CANCELLED

ⱼER L.

Remember i
The item is ᵤ

WORLDCALL

WORLDCALL

Global Perspectives on

Computer-Assisted Language Learning

EDITED BY
ROBERT DEBSKI
AND
MIKE LEVY

SWETS & ZEITLINGER
PUBLISHERS

LISSE   ABINGDON   EXTON (PA)   TOKYO

Library of Congress Cataloging-in-Publication Data

(applied for)

Cover design: Paula van der Heijdt
Illustration: Paula van der Heijdt
Printed in The Netherlands by Krips, Meppel

Copyright © 1999 Swets & Zeitlinger B.V., Lisse, The Netherlands

All rights reserved. No part of this publication may be reproduced, stored in a retrieval system, or transmitted in any form or by any means, electronic, mechanical, photocopying, recording, or otherwise, without the prior written permission of the publisher.

ISBN 90 265 1555 3

418.00285   DEB

001484370

Contents

Introduction

The tacit assumption with the use of WorldCALL as a label is that there is some value in reflecting upon Computer-Assisted Language Learning (CALL) holistically, as a worldwide phenomenon. Ten years ago, the technological infrastructure which could be used to underpin support for such a position did not exist. CALL, as it was practised then, tended to be concerned with the use of programs that existed as separate, disconnected artefacts, along the lines of one program one activity. The learning environment was clearly bounded. Language learners might work individually, or even collaborate in small groups, but always within the same physical space. Language teachers were restricted to the use of local resources to meet local student needs.

A decade later, the potential to engage native speakers at a distance, to utilise authentic materials and to enable learners to interact with rich, multi-dimensional learning environments has been realised. A more holistic view of CALL is justified, what might be termed a macroview, or even a world view as in WorldCALL. As today's learning environments are largely unrestrained in time and space, the location of resources is increasingly becoming less important. What learners need to know is how to tap into these resources and use them to their advantage. Teachers have a crucial role as managers of such world-distributed learning environments, always in search of new online materials and electronic partners who might enrich the experience of their students.

   That the power of the mind can emerge from the cross-connectedness of its parts, in themselves being simple and unintelligent, is the basic premise of Marvin Minsky's *The society of mind*.[1] We might risk the view that this premise can be extended to illustrate the shift we have recently experienced in conceptualising computing as well as the progress in its educational applications. At the time when we seemed to have been completely taken up by measuring the potential of a single machine, a new quality emerged from cross-connecting machines and joining the efforts of people standing behind them. With this qualitative shift come new questions and new ways of looking for answers have to follow. Our desire to understand what is happening when a learner or a group of learners are using a computer has been extended to involve situations when learners collaborate over distance and interact with virtual communities to accomplish creative goals. Research agendas are expanding to include issues of social computing and networked cultures and specific methodologies such as ethnography and ethnomethodology, designed to further our knowledge in this area.

   Although the phenomenal growth of networked communication has captured our attention, the way in which the globally interconnected systems function for individual students also continues to warrant careful investigation. The view taken by many of the 20 contributors to this volume is that the focal point of our attention should be the learner. And it is the learner's diverse experiences and attitudes that provide us with a point of departure for an alternative view on CALL, one that might be termed the microview. We need to learn much more about what the learner brings to the computer and the CALL activity, and once active on the computer we need to understand what particular factors impinge on learning success and what learning strategies are favoured and why.

   As technology may assist students in taking more responsibility for their learning as well as in situating them in networks animated by social interdependence, a humanistic perspective of CALL comes into view. This perspective strikes a chord with a recent image of technology drawn by Mark Stefik in his *Internet dreams*,[2] one that seems to be gaining popular acceptance. In this vivid book, today's electronic mail, marketplace, digital libraries and worlds are paralleled with human archetypes such as Communicator, Trader, Keeper of Knowledge, and Adventurer. This comparison teaches us that technological development may not after all be in dissonance with humanism; it also indicates that technology may assist us to implement humanistically motivated pedagogy where student skills, modes of thought and motivations are the centre of attention.

   As many contributions to this volume suggest, to develop insight about the processes of learning with computers from the learners' point of view, we need to develop more naturalistic and qualitative ways of going about research. Naturalistic investigation implies that there is a lot we can learn if certain phenomena are studied in their natural state, rather than in artificially constrained environments. Such thinking should initially focus on the learner's background, experience and mental model, and research studies should occur over time so that the findings really do capture significant events in the processes associated with language learning and in coming to terms with the technology. Longitudinal studies are especially needed because of the novelty effect to which learning with technology is prone.

The teacher's point of view provides us with another vital perspective at the micro level. And it is a view that must be carefully acknowledged if CALL is to be successful. The teacher not only has to attend to the needs of the students in a CALL environment, but his or her choices will also be governed largely by the conditions set by the local context, especially the technological resources, levels of access to computers, technical support, and the institutional, educational and cultural priorities.

Taking a macro or global view and considering those factors pertinent to the successful development of CALL, we are faced with enormous diversity. The technological resources, educational goals, cultural aspirations, language focus, institutional settings, clearly all vary significantly from place to place. Therefore, though the potential is there for a certain kind of shared, global technological infrastructure to be set in place, it is vital to remember that technology does not exist in a vacuum. Its introduction is governed quite rightly by the goals and aspirations of its users and the resources that are available: what is judged to be appropriate in one context may simply not be appropriate in another.

As we reflect upon the changes that new technologies have the potential to bring about, the path we choose will require the micro and the macro perspectives if the optimum decisions are to be made. The macroview, the one that is represented in the WorldCALL concept, provides a window onto the many ways that are now available to learn a language. These involve networks and systems of communication that are multi-faceted and global in their reach. In contrast, the microview reminds us that we are a long way from providing access to all. Further, the local context has always exerted an important influence on the texture of CALL as it is practised, and the preferences of the learner, the teacher and the culture need to be properly acknowledged and respected. So, in the end, we need both the macro and the micro perspectives: to work together and to collaborate where we can, sharing human and material resources; and to embrace and value difference in a world where communication across different languages and cultures continues to evolve and grow through the development of new technologies.

Context and acknowledgments

This volume has grown out of the inaugural WorldCALL Conference held in Melbourne on 13–17 July, 1998. The Conference gathered 320 CALL specialists from 28 countries. All chapters presented in this edited collection trace their genesis to the original Conference presentations. They have been selected for inclusion in response to a call for contributions first announced at the Conference and then on the Conference web page and via email. The call for contributions resulted in the submission of over 40 proposals, out of which 20 have been finally selected to be edited and expanded to chapter length.

Work on this volume has been assisted by extensive consultation with WorldCALL presenters, first at the Conference, and later through a web-based discussion forum and email. Our objective has been for the collection to capture the unique atmosphere of WorldCALL and the diverse perspectives on the use of computers in language study presented there.

Many people were instrumental in the production of this volume. This book has been supported generously by June Gassin, the WorldCALL Conference Convenor, and the Horwood Language Centre at The University of Melbourne. Sue Otto has made her impact on this volume as Chair of the Program Committee.

Many others have contributed to the production of this collection and we would very much like to thank them. Foremost among these are the authors themselves who have spent a great deal of time and effort in developing their initial concepts into the high quality collection presented here. Last but by no means least, we would like to thank Frances O'Sullivan for copy-editing all the contributions, and Mike Smith for preparing a camera-ready copy of the manuscript.

Mike Levy
Robert Debski
Melbourne
May 1999

Notes

[1] Minsky, M. (1988). *The society of mind.* New York: Simon & Shuster.

[2] Stefik, M. (1996). *Internet dreams: Architypes, myths and metaphors.* Cambridge, MA: MIT Press.

1

Dealing with Double Evolution: Action-Based Learning Approaches and Instrumental Technology

John Barson
Stanford University, USA

> Teach children what to think and you limit them to your ideas.
> Teach children how to think and their ideas are unlimited. (anon.)

The art of listening

The art of listening – taking the time to enter another person's narrative world in a respectful, self-effacing manner – is an essential ability for dedicated teachers. By relying on an innate predisposition enhanced by training, they give students the greatest gift of all, the freedom to think and express themselves independently. Students thus develop a sense of their being, realising actions affirming their uniqueness in society's collaborative environment – a mind-set currently capturing attention on a global scale. Through their creative ability, students leave in their wake meaningful artefacts for others. In achieving these ends, they engage in a process referred to in this chapter as 'self-realisation learning' (SRL), a concept affecting the nature of education and the role of students, teachers and technology.

SRL applies to students and teachers alike. Students engage wholeheartedly in the process of their own development and edification (i.e. growth in wisdom and growth in the ability to act). *Education* and *edification* share a purpose: building the self and the world to which one contributes. With a few drops of nascent thought, learners proceed to the development of a plan and to the execution of a project, involving themselves, their peers, and frequently technology. Ben Shneiderman (1997) expresses similar views in his formula *relate–create–donate,* especially emphasising the importance of learning projects and their immediate impact on society.

The acronym CALL, in widespread use to mean 'computer-assisted language learning,' could just as readily signify 'concentrated attention to liberated learners'. It would seem useful to position the instrumental use of technology in this particular interpretation of the act of learning. Evolutionary process shapes technology, just as we immerse ourselves in the development of new learning theory and practice in an ever-changing world. 'Dealing with double evolution' is clearly the story of achieving a single goal when one finds oneself in the arena of *edification*. One could speak of a three-part, parallel process involving education, edification, and life-long integration into society. Students adopting a self-realisation approach, engage in action to the point of abandoning the self. They experience a surge of energy and joy associated with acts of human ingenuity. Attentive teachers, disposed to listening, are their guides.

Mouse and metaphor: *The Colors* by Monique Felix

From lullabies to picture books to great works of literature, there seems to be no end to the power, attraction and metaphorical significance of the human message, irrespective of its form. A delightful picture story without words for children by Monique Felix, entitled *The Colors,* chronicles the adventures of an intrepid and creative mouse fascinated by painting. In the section below, one possible interpretation of the picture story can serve as a central metaphor representing curiosity, initiative, creativity and freedom – all essential qualities for students working in action-based learning models. The suggested story-line is interspersed with commentary.[1]

Once upon a time, an intrepid mouse, more ingenious than many of its kin, entered a book by nibbling away at the cardboard cover.

Primordial curiosity, by no means limited to the human species, is the precursor of discovery. In the beginning lies a question mark.

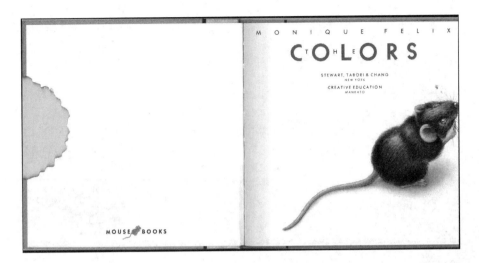

The mouse, finding itself on the title page, is curious to see what lies beyond it.

The readers no doubt share the mouse's curiosity. The page turn, from the perspective of a student, could represent the passage from the name of a course to the reality of the first day of class.

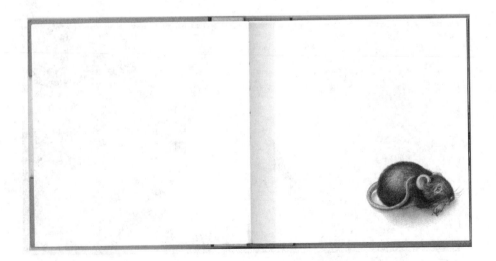

When the mouse finally makes its way to the following page, it discovers that nothing seems to be going on. At this point, the mouse appears condemned to leading a rather dreary existence on a deserted white page. With a sly look on its face, it begins to poke a hole in the blank page.

We see here the earliest awakenings of a disposition to tinker.

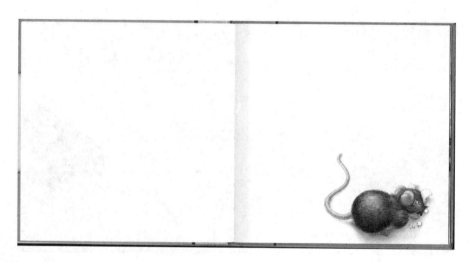

The mouse, reaching the next page, finds it blank. The creature, spurred on by its natural talents and curiosity decides to investigate again.

Idle curiosity may not be so idle after all! The blank page is an eternal challenge for creative artists.

True to its rodent nature, the mouse widens the hole until it can push its head through the page and gaze in fascination at a newly discovered universe filled with the most puzzling of objects. Displaying intrinsic motivation to investigate, the mouse begins to explore.

Books contain marvellous surprises and opportunities to learn – as does life – provided one knows how to interpret them. Just as the mouse's life unfolds in a book, so do students reside in appropriate learning environments, including the world in which they live. The new page in the mouse-student's life is an Art 101 studio. Generically, it could become a field-specific learning environment if appropriately adapted to other disciplines (e.g. physics, biology, chemistry, neuroscience, psychology, computer science, or foreign languages).

The mouse, having escaped from its initially sterile surroundings, tours its new environs, discovers a box containing carefully aligned tubes of paint, but is still not sure how to proceed.

A period of investigation and reflection familiarises learners with their environment. Students eventually become avid creators, thus initiating their own self-realisation. The book of life in the hands of learners ready to act is dependent on the situations encountered.

Picking up a tube of red paint, the mouse examines it, as would a child, by dipping a finger in the gooey substance, taking a small lick, and concluding that it is definitely not cheese.

Observers of young children are familiar with the discovery process consisting of touching, tasting and smelling. Often, these initial explorations determine what something is not (e.g. paint is not food) and push the experimenter to manipulate objects until constructive functions are identified. This situation characterises the use of digital tools. While they may offer some clues regarding their function, we can only master them by concerted tinkering, or by obtaining information regarding their use.

The mouse, displaying great concentration and wielding the large paintbrush with care, produces his first mark on the otherwise white page.

By perceiving a connection between the paintbrush and some potential activity (e.g. applying red-coloured gooey substance to paper), the mouse, lacking any previous experience, has made an untutored creative leap. One could easily substitute for the artist's implements the chemicals, test tubes and pipettes of a chemistry laboratory. Likewise, a computer is indispensable in preparing multimedia web pages, and email is a powerful tool for contacting distanced partners half way around the world, collaborating on a project. The significance of tools lies in their use.

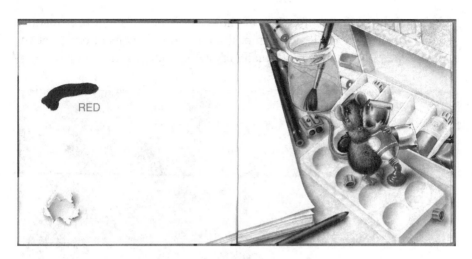

Inspired by its success with red, the mouse grabs a tube of blue paint and squeezes mightily. The painter-mouse also transforms the egg carton into a makeshift artist's palette.

Important here is the gestation of actions a learner may take with given tools. The mouse will most likely continue painting. Were the import of the brushstrokes extended to other disciplines, they would become foundational acts (e.g. the opening statement of a thesis, the corner stone of some great edifice, the theme of a musical composition).

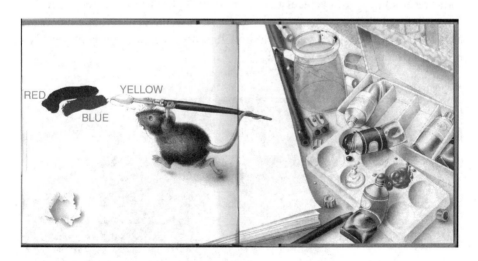

The mouse, wielding the paintbrush with growing skill, rushes across the page to apply yellow above the red – as the next page reveals – rather than below the blue, for reasons forever buried in its mousy brain.

In the realm of design, freedom of choice for learners is a respect-worthy quality, especially when it stems from ill-understood sources of our creative ability. Repeated endeavour eventually crystallises into form.

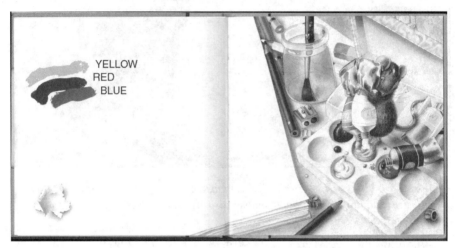

In the next manoeuvre, the mouse, having completed its dealings with the primary colours, displays intuitive talent for expanding the colour spectrum.

One might posit innate propensity in the mouse or, better yet, attribute his actions to pure tinkering. Consequently, tinkering becomes a very productive activity, especially when practiced by motivated learners. Judging from its exertions, the mouse has reached the limit of its capacity. This situation bears some resemblance to a typical learner's mental plight when faced with the rigours of unfamiliar concepts (e.g. quantum mechanics, verbal aspect, or Maxwell's equations). Acquiring knowledge does not always come easily. Mind transformations are required.

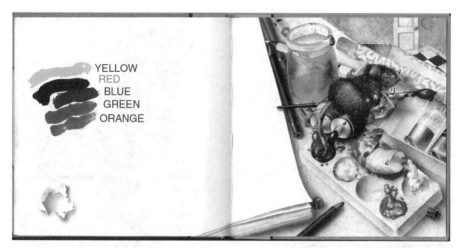

The mouse's fervour grows with every new colour discovered – orange from the mix of yellow and red, and purple from the combination of red and blue.

Free to act as inspiration dictates, the mouse is experiencing the special problem of design in its battle royal with paint and brush. The splotches on the fur coat and hand-like paws of the painter-mouse indicate enthusiasm and a fervent sense of purpose. Creative genius no doubt prompted the budding artist to place the slightly irregular brushstrokes one beneath the other. The painting represents the best efforts of a novice attempting to produce a thing of beauty. The mouse is enthralled, oblivious to its surroundings, experiencing special movements of the mind and soul, if one may attribute such qualities to a mouse. In speaking about human beings, Mihaly Csikszentmihalyi (1996) uses the term 'flow' to identify this unconstrained engagement of the mind, the complete surrender of one's entire being to an activity for the sheer pleasure derived from its accomplishment. Students experiencing flow become as vigorously engaged as the mouse in the disciplines they are studying, a situation bound to affect long-term learning.

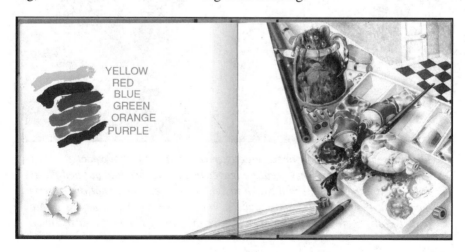

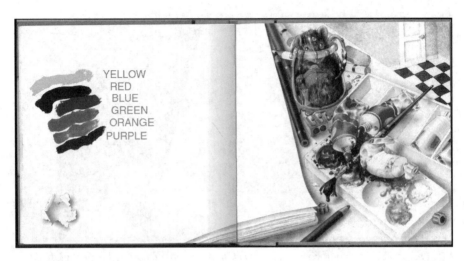

In its zeal, the mouse finally stumbles and finds himself inside a water jar. The mouse's previous gleam of exultation becomes a woeful look.

Occupational hazards. One can hardly represent education as a gentle (or not so gentle) slope ever rising toward guaranteed success. Setbacks, surprises, contingent events, constraints and sudden inspiration are an integral part of learning. The mouse has discovered that watercolours are soluble and has bathed in purifying liquid removing most of the stains connected with its productive foray into the world of art.

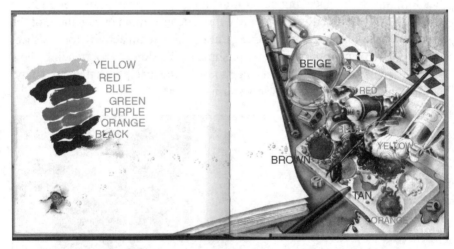

The mouse decides to bow out discreetly, perhaps due to the unexpected return of the young girl. The furry creature leaves behind the brightly painted page, to which it has brought life through insight, cleverness, imagination, experimentation, perseverance, and maybe a fair bit of luck. The opening in the page begins to close without completely sealing over. The mouse-artist may,

one day, return to sign its masterpiece, pursue its newly found talent, and take its place with the abstract expressionists of this world.

The judgment passed on the mouse's art is essentially subjective although it will invoke criteria such as form, colour and design. One will also have to take into account personal taste of the critic. Similarly with respect to students, teachers will apply a qualitative system of evaluation, in keeping with appraising students involved in action-based learning.

Triumphant and happy, the mouse now sports blobs of paint on its tail, a paintbrush for the future.

The mouse has learned to think and act as a painter. It has invested its entire being in artistic endeavour, experiencing flow, getting soaked in the process and surviving the experience with newly developed talent. The blossomed tip of its tail, now transformed into a multi-coloured palette, symbolises this newly acquired ability. The same principle applies to human beings as they engage, through action, in learning and living. Life and learning remain forever linked within the many narratives we develop for dealing with our world. Education has transformational power. At stake is the development of human potential within all disciplines as it affects activity and the development of personal identity.

From mouse to metaphor

The sprightly mouse story *The Colors* illustrates perfectly certain ideas having immediate application to the process of learning. Theory and story-telling become joint narratives of our efforts to deal with the world – a double approach to achieving a single goal. Each in its own way sheds light on an endless quest, a never-ending story – the history of humanity.

Activity theory

Foremost is the concept of 'learning by doing', a notion with us from time immemorial. Strongly propounded by John Dewey, early in the twentieth century, other thinkers have more recently dealt with the concept, among them Alexei Leontiev. 'Learning by doing' describes the process by which we come into knowledge of ourselves, of the world, and of our special talents as they relate to our potential contributions to society. In the beginning lies an impulse to act, individually or cooperatively. Activity, the concatenation of learner-initiated actions, imparts identity both individually and collectively to students taking a course. Leontiev succinctly and precisely summarises the principle tenets of activity theory. One achieves success by appealing to a person's fundamental 'intrinsic propulsive force.'

a) A man's activity is always material and significant. Man does not simply "behave", nor does he simply perform abstract deeds: any one of his actions constitutes at the same time an interaction with objects outside himself, and it can influence or alter them.

b) Man's activity is primarily social and embodies his social relationships. It is never the activity of a given concrete individual, considered separately from society; and it only emerges as material and meaningful action rather than a mere manipulation of things. ...

c) Man's activity has a systematic structure ... Let us start by saying that it is characterized by motive and aim. ...

... any language teacher knows how important it is for the success of his teaching to make mastery of the language not a compliance within a tedious obligation, but the additional or even fundamental "intrinsic propulsive force" of the cognitive activity of the learners. (Leontiev 1981: 13–16)

Applying the above statement from Leontiev, one may state that the substance of a course derives from the activity of the class members – learners and teacher engaged in action over time. Course specified as content is superseded by course viewed as a kinetic, modifiable process: the unique intertwining of student-generated actions, interacting, jumping ahead, looping back, but ultimately achieving coherence and conferring identity on the society of students. Participation and performance draw on the 'propulsive force' mentioned by Leontiev or on 'intrinsic motivation', the term used by Deci (1995). Students, after selecting topics deemed 'pursuit-worthy', proceed on their own initiative or with help from the teacher and like-minded peers. Decisions and strategic planning frequently appeal to all the students in the class taken as collective social unit. It is the coming together of many independent actions that 'merge into one single activity' (Leontiev 1981). The product of combined actions – the result of propulsive motivation – contributes to students' sense of accomplishment and to the concept of self-realisation. SRL is applicable to all disciplines and concentrated on the development of mind and life-experience. In this regard, all learning is experimental. Through the concepts of *action* and *activity*, we establish ourselves in society as well as in field-specific learning environments.

Freedom to invent
Inventiveness and innovation are essential to the learning process. Tapping into this fundamental creative spirit produces incomparable elation. With inspiration and insight, we can operate beneficially on the wealth of information contained in the world, thereby creating our own fund of knowledge. Clearly, one has to sort and choose in the name of synthesis and even survival. One strives for organisation and compaction in creating concise and aesthetically conceived artefacts revealing the profundity of their vast information content.

Motivation
Intrinsically motivated action has a central role in providing direction for learners. It drives experimentation in all human endeavours, orienting them towards a subject under investigation or suggesting the development of effective interpersonal (societal) contacts. Deci (1995) delves into a lengthy discussion of intrinsic motivation and its relevance to quality learning. Motivation provides a strong connection between plans and actions, an essential quality if learners are to benefit from the exchange of viewpoints and from a sense of solidarity capable of binding individuals working in collaboration. From the teacher's point of view, the art of listening to student voices is a prerequisite to fostering motivation in learners.

Tools and information
From paintbrushes to computers to land levellers, tools are forever capturing our attention as they facilitate human tasks. In the case of the mouse-painter, the tools were conventional brush and paint, but digital painting with multimedia applications (e.g. Photoshop) has also become an art in its own right. The Internet, the World Wide Web and innumerable computer applications for the manipulation of digital information have augmented the possibilities of creation and communication using digital media. Students will have to

learn to move through rapidly accumulating information in order to form their own syntheses.

Contingency
Although educational procedures call for some degree of organisation, one must also underscore the role of chance. The world we move in is chaotic, unpredictable, not necessarily well organised. Unexpected events and fortuitous accidents are very much a part of life and can provide strong incentives to student imagination and efforts. Remaining favourably disposed towards contingency is important, hence the value of listening and perceiving, mentioned at the outset. Fixed syllabi tend to play havoc with these subtle, unpredictable events regularly occurring in courses of instruction.

Real and virtual space
The mouse tale is an ingenious pictorial representation of the passage from real physical space to the more ethereal environment of the digital world. The mouse's exploratory dynamic pervades the book. The pages actually have dimensionality. The discovery of the painting studio plunges the mouse into an intriguing, if somewhat turbulent, virtual reality.

The mushrooming Web is a prime example, but not the only one, of this bridge into a digital perceptual system and a worldwide networking environment. Digital media encourage human endeavour in the form of endlessly varied *compositions*. Users will have to develop selective strategies in their use of multimedia in order to steer a productive course. Search engines and intelligent electronic agents are rapidly becoming indispensable tools in our technological times. Without them, we surely would become the victims of pointless meandering in an electronic labyrinth of our own making.

Composition, a setting down of synthesised material in whatever language or symbol system is appropriate to a given discipline, becomes a primary concern of learning theory. Students using multimedia resources will redefine learning itself, making the learning process inseparable from contributing to the world's store of knowledge.

Liberating learners
By extrapolating from the mouse's fascination with colours, we can take the exploration of the world of art as one instance, among many, capable of attracting a learner's attention in an information-rich environment. During the course of their education, students, lucky enough to be living in the enticing array of opportunities offered by academic life, explore a wide range of interests. Teachers serve as intellectual guides. Learners will eventually leave their mentors and fly on their own. One can view learning as the process of achieving uniqueness and independence.

Tinkering

Tinkering is also a pervasive strategy in student-focused learning approaches. Sherry Turkle (1995) writes pertinently on this subject. Children base their earliest learning efforts on the exploratory manipulation of objects, tools and people in an effort to understand how the world works. Adults as well. Tinkering plays a role in discovering how technological tools can facilitate new patterns of thought and the realisation of plans. Technological advances have brought forth a fascinating gamut of equipment well adapted to encouraging exploratory activity.

Assessment

In dealing with student projects – the mainstay of action-based learning – we have reached the point where statistically based testing instruments can no longer be used in good conscience, as they simply do not fit the process being evaluated. We are dealing with an act of subjective appreciation, invoking appropriate qualitative criteria. There is a troubling lack of correlation between standard achievement tests and the complex of values requiring assessment and appreciation in self-realisation learning. Elaine Shohamy (1993, 1996) speaks cogently to this topic, suggesting that teachers often use testing as a means of wielding power over students. The challenge will be to devise qualitative evaluation procedures capable of dealing with the complex, cognitive and interpersonal qualities attending human achievement (e.g. originality, organisation, facility, determination, collaborative skills, degree of discourse appropriateness, interpretive ability, sense of humour). Testing will have to be diagnostic in nature and better adapted to the performance levels expected by new learning approaches.

Satisfaction and a sense of fulfilment

When the mouse made its exit from the art studio, its satisfaction and sense of fulfilment were clear. One may say the same about students when they present their completed work at the end of a project-oriented course of learning. Their exuberance is palpable, the praise they receive well deserved. They have accomplished a self-set goal and communicated to their peers and teachers their interests, skill and originality. This fundamentally creative approach – using performance as means of acquisition and learning – provides students with a deep sense of accomplishment and an ability to be discipline-specific practitioners.

To summarise the above discussion, one can view the mouse tale as a metaphor for the entire process of education and its positive effect on learners. Education should be conducive to self-discovery and creativity through the instrumental use of tools in well-designed environments.

Student projects

In our technology-rich society, certain traditional environments familiar to students will inevitably expand to include new ones emerging from the growth of networks and the expansion of computer tools. The execution of projects in a self-realisation perspective provides us, metaphorically speaking, with the DNA of learning. These projects cover a considerable range from web pages to live individual presentations to films, sometimes made by an entire class. Student initiative and self-management replace teacher assignments. To proceed otherwise would be in contradiction with the basic premise that student action produces innovation and individual discovery.

Harvard–Stanford collaboration

In 1988, with funds from the Consortium for Language Teaching and Learning, Harvard and Stanford students in two French classes collaborated using email and file transfer protocols, to publish a magazine on themes of shared interest (Barson, Frommer & Schwartz 1993). This early venture proved successful and confirmed that collaboration and interaction – both face-to-face locally and cross-country using email – provided strong motivation.

When the World Wide Web appeared, preparing magazines and newspapers gravitated to the medium of digital bits. The project became the preparation of web pages (a new medium). The classroom dynamic, however, stayed the same: breaking into subgroups, appointing group-leaders, intense use of email (all corrected by the teacher online), submission of multiple drafts, class discussions devoted to management issues, design, or preliminary viewing of material. The goal was to portray university life as seen from each of the participating institutions. The overarching goal was the creation of a web site with contributions from numerous universities, all conveying information about students' points of view in higher education.

Multiple projects

Initially, a Web project was a central task focusing the energy of students for the entire term. In continuing experiments, it became clear that students prefer latitude to engage in other projects (e.g. filmmaking, theatre, written reports, cooking demonstrations, ballet demonstrations, guided tours of campus). Supporting all means of expression is consonant with student freedom. This diversity of pursuits constitutes a challenge to classroom management but results in absorbing and entertaining presentations. The following two may serve as examples.

The bronze arm

Using the Web, a student of French, majoring in engineering, wrote and presented orally in French a fully illustrated description on how to make a bronze casting of his own arm, a project he had undertaken in an engineering course. The bronze arm was to serve as a trumpet holder. At the conclusion of the presentation, the student displayed his bronze arm trumpet holder for all to admire.

Gecko film

Another group of students improvised and filmed a story involving puppets. The reading of *The Little Prince* and the chance appearance in class of two Styrofoam Hawaiian geckos on metal leashes served as inspiration. The film, entitled 'La Planète des Geckos,' involved two creatures that had somehow grown enormous teeth. Their terrifying smile scared away all visitors except the little prince, who was delighted to make friends. The students improvised a set, using two beanbags to represent mountains. Some students (off camera) controlled the puppets. Others (also off camera) read from laptops serving as telepromters. The interactive qualities of improvised projects are remarkable and exemplify the role of happenstance in activity-driven courses.

Technology as a partner

Technology (e.g. computer applications, networking protocols, local servers and the digital infrastructure supporting distribution) has currently developed to the point at which one can rightfully consider the digital world as a partner to pedagogy. Technology is a constantly changing phenomenon, offering a hitherto unknown interaction with mainstream and innovative approaches to learning and teaching. The goal for the profession is to find the most cogent points of intersection between this double evolution, since change is occurring in both sectors. This is simultaneously an issue of practice and research (Debski 1998).

The integration of learning and technology poses a special challenge. The evolutionary speed of technology surpasses the ability of the average user to adjust to change or, for teachers and specialists in pedagogy, to assess the impact of new technological potentiation. Since the understanding of evolution is itself a dynamic process, proposing definitive answers may be less important than progressive growth in understanding through experimentation.

Shifting perspectives
In self-realisation models, *teacher–student* joint participation in the learning process curtails teacher control. The hierarchical gap between teachers and students narrows significantly, in some cases disappearing entirely.

Technology, in this regard, is a great leveller, promoting change in more traditional relationships between teachers and learners.

Destined to become more peripheral than central, textbooks take their place as one among many resources available to students. Teachers, authors and publishers will have to reformulate the nature and functions of the textbook in order to understand its new position and role in action-based learning approaches.

Academics will have to reconsider their deep belief in a pervasive causality between specific teaching acts and subsequent learning. Enlightened teaching – bypassing canonic methodology – consists of identifying with finesse student actions establishing individual and group identity. It is important to view teaching as a form of guiding learners' efforts. Human imagination and endeavour are essential to any core-curriculum in both the humanities and the sciences, disciplines remaining by necessity in close relationship.

While the traditional classroom has its purposes, technological innovation has been instrumental in the creation of a new type of classroom, springing up in universities around the world. Often referred to as computer and multimedia classrooms, these high-tech environments offer great flexibility in terms of student grouping, so that function – the activity at hand – defines the form of classroom sessions. Laptops provide access to file servers and to the Internet. Tools for handling digital material are also available. In such classroom labs, physical learning space and virtual space have combined to form a very unified and effective environment in which technology is ubiquitous but unobtrusive. The task of educators will be to discover the full potential of these learning spaces making a clear call to revised teaching and learning strategies.

Resources
Teachers and students need skills to deal cogently with the sheer mass of resources now available electronically. Selecting useful and accurate information from the electronic quagmire housed on the Internet poses genuine difficulties, leading ultimately to sensory overload. Learning how to discard information (or at least ignore it) in our efforts to put information to good use is essential. Students will have to develop good filtering talents in order to construct knowledge, as they extract their own narratives from vast stores of information, the Web among them. The growing power of search engines and of intelligent electronic agents is essential to this process.

Courseware development
We live in an era in which it is relatively easy for teachers and learners to elaborate materials for themselves and for future generations of students. Teachers wishing to engage in courseware development are in need of more

copyright free materials that they can combine and rearrange in suitable ways. Small- as well as large-scale projects are possible.

GLEn

The Global Learning Environment (GLEn) project (Barson & Debski 1996, Barson 1997) directly addresses issues connected with distributed computing models in education. Currently in use at The University of Melbourne's Horwood Language Centre, GLEn provides a self-contained system of access to resources composed of modules designed to foster learner-initiated action. GLEn is comparable to a generic, electronic foyer, accessed from the computer desktop and dealing with all aspects of learning in a digital world. Learners function both in a physical space classroom and in coherently linked virtual environments accessible from the classroom, from computer clusters, or from student residences or homes.

Kiswahili

In his custom-designed first-year course in Swahili, *Tujifunze Kiswahili,* John Mugane (1999, forthcoming) offers an excellent example of adaptive, flexible and cohesive course design (see Mugane's chapter in this volume). Students learn, using free and customised browsing on the Web, along with special applications (e.g. *Stay Tooned*; and *Media-Driven Learning System,* Mugane 1998) for providing meaningful language practice based on student creativity.

Conclusion

Although digital communication and interconnectedness have become a global reality in many sectors, we must also acknowledge that the installation of technology on a global scale will take considerable time to reach its full potential. The catalytic force and richness of technology stimulate the mind, opening new modes of expression and living. Both will be forever evolving, due to human endeavour and to contingent events.

The extraordinary narrative in which we are both authors and main characters remains only partially known. In this ever-changing sea, educators must avoid the pitfall of looking for permanent solutions to learning issues. Evolution affects both learning philosophy and technology. We must remain focused on the generative process to which we all contribute, one forever leading to new solutions responsive and appropriate to the cultural milieu in which they are applied.

Coherent connectionism – to coin a phrase – expresses the many levels at which meaningful contact and exchanges especially inform the educational process. Coherence implies a continued selection of viable goals, in the knowledge that contact between students, teachers and technology forms a solid base, enabling people to create – in a spirit of collaboration – the innovations upon which our civilisations are built. Many universities have already implemented reliable infrastructures capable of providing the technological coherence and transparency on which computer-mediated learning depends.

Certain questions, however, remain ever present. Will a deep alliance between education and technology contribute to making known approaches more effective? Can technology and innovative pedagogy co-construct a new teaching and learning reality? Will learner-focused approaches encourage students to assume individual and collective responsibility, possibly on a global scale?

In the search for answers to the restructuring of education, we must apply our imagination and cognitive abilities to the nature of learning – forever growing more complex – and strive to comprehend the brain in its awesome complexity. Remaining conscious of what learning entails is vital to maintaining and developing our understanding of human consciousness and its role in the development of the species. For a task of this magnitude, innovation centres are called for to bring faculty, technical support, ethnographic researchers, administrators, and even students, together to plant the seeds of change. Implementations along these lines are already in place in the School of Languages at The University of Melbourne (Debski 1998). Humanistic concerns should guide our actions as Jerome Bruner aptly points out:

> ... effective education is always in jeopardy either in the culture at large or with constituencies more dedicated to maintaining a status quo than to fostering flexibility. The corollary of this is that when education narrows its scope of interpretive inquiry, it reduces a culture's power to adapt to change. And in the contemporary world, change is the norm. If pedagogy is to empower human beings to go beyond their "native" predispositions, it must transmit the "toolkit" that culture has developed for doing so. (Bruner 1996:17)

In his use of 'cultural toolkit' and in his call for change and flexibility, Bruner has offered us a considerable challenge. We must instil in learners the mental capacity to acquire disciplines purposefully and to make field-specific discourses their own through concerted action. Students also need to become aware of languages as symbolic systems. Language forms essential bonds between human beings. It is a primary means of self-knowledge, of sharing insights, and of relating one's inner being to the created *word* and to the perceived *world*.

Current and future generations of students must also be willing partners in the reconstruction of learning approaches and the propagation of their 'cultural tool kit'. In assuming this responsibility, they become co-investigators with their teachers in determining the most beneficial progression of academic courses and the most applicable uses of technology. Learners will address their primary goal in all disciplines: understanding how their different studies cohere in order to impart unique character to the mind.

Creativity must remain in a permanent state of evolution, forever contributing to our future. The task is to make our offerings, as circumstances warrant, to the evolutionary narrative in which we live, a narrative that in time will outlive us. In the future, we may achieve such a tight bind between technological developments and pedagogical issues that we shall no longer need the term 'double evolution' mentioned in the title of this chapter. We shall speak about the evolution of education as a single phenomenon co-mingled with technology. At that point, the term integration of technology and education will have turned from a goal into a reality.

The end, or maybe just the beginning!

Notes
[1] Since the original colour pictures have been rendered in grayscale, critical colours in the Felix book are indicated editorially in capital letters (e.g. YELLOW, RED and BLUE).

Acknowledgments
I wish to express my deepest admiration and gratitude to June Gassin, Director of the Horwood Language Centre at The University of Melbourne. Her leadership in the evolutionary betterment of education, culminating in the 1998 WorldCALL Conference at The University of Melbourne, is without equal. I also wish to thank the coeditors of this volume:
Dr Robert Debski, University of Melbourne, who so well embodies dedication to quality teaching, research, publications and technological development;
Dr Mike Levy, University of Queensland, for his professional contributions to CALL-based language learning and for his efforts in the realisation of this volume.
I am deeply indebted to Creative Education (123 South Broad Street, Mankato, Minnesota 56001) for granting permission to use *The Colors* by Monique Felix. Words cannot do justice to Felix's enchanting pictorial visions, a stellar example of the adage: One picture is worth a thousand words.

References

Barson, J. (1991). *Stay Tooned* (Multimedia application for the Macintosh). ©John Barson and the Board of Trustees of Leland Stanford Jr University.

Barson, J. (1997). Space time and form in the project-based foreign language classroom. In R. Debski, J.Gassin & M. Smith (Eds), *Language learning through social computing*. Melbourne: ALAA & LC.

Barson, J., Frommer, J. & Schwartz, M. (1993). Foreign language learning using email in a task-oriented perspective: An interuniversity experiment in communication and collaboration. *Journal for Science Education and Technology 2*, 4, 565–583.

Barson, J. & Debski, R. (1996). Calling back CALL: Technology in the service of foreign language learning based on creativity, contingency, and goal-oriented activity. In M. Warschauer (Ed.), *Telecollaboration in foreign language learning*. Second Language Teaching and Curriculum Center, University of Hawai'i at Manoa.

Bruner, J. (1996). *The culture of education*. Cambridge, Mass.: Harvard University Press.

Csikszentmihalyi, M. (1996). *Creativity: Flow and the psychology of discovery and invention*. New York: Harper Collins.

Debski, R. (1998). Implementing and evaluating project-based language learning with technology: A progress report. In *CALL to Creativity:* Proceedings of the 1998 WorldCALL Conference, University of Melbourne.

Deci, E. L. (c1995). *Why we do what we do*. New York: Putnam's Sons.

Leontiev, A. (1981). *Psychology and the language learning process*. Oxford: Pergamon Press.

Mugane, J. (1998). MDLS (Media-Driven Learning System). URL <http://www.aramati.com/~salama.html>

Mugane, J. (1999). Digital arenas in the delivery of African languages for the development of thought. In R. Debski & M. Levy (Eds) *WorldCALL*. Amsterdam: Swets & Zeitlinger.

Mugane, J. (1999, forthcoming). *Tujifunze Kiswahili* (Let's learn Swahili).

Shneiderman, B. (1997). *Relate, create, donate*.
URL <http://www.cs.umd.edu/users/ben/index.html>

Shohamy, E. (1993). The power of tests: The impact of language tests on teaching and learning. In *NFLC Occasional Papers*. National Foreign Language Center. June 1993. Washington, DC: Johns Hopkins University.

Shohamy, E. et al. (1996). Test impact revisited: Washback effect over time. In *Language Testing 13*, 3, 298–317.

Turkle, S. (c1995). *Life on the screen*. New York: Simon & Schuster.

2

Digital Arenas in the Delivery of African Languages for the Development of Thought

John Mugane
Stanford University, USA

Introduction

The Internet has expanded and altered the definition of 'community' profoundly. Electronic interaction encourages and amplifies community activities in physical space, since activity in virtual space is dynamically relevant to activity transpiring in the classroom. People have expanded conventional understanding of concepts such as distance, space and even identity. Physical space becomes significantly enriched when specialised computer applications are pervasively integrated into the modern classroom. The learning arena, traditionally in lecture halls, classrooms, seminar rooms and laboratories has expanded to include the global digital Internet housed in its many servers and fully searchable by high-powered browsers. We are dealing with an access-to-resources model that tends to override the more specific issue of where one is in physical space. To the question 'where can learning take place?' the answer is 'anywhere', so long as stimulating materials are available and potential for interaction present. Developing an understanding of the interplay between learning events occurring in real space and those fostered by virtual environments constitutes the main challenge facing education today.

The Stanford African Languages And Multimedia Applications site (henceforth SALAMA, the Swahili word meaning 'peace') located within <http://www.aramati.com> is a detailed implementation of customised web browsing environments for language teaching and learning. Making use of the basic web metaphor of branching, it constitutes specific learning space as arenas which embody clusters of asequentially related material. As is typical of web design, these roots form a growing network of deeply embedded connections because they are often offshoots of each other.

This paper illustrates the use that can be made of customised web browsing in a cohesively designed language learning arena, with specific reference to developing communicative competence and cultural awareness in Swahili.

The co-mingling of real space and virtual space as a means of promoting coordinated action in the large physico-spatial and digital world in which we live, prompts the use of the word 'arena'. Within this locally fused and globally oriented space, learners discover the importance of accessing resources and of being in partnership with others, including distanced learning partners. The joint efforts of learners expand their conception of our infinitely varied linguistic and cultural heritage. As we proceed to the 21st century, the teaching of African languages and the dissemination of African culture have to remain closely linked to African people's unique experience, which is often shared across ethnic and cultural boundaries. That experience, in the context of the African continent, has shaped the African world view. Ali Mazrui (1986), a world renowned thinker in African studies, astutely describes the African experience in the context of his own people – the Waswahili (Swahili people): 'geography is the mother of history', that is to say, one understands the history of the Waswahili by attending to their geography. This notion is extensible to the African continent as a whole. Geography (the physical space) is a primary contributor to the African world view. The arenas in which people find themselves greatly influence the manner in which individuals of a particular community interpret experience, make their history, construct a belief system, evolve a culture, and eventually leave a legacy. In like manner, technological innovation will significantly influence the practice and evolution of the teaching and learning enterprise in the next millennium.

The development of new tools – often referred to as technological innovation – brings with it the elaboration of new arenas. Postman (1993:18–21) observes that 'new technologies alter the structure of our interests, the things we think about. They alter the character of our symbols: the things we think with. And they alter the nature of community: the arena in which thoughts develop'. Likewise, Sherry Turkle (1995:232) finds that 'technology changes us as people, changes our relationships and sense of ourselves'. In fact where Multi User Dungeons (MUDs) are concerned, Turkle presents evidence that for some people the Internet has become a 'psychological adjunct to real life'.

Thus, in addition to dealing with issues of identity that plague the physical world, we now have to locate ourselves in virtual space as we form digital communities and identities. Psychological considerations and socialising in technological arenas are also a part of educational use of the Internet.

New and emerging arenas call for major intellectual and institutional shifts, especially in the way all relevant content (curricular, cultural, linguistic, etc.) is elaborated and explored. These shifts affect student and teacher roles as one expands the interactional learning space. Contact hours, no longer limited to regularly scheduled courses taking place in physical space classrooms now include cyberspace, harvested at will for educational purposes. The utilisation of digital arenas for the purpose of establishing relationships, for negotiating meaning, and for executing duties, is at present widespread and relatively free from constraints or controls. It would be shortsighted to attempt controlling how people accomplish their ends or even to anticipate which directions of inquiry or levels of negotiation are likely to be most profitable to them. An innate fluidity attends Internet affairs. Whom or what one might encounter remains quite open and subject to contingency. Internet functions enable productive states of connectivity and retrieval of information. The implications for education are obvious: learning can take place in a significantly wider frame of reference than the one provided by traditional classrooms.

Asequential learning strategies enhance learner-centred activity by leaving the student free to make individualised use of customised browsing environments. Shifting responsibility to learners, in the matter of determining their idiosyncratic styles, represents a major departure from the prescriptive nature of teacher-suggested curricular paths. In a telling sense, learning of specific material is permanently bonded to meta-cognitive consideration of what learning is about in the first place.

Customised Web

The SALAMA site is an arena built on a complex branching system of roots that rejoin each other at various points, thus forming a rich tapestry of organic, deeply embedded connections. Travel in any direction is possible and students may choose paths at random or follow pre-selected ones (Mugane 1997). Unrestricted asequential movement in a multi-directional Web setting is governed by the learners' search for areas consonant with their unique learning pace. The environments of the SALAMA site make it possible for learners at different levels of sophistication in the language to work on different content under the facilitation of the instructor who serves as a monitor of perceptive and purposeful browsing. The SALAMA site provides both free and guided browsing.

Free browsing

The free browsing environment is one for which no suggestions are provided on how to use the SALAMA site to facilitate the building of communicative competence in Swahili. A learner is provided with a menu as shown in figure 1.

Figure 1: The SALAMA menu

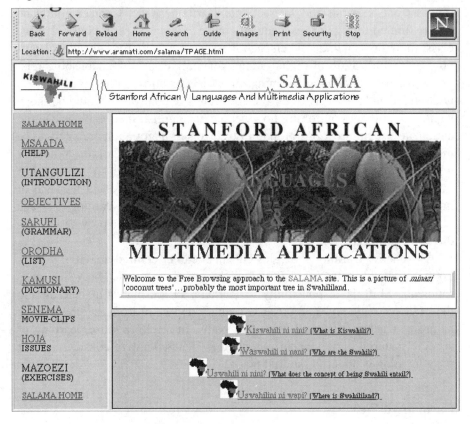

The menu contains a list of topics:
- *msaada* 'help'
- *utangulizi* 'introduction'
- objectives
- *sarufi* 'grammar'
- *orodha* 'list'
- *Kamusi* 'dictionary'
- *senema* 'movie-clips'
- *hoja* 'issues'
- *mazoezi* 'exercises'

These topics are the gateways to elaborated multimedia content and fall into three groups:

- gateway to cultural content
- grammar and vocabulary portals
- exercises and quizzes

In what follows, one element within *Hoja* (issues); the *Kamusi* (dictionary); and one element in the *Orodha* (list) are described to serve as illustrations.

Hoja (issues)

Hoja consists of the top-level questions for the SALAMA site. At the lower portion of the right side of figure 1, there are four fundamental questions, which are the focus of the elaboration within the SALAMA site:

- Kiswahili ni nini? (What is Kiswahili?)
- Waswahili ni nani? (Who are the Swahili people?)
- Uswahili ni nini? (What does the concept of being Swahili entail?)
- Uswahilini ni wapi? (Where is Swahililand?)

In researching a question such as *Kiswahili ni nini?* (What is Kiswahili?), a list of categories (figure 2) opens up from which learners must choose according to what they consider to be potentially fruitful. Although some categories are more amply developed than others, each category has material relevant to the query. The learner exercises some judgement to yield satisfactory responses. This approach has many desirable outcomes when used in the context of teaching and learning. More often than not, learners generate varying responses and reactions to what they find. Some browse thoroughly by exploring all of the categories, others pursue some topics partially while yet others leave some categories unexplored. The individual experiences of students serve as conversation inducers when they meet in the classroom or when they communicate by email or newsgroups.

As the course progresses, the list of topic categories grows, based on input from the students and the teacher. It is worthwhile to note that the SALAMA site offers state of the art content-based instruction, including links to the vast pool of information beyond SALAMA. Freedom of exploration is encouraged. Students explore issues regarding how language relates to history, politics and the environment to mention only a few areas germane to the acquisition of Swahili. Instruction, then, finds immediate connections to other disciplines while at the same time providing examples illustrating the use of Swahili both socially and academically. Many students have been involved in the construction of the SALAMA site and have influenced and continue to influence its evolution. Students using the SALAMA site have clearly

Figure 2: Categories for researching 'What is Swahili?'

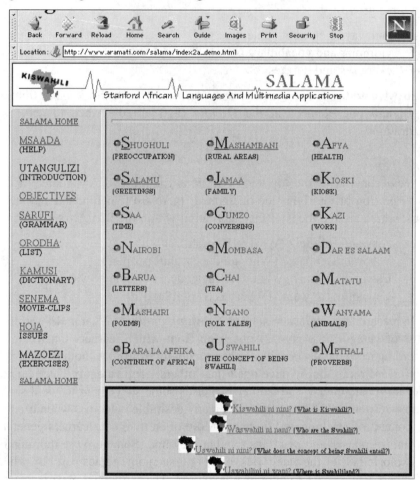

benefited from systematic use of the Web. Upon their return from travel or employment in Eastern Africa, they have asserted that the SALAMA site proved extremely useful in preparing them for their experiences abroad.

The Kamusi

The dictionary within the SALAMA site consists of words which are typical of first-year Swahili instruction. Most of the words have been gathered from classes taught at Stanford University since 1994, The University of California at Berkeley in the summer of 1995, and The University of California in Los Angeles in the summer of 1997. Throughout that time, some students kept records of all of the nouns and verbs used in class. These were taken and added to those used in the course reader *Tujifunze Kiswahili 1.0*

(Let's Learn Swahili) (Mugane, forthcoming), their own essays and class assignments. The *Kamusi* is organized as shown in figure 3.

Although this specialised dictionary presents words in alphabetical order for ease of reference (top frame), the words associated with a given letter appear in the lower left frame and are enhanced with links to culturally relevant explanations and illustrations found in the lower right frame. Figure 3 shows that M has been selected and the list of M words used in the SALA-MA site is provided on the lower left frame. Students recognise the usefulness of this dictionary because it is immediately accessible and provides a representative compilation of words most likely to be encountered in the early stages of learning Swahili.

Figure 3: The dictionary within the SALAMA site

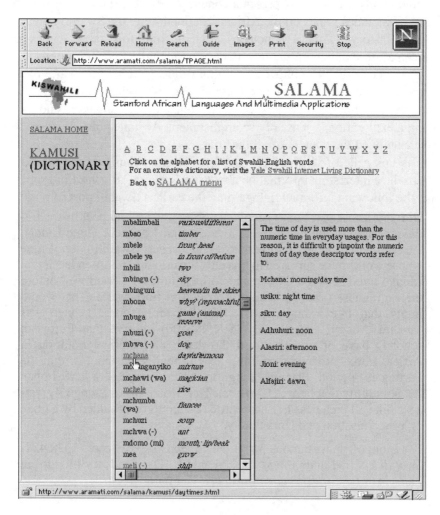

Some students say that they often visit the *Kamusi* just to peruse through lists of words and the associated cultural notes. In the future, the dictionary will include sound as well, which is something several students have inquired about. Note that a link to the *Yale Internet Living Dictionary* <http://www.cis. yale.edu/swahili/> (an extensive resource) is also provided so that users of the SALAMA site can look up word meanings not included in the first year Kamusi (Benjamin 1997).

The Orodha

The *Orodha* (list) provides specific content on East Africa combining text, audio, graphics, pictures and video-clips. There are over thirty different titles on the *Orodha* grouped in thematic zones organised on an increasing scale of difficulty. Zone I, shown in figure 4, includes preliminary topics such as greetings, self introductions, speaking about intimate subjects such as family, community etc. Zone II presents content on places, rural and urban life. Zone III includes issues on the African continent (e.g. the Swahili language, Swahili history). Zone IV includes content from folk tales, games and African art to mention only a few. Each zone includes review portions.

The zones provide sophisticated cultural information, grammar, vocabulary and subject matter with careful attention to comprehensibility. The zones also give goal-driven learners concrete fields of investigation and offer, through exploration, a sense of accomplishment. At some point, students will have examined the content of all the zones.

The link called *Je Wajua?* (do you know?) is a column whose purpose is to introduce interesting information about sub-Saharan Africans. For example, take the following information regarding the earliest Swahili poet of note:

> **Did you know** that Fumo Liongo a noble, warrior and poet, is the traditional hero of the Swahili. He lived around 1200 AD. Fumo Liongo is regarded by the Swahili people as the earliest Swahili poet of note whose works have survived to this day. Swahili oral tradition has it that Liongo lived between the 9th and 13th centuries, a period well before the Portuguese (and Christianity) arrived in East Africa. That would imply that like a majority of Swahili people today, Liongo was Muslim. Mazrui and Shariff (1994:98–100) observe that European scholars have often questioned the depth of historical tradition in Africa. Eurocentric scholarship places Liongo's existence within the Portuguese period. Placing Liongo in the Portuguese era leaves open the possibility that he was Christian. That would mean Liongo's greatness (like all greatness in Eurocentric conception) was aided by a tinge of Westernisation and Christianity.

> For Liongo's most famous poem the *Takhmisa* see: Steere (1928:454) *Swahili Tales*, London; and Carl Meinhof, 'Das Lied des Liongo' in *Zeitschrift fur Eingeborenen-Sprachen* Hamburg, 1924/5.

These items offer references for interested learners to pursue the issue should they wish to. Eventually, these notes will have links to a dedicated cultural database allowing for open access to information.

Guided browsing

The guided approach to the SALAMA site is recommended for beginners. Using the same material available for free browsing, guided viewing includes navigational procedures designed to help students focus rapidly on a particular cultural or environmental theme, a grammatical concept, or thematic vocabulary (e.g. professions, time division, numbers). Figure 5 shows a segment within SALAMA entitled SALAMU: WATU WAWILI (greetings between two people). This cluster of information – containing simple material and abundant illustrations – is available at the outset within the guided

Figure 4: The *Orodha*

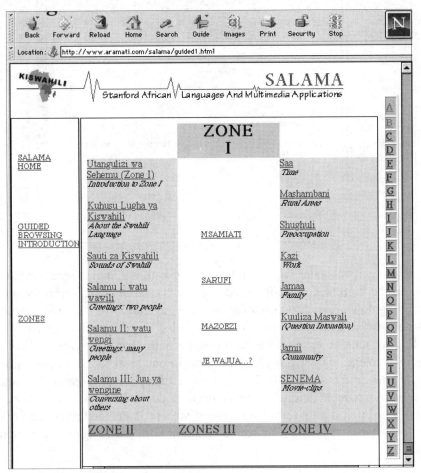

browsing environment. The strategy here is to provide direct experience of language use, an aim reinforced by a video clip exemplifying greetings.

Figure 5: Greetings between two people

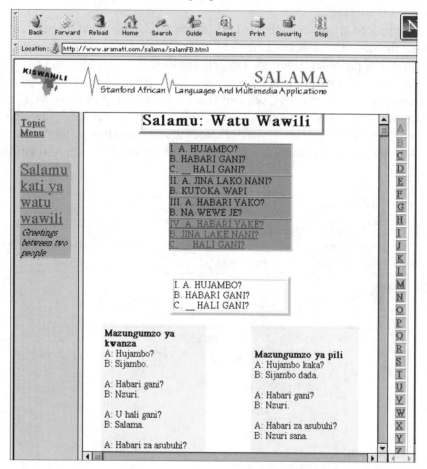

Each segment states what is to be covered within it, including a specification of the kind of knowledge needed for successful navigation in the area. Scrolling down reveals text with accompanying audio. Importantly, a dictionary is always available throughout the guided browsing environment, providing constant access to word definition. A control bar is provided with each audio segment, allowing students to listen to one sentence at a time, meanwhile attempting to repeat it. The usefulness of repetition to internalise intonation and pronunciation has never been in doubt. It is also already well established that digital retrieval of sound presents a decided advantage over analogue tapes. Students can access sound at will, easily associating sound and text if they wish.

Throughout the SALAMA site, comprehension questions associated with the various texts are provided. These questions have sample answers that pop up when questions are submitted. Since comprehension questions are frequently open-ended, difficulties arising in student responses are dealt with either digitally – using email and newsgroups – or in the classroom. Immediate feedback is crucial for any language learner as it aids comprehension and general progress. There are also buttons that enhance movement back and forth over large chunks of material with considerable ease.

Merits of the SALAMA site

Within the SALAMA site a bi-modal search procedure has become the principal dynamic of a new pedagogy, targeting enlightened exchange between individual learners. The goals of the lesson are mastered when information gained from browsing is taken and redirected or applied in correspondence, actual conversation and whatever other uses language is put in.

A customised assisted browsing environment provides some measure of cohesion while the Web remains accessible at the same time. Thus, there is a place to begin study and engage in purposeful activity, before using the Web at large. Customised environments will not curtail the learner's freedom of navigation: rather, they will benefit the learner constrained for time and eager to find quality materials quickly and consistently. Furthermore, the SALAMA site has taken into account student reactions to materials. Sites such as SALAMA are launching platforms from which learners can use circumscribed material to increase their knowledge of Swahili and African cultures in preparation for exploring all resources found on the Web. SALAMA is a home base to which learners can always return to seek clarification, continuity, and even evaluate their own progress relative to a significantly broad instructional base.

Digital space can be likened to an enormous tapestry on which everyone is welcome to place multimedia and textual resources. The challenge of exploration on the Web is the fact that the user is often distracted by catchy information strewn across individual pages by use of endless attention-getting gimmicks (such as 'click here for a free gift' etc.) which frequently derail the attention of the viewer trying to concentrate on language acquisition matters. The determination to advertise at all costs fractures the aggregate quality of the page. This may have its legitimacy in the commercial world in which competition reigns supreme. Its effectiveness is highly questionable in academic settings. The wizardry of computer interfaces requires close assessment to determine the appropriacy of technological devices to a given digital presentation of material. What a computer can do is not *a priori* what a computer should do. The power of gadgetry can easily overcome the virtue of human discernment. In the end analysis, quality of materials and transparency of presentation are the main considerations in providing authenticity and insight. The glamour inherent in Web presentations can readily form a misleading veneer, banishing any thought that the materials themselves could be incomplete, inaccurate, or completely false or misleading. Likewise, the power of linking can serve up chaos just as easily as order and higher levels of understanding. *Caveat emptor* applies here rephrased as 'browser beware'.

The Web has been praised for its access to authentic materials yet academics, including colleagues attending WorldCALL Conference, have referred to the Web as 'a library with all books piled up on the floor'. Stemming the navigational cost of time wasted in irrelevant searches is a primary problem in Web design. The SALAMA site offers a customised browsing environment as a means of addressing this problem. With a specifically constructed site, information of one kind is presented with links to other relevant sites. The presentation of materials fully emulates the Web style. At the same time, it also reflects attention given to pedagogical issues and purposeful exploring. Customised environments like SALAMA respect learner autonomy. Self-pacing, freedom from instructor-imposed methodological constraints, freedom to select links and explore at random within an information-rich milieu, can all be efficiently optimised, given the need to accommodate to reasonable expenditures of navigational time.

Web materials for language teaching, according to Robinson (1994) could be divided into three types: (a) informational – presenting cultural information; (b) behavioural, including video and audio clips of interviews; and (c) achievement – offering clips of interviews demonstrating discourse strategies. The customised web-browsing environment presented by the SALAMA site goes beyond the three-part categorisation of Web sites suggested by Robinson. In addition to assembling information, the SALAMA site provides numerous adjunct utilities enabling the learner to maximise investment in learning within a Web environment. The view of the Internet as an arena for thought development embodied by the SALAMA site cautions against any attempts to categorise Web materials. The Web's full potential both in its evolution and integration into modern teaching and learning has yet to be seen and clarified in research.

According to Moeller (1997:8), the teacher is involved with the introduction of 'content which involves learners in comprehending, manipulating, interacting in the focus language, attending mainly to meaning rather than form'. The SALAMA site incorporates state of the art resources from other African language teaching centres – the most significant of these being video-clips from the University of Georgia (Moshi 1996). SALAMA also calls on leading scholars in African linguistics and in language teaching and learning to serve as pedagogical consultants. Indeed, customised Web environments will make it possible for language professionals to judge for themselves what constitutes quality applications and materials. The transparent, customised browsing environments within SALAMA will point up certain limitations presented by the Web at a more general level. They will also temper the currently widespread belief that the Web, in and of itself, is capable of solving fundamental questions in the domain of language learning. We will have the rationale for answering questions inevitably springing to mind, instead of only posing them.

1 Are customised Web environments a good idea?

2 What can be accomplished using the Web for language learning?

3 What learning and teaching styles can the Web support? Will learners experience more freedom when content allows for exploration or will it be expository at best and rigorously regimented at its worst, leaving learner curiosity and inventiveness curtailed and teachers firmly in control?

4 What kinds of learners and instructors are likely to benefit from customised environments?

Clearly, the Web does not offer a universal solution to educational issues. Some purposes are more readily and efficiently accomplished using specially designed applications. The Stanford Swahili Project, recognizing the value of pulling together well-adapted tools, calls upon other applications instrumentally to accomplish a wide range of language learning tasks, specifically calling upon students' initiative and spirit of innovation.

The specific use of *Media-Driven Learning System* (Mugane, in preparation) and *Stay Tooned* (Barson 1994) programs are described in Mugane (1997, 1998). Optimal applications are necessary when computers are used to facilitate second language acquisition. As Levy (1997:30) points out, we have to 'shift from a naïve search of a superior teaching machine to a more atomistic study of the characteristics of new media in relation to key factors associated with learning, the learner, and the learning context'. It is the complex of the language learning process coupled with learner individuality that prompts the planning of effectiveness research for all CALL activity (Chapelle 1989). The instrumental use of computers will prove useful in the selection of applications ensuring learner autonomy rather than hindering it.

Conclusion

The architecture of the Stanford Swahili Project is based on a coherence-directed curriculum. Partially conceived in advance, the curriculum is a set of exploratory paths. Students, in following leads and satisfying their curiosity, contribute to an emerging syllabus in which content, communicative acts, development of grammaticality and productive feedback must all be present and valued. The curriculum must also be capable of generating meta-level considerations about language function, learning space, and the role of cogent, communication-oriented learning space. Just as language is a system of embedded subsystems, our approaches must be multifaceted rather than linear, parallel rather than sequential. The technology selected or developed for language teaching and learning also must take into account the nature of language and recognize the considerable mystery still surrounding the process of language acquisition.

In the SALAMA arena presented here, balance is essential to carving out an adequate learning experience and cultivating efficient learning techniques among students and instructors. The project – its methods, approaches and materials – is evaluated in terms of its success at promoting cohesion. In attempting to achieve this goal – the coherence of learning and reality. The most vital concerns are insuring learner participation, learner-determined acquisition of knowledge, learner initiative, activity and reflection.

A true integration of computer technology and learning exists precisely when computer applications are utilised instrumentally, in the context of accomplishing specific tasks. Digital applications grounded on pertinent the-oretical premises regarding life and education in our networked era do offer promise. They ensure that theoretical and pedagogical considerations related to the development of Mind will be able to weather the flux attending tech-nological evolution today—and something else; we might, perchance, build the 'good society' Mihaly Csikszentmihalyi so eloquently describes:

> A good society is one that helps each individual develop his or her genetic potential to its fullest. It provides opportunities for action to everyone: to the athlete and the poet, the merchant and the scholar. It does not bar anyone from doing what he or she does best, and guides everyone to discover what it is. A good society makes it possible for each person to develop the skills necessary to experience flow in socially productive activities. … freedom does not apply to *doing* but to *being*. (Csikszentmihalyi 1993:269)

In constructing SALAMA, African languages and cultures were central. The project itself, however, and the knowledge gained from its implementa-tion and use can serve as a prototype for builders of other learning environ-ments customised for specific disciplines. The integration of computers and networking with learning is, without a doubt, a cross-disciplinary venture.

Acknowledgements

The writing of this paper has been greatly aided by a major grant from The Consortium of Language Teaching and Learning and also by numerous discussions with John Barson, Emeritus Professor of French and Italian, Stanford University. All shortcomings of this paper are solely the responsibility of its author.

References

Barson, J. (1994). *Stay Tooned application*. Palo Alto, Calif.: Stanford University.

Benjamin, M. (1997). Malangali and the Cyberians: Reflections on the Internet living Swahili dictionary, *Africa Today 44*, 3, 339–355.

Chapelle, C. (1989). CALL Research in the 1980s: Setting the stage for the 1990s, *CALL Digest 5*, 7: 7–9.

Csikszentmihalyi, M. (1993). The evolving self: A psychology for the third millenium. New York: Harper-Collins.

Levy, M. (1997). *Computer-assisted language learning: Context and conceptualization*. Oxford: Clarendon Press.

Mazrui, A (1986). *The Africans: A triple heritage*. Television Series. London: BBC.

Moeller, A. (1997). Moving from instruction to learning with technology: Where's the content? *CALICO Journal 14*, 5–13.

Moshi, L. (1996). *Kiswahili* [video recording]: *Lugha na Utamaduni*. Produced by the Office of Instructional Development, Instructional Resources Center, University of Georgia.

Mugane, J. (1997). Learning african languages with evolving digital technologies. *Africa Today 44*, 4, 423–442.

Mugane, J. (1998). Episode-generated instruction: A digital approach towards dealing out sequentiality. *Journal of the African Language Teachers Association* (forthcoming).

Mugane, J. (forthcoming). *Tujifunze Kiswahili 1.0*: Let's Learn Swahili

Mugane, J. (in preparation). Media-driven learning system (MDLS).

Postman, N. (1993). *Technopoly: The surrender of culture to technology*. New York: Vintage Books.

Robinson, G. (1994). *Culture learning in the foreign language classroom. A model for second culture acquisition in culture and content: perspectives on the acquisition of cultural competence in the foreign language classroom*. Southwest Conference on Language Teaching. Monograph series no. 4. Tempe, Az.

Turkle, S. (1995). *Life on the screen: Identity in the age of the internet*. New York: Simon & Schuster.

3

Interactivity in L2 Web-Based Reading

Roger Ganderton
Education Queensland, Australia

Introduction

Use of the World Wide Web in second and foreign language (L2) teaching is an area of ever-increasing interest, with respect to both the technological developments and the variety of learning activities the Web now facilitates (Ganderton 1996). As well, its role in creating new forms of literacy which challenge some of our current educational practices has been the focus of much consideration (Dudfield 1998; Levy 1997b). The primary importance of reading and the Web's usefulness for authentic language reading activities are highlighted (Ganderton 1996; Mak 1996; Prokop 1996), although Mills (1995) outlines other uses, such as searching for information, downloading materials, and also as a forum for publishing of student work. Warschauer (1995) also notes the increased use of the Web for computer-mediated communication such as Chat, while Godwin-Jones (1998) discusses development of 'interactive' web pages for the delivery of learning materials.

Here, the examination of Web use will be on two key aspects. The first of these is its importance in L2 reading, especially given its facility of being able to provide access to authentic language material (Cangiano, Haichour & Stauffer 1995). The second, in relation to this, is the concept of interactivity with regard to web-based reading. The term 'interactive' is used by Godwin-Jones (1998:par. 4) with a specific focus, namely the design of 'pages which allow (or require) user input (typing, clicking) with appropriate responses to that input or pages which enable users to work collaboratively, particularly in written form'. Dudfield (1998) likewise refers to 'interactive' web pages with reference to their inviting of user input and collaboration. However, in considering use of the Web from the L2 learner's perspective, particularly with respect to reading, the concept of interactivity needs to be extended beyond the scope of interaction between the learner and the computer. Devitt (1997) outlines the various types of interaction examined in language learning generally, such as face-to-face interaction, interaction of the reader with the text or writer, interaction within the reader of various subprocesses, and interaction between the language learner and the input provided by texts in the L2. Similarly, Barty (1998), in discussing interactive television technology in distance education, expands the notion of interactivity to include not just interaction between teacher and learner via the television medium, but also interaction between learners in the remote group, and indeed interaction between the learner and the course materials.

In a similar way, it is argued here that reading of authentic L2 texts on the Web can be interactive in the fuller sense of the word, when considered as interaction not just between the learner and the computer, but also between the learner and the text, and indeed among the various mental processes occurring within the learner themselves. This proposition will be expanded through examination of previous research on L2 reading in general, as well as the nature of the medium of the Web, and a recent study observing reading strategies used by L2 learners performing web-based reading tasks.

Literature review

L2 reading

Interactive models of L2 reading view it as a combination of lower level processes (i.e. vocabulary and syntactic knowledge and automaticity of text decoding at the sentence level) and higher level processes (i.e. formal and content schemata, skills monitoring, metacognitive knowledge and use of reading strategies) (Grabe 1991). Such models are also seen as combinations of bottom-up orientations, which assert the primacy of the text and its decoding by the reader, and top-down orientations, which emphasise reader interpretation and prior knowledge (Bernhardt 1991; Chun & Plass 1997; Swaffar, Arens & Byrnes 1991).

In addition to examination of reading processes, reading strategies is another major area of L2 reading research. Use of the term 'strategies' for many authors entails a focus on conscious behaviours exhibited by L2 readers in comprehending text, such as decoding vocabulary, predicting or invoking prior knowledge (Jiménez, García & Pearson 1996; Swaffar et al. 1991). This is in contrast to reading 'processes', which in reading research and cognitive psychology refer more to unconscious or automatic mental operations (see e.g. Horiba 1996).

Of particular interest in the L2 reading situation is, also, the relationship between reading ability and language proficiency. Carrell (1988) highlights the importance of vocabulary development and word recognition, areas that function as parts of L2 proficiency, and more recent research suggests that L2 readers pay more attention than L1 readers to these lower level processes (Chun & Plass 1997). Taillefer (1996) concludes that, for L2 readers of lower language proficiency, factors such as lack of confidence in the L2 or anxiety may make them afraid of incorporating their L1 reading knowledge into the L2 situation. Therefore, she advocates the incorporation of metacognitive awareness and training in reading strategies into the teaching of L2 reading. Determining effective reading strategies for L2 learners and training them in their use has long been called for in the language teaching field (Barnett 1989). Similarly, design of reading tasks by teachers should take into account the strategies required (Cicurel 1991).

Reading on the Web
However, while there may be a significant amount of research available to support use of specific strategies for printed text, there is a paucity of information and research that documents exactly what reading strategies L2 readers exhibit when accessing text in electronic form, specifically through the hypertext medium of the Web. Many proposed strategies for web-based reading (Johnson 1996), as well as suggestions for reading tasks (Australian Federation of Modern Language Teachers Associations Inc. 1997), are based mainly on anecdotal evidence or teachers' experiences, rather than from specific research data (e.g. Ganderton 1996; Mak 1996; Prokop 1996). In some cases, the Web is seen as having potential benefit based on the characteristics of the technology itself (Cangiano et al. 1995), although, more recently, studies reporting on the piloting of particular web-based activities, learner feedback, and observation have offered some confirmation of this benefit (Collombet-Sankey 1997; Osuna & Meskill 1998).

Major differences between the reading of printed text and hypertext derive from the particular properties of the different media. Kaplan (1995) notes, for example, the need for understanding not just of the written language system, but also the computer's interface. Similarly, graphic images can assume increased importance in hypertext documents, as they can be used not just as accompanying illustrations, but also as icons to assist in navigation (Barnes 1994) or as hyperlinks themselves.

However, perhaps the most crucial feature of hypertext is its nonlinear structure. This stands in contrast to print media, like books, which are 'essentially repositories for the sequential storage of information' (Snyder 1996:17). This has profound implications for the interactive view of L2 reading and the processes and strategies associated with it. For higher level processes, looking at text structure or skimming or scanning can now only apply to the portion of text located on a particular web page, as the rest of the site (i.e. related text linked to that page) is not visible without physically linking to it. In fact, how (or whether) the reader perceives a hypertext document as a whole is problematic. Levy (1997b:40) points out that 'the reader quite probably never reads or sees all the text that has been written' in a hypertext document, an observation supported by Quentin-Baxter's (1998) study of L1 students accessing hypertext learning materials.

On the positive side, the possibility of linking to other sites from a web document may be able to enhance readers' background knowledge (cultural or linguistic) when dealing with a particular portion of text on the Web and in fact alter or enhance their comprehension of it. Collombet-Sankey (1997) points to the constructive role the learner may play in reorganising and restructuring information encountered in the nonlinear environment of the Web when researching information for incorporation into their own language production. A similar view is seen in the area of multimedia learning, in particular the 'generative theory', which portrays the learner, or user, as actively constructing knowledge by selecting relevant words and images from information presented and organising this selected information into a coherent mental representation (Mayer 1997).

The fact that linked portions of text on a web page are strongly highlighted may also have some implications for lower level reading processes. L2 vocabulary and syntactic knowledge are crucial, as they are in all L2 reading (Carrell 1988; Grabe 1991), in recognising which hyperlinks to click to seek specific information. However, it may also have some effect in drawing the reader to particular textual items merely because of their physical emphasis rather than their importance. This points to a problem in the lack of direction L2 learners may encounter when using the Web if they have no specific goal or task in mind (Mak 1996). The range of choices, links, starting points and navigation paths offered by hypertext can very easily find the learner 'lost in cyberspace'. The importance of other elements, apart from the physical reading medium alone, therefore play a role. As Cobb and Stevens (1996:117) suggest, 'there is no guarantee that making large and varied amounts of online text available automatically promotes particularly deep processing'.

Reading tasks on the Web

With respect to the actual tasks that readers can perform with web-based texts, Tuman (1996) highlights the strength of the Web as an instrument for browsing and locating information that one is interested in. In fact, Slatin (1990:875) makes an important distinction between 'browsing' and 'using' on the Web. The former is a more non-directed activity, where the computer user follows links in the hypertext environment as momentary interest dictates, while the latter involves accessing a hypertext document for the purposeful seeking of specific information.

Tuman (1996) notes that, with traditional printed text, the finding of a particular text holds much less status and is considered more a preliminary step to actual reading. In contrast, in the Web environment, such location of text involves particular skills and has increased importance. However, in the L2 context, the mere recognition and comprehension of specific items of text may be difficult enough for some learners, let alone actual critical reading of larger volumes of text. Therefore, browsing or using tasks on the Web have the potential to challenge L2 readers and engage their reading skills at all levels.[1]

Just how such tasks can be applied in the L2 classroom and what strategies learners require to complete them need more investigation. Long (1980) argues that in second language acquisition (SLA) research, the research cycle should progress from descriptive to correlational to experimental studies. In the area of L2 reading strategies on the Web, as Chapelle (1990) notes for CALL in general, the descriptive phase has barely begun. With this focus in mind, the aim of the study described here was to describe the strategies exhibited by some L2 learners reading hypertext documents in the target language on the World Wide Web. The observations of these learners performing web-based reading tasks were analysed in relation to taxonomies of reading strategies proposed in other research on L2 reading with printed text.

Method

In line with the descriptive orientation of this study, a variety of qualitative methods were employed to collect data (Larsen-Freeman & Long 1991). The primary focus of this data collection was the observation of the participants performing reading tasks on the Web, with data collection occuring before, during and after the performance of these tasks. Six high school intermediate learners of French as a foreign language were selected at random from a Year 10 French class at a private girls' school in Brisbane to participate in this study. The participants were divided into three pairs.

Prior to the reading tasks, background information on the participants was sought via a questionnaire on basic biographical data, language background and previous experience with use of computers and the Web. In addition to the questionnaires, the class teacher was consulted on the participants' latest achievement levels in the reading skill in French, as well as their overall French achievement.

Two reading tasks were then given for each pair of participants: one involving information retrieval and one involving free browsing, in line with Slatin's (1990) using–browsing distinction. The information retrieval task involved searching for daily weather forecasts for two cities – Bordeaux, France and Stockholm, Sweden – starting from the home page of *Météoconsult*, a French commercial weather forecasting agency.[2] The browsing task was from the *DouceFrance* home page, a French-language links page containing a range of diverse topics.[3] Unlike the information retrieval task, no specific instructions were given apart from requesting the participants to pursue links that were of interest and to stay, where possible, on web pages in the target language.

From the actual reading tasks, data was obtained through three main sources: videoscreen recording, audio recording of the participants' discussion during the tasks, and a post-task interview. Use of recording techniques to monitor participants' navigation paths is a common technique in researching hypertext use (McKnight, Dillon & Richardson 1991). The use of video for this work not only allowed tracking of web pages accessed, but also monitored the sections of a page that were being viewed at any particular time, as well as mouse movements and clicks. In conjunction with this, a 'pair talk' protocol was employed to record participants' discussion during the tasks (see figure 1). This technique differs from the 'think aloud' protocol commonly used in reading strategy research (Jiménez et al. 1996), most obviously as it is used with pairs of subjects rather than individuals. However, it also offers added advantages in that it gives a more naturalistic setting and creates a need for participants to justify or explain their ideas or actions, and thereby verbalise thought processes (Trollope 1995).

Introspective (during task) and retrospective (post-task) data collection techniques have been combined in a variety of studies previously (Nunan 1992). Haastrup (1987) highlights the advantages of combining introspection and retrospection to help compensate for shortcomings of each method individually. The point is made, however, that the introspective data is the chief source, with the retrospective data supplementing or filling in the gaps. Such an approach was implemented in this study through the post-task interview, in order to provide a larger quantity of data to draw from and to utilise retrospection as a means of further enriching and clarifying elements arising from the introspective data (Nunan 1992). In this regard, a 'stimulated recall' interviewing technique was employed (1992:124), in which participants were shown particular segments of the video recording, which served as prompts for clarification and discussion of their strategy use. Questions posed by the researcher were initially general ones, with more specific questions added in response to points raised by participants, an approach described by Haastrup (1987:204) as 'researcher-controlled and informant-initiated'. This looser interviewing style therefore allowed the researcher to pursue other topics not considered prior to the interview in response to participants' feedback (Guthrie & Hall 1984).

Figure 1: Technical setup for data collection during reading tasks

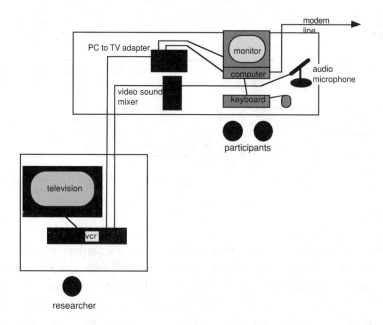

The video recordings and post-task interviews were transcribed using common transcription conventions (see Schiffrin 1994:422–433), with a 'storyboard' technique used for the video transcripts; that is, two columns were given with one presenting the verbal transcript, and one indicating web pages currently on the screen and actions performed by the participants (e.g. mouse movements and clicks). Strategies observed from the transcripts were categorised according to a framework of five categories of reading strategy use, based on Grabe's (1991) outline of component skills and knowledge areas in L2 reading. These categories were chosen as they cover a wide range of aspects of the L2 reading process and cater for the interactive model of L2 reading prevalent in the field. The categories and their definitions are given in table 1.

Table 1: Categories of component skills and knowledge areas in L2 reading
used for data analysis

Category	Definition
Vocabulary and syntactic knowledge	Explicit recognition of words or phrases, use of knowledge of L2 vocabulary and language structure (Carrell 1988; Grabe 1991).
Formal discourse structure knowledge	Knowledge of text structure and use in comprehension of text (Grabe 1991), strategies of navigation demonstrating text structure knowledge.
Content and background knowledge	Readers' prior knowledge of text-related information and content, including cultural knowledge (Grabe 1991).
Synthesis and evaluation skills	Evaluating text information, integrating or comparing with information from other sources, prediction of upcoming portions of text (Grabe 1991).
Metacognitive knowledge and skills monitoring	Knowledge and regulation of reading processes (Grabe, 1991), dealing with problems in comprehension or task completion (Jiménez et al. 1996).

Findings

Grabe (1991) notes the particular importance of vocabulary in L2 reading in
general. This importance was evident in the web-based reading observed.
There was a strong focus on reading of words and phrases, and not so much
on reading of larger portions of text. In particular, participants focused very
heavily on hyperlinks on the web pages, as well as other text with a similarly strong physical emphasis. While many of the pages visited consisted
almost exclusively of hyperlinks or text buttons, particularly in the first task,
this focus on hyperlinked text was also evident when viewing pages containing long paragraphs of text. This aspect could be related in part to the content
of the web pages but could also be a function of participants' lower language
skills and their inability or unwillingness to negotiate larger portions of text.
    Focusing on known vocabulary or easily recognisable cognates was a
common initial strategy used by all participants in both tasks. In some cases,
recognition of vocabulary was immediately followed by linking to that page.
One group, in commencing the first task, noted the word *jours* ('days') on the
link *Prévisions à 10 jours* ('10-day forecasts') and immediately went to it,
only to return subsequently to the beginning when that link proved fruitless.
In contrast, other groups commenced by scrolling and scanning the page,
considering the various links available, and then making a selection.

Reference to the task objectives, as well as comprehension of text, was significant in the participants' decisions on what links to follow. In the first task, all participants knew the word *sur* ('on') and could therefore deduce the link *Prévisions sur la France* (literally 'Forecasts on France') for finding Bordeaux. However, the word *hors* ('outside') in the link *Prévisions hors de France* ('Forecasts outside of France') was not known. Nevertheless, all participants were able to correctly infer its meaning and successfully locate the forecast for Stockholm in Sweden. Similarly, the word *aujourd'hui* ('today') in the link *Le Temps d'Aujourd'hui* ('today's weather'), was also commonly known and its significance recognised. Some participants recognised *le temps* as 'weather', but there was also some mistranslation, in part based on cognates, a common source of inferences and errors in this study.

However, in hypothesising the meaning of this and other words or phrases, a strong effect of hypertext was observed. One group was able to revise an initial hypothesis on the meaning of *le temps* based on subsequent hyperlinking. There were also numerous instances of participants opting to 'let's click on it', when reading hyperlinked text the meaning of which they were not certain. Nevertheless, participants' inferences on vocabulary meaning were not always actively tested in this way and in some cases such inferencing was abandoned in order to focus on other links deemed more interesting or relevant.

In addition, use of cognates or context, while common, were not the only sources for making inferences with vocabulary meaning. One interesting case was noted in the first task with one participant, who suggested that the *Validez* ('confirm/validate') button used in selecting towns for weather forecasts might be referring to a 'search' function. In this case, her inference was based more on the physical form of the web-based text. In the post-task interview, she compared the appearance of the scrolling list with the button next to it to similar formats she had seen on English language web pages. Inferring its meaning by other means might well have yielded a very different result.

With respect to the second task, where interest was the chief criterion for linking, a lack of direction was observed in some cases. For example, in some instances, participants chose links more or less at random or by processes of elimination. Nevertheless, one group's linking to *mode* ('fashion') was made with a specific goal in mind, namely to compare Australian and French fashion trends. Also, another participant's specific interest in *l'équitation* ('equestrianism') was shown while browsing a sports page. In both such instances, student interest in and language knowledge of the topic were combined. As well, in the second instance, the navigation trail to *l'équitation* showed some evidence of associative knowledge, a key aspect of hypertext reading (Slatin 1990; Tuman 1992), in that the participant was able to select *sports*, and then discriminate between different categories such as *sports d'équipe* ('team sports') and *sports individuels* ('individual sports').

While graphics are seen as potentially helpful in the learning of vocabulary in a multimedia environment (Chun & Plass 1997), it did not appear they were drawn upon strongly by participants in this study, especially with respect to the icons for the different topics on the *DouceFrance* page in the browsing task. In fact, one participant referred to these when stating that they were 'hard to understand if you didn't know the French words'. In addition, in the first task, graphical navigation icons on the *Météoconsult* pages were completely ignored.

In considering the participants' knowledge of overall text structure, it was clear that they were basically familiar with the web environment, based on their background information and their task performance. All were able to navigate reasonably successfully through the different sites visited, largely by use of the browser's 'Back' and 'Forward' buttons. In one case during the first task, the participants were able to note a page viewed earlier and return to it when they later required it. In this respect, it appeared that the branching structure of the site was noted and used by all three groups. In the second task, however, all participants encountered difficulties with the introduction of a second browser window, which appeared for links outside the *DouceFrance* site. They appeared unfamiliar with this hyperlink format, although two of the groups were able, by trial and error, to eventually close off the window and thereby return to the topic page. One group in particular noted this structure and used it again later in the task.

Scrolling and scanning of the whole page before linking to another was a strategy commonly used by all three groups. This suggested awareness of the structure of individual web pages by participants, in particular by use of scrolling to view the whole page first, as well as the need to wait for the whole page and graphics to load. This was particularly important with the *DouceFrance* page, which had a large number of graphical icon links. In this regard, one strategy observed in several instances was to move the mouse over a web page and check for clickable links, especially with large graphics.

Discussion

Interactive reading
While participants' reading strategies were categorised separately in this analysis, it is reasonable to conclude that these strategies within the different component skills and knowledge areas did work together in the overall reading process, in accordance with the interactive models of reading discussed

earlier. In fact, it is difficult to consider the strategies within one area without reference to those of another.

Looking firstly at the vocabulary knowledge demonstrated by the participants in this study, several interesting points emerge. Firstly, the gap in knowledge with regard to *le temps* ('weather') illustrates an interesting implication for web-based reading. As one participant wryly remarked about their class learning, 'we've done "rain" and "snow" and stuff, nothing about, not the actual weather'. In this light, a knowledge of subordinate terms like 'rain' without the corresponding knowledge of superordinate terms like 'weather' could present difficulties in linking to the subordinate, given that many such links on web pages are built on this superordinate–subordinate relationship. In fact, using semantic relationships as a strategy for learning of vocabulary ('semantic mapping') is an approach already incorporated in some CALL environments (see Svenconis & Kerst 1994/5). How semantic mapping may be applied to reading of authentic web-based documents, particularly with respect to different semantic relationships, is a topic worthy of deeper examination.

In the second task, the intersection of interest in particular topics (e.g. *mode, l'équitation*) and motivation to acquire or engage language knowledge in these topics was coupled here with the capacity on the Web to utilise that knowledge for the learner's own means. Such incidental application of participants' language skills and learning across diverse topic areas was a salient feature of the second task overall and represented a positive aspect deriving from the open-ended nature of this task. This is in contrast to the first task, in which the clearly defined objectives appeared to lead to more focused reading. One group in particular showed much more propensity to take risks in the first task than in the second, and to try out links of whose meanings they were not certain. Therefore, the motivation provided by the freedom of choice of the second task shows some different characteristics from the goal-based motivation of the first.

Another crucial difference between the two tasks used in this study is seen in the scope of pages visited in the first and the second reading tasks. The fact that the first task was limited to the pages on the *Météoconsult* site meant that it was more predictable where the participants might go, and indeed participants' prediction of content to be visited when hyperlinking was generally more accurate. In the second task as well, participants had a defined number of links that could have been followed from the *DouceFrance* home page. However, from there, their paths were very diverse. Clearly, it could not be so easily foreseen what links might be chosen overall and what language and content they might encounter in such a free-browsing task.

At this point it is worth noting that, while the participants' skills and knowledge areas were 'interactive', this notion of interactivity in reading can also be applied 'to the general interaction which takes place between the reader and the text' (Grabe 1991:384). In the context of web-based reading, this view is also significant. Different groups in the study did follow different links, thereby in effect creating different texts to be read. In the key area of hypothesising specific meanings of language items or content, this involved direct 'physical' interaction with the document, in the form of selecting and clicking links, to address their hypotheses.

While the use of authentic texts in these reading tasks did provide many opportunities for such interaction, there were difficulties and limits based on the content and structure of the texts themselves and the fact that they were authentic texts (i.e. written for a target audience of native speakers). For example, when participants accessed the *Météoconsult* pages discussing *Minitel*, they appeared unfamiliar with what *Minitel* was and were confused by the graphics showing sample *Minitel* screen captures.[4] However, on these pages, there were no links available to other pages or sites that might help them obtain the necessary background knowledge on *Minitel* to assist in comprehending what was shown on these *Météoconsult* pages. From the web page author's point of view, such links would be redundant if the target audience is assumed to be French nationals or native speakers, virtually all of whom would already be familiar with the concept of *Minitel*. Therefore, while it can be argued that the participants' lack of native speaker intuitions about certain vocabulary, subject matter, or graphical content could in part be overcome by hypothesising and hyperlinking, in this case a limit is clearly drawn due to the linking structure of the document. This issue highlights the importance in task design of considering the nature of the text to be used and what pages, content, and prior knowledge a learner will require in order to complete the task.

Conversely, one would also need to consider exactly what unfamiliar language or content could reasonably be inferred through the task, and indeed what strategies or support the learner would need for such inferencing. In this regard, the variety not just within texts to be used but in learners to be using them is a significant factor, as it is in examining L2 reading comprehension generally (Chun & Plass 1997). For example, one interesting contrast between two groups of participants in this study was seen in their cognitive styles, specifically with respect to reflection and impulsivity (see Jamieson 1992). One group, in commencing the first task, spent a long time scrolling and scanning the first screen before selecting a link, whereas the other, without any scrolling, clicked on the first link in which they recognised a word. Significantly, the first group were able to make their way directly to the information required through several links, whereas the second group experienced difficulties and eventually had to return to the starting page. On the other side, the first group appeared less ready to take risks with unfamiliar material and, when they did encounter difficulties with navigation, remained in that difficulty for some time. The second group tried several unfamiliar links in both tasks, with varying degrees of success. The reflective (slow-accurate) approach of the first group therefore contrasted heavily with the impulsive (fast-inaccurate; Jamieson 1992) approach of the second. This, of course, is only one example of individual differences that learners may exhibit, but it highlights the importance in task design in considering not just characteristics of the text, but of the learner as well.

The issue of the learner's holistic view of web documents, referred to earlier, also needs to be considered in relation to the nature of the reading task. Quentin-Baxter (1998: sect. 4) says as much in stating that 'hypermedia is ideal for case-based teaching materials where students are expected to identify the important as opposed to the redundant information', that is, students do not have to access all the information available but select the information 'of greatest relevance to the learning objectives'. Conversely, Collombet-Sankey (1997) uses a more learner-centred approach in having the learner determine the objectives for their web use by defining their own topic for their oral presentations in their language class, which are to be researched using the Web. This approach highlights the importance not just of learners using the existing structure of hypertext documents to access information, but also of their own structuring of the information that they access in order to create their own text (Snyder 1996).

This contrast between approaches using prescribed web documents with prescribed learning objectives and approaches emphasising learner choice, both in terms of documents to be accessed and information to be sought, maps well onto the using–browsing distinction outlined by Slatin (1990). While the different studies mentioned above may suggest the superiority of one approach over the other, the findings presented in this study point to different advantages for the different uses, especially with respect to learner motivation and inferencing. What is also important in this regard is the point made by Slatin (1990:875) with reference to using and browsing that, in practice, one can tend to switch from using to browsing and vice versa while working in a hypertext system.

Conclusion

Given the variety of uses of the Web outlined earlier, determining what role web-based materials may play in encouraging interactive reading requires some consideration. In this regard, Levy's (1997a) tutor-tool distinction is helpful. Godwin-Jones's (1998) focus on 'interactive' web pages, discussed earlier, suggests a more tutorial role for these web pages in evaluating and responding to the user's input (Levy 1997a). This also implies a 'stand-alone' role for the computer, in that all that is required to perform the task is there on the web page. Cangiano et al. (1995) similarly propose a total learning environment on web pages by use of browser frames, one of which would contain an authentic text for reading. Other frames would then be used for task instructions, or even support materials, such as links to cultural notes, online dictionaries, structured lesson notes, and an online writing environment. This latter proposal falls more in the 'tool' role for the computer as described by Levy (1997a). The materials presented on the web page are available for the learner to use for reading, writing and participation in lesson activities, although the actual evaluation of learner input is done by the teacher rather than by a computer program.

The approach used in this study, however, was to have participants use the computer solely for reading of authentic text. Within Levy's (1997a) tutor-tool framework, such an approach would conceivably fall more within the tool category, that is, using the computer as a tool for accessing text, although Ganderton (1997) posits a separate 'resource' category for such applications where accessing linguistic material – as opposed to creating, manipulating, or responding to it – is the primary role of the computer.

It is not the contention here that one approach is necessarily superior or inferior to another in promoting interactive L2 reading. Nevertheless, limiting the computer's role to that of presenting material is equally justifiable, especially as the other roles assigned to the computer above could well be better handled by participants other than the computer in some situations. Chapelle's (1998) suggestion that authentic web-based materials may only provide input, whereas multimedia CALL materials allowing for modifications of linguistic material may provide comprehensible input, should be qualified in this light. The important process of negotiating meaning, highlighted by Chapelle as part of the interactionist model of SLA, need not be handled by the computer and learner alone.

In fact, in print-based reading, such negotiation can be actively pursued between the reader and their own language and knowledge base, in conjunction with the text input (Grabe 1991), and the benefits of authentic texts in challenging the learner in this should not be overlooked (Leow 1993; Vale, Scarino & McKay 1991). Devitt (1997), in advancing an approach for (print-based) reading of authentic text, even sees native speakers as potential participants in the negotiation of text meaning with the learner, drawing on links between interaction research in SLA and L2 reading. While Chapelle (1998:27) sees modifications of input provided by multimedia CALL materials coming 'in the form of repetition, simplification through restatements, non-verbal cues, decreased speed, reference materials, and change of input mode', Devitt (1997:463) notes that texts modified 'along the lines of the interactional adjustments native speakers make in face-to-face conversation' tend actually to be more elaborate, rather than simplified. But they are still being effective in making the original text comprehensible (Yano, Long & Ross 1994), as well as enhancing linguistic intake by the language learner (Leow 1993).

There is, therefore, a danger in designing L2 reading approaches of possibly making the computer do too much, or take on roles perhaps best left to human interactants (e.g. teacher or native speaker). Authentic texts in and of themselves can still provide appropriate 'comprehensible' input to encourage interactive reading and negotiation of meaning, and the computer's role can be limited to that of provider of this authentic text. The importance here, however, is on the selection of texts, design of tasks, and utilisation of the Web and its characteristics for their natural advantages.

This returns the focus to the central point of interactivity needing to be considered beyond the scope of interaction between learner and computer. Some of the interactions outlined by Devitt (1997), such as learner with text, learner with input, mental processes within learner, or indeed learner with fellow learner (Barty 1998), are all worthy of deeper examination in the context of researching, planning, and evaluating CALL activities.

The study presented here has described just some of these interactions in the context of observing learners' reading strategies in performing reading tasks with L2 web-based authentic texts. The strengths and limitations of the medium of the Web for the development and application of specific reading skills and knowledge areas, such as inferencing, use of text structure and synthesising new information, have been discussed. In addition, some successful reading strategies used by participants in this study have been outlined, although the initial focus of the study was descriptive only. Clearly further research is needed to examine the generalisability and applicability of such strategies in the L2 teaching situation.

There is much still to be learned about using this comparatively new medium, which offers much that can be beneficial to the L2 learner and teacher. On the other hand, in some aspects 'new' is not always 'better'. The challenge for teachers and researchers is to understand and apply better the new technologies for the purposes for which they are best suited.

Notes

[1] In fact, in some tasks, the media of print and the Web can be readily combined (AFMLTA 1997). Taking into account Taillefer's (1996) distinction between the three types of reading (skimming, scanning and reading for meaning), learners could use the Web to skim or scan to locate particular texts, which could then be printed out for more concentrated reading for meaning.

[2] http://www.meteoconsult.fr

[3] http://www.doucefrance.com

[4] *Minitel* is a French-based computer network, through which home users can access public information.

References

Australian Federation of Modern Language Teachers Associations Inc. (1997). *Language resources on the Internet: Guidelines and tasks*. Canberra, Australia: AFMLTA.

Barnes, S. (1994). Hypertext literacy. *Interpersonal Computing and Technology 2*, 4, 24–36.

Barnett, M.A. (1989). *More than meets the eye: Foreign language reading: Theory and practice*. Englewood Cliffs, NJ: Prentice Hall.

Barty, K. (1998). Interactive television: How interactive is it? *Babel 33*, 1, 28–30, 36–38.

Bernhardt, E.B. (1991). *Reading development in a second language: Theoretical, empirical, and classroom perspectives*. Norwood, NJ: Ablex.

Cangiano, V.J., Haichour, E.H. & Stauffer, S.J. (1995). Taming the electronic lion, or how to shape a language-learning environment out of the chaos called the Internet. In *Georgetown University round table on languages and linguistics 1995* (pp. 512–525). Washington DC: Georgetown University Press.

Carrell, P.L. (1988). Interactive text processing: Implications for ESL/second language reading classrooms. In P. Carrell, J. Devine & D. Eskey (Eds), *Interactive approaches to second language reading* (pp. 239–259). New York: Cambridge University Press.

Chapelle, C. (1990). The discourse of computer-assisted language learning: Toward a context for descriptive research. *TESOL Quarterly 24*, 2, 199–225.

Chapelle, C. (1998). Multimedia CALL: Lessons to be learned from research on instructed SLA. *Language Learning and Technology 2*, 1, 22–34.

Chun, D.M. & Plass, J.L. (1997). Research on text comprehension in multimedia environments. *Language Learning & Technology 1*, 1, 60–81.

Cicurel, F. (1991). *Lectures interactives en langue étrangère* (Interactive reading in a foreign language). Paris: Hachette.

Cobb, T. & Stevens, V. (1996). A principled consideration of computers and reading in a second language. In M.C. Pennington (Ed.), *The power of CALL* (pp. 115–136). Houston, TX: Athelstan.

Collombet-Sankey, N. (1997). Surfing the net to acquire communicative competence and cultural knowledge. In R. Debski, J. Gassin & M. Smith (Eds), *Language learning through social computing* (pp. 141–158). Melbourne, Australia: Applied Linguistics Association of Australia.

Devitt, S. (1997). Interacting with authentic texts: Multilayered processes. *Modern Language Journal 81*, 4, 457–469.

Dudfield, A. (1998). Cyberliteracies: Implications for education. *On-CALL 12*, 3, 25–34.

Ganderton, R. (1996). Internet tools in language teaching. *MLTA Quarterly 104*, 4–10.

Ganderton, R. (1997). *Using computers in the LOTE classroom*, Paper presented at the Queensland Society for Information Technology in Education Primary Distributed Conference, Brisbane, Australia.

Godwin-Jones, R. (1998). *Language interactive: Language teaching and the Web.* URL <http://www.fln.vcu.edu/cgi/1.html> (26 March 1999).

Grabe, W. (1991). Current developments in second language reading research. *TESOL Quarterly 25*, 3, 376–407.

Guthrie, L.F. & Hall, W.S. (1984). Ethnographic approaches to reading research. In P.D. Pearson (Ed.), *Handbook of reading research* (pp. 91–110). New York: Longman.

Haastrup, K. (1987). Using think aloud and retrospection to uncover learners' lexical inferencing procedures. In C. Faerch & G. Kasper (Eds), *Introspection in second language research* (pp. 197–212). Clevedon Avon, England: Multilingual Matters.

Horiba, Y. (1996). Comprehension processes in L2 reading: Language competence, textual coherence, and inferences. *Studies in Second Language Acquisition 18*, 4, 433–473.

Jamieson, J. (1992). The cognitive styles of reflection/impulsivity and field independence/dependence and ESL success. *The Modern Language Journal 76*, 4, 491–501.

Jiménez, R.T., García, G.E. & Pearson, P.D. (1996). The reading strategies of bilingual Latina/o students who are successful English readers. *Reading Research Quarterly 31*, 1, 90–112.

Johnson, L. (1996). *Reading strategies for web activities.* URL <http://members.aol.com/maestro12/web/strategies.html> (26 March 1999).

Kaplan, N. (1995). *E-literacies.* URL <http://raven.ubalt.edu/staff/kaplan/lit/E-literacies_612.html> (26 March 1999).

Larsen-Freeman, D. & Long, M.H. (1991). *An introduction to second language acquisition research.* New York: Longman.

Leow, R.P. (1993). To simplify or not to simplify: A look at intake. *Studies in Second Language Acquisition 15*, 333–355.

Levy, M. (1997a). *Computer-assisted language learning: Context and conceptualisation.* Oxford: Clarendon Press.

Levy, M. (1997b). Technological determinants in reading and writing linear and nonlinear texts: A comparison. *On-CALL 11*, 2, 39–45.

Long, M.H. (1980). Inside the 'black box': Methodological issues in classroom research in language learning. *Language Learning 30*, 1–42.

Mak, L. (1996). *Language learning of a new kind.* URL <http://www.hku.hk/ssrc/newLearn.html> (26 March 1999).

Mayer, R.E. (1997). Multimedia learning: Are we asking the right questions? *Educational Psychologist 32*, 1, 1–19.

McKnight, C., Dillon, A. & Richardson, J. (1991). *Hypertext in context*. Cambridge: Cambridge University Press.

Mills, D. (1995). A home on the Web: Our experience. *CAELL Journal 6*, 1, 10–16.

Nunan, D. (1992). *Research methods in language learning*. Cambridge: Cambridge University Press.

Osuna, M.M. & Meskill, C. (1998). Using the World Wide Web to integrate Spanish language and culture: A pilot study. *Language Learning & Technology 1*, 2, 66–87.

Prokop, M. (1996). *Using the web for language exercises and readings of authentic texts*. URL <http://www.ualberta.ca/~german/present.htm> (26 March 1999).

Quentin-Baxter, M. (1998). *Hypermedia learning environments limit access to information*. Paper presented at the WWW7 Conference, Brisbane, Australia. URL <http://www7.scu.edu.au/programme/docpapers/1941/com1941.htm> (26 March 1999).

Schiffrin, D. (1994). *Approaches to discourse*. Cambridge, Mass.: Blackwell.

Slatin, J.M. (1990). Reading hypertext: Order and coherence in a new medium. *College English 52*, 8, 870–883

Snyder, I. (1996). *Hypertext: The electronic labyrinth*. Melbourne, Australia: Melbourne University Press.

Svenconis, D.J. & Kerst, S. (1994/5). Investigating the teaching of second-language vocabulary through semantic mapping in a hypertext environment. *CALICO Journal 12*, 2/3, 33–57.

Swaffar, J.K., Arens, K.M. & Byrnes, H. (1991). *Reading for meaning: An integrated approach to language learning*. Englewood Cliffs, NJ: Prentice Hall.

Taillefer, G. F. (1996) L2 reading ability: Further insights into the short-circuit hypothesis. *Modern Language Journal 80*, 4, 461–477.

Trollope, J. (1995). *A comparison of reading strategies in a computerised reading situation and in a non-computerised reading situation*. Master's thesis, Bristol University, United Kingdom.

Tuman, M. C. (1992). *Word perfect: Literacy in the computer age*. Pittsburgh, Pa.: University of Pittsburgh Press.

Tuman, M. C. (1996). Literacy online. *Annual Review of Applied Linguistics 16*, 26–45.

Vale, D., Scarino, A. & McKay, P. (1991). *Pocket ALL: A users' guide to the teaching of languages and ESL*. Carlton, Australia: Curriculum Corporation.

Warschauer, M. (1995). *E-Mail for English teaching*. Alexandria, VA: TESOL Inc.

Yano, Y., Long, M.H. & Ross, S. (1994). The effects of simplified and elaborated texts on foreign language reading comprehension. *Language Learning 44*, 189–219.

4

A Vocabulary-Based Language Learning Strategy for the Internet

Chris Greaves & Han Yang
Hong Kong Polytechnic University

Introduction

This paper describes the vocabulary-based strategy adopted in implementing the Hong Kong 'Virtual Language Centre' (VLC) as an integrated language learning and study platform run from a dedicated web server. The VLC integrates on a single platform methodologies from computer-assisted language learning (CALL), data-driven learning (DDL) and corpus linguistics, electronic dictionaries and multimedia design, in a way that offers a comprehensive learning facility that combines ease of access with integration of the fullest range of these resources. The Virtual Language Centre includes the following features:

- the *South China Morning Post* ESL Corner with regular updates of exercises using *SCMP* articles;
- a variety of English language study materials and tests;
- English/Chinese lexicon (an online electronic dictionary);
- a web concordancer;
- a Putonghua (Mandarin) course for beginners; and
- authoring utilities for teachers.

Electronic dictionaries

One of the most powerful language-learning tools to have come about
through computer technology is the electronic dictionary. Ranging from the
authoritative Oxford English Dictionary on CD to the hand-held pocket-sized
bilingual dictionaries which are popular with Hong Kong students, these
have transformed the way in which we can look up a dictionary entry to find
meanings, translations and examples of use. Nothing is easier or faster than
doing a search and retrieval by simply typing in the search string, or better
still copying and pasting it from a text, as compared to the often laborious and
time-consuming process of finding the desired entry by leafing through a
bulky, heavy tome with minuscule typeface. Yet, this is still an under-exploit-
ed resource and the full potential for linking texts to an electronic dictionary
is seldom achieved, with a few noteworthy exceptions such as Microsoft's
Encarta encyclopedia. Figure 1 shows how easy it is to look up the meaning
of a word with *Encarta* simply by double-clicking the mouse on the word.

Using electronic dictionaries in the classroom

Despite the power and ease of use that electronic dictionaries provide, they
are still an under-used resource and very little teaching actually goes on
where they are available. This is a pity, as linking an electronic dictionary to
reading or other activities is easy to do and can be a powerful learning tool,
as the example of *Encarta* in figure 1 illustrates.

Figure 1: Double-clicking a word invokes the dictionary reference in *Encarta*

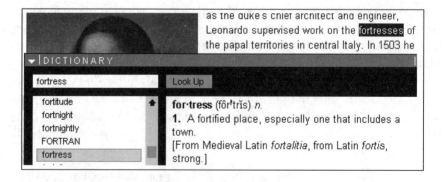

Electronic dictionaries can be effectively integrated with CALL activities
on a stand-alone PC or across a local network, and can easily be employed in
conjunction with other programs. Some dictionaries (Collins is a good example) have keyboard shortcuts such as Alt/Ctrl/D to automatically initiate a
search from a highlighted word in a text, making looking up entries even

simpler. It is also easy for students to build vocabulary lists by reversing the copy/paste procedure to copy dictionary entries into a wordprocessor. The experience of doing activities such as these in the classroom is the inspiration for the VLC lexicon, for the electronic dictionary is most effective and supportive when it is integrated into some other language-learning activities, whether CALL or otherwise.

Online web dictionaries, such as *Webster's Online* and *Newbury House Online,* are independent search resources which are freely available to users. Originally, it seemed like a good idea to place links for students to be able to look up words in these sources directly, but apart from the problem of linking across different servers and countries, which can lead to delays, the main dissatisfaction lay in the fact that the entries in these dictionaries are not aimed at our students, and are not always suitable. In fact, the monolingual dictionaries often contain difficult explanations – in some cases the explanations are written in words which are more difficult than what is being explained. *Cliché*, for example, is defined in *Webster's* as 'a trite, stereotyped phrase'. The solution was, therefore, to start building a customised bilingual lexicon specifically designed to help Chinese students, which at the same time could be fully integrated into diverse language-learning activities on the VLC. The lexicon is implemented as a database table, with a dedicated access program which is invoked from HTML forms by means of hyperlinks.

The lexicon can be accessed in several ways:

- from the browser window, using record navigation and 'Find' buttons;
- by directly typing (or copying and pasting) the lookup word into the edit box and pressing the 'Go' button in the lexicon lookup form; or
- by clicking on items in the text which have been linked directly to the lexicon.

The third of these techniques will be described more fully below.

The web concordancer: Extending the lexicon as a reference tool

The lexicon also provides the additional feature of a direct link from the lexicon entry to a corpus search for concordance examples of the word. Corpus-based classroom concordancing is another teaching approach which has attracted a lot of interest, although perhaps not as much as it deserves due to the relative difficulty of gaining access to such resources, at least until recently. A number of commercial as well as freeware programs are available, however, and the availability of large amounts of text on CD makes obtaining text sources for a corpus fairly easy. For teachers and students the corpus can provide an invaluable source of 'raw' data, and with even a simple concordancing program it is possible to find interesting examples and create simple activities such as gapped keyword strings (Tribble & Jones 1989). The integration of corpus-based techniques within a broader CALL environment is a useful resource when applied using LAN technology (Milton, forthcoming).

By providing integrated access to corpus source texts via concordance search software, the VLC can provide not only a resource for students, teachers and researchers alike, but can familiarise more people with this approach to language study. The concept of data-driven learning needs to be more widely understood and appreciated, and the integrated learning platform which the VLC provides is an important step in helping to achieve this. By integrating the facility with other more familiar language-learning materials many more people will be introduced to this effective resource. A web concordance search facility is a valuable addition to the language learner's range of learning aids and, by providing links to other sites such as Tim Johns' *Virtual DDL Library* (Johns 1997), the techniques and value of this approach will be better understood and reach a wider audience than would otherwise be the case.

By providing such links from the lexicon, a mouse click is all that is needed to see a concordance search for the item. Figure 2 shows the outcome of this for the selected word 'premiere'.

Figure 2: Concordances invoked from the lexicon entry for *Premiere*

```
Concordances for premiere = 21
 1    full of Foreigners is a   Playhouse  premiere  and it runs until September
 2    full of Foreigners is a   Playhouse  premiere  and it runs until September
 3     and auction to coincide  with the   premiere, are still hoping to bring
 4    nt. /article   headline   Charity    premiere  article  CHARITY alert! Th
 5    .   /article   headline   Exclusive  premiere  article  OUR arts corresp
 6    stensibly dissuaded from a Russian   premiere because of the    disarray s
 7     city's wretched poor.  para  Its    premiere here is in aid of Future F
 8    at he will visit  Hongkong for the   premiere here of his new movie, City
 9     fruit of the new link will be the   premiere in Birmingham on    March 5
10    i Nabokov (son) who attended the     premiere, must be quite the most ove
11    ions at the carnivals included the   premiere of a  Cantonese opera, The
```

In the context of Hong Kong, as elsewhere, the potential for parallel corpus concordancing is also a stimulus to do more in this area, and access via the VLC to such a parallel corpus could be of relevance to anyone interested in translation. In the next section, we shall describe how this process of integrating the lexicon and concordancer with conventional CALL activities has developed into the strategy of 'lexicon-driven learning', and its extension to include multimedia content as well.

Integrating CALL activities via the World Wide Web

A wide range of interactive CALL activities can be implemented in web documents. A characteristic of this technology is the ease with which diverse types of data may be integrated, so that data stored in a database table and images produced by a 3D-graphics generator can be merged in a single document. The interactive nature of the Web means that the VLC can provide a platform for two-way communication between user and server which allows the VLC to supply a combination of services, providing feedback to a wide range of requests and needs.

The VLC server can be understood as providing two distinct levels of functionality:

1. the provision of a range of language study materials, reference sources, exercises and so on for users who may be students or teachers; and

2. the processing of information, requests and messages received from users and the provision of feedback to the users.

Programs placed on the server will retrieve the data sent by the client and then post back an immediate reply which will be printed out on the client's screen. Messages and requests are posted via HTML forms which direct the message to a specific program on the server, and the program which receives the message handles it accordingly. This method applies equally whether for checking a student's answer sheet, looking up the meaning of a word in a table, or carrying out a search for concordances in a corpus. Performance can be monitored by keeping a score with reference to an answer key. Figure 3 shows a vocabulary exercise in which the student's answers are checked against the key, scored, and a report sent back to the student as in figure 4. This is an example of multiple-choice vocabulary exercises which are easy to implement and use server automation to do the scoring. No answers are given until the student has completed all the questions. Then the form is submitted to the server, the student's answers are checked against the key, scored, and a report sent back to the student. This makes an ideal type of exercise for regular updates, and is used for many of the '*South China Morning Post* ESL Corner' passages which appear as a regular feature.

Figure 3: A reading exercise implemented as a test with multiple-choice list boxes

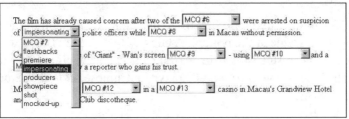

The VLC is fortunate to have the support of the *South China Morning Post* which allows up to ten of its articles per month to be adapted for use as exercises. Such sponsorship is invaluable in providing a source of topical, professionally written and entertaining English texts which, when implemented as VLC materials, serve as a useful teaching and learning resource for teachers and students alike.

Figure 4: The score report sheet returned by the server

You scored	6	out of	13		
Check your score sheet					

Question	Answer	Submit	Score
1	premiere	MCQ #1	0
2	producers	MCQ #2	0
3	showpiece	MCQ #3	0
4	open	MCQ #4	0
5	publicity	publicity	1
6	cast	producers	0

Figure 5 shows how linking items to the lexicon enables students to practise the vocabulary items before doing a similar test from one of the '*South China Morning Post* ESL Corner' selections.

Figure 5: A vocabulary list linked to the lexicon

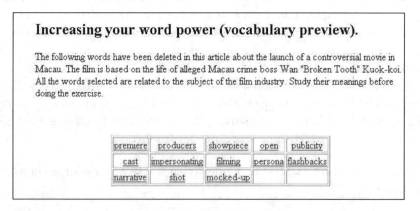

Increasing your word power (vocabulary preview).

The following words have been deleted in this article about the launch of a controversial movie in Macau. The film is based on the life of alleged Macau crime boss Wan "Broken Tooth" Kuok-koi. All the words selected are related to the subject of the film industry. Study their meanings before doing the exercise.

premiere	producers	showpiece	open	publicity
cast	impersonating	filming	persona	flashbacks
narrative	shot	mocked-up		

The vocabulary items are first listed in a table in the main frame with links to the lexicon frame at the bottom. A click of the mouse is all that is required to produce the result shown in the lexicon frame in figure 6. The lexicon lookup has found the entry and displays its Chinese and other entries in the table as shown.

Figure 6: The lexicon entry for *Premiere* with sound and concordance link

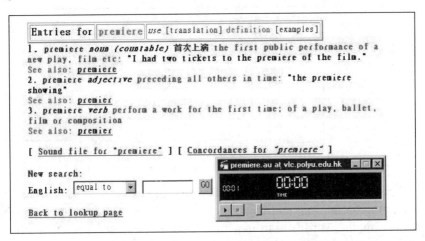

This also provides a good illustration of the fundamental principle of the VLC strategy, which is the *integration* of vocabulary, lexicon, concordancing and multimedia on a unified platform. Going directly from the text, the student can link seamlessly to a lexicon providing translation and examples, concordance examples, and listen to the pronunciation.

Implementing the bilingual lexicon

In this section we shall describe in some detail the processes involved in the implementation and design of the online lexicon, and some of the lexicographical and practical problems involved. From the example in figure 7 we can see the structure of the lexicon database, which has fields for definition, comments and synonyms, as well as having fields for the English and Chinese equivalents. The input method uses an HTML form to display the data entries, which can be edited and updated from any PC with Internet access. Figure 7 illustrates the process of creating lexical entries on the Edit Record form.

Thus, for example, if the word *alcohol* is the lexical item we want to add to a new record, *alcohol* is entered in the box marked 'English'. One of the Chinese equivalents for *alcohol* is entered in the box marked 'Chinese'. The Chinese characters can be converted from the traditional version to the simplified version and vice versa to suit the needs of the Mainland and Hong Kong, as well as other Chinese-speaking regions. The grammatical category of the entry word is entered in the 'Comments' section together with any other relevant grammatical information such as transitivity (in the case of verbs) and plurality (in the case of nouns), as well as its collocation with

Figure 7: The Edit Record form

English	alcohol
Chinese	酒
Definition	(n) drinks such as beer or wine that contain a substance that can make you drunk
Comments	noun (uncountable)
Examples	You bring your own alcohol to most restaurants here.
Synonyms	liquor, booze, spirits
Sound	0

other lexical items where necessary. The 'Examples' section is designed to illustrate the 'definition' and 'comments' of the entry word and to show the students how the word is used in actual texts. The examples are taken from the corpus using the concordance search tool (see figure 2 for one such example), and copied and pasted into the database. 'Synonym' items are entered as appropriate and the 'Sound' field is used to show a link to the corresponding audio file. Using the Web to directly edit and add records means that editors can work from anywhere, whether New York, Beijing or Hong Kong, simultaneously updating the lexicon. At the same time, it is easy to open any number of online dictionaries to compare various interpretations. The following are examples of the definitions of *alcoholism* taken from some of the online dictionaries:

(1) *WWWebster Dictionary* (Merriam Webster, online)

alcoholism n

1: continued excessive or compulsive use of alcoholic drinks
2: poisoning by alcohol; *especially*: a complex chronic psychological and nutritional disorder associated with excessive and usually compulsive drinking

(2) *The Wordsmyth English Dictionary-Thesaurus* (online)

alcoholism
DEF: a pathological condition resulting from habitual overuse of alcoholic beverages, characterised by dependence on alcohol, difficulty in functioning properly, and severe withdrawal symptoms when alcohol use is stopped.

(3) *Random House Webster's* (Random House, online)

al-co-hol-ism (al'kuh h?liz uhm, -ho-) n.

1 a chronic disorder characterised by dependence on alcohol, repeated excessive use of alcoholic beverages, and decreased ability to function socially and vocationally. [1855-60]

Since the VLC bilingual online dictionary is designed primarily for Chinese students of English, it is important to make the definitions as simple as possible, and avoid using only definitions that involve some complicated vocabulary that requires further explanations such as: 'a chronic disorder characterised by dependence on alcohol, repeated excessive use of alcoholic beverages' (*Random House Webster's*). By contrast, the VLC lexicon entry for one definition of *alcoholism* is simply: 'being addicted to alcoholic drinks'.

Lexicographical considerations in creating an online lexicon for students from a Chinese background: The problem of 'alcoholism'
An important consideration that we must bear in mind is that different cultures have different culture-specific items in their languages, and for such linguistic items lexicographers often have to resort to some lengthy explanations to make the concepts clear to dictionary users. For example, 'fish 'n' chips', and 'football hooliganism', to name but two, are phrases that identify culturally specific behaviour and require background awareness. Many problems in translation and explanation seem to arise where just this type of consideration has not been given, and lexical items have been treated as being 'universal' when they are in fact culture-specific. The example of *alcoholism* cited above exemplifies this problem.

Almost all the available English–Chinese dictionaries have translated this word as:

酒 精 中 毒

When translated back into English, this means 'alcoholic poisoning', a serious medical condition which may result in death. *Alcoholism* on the other hand refers to a chronic social and physiological problem which is more common in northern-European countries.

Perhaps this prolonged and excessive drinking habit is less common in Chinese culture, and therefore alcoholism is not a social problem as we know it in the West; hence the lack of suitable vocabulary in Chinese for 'alcoholism'. Or else, dictionary makers have in the past simply followed previous examples that were erroneous in the first place. The following examples, taken from a couple of the most commonly used English–Chinese dictionaries, illustrate this problem:

1 *The English–Chinese Dictionary* (unabridged) (Shanghai Yiwen 1996)

Alcoholism:　　1.酗酒　2.酒精中毒

2 *Longman Dictionary of Contemporary English (English–Chinese)*
   (Longman Asia 1997)

   Alcoholism: 酒精中毒

Figure 8: A problem of translation

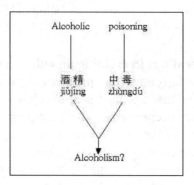

Is 'alcoholism' equivalent to 'alcoholic poisoning'? The problem becomes
even more confusing when we find that many of the well-known English
monolingual dictionaries also treat alcoholism as a medical condition and
some even regard it as a disease (e.g. *Oxford Advanced Learner's
Dictionary*). And so, perhaps the bilingual dictionary makers might well have
been influenced by the definitions provided by the monolingual dictionary
writers such as the ones below:

1 *Longman Dictionary of Contemporary English*, third edition (1985)
   Alcoholism: the medical condition of being an alcoholic.

2 *The Collins Cobuild Student's Dictionary Online* (1998)
   Alcoholism is a kind of poisoning caused by drinking too much alcohol over a
   long period of time.

3 *Oxford Advanced Learner's Dictionary of Current English* (1989)
   Alcoholism: (disease caused by) continual heavy drinking of alcohol.

Perhaps the most extraordinary of all these entries is the one which we
find provided by the online version of the popular *Cobuild Dictionary*, defining *alcoholism* as 'a kind of poisoning'. Since our aim is to help the Chinese
learners to improve their learning of English, it would obviously be misleading if our students started believing that *alcoholism* is some kind of English
medical problem!

So after all these considerations, in writing our own entries for the VLC lexicon, we have arrived at the following translations and definitions for *alcoholism* as shown in figure 9:

Figure 9: The VLC lexicon entries for *alcoholism*

> **1.** alcoholism *noun (uncountable)* 飲 酒 上 癮 being addicted to alcoholic drinks :
> The International Red Cross is working to provide activities for the refugees and
> to counter social and psychological problems such as alcoholism.
> See also: <u>dipsomania , potomania , addiction</u>
> **2.** alcoholism *noun* 嗜 酒 成 性 prolonged and excessive intake of alcoholic
> drinks leading to a breakdown in health and an addiction to alcohol such that
> abrupt deprivation leads to severe withdrawal symptoms : [null]
> See also: <u>alcohol addiction , drunkenness , alcoholic abuse , alcoholic</u>
> <u>poisoning</u>

And finally, we have added a separate entry for *alcoholic poisoning* with the appropriate Chinese equivalent which is included in the lexicon, as illustrated below (figure 10).

Figure 10: A new entry for *alcoholic poisoning*

> **1.** alcoholic poisoning *noun phrase* 酒 精 中 毒 a medical condition that results
> from drinking an excessive amount of alcohol, often resulting in death;
> especially after drinking low-grade or home-made alcoholic drinks such as fruit
> juice mixed with alcohol: Ultimately, he was found in the road and in the
> institution where he was taken, the chart at the end of his bed read: "Died of
> alcoholic poisoning, name unknown."
> See also: <u>alcoholism</u>

We have discussed this problem in some detail not because it is an isolated problem, but because, on the contrary, it is typical of the problems faced in lexicography. When one considers that there are thousands of other entries which present similar difficulties in varying degrees, what we have come to refer to as 'the problem of alcoholism in lexicography' exemplifies some of the difficulties faced in implementing the task of developing a comprehensive and trustworthy online bilingual lexicon.

'Big brother' is watching
In addition to full-time staff, quite a number of other people (e.g. bilingual and translation student assistants and part-time lexicographers) may be involved at different stages of the development of the lexicon, working from

different locations and even different countries, so an 'editorial log' has been developed to keep track of the new entries added by the individual members of the team. This enables the chief editor(s) to check and revise the new entries as necessary without having to go through the main body of the lexicon to locate the new entries. Figure 11 shows an extract from this log, which stores the developer's name at login and their computer ID, data for the new entries, as well as the date and the time when the individual entries were recorded. Thus, each transaction can be monitored and all information pertaining to it easily accessed at any time, ensuring that there is always a strong editorial control.

Figure 11: An extract from the editorial log file

```
Login by: 202.77.160.23
Date: 09/23/98  Time: 17:53:38
User: frances
================================
Edit update by: 158.132.164.96
Date: 09/23/98  Time: 17:54:02
English: ideological
Chinese: 思想的;思想意識的
Definition: (adj) Ideological means relating to principles or beliefs.
Comments: adjective
Examples: The ideological divisions between the parties aren't always obvious.
Synonyms: (null)
================================
Edit update by: 202.77.160.23
Date: 09/23/98  Time: 17:55:23
English: near
Chinese: 接近
Definition: (v) If a time nears, it gets closer and will come soon.
Comments: verb (intransitive)
Examples: He got more and more nervous as the day of his departure neared.
Synonyms: approach
```

The integration of database technology with the HTML client–server interaction is one of the most versatile tools on a web server, and allows us to take advantage of the full range of database searches in providing access to the lexicon. By linking directly from the text to the database as shown in the above examples, the student has a translation and explanation for any difficult words returned immediately at the click of a mouse. Reading activities and texts containing advanced and difficult vocabulary can be transformed into relatively easy vocabulary-building experiences, simply by anticipating what items in the text are likely to cause most difficulty. Provided the lexicon contains entries for these respective items, it requires only a few minutes of editing to place hyperlinks to the lexicon directly in the text.

This strategy can aptly be described by the phrase 'lexicon-driven learning', which is not merely a pun on the 'data-driven learning' concept, but in fact describes one of the key notions of integrated language learning which underpins the fundamental concept of the Virtual Language Centre. The electronic lexicon is at the heart of the VLC strategy, and is one of the principal tools helping the language learner to develop the vocabulary base and skills for mastery of the target language. However, having adopted this approach, it clearly becomes an important priority to ensure that any language that students encounter in the various activities on the VLC can also be found in the lexicon.

Ideally, a lexicon requires at least 40 to 50 thousand entries to serve as a generally useful reference. This is obviously a challenging and long-term goal, and requires a large team of lexicographers if all the entries are to be original. However, there are public-domain lexical databases which can be used initially, and the most useful of these is the well-known 'Word Net' database developed at Princeton University, which can be accessed and freely downloaded from their web site. By incorporating this database into our own, we have been able to create a lexicon with at least a sufficiently large number of basic English entries to be a practical and useful reference tool. However, most of these entries do not yet have Chinese translations, and many of the definitions also suffer from the same deficiencies as those examples given above in that they are not intended for second-language learners. Nevertheless, by using the strategy of text hyperlinks direct to the lexicon table, entries can be built up gradually, while the lexicon is still available and fully functional as an integral part of the language-learning activities. Lexicon-driven learning is thus a flexible, ongoing strategy of development. Indeed, the characteristic of this approach is its flexibility, and that publishing can take place 'while the ink is still wet'. It is not necessary to complete chapter 10 before publishing chapter 1. The lexicon, as indeed other web documents, can be built up gradually and still be used effectively at the same time as it is being developed. Eventually, the lexicon will have sufficient fully edited and translated entries to serve as a general reference for all users.

Designing customised 'lexicon-driven learning software'

We have discussed the strategy of lexicon-driven learning as the approach which basically seeks to draw together the use of an online dictionary, concordance searches and CALL activities in a coherent and integrated way that gives maximum support to the student. In this section we shall discuss some of the ways this strategy has informed and influenced the design and implementation of VLC software and web page design. The VLC features many diverse activities which have been influenced by this strategy in various ways, including for example the 'WordTrap', a synonyms-matching game which gives students the chance to study the vocabulary items with the lexicon (in the same way as illustrated in figure 5) before running the program.

Another example is the web-authoring utilities, some of which, such as ClozeMaker, can generate word lists linked to the lexicon.

However, it was the experience of using electronic dictionaries in the classroom which provided the original inspiration for the concept of lexicon-driven learning, and it is this application that we shall return to for our example. *Encarta* was cited as a model of this approach, and how easy it is to look up a word in the dictionary just by double-clicking it in the text. Windows programs support this functionality as a normal feature, and programmers can easily build it into their programs using the standard Windows programming tools. However, web documents must be displayed in browsers such as Netscape and Internet Explorer, and this kind of functionality is not so easy to replicate. Both browsers support the feature of highlighting a single word which has been double-clicked, but normal web page HTML formatting or even Java script does not allow us to retrieve the selected text and do something with it such as search for it in the lexicon. What we can do, however, is to use the standard copy and paste functions which all browsers support and thereby enable the user to make a relatively easy reference to the lexicon.

Our original design to facilitate this functionality was simply to provide a separate frame for the lookup edit box. This has remained a basic design feature for many VLC activities, including of course the *South China Morning Post* articles which are published as exercises. In this model, the reader can make reference to the lexicon for any word that appears in the text by following a few simple steps: double-clicking the word to trigger the highlighting, selecting the 'copy' function (either from the menu or by using keyboard shortcuts), positioning and clicking the mouse in the lookup edit box to set the focus, selecting the 'paste' function, and finally clicking the 'Go' button to do the search. This is not a difficult or particularly slow set of steps to follow and, given the wide distribution of Internet documents, is certainly a relatively easy way to gain access to this resource. Nevertheless, it obviously lacks the immediacy and simplicity of a customised program like *Encarta*. In an effort to streamline and simplify this and develop a web interface specifically to achieve integrated support for readers and with immediate access to the lexicon, we developed the VLC Text Reader as a Java applet.

The Text Reader: A customised Java applet interface to the lexicon
Although we cannot implement the full range of functions in web documents that we might expect in a stand-alone Windows program, the Java programming language gives us an interface that goes beyond what we can do with ordinary web documents. The Java classes provide many of the functions we need to develop programs that can be embedded and distributed in HTML documents and which contain functions such as text processing that we would find in ordinary programs. The Text Reader was designed to provide

the best and smoothest functionality for accessing the lexicon while reading a text. It has been designed to allow users to select a text of their choice (at the moment these are also articles from the *South China Morning Post*), and its purpose is to provide the user with the easiest and most enjoyable framework in which to read, understand and learn English. There is no element of testing involved; the emphasis is instead entirely on providing the student with a context of reading for pleasure. Figure 12 shows its basic operation, where a text is displayed in a text window, and the standard double click invokes the highlighted word in the text area, so that all the user has to do to invoke the lexicon search and display function is to click the 'Check dictionary' button.

Figure 12: The Text Reader Java applet

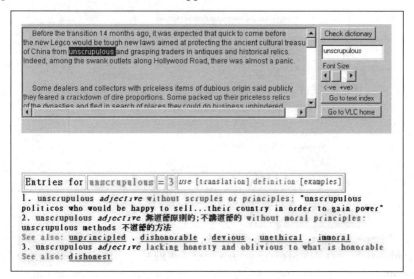

It is also possible to select a phrase or group of words by dragging the mouse across the selection. This functionality is achieved in our applet by using the Java function 'GetSelectedText'. The Text Reader applet thus exemplifies the lexicon-driven learning strategy as a technique, a programming model and as a basic concept for web-page design.

Multimedia resources on the Web

Before concluding this overview of the Virtual Language Centre, we should also make some reference to the challenges and problems posed by multimedia formats, and some of the strategies which we have adopted. There are well-known commercial multimedia dictionaries which successfully integrate sound and video, and the online version of the Cobuild dictionary features sound files for its entries. As we have seen in figure 6, we can also provide similar links from the VLC lexicon to sound files with relative ease, although building up a library of such multimedia resources is itself a huge undertaking requiring considerable investment in financial and human resources. The growth in the provision of third-party client plugin technologies such as QuickTime, RealAudio and ShockWave is also greatly extending the possibilities. Figure 13 shows an example of QuickTime controls together with an ActiveX control.

Figure 13: The VLC ActiveX recording control

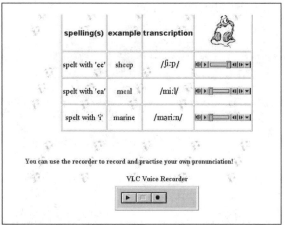

Although Internet technology has been developed to allow a wide range of multimedia extensions, developers run up against the problems posed by the competing technologies offered by rival companies. Since practically all Internet access involves either the use of Netscape or Internet Explorer browsers, the differences between these programs and the support they offer becomes a crucial concern for anyone trying to develop materials with multimedia content and support. This is particularly so in the case of programming technologies such as Java and ActiveX, which allow developers to write their own customised controls for their web pages. For PCs running Windows, ActiveX allows the widest range of functionality to be employed in controls. But choosing ActiveX obliges developers to make a hard choice: whether to limit their scope to producing materials that can be displayed in both browsers, or to develop customised controls which best achieve the purpose but which will only be supported in one browser. Figure 13 shows an example of this dilemma in the ActiveX recording control developed for pronunciation and oral practice. This is a simple control which utilises the

Windows Media Control Interface, and is embedded along with other plug-ins in the HTML document to provide students with the opportunity if they wish to practise their own pronunciation in conjunction with the examples. However, until the time when support for ActiveX controls is added to Netscape, this control will only work with the Internet Explorer.

Conclusion: The strategy of lexicon-driven learning

The fundamental principle of the VLC approach is the *integration* of vocabulary, lexicon, concordancing and multimedia on a unified platform. It results from the convergence of the various traditions in CALL and is the primary characteristic of the VLC. The VLC web server is an effective and accessible medium for the integration of all these approaches *with the potential of bringing these disparate traditions to a wider and more diverse audience than has hitherto been possible.*

We have suggested the phrase 'lexicon-driven learning' to describe this strategy of integrated language learning and online dictionary which underpins the whole concept of the Virtual Language Centre. This is at the heart of the VLC approach, and the electronic lexicon is one of the principal tools helping the language learner to develop the vocabulary base and skills for greater mastery of the target language. At the core of the language-learning process is the basic problem of vocabulary building and, in the final analysis, the pace at which the student learns the language is limited to how fast the vocabulary can be absorbed. Aiding or simplifying dictionary searches, therefore, must pay dividends. This is precisely the rationale behind the notion of lexicon-driven learning, which can help to eliminate or reduce much of the time and effort otherwise spent in lexical research, by integrating the lexicon into a broad range of language-learning activities such as reading, gap filling, synonym practice exercises and so on. *The goal of lexicon-driven learning is to speed up the process of vocabulary development and at the same time take some of the drudgery out of the process.*

References

Collins Cobuild Student's Dictionary Online (1998).
   URL <http://www.linguistics.ruhr-uni-bochum.de/ccsd>
Hong Kong Virtual Language Centre. URL <http://vlc.polyu.edu.hk>
Johns, T. & King P. (Eds) (1991). Classroom concordancing. *ELR Journal (New Series) 4*. Birmingham: Centre for English Language Studies.
Johns, T. (1997). *Lingua multilingual concordancer.*
   URL <http://sun1.bham.ac.uk /johnstf/lingua.htm>

Merriam-Webster WWWebster dictionary. URL <http://www.m-w.com>

Milton, J. (forthcoming). *Exploiting L1 and L2 corpora in the design of an electronic language learning and production environment.* In S. Granger (Ed.) *Learner English on computer.* Harlow: Longman.

Perry, P. (1996). *Creating cool web applets with Java.* IDG Books.

Random House Webster's college dictionary – Newer words faster.
   URL <http://www. vintagebooks.com/features/rhwebsters/>

The English–Chinese Dictionary (Unabridged) (1996). Shanghai: Shanghai Yiwen Publishing Co.

The Wordsmyth English Dictionary-Thesaurus.
   URL <http://www.lightlink.com/bobp/wedt/site.htm>

Tribble, C. & Jones, G. (1989). *Classroom concordancing.* Harlow: Longman.

WordNet, Princeton University.
   URL <http://www.cogsci.princeton.edu/cgi-bin/webwn>

5

Web-Based Language Learning: A Window to the Authentic World

Uschi Felix

Monash University, Australia

Introduction

During the relatively few years in which language learning materials have been available on the Web, the technology has evolved tremendously in terms of the types of interactivity on offer, with text-based environments gradually being replaced by virtual classrooms. If we compare an early electronic text-book in German (Smith 1995) with sophisticated recent materials (Goelz 1998; Kretschmer et al. 1997), the advances are obvious – from a grammar text presented electronically with some added sound, to sound with some video, grammar exercises with online feedback, interactive tasks linked to authentic web sites, and direct communication with the teacher and others. Smith's own site illustrates the advancing technology with the latest version moving further away from being a textbook on the screen. While there are many sites of the earlier sort in a large variety of languages, and particularly in a dialogue-driven format, only a handful of sites of the latter sort have so far appeared, though not in the form of fully fledged courses (Felix 1998a).

What is clear about the development is that pedagogy has been driven largely by technology, with the advent of CGI, helper applications, plug-ins, JavaScript and Java adding interest to the material (for excellent online demonstrations see Goodwin-Jones 1998 and Mills 1998). Developers have been excited from the start by what could be done with little effort, and recent authoring resources that need no programming knowledge have made the enterprise even more tempting (Holmes & Arneil 1998).

This chapter describes the variety of ways in which the Web is being exploited for language teaching. Since the environment is still evolving, any picture of what is available will be a mixed one, with approaches ranging from fairly traditional grammar teaching at one end to experiential learning at the other. Nevertheless, the direction of the developments is becoming clear. There appears to be a gradual shift from teacher-centred approaches, largely reflected in the explicit teaching of grammar, which exploit the technical potential of the Web, to student-centred learning, reflected in meaningful task-based activities, which exploits the new medium's unique potential for authentic learning experiences. This contribution also focuses on how an environment often perceived as uncontrollably chaotic can be harnessed for meaningful language learning, especially in terms of interactivity and authenticity.

Grammar teaching on the Web

Even on the Web, the attractions of grammar explanations as well as drill and practice and online testing continue to be evident. Grammar explanations often take the form of daunting slabs of complicated explanatory material filled with specialised vocabulary, with few even offering the clean layout heightened by the use of contrasting colours found in Smith (1995). Grammar drills are typically limited by the fact that the same few questions are presented every time the exercise is repeated, and by non-existent or not particularly helpful, or appropriate, feedback. Notable exceptions are Friedman (1997), Lee (1998), and especially Arana (1998). The latter provides an excellent example of what is possible: students choose an appropriate response in Spanish to a given situation from a list where none of the choices is obviously ludicrous and more than one might be 'correct', and each response generates a sentence in Spanish explaining why that answer is right or why it is not fully appropriate.

Testing can range from purely grammatical questions in English to the ubiquitous fill-ins, often in multiple-choice format. Many sites at least seek to provide a coherent context for the questions in the form of complete sentences with fill-ins, while a few go further and locate the work within an extended and coherent narrative (Friedman 1997; Arana 1998). Coherent narrative is not the same thing as authentic material, however, and it is rare to find a site that bases grammar on fully authentic texts as the ALFAGRAM project aims to do, for example (Melis et al. 1998).

Where the whole approach to grammar is concerned, web sites continue to illustrate the central dilemma of course designers and their pedagogical beliefs. If the coverage of grammar is to be systematic and comprehensive (Blyth 1997), then it is virtually impossible for the material to be extended, coherent and authentic because control of structures and vocabulary is so difficult to achieve. To put this the other way, if the course is based on authentic material (Biddulph 1998; Calvi et al. 1998; Melis et al. 1998), then it is virtually impossible to provide systematic and comprehensive coverage of grammar, particularly in any logical progression of difficulty.

What is obvious from a survey of a large number of sites (Felix 1998a) is that the current level of sophistication is not high. The day when the Web might provide an extensive and changing range of grammar exercises with helpful feedback and storage of student results – still less, an analysis of student weaknesses to allow both for appropriate and helpful feedback and for the tailoring of future work to identified needs – is some way off. As Lamy (1997) has already shown for French grammar, web sites fall well short of the potential, and even her favourite site *France à la carte* does not meet her own rigorous criteria of excellence. The situation has not changed much in the period since she reported, even though the technology has become more flexible and some sites are focussing more on interactivity and authenticity.

Given the limitations of existing web-based grammar programs, the reader will inevitably wonder what the point is of using the Web for this purpose when CD-ROMs offer obvious technological advantages, especially in terms of speed.

The most convincing answer to this question is that the Web is accessible in a way that a CD-ROM is not: resources can easily be updated (this is not to say that all material is, in fact, regularly updated), and communication facilities can be integrated. In any case, distance education courses will naturally want to provide a complete teaching and learning package, and so will include explanations of grammar. In addition, it must be tempting to offer grammar exercises as well, even if the Web, stricken as it is by the slowness of the connections, is not a particularly attractive medium compared with a CD-ROM loaded into a local computer. Mastery of structures remains a popular goal: students constantly surprise by their interest in grammar drill and practice (at least in an environment where grammar is tested), second only to their enthusiasm for games (Felix 1997).

Nonetheless, the basic point is persuasive. The Web should most sensibly be used for the unique potential that it offers. Whatever legitimate place traditional teaching content and styles may have in a web-based course, it seems odd to use the Web to focus on them instead of exploiting the new medium for student-centred, task-based, and collaborative learning in true-to-life or, better still, authentic settings.

Rethinking the teaching approach: From teacher-centred to student-centred

Materials on the Web reflect teaching approaches. The teaching of grammar as illustrated above, whether contextualised in authentic materials or not, reflects a teacher-centred approach, one that is systematically controlled, pre-scriptive and linear. The attractions are immediate feedback, the potential for less marking and a definite sense of what has been learnt. Drawbacks are the failure to allow for differences in students' learning strategies and styles, motivation, attitudes, preferences, backgrounds and personalities.

In his keynote address at WorldCALL, Barson (1998) boldly put the view that the biggest hindrance to learning is … teaching! This may sound radical, but it makes sense in a world in which we are dealing with 'children of chaos' (Rushkoff 1996), nonlinear thinkers used to negotiating complicated intuitive computer games, and comfortably navigating cyberspace communities and resources. (For discussions of the implications of cyberliteracy for education see Snyder 1997 and Dudfield 1998.)

Caution is still needed. The conclusion should not be simply to adopt a student-centred approach which hands over all responsibility to the learner, in the hope that autonomous learning will turn out to be a natural skill and that knowledge will be acquired by osmosis. Students may have the technical skills and the inclination to negotiate hypertext and images, but the acquisition of how-to-learn skills, however individually based, still requires help. A more desirable and more effective approach, therefore, may be to hand over control to the students in an environment where some guidance is provided (Hoven 1998). In most recent times the Web has become a treasure trove for finding ready-made or creating meaningful interactive tasks to support this approach.

Meaningful interactive tasks in authentic environments

Since the early days of communicative teaching the goal has been to make learning a language meaningful and authentic. To this end, attempts have been made to inject an air of authenticity into the classroom by means of simulations and role-plays that reflect, mirror or represent authentic settings. My own experience as a native speaker of German teaching French to Australian students highlighted the problem of providing truly authentic experiences. Even authentic materials in videos, newspapers or magazines were often out-of-date, and it was not until the arrival of real-time television news that students were brought into contact with topical, up-to-date and authentic resources.

All this has changed radically. With the advent of the Web, activities no longer have to be simulated or artificially contextualised but can be excitingly authentic. The real world of the target language can now be brought into the students' experience with the creation of meaningful tasks tailored to their interests and capabilities at different levels of interactivity.

Low level interactivity: Point and click activities
The lowest level of interactivity resides in point and click activities. However, these can now be located in settings that offer greater cultural and linguistic richness. In the Vietnamese materials (Felix 1998b), beginning students can click into sections on geography, economy, history, people, politics and culture, illustrated with maps and photographs; switch to language exercises; practise pronunciation; read simple poetry; attempt translations; and analyse culture-specific behaviour in videos. What makes this resource different from similar ones on CD-ROM is that students can also visit a number of sites in Vietnam to get authentic information about such things as poetry, songs, street signs or recipes.

While this particular course provides a structured virtual classroom for beginning students, other sites adopt a more open approach. The German course at the University of Victoria, Canada (Goelz 1996), through its strategic links to other sites, includes a vast variety of materials from which students at any level can profit. A simple click will immerse an intermediate student in authentic German literature forums, the web site of the hottest German pop group complete with song clips, or German *film noir*. Similarly, an advanced student can enter the world of real-time German television news.

Medium level interactivity: Resolution of information gaps
A higher level of interactivity involves some form of information gap which has to be resolved using language as a communicative tool, with the learners having a limited influence over the outcome (Foot 1994). There are a large number of sites, mostly in European languages, which offer creative activities of this sort. In *Adesso* (Di Fabio & Hemment 1997), a beautifully presented site sponsored by Heinle & Heinle, students are asked to answer questions by collecting information from linked sites, to fill in forms, or to prepare challenging materials, such as an advertisement for the Caffé Florian in Venice.

While most such tasks in a variety of languages are presented on proformas to be printed out and delivered to the teacher in class, some can be submitted electronically. They range from self-contained brief tasks designed to be completed in a relatively short time, as in the information-collecting exercise on Bavaria (Prokop 1997), to extensive problem-solving activities, as in the Chinese Long Walk (Clayton 1998). The latter is one of a series of structured teaching plans by a variety of contributors to an Australian Federation of Modern Language Teachers Associations (AFMLTA) project. The target audience are students in the school sector and contributions so far include Chinese, French, German, Indonesian, Italian, Japanese and Turkish. Activities vary in approach, content and scope but all provide interesting ideas to cover several teaching sessions. A site listing similar activities for school students in a range of languages has been produced by teachers in the California Foreign Language Project.

This type of interactivity can also be created in MOO and Chat sites (Fanderclai 1995; Truna 1995a). Chat facilities, through which users can interact in real time by way of written communication, are now available in a large variety of languages (Felix 1998a). They tend to be more user-friendly than MOOs even though they do not offer the same scope for creative interaction offered by the best MOOs. The essential advantage of the MOO space is that it is an object-oriented environment in which users can create and manipulate objects. In most MOOs this is still restricted to text-based creations, such as descriptions of rooms, people or objects, which can be demotivating for students expecting a world full of colourful graphics or animations. However, the environment is changing as rapidly as everything else on the Web, and sophisticated MOOs like *Active Worlds* are appearing where users can create virtual objects represented graphically.

There are two interesting examples of how a potentially chaotic environment can be used with some guidance while still allowing students room for individual contributions. One is the treasure hunt in Truna (1995b) where a variety of objects are left in different locations of the MOO for students to discover; another is the topic-related chat sessions suggested by Ferguson (1998). An attractive idea in the latter is the presence of native speaker experts to avoid the artificial situation of students chatting only to students and recycling their own varieties of interlanguage, potentially leading to what Garrett (1986:133) termed so aptly 'irremediably inaccurate fluency'.

High level interactivity: Experiential learning
The highest level of interactivity offers a range of experiential learning, involving users in real interaction in authentic or virtual true to life settings, quests with a meaningful goal, or the production of materials.

The most authentic interaction can be achieved in MOO and Chat sites operating in the target language country rather than those created especially for language teaching purposes. The latter may have the advantage that more guidance can be given, but there is a contrived and simulated feeling to them, with many instructions in English and large amounts of inaccurate language generated, especially when the environment does not support accents. Sites situated in the target country, by contrast, operate exclusively in the target language and have native speakers engaging in authentic conversation online. This can be seen as either challenging or threatening: while it may be an excellent environment for advanced students, beginning and intermediate students may not have the courage or skills to attempt it. All the same, a simple exercise like discovering where people are, who they are and why they are there should not be beyond students at any level. In any case, a useful aspect of this environment is the possibility of communicating through assumed identities which can have a liberating and empowering effect (Turkle 1995). Then no one ever needs to worry about exposing their mistakes, a common complaint in the communicative classroom.

The difference between the two types of site is illustrated by the contrast between the MUSH Peter Goelz created for students at the University of Victoria in Canada as early as 1996 (Goelz 1996), and *Planet Talk*. The former allows students to meet in different teaching rooms and in other locations resembling a university environment. The site also operates in French, Spanish and English and offers its own novice tour in English which is highly recommended for anyone new to this environment. While this may well be a good starting point for beginners, these types of multi-user domains tend to be limited in the sorts of interactions that take place, and generally need some initiative from the teacher if interesting exchanges are to be set up. They also do not support the creation of accents, at least so far, and instructions are generally in English. The reason for this – another illustration of pedagogy being hampered by technology – is that they operate via Telnet, and tend to use standard MOO commands

Planet Talk, by contrast, is one of the most user-friendly chat sites imaginable, on the subject of love and fun in Germany. There are people online at all hours offering instant communication with native speakers. The site also supports extended characters so that the writing is, by and large, accurate. Interaction tends to be very fast if many people are online but users can choose to respond just to one person. These sorts of sites are ideal vehicles to expose intermediate students to the specific 'netspeak' discourse of young people in the target language. When testing the site I got a severe grilling from one of the 22 people online, about whether I was really in Australia, and had to give information on population, animals and geography in a naturally authentic, information-gap exercise.

A challenging site for students is *Active Worlds*, a three-dimensional environment available in German, Spanish, French, Russian, Italian and Norwegian with each site located in the country of the language. Here, users can explore many virtual worlds and even create their own. They can meet others and interact as a 3D, lifelike, animated figure. Sites use objects just like hyperlinks to send mail and surf the Web, and include games, puzzles and mazes.

Quests with a meaningful goal can be found in many, mostly European, languages (Felix 1998a). They are often beautifully produced by publishers as teachers' resources linked to a specific textbook. One example has been given above in *Adesso* (Di Fabio & Hemment 1997) which offers 17 further activities of a similar kind. An equally impressive site, produced by Prentice-Hall, is *Mosaicos* (Lee 1998), which provides excellent examples of goal-oriented tasks, explicitly covering activities for the development of all four skills. In chapter 7, for instance, students are asked to identify the capital, cities and artists of Venezuela; to find information and write about one of the states in Venezuela; and to exchange ideas and cultural information with native speakers via email and a chat room, and discover more about the geography, president, museums, cities and artists of Venezuela. Of course, even the best designed activity risks running foul of a lack of interest in Venezuela on the part of the student, but an impressive characteristic of such sites is the number and variety of the activities available.

Further models can be found in sites which are integrated into a particular course such as first-year French at the University of Texas (Blyth 1997). This provides 14 self-contained activities, such as the simple task of calling up the issue of *Paris Match* published on a student's birthday and describing what is on the cover, or finding vacation accommodation through real estate sites in France. The two series of structured teaching plans mentioned earlier also offer activities of this kind and in languages not normally covered. One example is the activity for background speakers of Turkish which requires students to search for subjects that interest them to obtain information for use in a trivial pursuit-type quiz (Sperou 1998).

Where the production of materials is concerned, it is becoming common for this to be part of the students' learning experience. The work might include one-off short tasks leading to a tangible product, or substantial longer-term collaborations that might even include negotiating the curriculum (Barson 1997). Tasks and projects can be generated through various modes. Commercial sites offer a variety of potentially meaningful activities, MOOs and Chats are ideal for constructing imaginary worlds or communities, and Web-distributed environments (Debski 1998) offer promising new ways towards process-oriented collaborative learning.

Of the commercial sites, *Virtual Florist* allows real or virtual flowers to be sent to a recipient, together with a message composed by the sender. The best version of the genre is the *Virtual Card Shop* which allows greeting cards to be sent in a choice of 14 languages. One advantage is that all instructions are given in the respective language. Another is the complexity of what can be done, with students able to create their own version of the available models by adding backgrounds, choosing colours and attaching tunes and links, and even to create entirely new cards, in each instance processing relatively sophisticated language items. This provides an excellent opportunity for goal-oriented learning in which students end up with a tangible product in the target language which they can keep in printed form or send to someone. This activity could easily be set as an assignment with a card to be sent to the teacher. A nice touch is that the email message that is automatically sent to the receiver is also in the target language – and in language of good quality rather than in some poor translation.

A similar activity is provided by the Singapore Tourist Promotion Board site in which users produce a collage that expresses their idea of Singapore. Initially this was set up as a competition with a prize which made it even more motivating and meaningful, but even without the prize users end up with something to show for their work.

Where MOOs and Chats are concerned, an interesting example of how to use them to create student-generated materials is demonstrated by *Jarp Town,* a creative writing experiment on the Integrated Cyber Environment and a cyber community created through collaborative narratives (Truna 1998). A group of ESL students in Brisbane, Australia, have developed a variety of characters who then interact in a village environment built in the cyber community, *Connections.* The results of these interactions are then turned into narrative writings and posted back on the Web. As the project progresses, it is hoped that readers will be able to 'walk into the community' and in their own turn join in the narratives.

There are many ideas for collaborative work using the Web, such as the five-week teaching plan in which online Indonesian newspapers are researched and ideas gleaned for use in the creation of a class home page (Elliott 1998). Taking the idea of collaboration still further to link groups in different countries, Debski (1997) reports on two groups of students – American and Polish – who created sophisticated web pages about their own campuses. A larger-scale version of this has been trialled at The University of Melbourne (Debski 1998) in a project in which teachers, students and different language groups collaborate in negotiated student work, supported by a Web-distributed Global Learning Environment especially created for the purpose. This approach certainly reflects a significant move away from teacher-centred approaches and, as such, would seem to require a great deal of courage. As Barson puts it:

> An activity-driven classroom cannot be fully known in advance, nor can an activity-based curriculum be prescribed without altering the fundamental charge to the learner to elect and engage their intellect and psyche in accomplishing a project. (Barson 1997:5)

Discussion

What has become obvious over recent years, noticeably through reports at the WorldCALL and EuroCALL conferences, is that technology is moving into the background. The fascination with gadgets and bells and whistles that characterised the early days of multimedia development has given way to a focus on the student, with a shift from what the technology can do for the student to what the student can do with the technology.

While there continues to be, for obvious reasons, an interest in instruction in grammar and structures, and while a renewed interest in the teaching of grammar has surfaced (Goodfellow & Metcalfe 1997), the Web is best suited for task-driven activities in which students, working individually or in groups, have some degree of control over their learning.

As yet, however, there is no documented hard evidence of any effects on language learning outcomes for this approach – as compared with the detailed knowledge we have of what has been achieved in grammar, even if the achievement is relative, and knowledge of structures, of course, does not naturally lead to communicative competence in the language.

There is a growing body of anecdotal evidence, however, suggesting positive effects of task-based learning using the Web in a variety of projects, approaches and languages (Barson et al. 1993; Meagher & Castanos 1996; Warschauer 1995). Some of these have been confirmed at Monash University, Melbourne, in a Web-enhanced Japanese subject where a positive effect on retention rates and on the volume and quality of work generated, especially by weaker students, has been observed. In addition, there has been greatly increased communication with the teacher by email, allowing for faster, more individualised and more frequent feedback. Similarly, positive judgments on the Vietnamese program have been reported, with the lecturer delighted that students could work simultaneously on different parts of the course at their own pace, allowing freedom to respond to questions and provide more detailed feedback (Felix 1998b). Higher motivation and a better attitude towards learning have also been reported in web-based teaching (Atkinson 1998), which seems to reflect general findings in CALL where effects on learning outcomes have always been equivocal at best, but where positive affective factors have been consistently reported.

Interestingly, less resistance to task-based learning on the Web appears to be reported than in the pre-Web era where students were often found to resist the use of technology, and to prefer to work with pen and paper (Felix 1997; Gillespie & McKee 1998). From observation, students seem fascinated with the vast variety of materials and approaches available to them now. An interesting example is the Vietnamese bulletin board at Monash University where students write to each other and to the teacher even when they are all in the same room together. The students are apparently fascinated by how the system works and are motivated to write more, and at what are reported to be surprising levels of accuracy. How far this is a novelty effect remains to be seen.

This is not to say that all problems have been solved. What appears to be the case is that any resistance now is more likely to be to the teaching approach rather than to the medium. As Levy (1997) observes, project-based collaborative learning is not necessarily every student's preferred learning style, and potential problems with assessment, group dynamics and time commitment need to be carefully considered (Barson 1997 addresses some of these). Similarly, the extra time teachers now spend on course development and responding to emails also needs to be taken into account.

The great advantage that web-based teaching and learning offers is variety of content, approach and media. It allows flexibility in finding meaningful activities, often available at no cost, for different students, and most of all it allows for authenticity. The Web is an exciting new tool for language teaching: it may have its own problems, but it can add a valuable dimension to face-to-face teaching by providing an environment for meaningful interactive tasks in authentic settings, or at least in settings that are rich in authentic language and culture. There is no sense in advocating web-based learning as the sole medium of instruction, but, used at its best, it can be seen as a uniquely valuable addition to already excellent teaching in the classroom.

Notes

Abstracts for WorldCALL can be accessed at
   <http://www.hlc.unimelb.edu.au/worldcall/abstracts.html>
Abstracts for EUROCALL 98 can be accessed at
   <http://www.arts.kuleuven.ac.be/eurocall98>

Refernces

Active Worlds. URL <http://www.activeworlds.com/> (accessed 29 October 1998).

Arana, J.R. de (1998). Spanish Language Exercises.
   URL <http://mld.ursinus.edu/~jarana/Ejercicios/> (accessed 29 October 1998).

Atkinson, T. (1998, July). *Researching language learning and technology.* Paper presented at the inaugural WorldCALL conference, Melbourne.

Barson, J., Frommer, J. & Schwartz, M. (1993). Foreign language learning using email in a task-oriented perspective: Interuniversity experiments in communication and collaboration. *Journal of Science Education and Technology 4*, 565–584.

Barson, J. (1997). Space, time and form in the project-based foreign language class-room. In R. Debski, J. Gassin & M. Smith (Eds), *Language learning through social computing*. Occasional Papers Number 16, 1–37. Melbourne: ALAA and the Horwood Language Centre.

Barson, J. (1998, July). *Dealing with double evolution: Action-based learning approaches and instrumental technology*. Keynote address at the inaugural WorldCALL Conference, Melbourne.

Biddulph, P. (1998, September). *Interactive exercises and authoring for language learning on the Web*. Paper presented at the EUROCALL 98 Conference, Leuven. URL <http://www.point2.co.uk/lnet/> (accessed 29 October 1998).

Blyth, C. (1997). First year french@ut.austin.
URL <http://www.lamc.utexas.edu/fr/home.html> (accessed 29 October 1998).

Calvi, L., De Riddler, I. & Geerts, P. (1998, September). *Non-linear learning in the open way: Language acquisition on the Web*. Paper presented at the EUROCALL 98 Conference, Leuven.

California Foreign Language Project: Internet activities for Foreign Language Classes. URL <http://members.aol.com/maestro12/web/wadir.html> (accessed 30 October 1998).

Clayton, J. (1998). *The long walk: A journey as a learning activity*.
URL <http://www.epub-research.unisa.edu.au/AFMLTA/> (accessed 29 October 1998).

Debski, R. (1997). Support of creativity and collaboration in the language classroom: A new role for technology. In R. Debski, J. Gassin & M. Smith (Eds), *Language learning through social computing*. Occasional Papers Number 16, 39–66. Melbourne: ALAA and the Horwood Language Centre.

Debski, R. (1998, July). *Goal-oriented foreign language learning: Research of atti-tudes and implementation guidelines*. Paper presented at the inaugural WorldCALL Conference, Melbourne.

Di Fabio, E. & Hemment, M. (1997). *Adesso.*   URL <http://adesso.heinle.com/> (accessed 29 October 1998).

Dudfield, A. (1998). Cyberliteracies: Implications for education. *On-CALL 12*, 3, 25–34.

Elliott, S. (1998). *Ayo, berselancar berita Indonesia!*
URL <http://www.epub-research.unisa.edu.au/AFMLTA/> (accessed 29 October 1998).

Fanderclai, T. L. (1995). *MUDs in education: New environments, new pedagogies*. URL http://sunsite.unc.edu/cmc/mag/1995/jan/fanderclai.html (accessed 29 August 1998).

Felix, U. (1997). Integrating multimedia into the curriculum: A case study evalua-tion. *On-CALL 11*, 1, 2–11.

Felix, U. (1998a). *Virtual language learning: Finding the gems amongst the pebbles*. Melbourne: Language Australia.

Felix, U. (1998b). Virtual language learning: Potential and practice. *ReCALL 10*, 1, 53–58. Beginners' Vietnamese course,
URL <http://www.arts.monash.edu.au/viet/> (accessed 29 October 1998).

Ferguson, A. (1998). *Chat session discussion for advanced learners of German.*
URL <http://www.epub-research.unisa.edu.au/AFMLTA/> (accessed 29 October 1998).

Foot, C. (1994). Approaches to multimedia audio in language learning. *ReCALL 6*, 2, 9–13.

France à la Carte. URL <http://www.francealacarte.org.uk/> (accessed 29 October 1998).

Friedman, E. (1997). *FLIQ! Friedman's little Interactive Quizzes.*
URL <http://eee.uci.edu/96s/24060/fliq.html> (accessed 29 October 1998).

Garrett, N. (1986). The problem with grammar: What kind can the language learner use? *Modern Language Journal 70*, 2, 133–148.

Gillespie, J. & McKee, J. (1998, September). *Resistance to CALL: Degrees of student reluctance to CALL and ICT.* Paper presented at the EUROCALL 98 Conference, Leuven.

Goelz, P. (1996). *German for beginners.* URL <http://web.uvic.ca/german/149/> (accessed 29 October 1998).

Goelz, P (1998). *Deutsch online.* URL <http://web.uvic.ca/german/dol-demo/> (accessed 29 October 1998).

Goodfellow, R. & Metcalfe, P. (1997). The challenge: Back to basics or brave new world? *ReCALL 9*, 2, 4–7.

Goodwin-Jones, B. (1998). *Language interactive: A trailguide to creating dynamic web pages.* URL <http://www.fln.vcu.edu/cgi/interact.html> (accessed 29 October 1998).

Holmes, M. & Arneil, S. (September 1998). *Hot potatoes: Free tools for creating interactive language exercises for the World Wide Web.* Paper presented at the EUROCALL 98 Conference, Leuven. URL <http://web.uvic.ca/hrd/halfbaked> (accessed 29 October 1998).

Hoven, D. (1998, July). *Modelling learner-centred CALL.* Paper presented at the inaugural WorldCALL Conference, Melbourne.

Kretschmer et al. (1997). *Texthaus.* URL <http://www.texthaus.com/> (accessed 29 October 1998).

Lamy, M-N. (1997). The Web for French grammar: A tool, a resource or a waste of time? *ReCALL 9*, 2, 26–32.

Lee, L. (1998). *Mosaicos: Spanish as a World Language.*
URL <http://www.prenhall.com/mosaicos/> (accessed 1 November 1998).

Levy, M. (1997). Project-based learning for language teachers: Reflecting on the process. In R. Debski, J. Gassin & M. Smith (Eds), *Language learning through social computing.* Occasional Papers Number 16, 181–199. Melbourne. ALAA and the Horwood Language Centre.

Meagher, M.E. & Castanos, F. (1996). Perception of American culture: The impact of an electronically-mediated cultural exchange program on Mexican high school students. In S.C. Herring (Ed.), *Computer-mediated communication: Linguistic, social and cross-cultural perspective*s. Amsterdam: John Benjamins Company.

Melis, L., Desmet, P. & Vleminckx, G. (1998, September). *The ALFAGRAM-project: Active learning environment for French as a foreign language – grammar*. Paper presented at the EUROCALL 98 Conference, Leuven.

Mills, D. (1998, July). *Interactive web-based language learning: The state of the art.* Paper presented at the inaugural WorldCALL Conference, Melbourne.

Planet Talk. URL <http://www.allegra.de/talk/> (accessed 29 October 1998).

Prokop, M. (1997). *Bayrische Landeskunde.* URL <http://www.ualberta.ca/~german/bayern25.htm> (accessed 29 October 1998).

Rushkoff, D. (1996). *Children of chaos*. London: Harper Collins.

Singapore Tourist Promotion Site. URL <http://www.newasia-singapore.com> (accessed 29 October 1998).

Smith, G. (1995). *The German electronic textbook.* URL <http://www.wm.edu/CAS/modlang/grammnu.html> (accessed 29 October 1998).

Snyder, I. (ed) (1997). *Page to screen: Taking literacy into the electronic era.* Sydney: Allen & Unwin.

Sperou, A. (1998). *Turkish quiz.*   URL <http://www.epub-research.unisa.edu.au /AFMLTA/> (accessed 29 October 1998).

Truna aka Turner, J. (1995a). *Using text-based virtual reality in the classroom - A narrative.* URL <http://elicos.qut.edu.au/moo/mpaper.html> (accessed 29 October 1998).

Truna aka Turner, J. (1995b). Virtual treasure hunt. In M. Warschauer (Ed.), *Virtual connections: Online activities and projects for networking language learner*s (pp. 242–244). Hawai'i: University of Hawai'i Press.

Truna, aka Turner, J. (1998). *Jarp Town*. URL <http://elicos.qut.edu.au/village/> (accessed 29 October 1998).

Turkle, S. (1995). *Life on the screen: Identity in the age of the internet*. London: Weidenfeld & Nicholson.

Virtual Card Shop. URL <http://www.bizshoppe.com/cardshop.html> (accessed 30 October 1998).

Virtual Florist. URL <http://www.virtualflorist.com/> (accessed 30 October 1998).

Warschauer, M. (Ed) (1995). *Virtual connections: Online activities and projects for networking language learners*. Hawai'i: University of Hawai'i Press.

6

Collaboration in a Virtual World: Groupwork and the Distance Language Learner

Lesley Shield
Open University, UK
Markus J. Weininger
Universidade Federal de Santa Catarina, Brazil

Overview

The Internet allows the use of communications technologies to promote collaboration between distance learners. For the language learner, the Internet provides myriad opportunities to consult authentic sources and to practise using the target language both with native speakers and other learners synchronously and asynchronously. This chapter describes the design, development and implementation of a language-learning activity using text-based virtual reality in conjunction with the World Wide Web. The pedagogical purpose underlying this activity was to promote autonomous learning behaviours by enabling geographically distant language learners to work with native and non-native speakers of the target language on an engaging and motivating task with a concrete and meaningful outcome.

We define 'learner autonomy' and outline why we believe text-based virtual reality is appropriate for our purposes. Next, we describe the design and outcomes of initial trials, examining participants' successes and difficulties. Finally, we reflect on how to improve such an activity to enhance the learning experience and support the development of the autonomous distance language learner still further.

Defining learner autonomy

'Autonomy' has become a widely-accepted concept in 'post-communicative' methodological discussions. Little (1991:1) holds that perhaps 'the most widespread misconception is that autonomy is synonymous with self-instruction, that is essentially a matter of deciding to learn without a teacher'. Little (1990:7) explains that learner autonomy is not about 'letting the learners get on with things as best they can ... something that teachers do to learners ... a single, easily described behaviour ... a steady state achieved by learners'. While 'learners are unlikely to become autonomous without active encouragement from their teachers ... learner autonomy cannot be programmed in a series of lesson plans'. Rather than a movement towards teacherless learning, autonomy is: '... a capacity – for detachment, critical reflection, decision-making and independent action' (Little 1991:4). It 'entails a capacity and willingness to act independently and in co-operation with others, as a socially responsible person' (Dam 1990:17) and 'contains the idea that learning arises essentially from supported performance' (Schwienhorst 1998b).

For our purposes, learner autonomy refers to the development of a capacity for engagement with and critical reflection on the learning process. Learners take responsibility for their own learning and groups of learners take collective responsibility for group learning. Behaviours that display features of learner autonomy include negotiation between facilitator and learner and between learner and learner about what is to be learned, when it is to be learned and how learning is to be achieved, as well as proactive, independent use of any and all potentially helpful learning resources. Such behaviours 'confer the *power* to carry out learning under conditions of total responsibility and total independence' (Holec 1988:6), even if the learner chooses not to exercise this power. Such knowledge empowers the learner, and the role of the teacher changes from 'fount of all knowledge' to co-learner, 'counsellor and manager of learning resources' (Little 1990:11).

Bringing together geographically distant learners
Schmooze University (Schmooze) is an ESL/EFL/cross-cultural communication MOO. Users from around the world log into Schmooze and regular users are frequently approached by guests 'because my teacher says I have to talk with people here'. Unsurprisingly, such guests do not return after classes end. For them, the MOO experience is related to their studies; something their teacher does to them, rather than something they have chosen or negotiated to do themselves. They log in only when they must.

Many learners, however, do log in regularly outside class time. Some come to Schmooze of their own volition, some initially at their instructors' suggestion – but all obtain permanent characters. For some, 'chatting' with virtual friends is sufficient. For others, the attraction of MOO lies in its ability to expand to incorporate their own ideas and creations. These users are autonomous learners in the sense we have defined. They take responsibility for what they learn – whether MOO programming, English or intercultural issues – and choose when and how to do this. They are not, however, 'teacherless'. Even if such learners do not consult their (language) tutors, almost every new Schmooze-user requests assistance and instruction from more experienced users when creating descriptions for their personae, simple objects, rooms and room entrances and exits. Learners may even use asynchronous, MOO-based tools to begin and maintain a dialogue with experienced, absent players. Finally, examining descriptions others have written probably contributes to learners' understanding of what they can do. Collaboration and co-learning of this sort continue even when players are absent, as indicated by Kolko (1998:267): 'when I am alone in a room, looking at objects ... I am collaborating, albeit asynchronously, with other players'.

Furthermore, whether chatting or expanding the MOO, learners are engaged in activities which are meaningful to them. Bruckman and Resnick (1995) point out that constructionism, a concept central to learning autonomy, involves two types of construction. Firstly, knowledge is constructed on experience – learning is an active process. Secondly, 'people construct new knowledge with particular effectiveness when they are engaged in constructing personally-meaningful products'.

For language learners, MOO has a special advantage; the learners must communicate with others, either directly by 'speaking' or indirectly in their descriptions of themselves and of the virtual space which is 'theirs'. Such activities and environments demonstrate the features we have stated to be central to our definition of learner autonomy. It was to exploit this sense of collaborative, autonomous learning that the activity for the Bamburgh Project was developed.

This project attempted to harness both the 'neutral, but potentially controllable environment' of MOO and to provide 'tools, resources and activities' (Schwienhorst 1998a) to support successful language learning and to promote learner autonomy among groups of geographically distant learners.

The Bamburgh Project

MOO has a steep initial learning curve. Learners who are physically in the same place when they initially come to MOO can collaborate with each other and with their tutor in a face-to-face as well as in a virtual environment. For learners who are at a distance from both their co-learners and their facilitator, the situation is different. They rely solely on keyboard-mediated communication. It was for this type of learner that the Bamburgh Project was developed.

Aims

Tandem language learning has been successfully used within MOO environments (Schwienhorst 1997a, 1997b, 1998a, 1998b; Donaldson & Kötter forthcoming). Tandem brings together groups of learners who are native speakers of each others' target language and is based on clearly described principles concerning reciprocity (each learner must benefit equally from the partnership), bilingualism (the same amount of the first and target language should be used) and learner autonomy (learners are responsible both for their own learning and for 'making the partnership as rich and beneficial to each partner as possible' (Schwienhorst 1997b).

The aim of the Bamburgh Project was slightly different: individual, geographically distant learners worked together in Schmooze using only the target language to identify a topic, design, develop, draft, redraft and publish a web page. Publication of the web page entailed using a specially designed web editor which allows even the least computer-literate user to produce a well-formatted web page and to publish it on the World Wide Web as the final outcome of the activity. This served to enhance student motivation by providing a concrete outcome and turning the collective writing activity into an authentic communicative act, as opposed to writing essays for the teacher alone.

Methods

To provide a focus and common but flexible topic area for the project, a work area was designed, set in a virtual representation of the north-east coast of England. A wide choice of in-MOO and web-based tools was offered, allowing learners to research and develop web pages according to any of the themes offered or to choose another topic entirely. Tools were minimal because, as Little (1991:51) points out, 'an autonomous learning scheme does not depend above all else on providing a great wealth of materials'. Learners were not constrained by the tools or materials provided; they could use other resources if they wished. They negotiated web page content and assigned specific tasks to individual group members. Thus, learners took collective responsibility for a successful outcome.

Asynchronous support was provided via the in-MOO bulletin board, MOOmail, online help and a web site, whilst synchronous advice was available from tutors and project designers. It was believed that all participants, both tutors and learners, should have access to the designers because a 'kind of constructionist culture often emerges when the tools designer is present to help grow a community of users' (Bruckman 1998).

The learning environment
The environment that was developed comprised:

- a virtual space in which participants could meet and work synchronously and asynchronously;
- a suite of in-MOO tools;
- a supporting web site for the project; and
- a specially created, easy-to-use web-editing tool.

The virtual space
Tools and 'rooms' in a MOO can be restricted to named players. The Bamburgh Project is mostly open to all, with certain exceptions. It was thought important that participants felt a sense of ownership of the project. To promote a sense of community, groups were provided with their own area. This comprised a shared workroom, project bulletin board and bookcase complete with books containing references to web sites which had been identified as being relevant to some aspect of the type of research learners might undertake. Only tutors or designers could write on the bulletin board, and books were 'programmed' in such a way that they could not be removed from the work area.

Three study areas, leading from the main workroom, were also developed. Each contained a MOO-based whiteboard on which learners could enter their ideas for their web pages. Once groups of learners had been established, whiteboards were 'locked' so that only members of the groups could use them. Initially, the study areas were not locked, but some project participants asked that this be done so they could work undisturbed, 'Can we lock the door or something like that to keep other people out of the room while we work?' (Participant's MOOmail).

Facilitators were also provided with a meeting area, or staffroom. Initially, only tutors could use it, but it was opened to all, on their request.

As well as making use of resources based in the shared workroom, students were able to explore a text-based representation of a section of the north-east coast of England which included links to web-based sounds, graphics and text.

For readability, descriptions for each 'room' in the project space filled no more than a single screen (figure 1), so that users did not have to scroll up and down to read them. MOO automatically adds exit names to room descriptions, but these can sometimes be 'lost' in text descriptions. In order to make them obvious, a blank line was added to the end of each 'room' description.

Figure 1: Room description

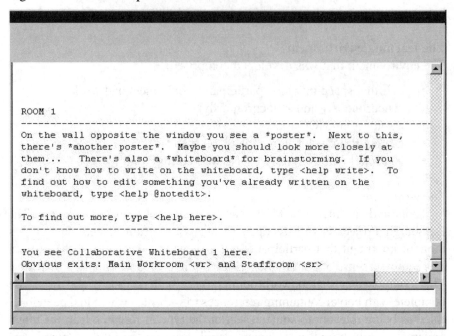

Further information could be obtained by examining words enclosed between asterisks (figure 2). The detail associated with such words could be accessed by typing <look <word>> and might be another textual description with further examinable detail or a link to a web-based sound, picture or text.

Users of the area can easily see their location at any time by typing <look>. Unlike hyperlinked texts, where it is possible to become 'lost in hyperspace', the type of extra detail offered in the MOO project area does not require learners to change virtual location.

In-MOO tools

The project work area offers a range of tools to learners. Some of these are MOO standards, while others are adaptations of existing MOO tools, tailored especially for this project.

There are two main types of asynchronous communications media in-MOO: CMC and one-way media. Both types of tool were available for the Bamburgh Project.

MOOmail is similar to email but available only to users of individual MOO communities; it is not normally possible to send MOOmail to a recipient who is not also a user of the MOO from which it originates. Like email, MOOmail allows users to send, forward or reply to single or multiple recipients. MOOmail messages can even be automatically forwarded to users' email accounts.

Figure 2: Further detail related to an asterisked word or phrase

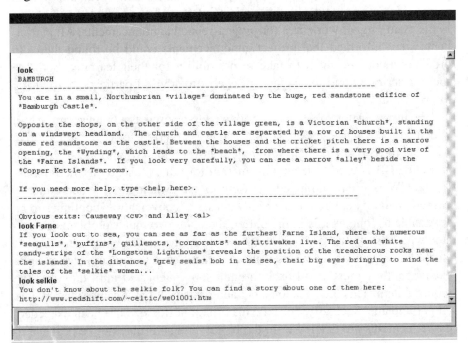

```
look
BAMBURGH
--------------------------------------------------------------------------------
You are in a small, Northumbrian *village* dominated by the huge, red sandstone edifice of
*Bamburgh Castle*.

Opposite the shops, on the other side of the village green, is a Victorian *church*, standing
on a windswept headland.  The church and castle are separated by a row of houses built in the
same red sandstone as the castle. Between the houses and the cricket pitch there is a narrow
opening, the *Wynding*, which leads to the *beach*,  from where there is a very good view of
the *Farne Islands*.  If you look very carefully, you can see a narrow *alley* beside the
*Copper Kettle* Tearooms.

If you need more help, type <help here>.
--------------------------------------------------------------------------------
Obvious exits: Causeway <cw> and Alley <al>
look Farne
If you look out to sea, you can see as far as the furthest Farne Island, where the numerous
*seagulls*, *puffins*, guillemots, *cormorants* and kittiwakes live. The red and white
candy-stripe of the *Longstone Lighthouse* reveals the position of the treacherous rocks near
the islands. In the distance, *grey seals* bob in the sea, their big eyes bringing to mind the
tales of the *selkie* women...
look selkie
You don't know about the selkie folk? You can find a story about one of them here:
http://www.redshift.com/~celtic/we01001.htm
```

Participants in the Bamburgh Project were encouraged to use MOOmail to contact each other, their tutors and the designers asynchronously to discuss any aspects of the project or their chosen topic.

MOO mailing lists are similar to email mailing lists. They may allow threaded or unthreaded discussion. Once users have subscribed to a MOO-based list, they automatically receive copies of all messages sent to it, and any message they send to it is automatically distributed to all other sub-scribers.

It was decided to offer a mailing list to the participants in the project. The purpose of this list was to allow a forum for project-related or technical ques-tions. Such questions would build up into a Frequently Asked Questions list (FAQ) which would be dynamically shaped by project participants. This FAQ would be the first port of call for those with such questions. If they were unable to find the answer to their question on the FAQ, they would then either ask others synchronously or post a new query to the list, thus taking respon-sibility for their own learning.

It is possible to create an object known as a 'note' within the MOO envi-ronment. This can be written on by a restricted or unrestricted group of users and can operate as a Bulletin Board (BB). Unlike the CMC tools described above, the BB is a one-way communication medium. Specified users may post announcements to it, while both they and others with appropriate permissions may read it. For this project, a BB tool was provided and placed in the main project work area for project-related announcements. All participants were informed that project announcements could be found there. In order to encourage them to take responsibility for their learning, both the room description and the supporting web site advised participants to check the BB regularly.

The in-MOO note object can be adapted to be used as a brainstorming tool which, for the purposes of the project, was referred to as a collaborative whiteboard (CW). The main difference between the BB and the CW is that while the BB is used to leave information for others, usually asynchronously, the CW is often employed by users to share their ideas synchronously. Although all text entered into a MOO during a 'conversation' continues to be accessible as long as it is in the buffer, there are two major problems associated with this: firstly, text in a MOO scrolls up the screen with each new text entry. This means that if users want to consult something from earlier in an exchange, they must scroll back through subsequent text until they find the required item. This then has to be cut and pasted so that it can be shared with all participants. Secondly, once the maximum buffer size has been exceeded, earlier contents are deleted from the buffer, and so it may not be possible to retrieve the required information. The CWs for this project provided users with a permanent, easily accessible space in which to brainstorm ideas or to write and edit text in collaboration with others. A project-specific help text was also written to explain how to use the area (figure 3). Learners were able to access this by typing <help here> at any time while they were in the project-related virtual space.

One of MOO's most useful features for language learners is the opportunity it offers users to log events while they are online. While various ethical issues are associated with keeping MOO logs (permission should be obtained from all those involved before logging commences, for example) this tool allows learners to review, reflect on and exploit their online experiences in a way which contributes to their development as autonomous learners. For this reason, project participants were encouraged to log their project-related activities, and to share these logs with the project designers primarily to inform them of how the in-MOO tools were used. It should be noted here that the initial request to tutors that learners should log their project-related work was met with resistance, but, when learners were asked to decide whether or not they would keep logs, all agreed.

The supporting web site

The project's supporting web site (Weininger & Shield 1998) offered both learners and tutors:

- suggestions about how they might use the in-MOO project area;
- descriptions of the tools they would find there;
- technical advice about MOO clients;
- a 'map' of the virtual space in which the project was located; and
- an explanation about how to use the web editor (figure 4);

All the links to resources provided in-MOO were repeated on the web site to enable ease of access for learners whose MOO clients did not support hotlinking to the Web.

Figure 3: Project-specific help

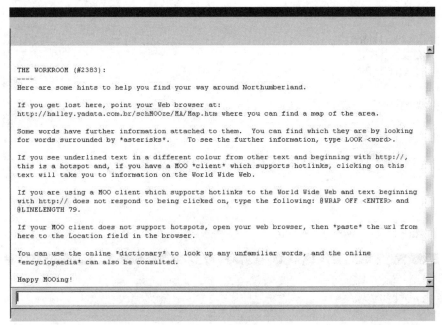

The web editing tool

Using CGI templates, a series of password-protected forms was developed to allow users to input web page content – including text, sound and graphics – which was then automatically formatted (figure 5). The templates also accept HTML code, so that users proficient in web page design can override the built-in formatting. A preview facility is included so that web pages can be edited before being published on the World Wide Web. A page developed using the web-editing tool is automatically published on the Web via a server in Brazil and an automatic link to it generated from the project support web site. Learners have complete control over when and whether their web page should be generally accessible. Firstly, they can edit its content until fully satisfied and, secondly, they can delete and replace it with another,

Figure 4: The project-support web site menu

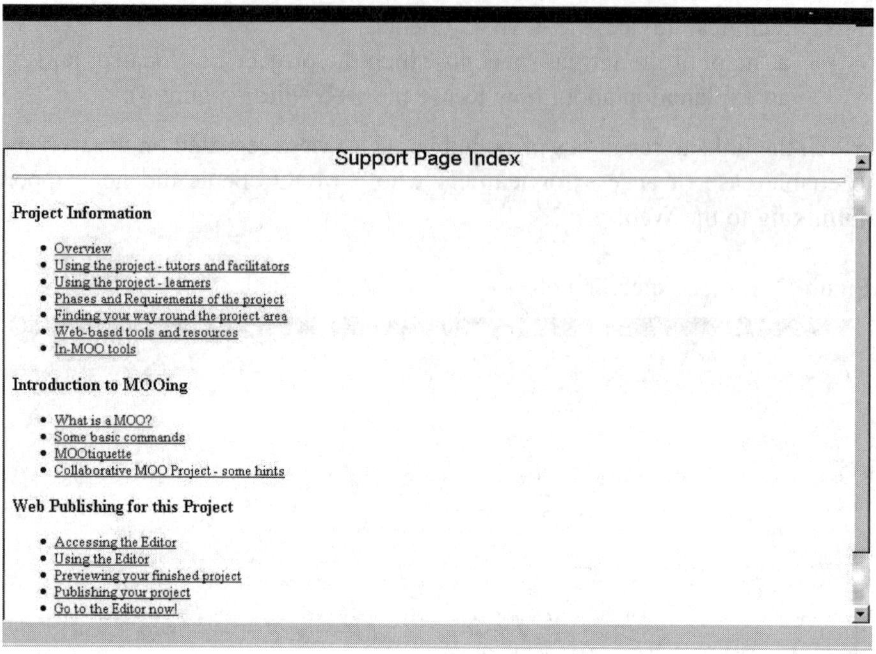

Figure 5: The web editing tool

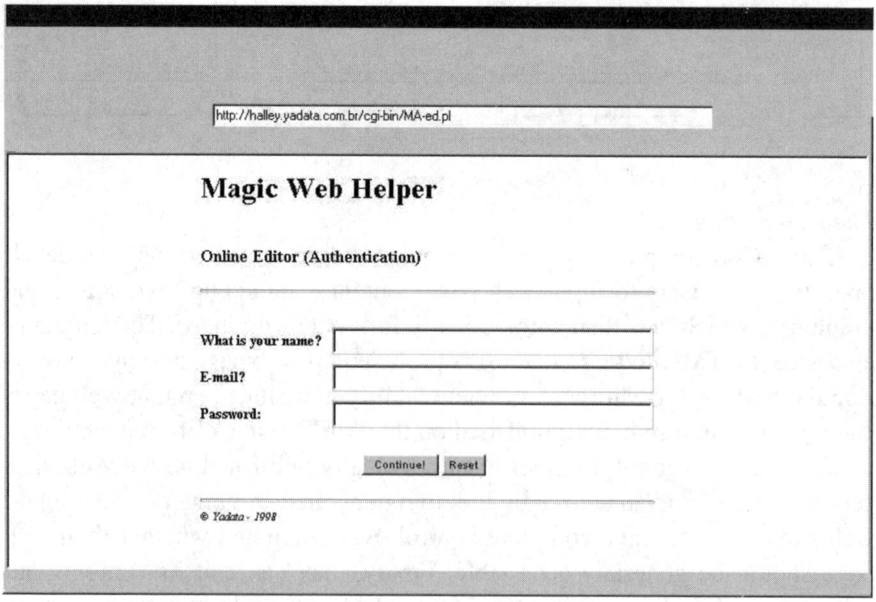

updated version, if they wish to make changes after publishing the page. Full instructions on the use of the web-editor are provided on the supporting web site.

This tool allows even the least computer-literate user to produce well-formatted web pages and thus to concentrate upon the content, rather than the form, of the final product.

The project trials

A series of informal, small-scale project trials was carried out over a six-month period. The project involved collaboration at three levels:

- The developers were based on different continents and all development work was carried out collaboratively via MOO.
- Tutors collaborated with each other, with their own and other tutors' students and with the developers.
- Learners collaborated with each other, with their own and others' tutors and with the developers.

The activity was intended primarily as an introduction for language learners to MOO and the possibilities of collaborative learning. Learners' use of language while preparing their web pages has not been analysed at this stage. What we were interested in was which tools they used and how they used them, and also, in the light of the collaborative possibilities offered by MOO, whether they worked with each other or separately.

The first trial

Once the virtual space had been designed and built and the supporting web site and web-editing tool completed, volunteers were requested from two sources; firstly, a description of the project and its aims was posted to the Teacher List at Schmooze, and secondly, personal contacts were made with teachers of English who had an interest in Internet-based language learning. Four volunteer groups were obtained (table 1).

Table 1: Volunteers for the first trial

Group	Located	No. of participants*	Lab/home	MOO-experienced
1	Brazil	L=4 T=1	Lab/home	L=No T=No
2	Brazil	L=1 T=1	Lab/home	L=No T=No
3	USA	L=2 T=1	Lab	L=Yes T=Yes
4	Japan	L=4 T=1	Lab/home	L=No T=Yes

* L = Learner, T = Tutor

Participants negotiated that both learners and tutors would have scheduled meetings once a week, while learners could arrange to meet outside those times in order to socialise, get to know each other and to work on the activity. The designers would be online during scheduled meetings in order to answer questions. It was made clear to all participants, both teachers and learners, that how the project was used was entirely a matter for negotiation. It was also explained that there were no lesson plans and that the purpose of the activity was to provide learners with an opportunity to work with others in different locations using the target language, English, to produce a web page about a topic area which interested them as a group. It was stressed that while the topic area could be related directly to some aspect of the virtual space in which they would work together, the link might be as tenuous as, for example, a comparison of the fishing industry in several different cultures.

Outcomes of the first trial

After two weeks, it became clear that the activity was not working as had been intended, although the designers had attempted to offer a supportive and nonthreatening learning environment which would allow learners to take responsibility for their own learning. Discussions with teachers revealed that a number of factors contributed to the failure of the first trial, as summarised in table 2.

Lessons of the first trial

Although this project trial ran for six weeks, there was no material outcome in terms of learners using the learning environment with the results defined in table 2 as being necessary to their successful development as autonomous learners. What did become clear, though, was that enthusiasm was not enough. The following conclusions were drawn:

- At least one member of each group of participants, whether teacher or learner, must be MOO-experienced.
- Greater use of asynchronous tools is needed to overcome scheduling problems and also to contribute to building a sense of community based on shared interests and goals.
- Teachers need more support and should work through the project themselves before asking learners to trial it.

The second trial

A repeated request for volunteers was sent to the Teacher List at Schmooze. Using this route, designers could be certain that they would have MOO-experienced volunteers. Responses to the request were encouraging – teachers from Australia, Japan, Germany, Italy and the USA asked for further information, and the designers set up a mailing list to inform these teachers of

Table 2: Reasons for the failure of the first project trial

Reason	Description
Technical	The USA group experienced frequent and frustrating technical problems including severe 'lag' (delay in transmission to and from the MOO server making synchronous exchanges difficult or impossible). They were thus unable to participate actively in synchronous meetings.
Personal	One teacher experienced personal problems and was unable to arrange for her learners to be available at all.
MOO experience	Only two teachers and one group of students were MOO-experienced. Although it is possible to operate effectively in a MOO environment whilst knowing only four commands, understanding what to do can be problematic for some learners.
Pedagogical	Not all teachers seemed clear about the underlying concepts of learner autonomy and collaborative learning. This emerged in their requests for 'lesson plans' and assertions that they did not understand the project's purpose since no information was available to them (despite having been told about the supporting web site on several occasions).
Motivational	As a result of technical problems, the US group lost motivation. This had a knock-on effect on other students who did not see the point in working without their peers. Furthermore, the promised Japanese group did not join the project, primarily because of time zone differences between this group, Brazil and the USA. The teacher in Japan had difficulty in persuading his extremely busy students that this would be a worthwhile activity, since the students did not get extra credit for participating.
Scheduling	The USA group persisted in their attempts to participate despite their technical problems, but experienced severe difficulties in scheduling synchronous meetings with their Brazilian counterparts.
Community building	Socialisation is one of the underlying principles of constructionist learning. This did not happen either between learners and teachers, or teachers and teachers, although both teachers and learners socialised with the designers on an individual basis.

developments. Unfortunately, the time of year – early May – precluded German learners, and time zone differences prevented participation from Italy, while the American teacher was unable to motivate his students to take part. However, interest from Japan and Australia continued, and the second small-scale trial began (table 3).

Table 3: Volunteers for the second trial

Group	Located	No. of participants*	Lab/home	MOO-experienced
1	Australia	L=4 T=1	Home	L=Yes T=Yes
2	Australia	L=2 T=1	Lab/home	L=Yes T=Yes
3	Japan	L=4 T=1	Lab	L=No T=Yes

* L = Learner, T = Tutor

Outcomes of the second trial

There were two groups of learners in the second trial: one comprising two Australian adult basic education students and two learners from the University of Nanzan in Japan, and the other made up of another Australian student from a different site and two more learners from Japan. Tutors and designers had suggested groups of students who did not know each other, but learners made an autonomous decision to divide in this way. Within these groups, students negotiated the topic for their web page. They organised their own meeting times and also worked individually on the project when other group members were not available.

The Australian students were fairly experienced MOO users and logged in from home via modem as well as from a computer laboratory, while the Japanese students were new to MOO and used their university's facilities to connect.

Initially, the Australian students found the Japanese learners' ignorance of MOO difficult to come to terms with. One even asked for advice about how best to deal with the fact that she felt she was 'speaking a different language' from her Japanese colleagues when she was explaining to them how to use MOO for the project: 'I must admit I was beginning to feel a bit frustrated with the communication barrier but I'm sure we will get over it!' (participant's MOOmail).

Once they became aware that they could substantially help their Japanese colleagues, the Australian students gained confidence and the groups began to cohere to the extent that the Australians felt able to make suggestions as to how to proceed: 'I took the time to make some very simple web pages so you could see examples of how web pages develop. You will see how we can build on something very simple and make a more and more complex web page. Have a look at the first one and follow the instructions to get you to the other three web pages' (participant's MOOmail).

Reflections

The small number of participants makes it impossible to draw any but the most general of conclusions at this stage. The activity was intended primarily as an introduction for language learners to MOO and its possibilities. We have not, therefore, examined learners' use of language here. What we were interested in was which tools learners used and whether they worked with each other or separately. In other words, we were interested in observing autonomous, authentic, online negotiations where learners help overcome each others' individual challenges, thus narrowing lexical, cultural and geographical distance through mutual respect, exchange and collaboration.

What has been emphasised during the course of the activity is that groups of this sort must include at least one member who is MOO-competent, and is prepared to help less competent members to use the technology. Facilitators, although physically in the same place as their own groups of learners, were not asked for help as frequently as other, geographically distant group members. Peer-knowledge shared in this way appeared to increase learners' confidence greatly, and also added to the sense of community within the groups. Group members could frequently be seen online with each other outside official meeting times.

From the point of view of learner collaboration, the project appears to have been successful as project participants started autonomous real-time interaction in-MOO, and engaged in reflective meta-communication by MOOmail. Further, they used the tools and materials provided to engage with the learning environment in a way meaningful to them.

A major problem experienced while setting up the project was obtaining volunteers to trial the activity. Although MOO provides the possibility of remote learners communicating with similar learners, time zones must be taken into consideration. The groups for the second trial were only one hour apart in time zones, and so were able to arrange mutually convenient meeting times. As a result of the experience of the first, unsuccessful trial, it was decided that the designers would be available at a specific time each week to answer facilitators' questions or discuss any points of interest or difficulty which had arisen. Learners also discussed issues with the designers, but on a more ad hoc basis.

As noted above, learner groups must include at least one MOO-experienced member. It is also apparent that facilitators must have some experience of MOO and an understanding of its possibilities in order for an activity to be successful. Learners must understand at least basic MOO commands and how to move within MOO-space before they enter it.

In spite of these operational difficulties, the project appears to have achieved its goals: learners worked collaboratively with each other towards developing web pages based on information in the project area. They autonomously found relevant links to additional web sites. Interestingly, the tools which they used most were the in-MOO dictionary, links to the Web and the collaborative whiteboards. MOOmail was initially ignored in favour of external email systems, although, more recently, participants have begun to use it. The in-MOO project mailing list was not used at all, despite one participant's suggestion via her group's whiteboard that it was a useful tool. It is not clear whether the mailing list was rejected because it was too complicated for MOO-inexperienced users or whether learner groups developed a degree of autonomy such that they formed self-help groups and did not require help from tutors or developers. While none of the groups has yet produced a finished web page using the web-editing tool, one of the learners has posted a guide to the project on his institution's own web site.

Most encouragingly, one of the groups which disbanded over the summer as a result of the summer break has now reformed of its own volition, as announced in this message:

> They (the Japanese students) have just returned from summer holidays and find that 1) they are very busy and can't meet so often and 2) their characters have been recycled. So at the moment we are waiting for them to get back on as characters and to work out a good time to meet. I suggested that we write an adventer [sic] story together which takes the reader around the island through links – that way we don't need to be online at the same time every time we have time to work on the project. (Participant's MOOmail)

It seems that the project has allowed this group to develop a degree of autonomy through working collaboratively, even though group members are not all in the same location. In the time they have been working together, they have moved from making tentative requests about who should and should not be able to use their study area to telling the designers what they have negotiated between them in terms of what they intend to learn (the content of the web page), and how and when they intend to do it.

Future directions

This project forms the first in a series of MOO-based activities to be trialed for language learners working at a distance from one another. Because of the small size of the sample during this trial, and the inconclusive nature of the outcomes, the trial will be extended to include a greater number of learners and sites. If these trials appear to replicate the successful outcomes experienced so far, the activities will be developed further.

The next stage is for learners to work in groups (perhaps drawing upon the Bamburgh Project area for ideas) to build a project area of their own, based on a topic negotiated within the group. This would introduce a new dimension to the activity, since MOO-experienced learners who had advanced beyond the 'player'-level character, could discuss project requirements with other group members before 'building' or 'programming' the objects involved. Less MOO-proficient learners could use in-MOO tools to write descriptions or specifications which could then be agreed within the group and incorporated into the project outcome. Learners might even develop a web site (using the web-editing tool) to provide support for their own area of the MOO. Finally, learners would explore each others' projects and web sites in more detail, meeting online (time zones permitting) to present, discuss and explain what they had developed.

This type of activity supports this suggestion made by Allison:

> The future utility of MOOs and MUDs lies not in their ability to recreate the classroom, but rather in their ability to place students in situations where they can develop team skills and tackle questions in a virtual sense that they would not have looked at in their traditional environment. (Allison 1995)

MOOs allow both teachers and learners to participate in a collaborative learning environment which develops autonomous learning skills by empowering learners to take charge of the what, when and how of their own learning.

References

Allison, J. (1995). *MOOs and education: Their role and relevance*. Unpublished paper presented in partial completion for Course 1514S The Internet and Education, Ontario Institute for Studies in Education (OISE), URL <http://www.oise.on.ca/~jallison/abst4.html>.

Bruckman, A. (1998). Community support for constructionist learning. *Journal of Computer Supported Collaborative Writing 7*, 47–86, URL <http://www.cc.gatech.edu/fac/Amy.Bruckman/papers/cscw.html>.

Bruckman, A. & Resnick, M. (1995). The MediaMOO project: Constructionism and professional community. *Convergence 1*, 1, Spring, URL <http://www.cc.gatech.edu/fac/Amy.Bruckman/papers/convergence.html>.

Dam, L. (1990). Learner autonomy in practice. In I. Gathercote (Ed.), *Autonomy in language learning* (pp. 16–37). Great Britain: CILT.

Donaldson, R.P. & Kötter, M. (forthcoming). Language learning in a MOO: Creating a transoceanic bilingual virtual community. In *Literary and linguistic computing*. Oxford: Oxford University Press.

Fernback, J. & Thompson, B. (1993). *Virtual Communities: Abort, retry, failure?*, URL <http://www.well.com/user/hlr/texts/Vccivil.html>.

Holec, H. (Ed). (1988). *Autonomy and self-directed learning: Present fields of application*. Strasbourg: Council of Europe.

Kolko, B. (1998). Bodies in place: Real politics, real pedagogy and virtual space. In C. Haynes & J.R. Holmvik (Eds), *High wired: On the design, use and theory of educational MOOs* (pp. 253–265). Ann Arbor: University of Michigan Press.

Little, D. (1990). Autonomy in language learning: Some practical and theoretical considerations. In I. Gathercote (Ed.). *Autonomy in language learning* (pp. 7–15). Great Britain: CILT.

Little, D. (1991). *Learner autonomy 1: Definitions, issues and problems*. Dublin: Authentik Language Learning Resources Ltd.

Marvin, L. (1995). Spoof, spam, lurk and lag: The aesthetics of text-based virtual realities. *Journal of computer mediated communication 1*, 2, URL <http://shum.huji.ac.il/jcmc/vol1/issue2/marvin.html>.

Schwienhorst, K. (1997a). Modes of interactivity: Internet resources for second language learning. In D. Kranz, L. Legenhausen & B. Lüking (Eds), *Multimedia – Internet – Lernsoftware: Fremdsprachenunterricht vor neuen Herausforderungen* (pp. 103–110). Münster: Agenda Verlag,
URL <http://www.tcd.ie/CLCS/assistants/kschwien/Publications/modinter.htm>.

Schwienhorst, K. (1997b). *Talking on the MOO: Learner autonomy and language learning in tandem*. Paper presented at the CALLMOO: Enhancing language learning through Internet technologies conference, Bergen, Norway,
URL <http://www.tcd.ie/CLCS/assistants/kschwien/Publications /CALLMOOtalk.htm>.

Schwienhorst, K. (1998a). *Co-constructing learning environments and learners identities: Language learning in virtual reality*. Paper presented at the EDMedia/ED-Telecom Conference, Freiburg, Germany. URL:
<http://www.tcd.ie/CLCS/assistants/kschwien/Publications/coconstruct.htm>.

Schwienhorst, K. (1998b). The 'third place': Virtual reality applications for second language learning. *ReCALL 10*, 1, 118–126. URL:
<http://www.tcd.ie/CLCS/assistants/kschwien/Publications/eurocall97.htm>.

Weininger, M.J. & Shield, L. (1998). *Collaborative MOO project for distance language learning*, URL <http://halley.yadata.com.br/schMOOze/MA/about.htm>.

7

Interactive Web-Based Language Learning: The State of the Art

Douglas G. Mills
University of Illinois,
Urbana-Champaign, USA

Introduction

The World Wide Web continues to explode, not only in terms of the numbers of users, registered domains and web pages available, but also in terms of web-based technologies. In the nine and a half months between 18 December 1997 and 1 October 1998, the World Wide Web Consortium (W3C), the group that develops and promotes standard protocols for web-based applications, approved eight specifications for industry-wide adoption (Berners-Lee 1998). Of these, five hold clear potential for use in web-based interactive language learning applications, and of these, two are completely new technologies on the Web: Extensible Markup Language (XML) and Synchronized Multimedia Integration Language (SMIL – pronounced 'smile'). In terms of the available tools for implementing interactive language-learning activities on the Web, the landscape is continually changing.

This constant development should encourage those developing web sites for language learners. In a personal conversation in March 1998, a seasoned CALL veteran summed up her view of the current state of interactivity in web-based language learning by comparing it to the early days of CALL: ' ... so now we can do stupid things again'. This viewpoint was echoed by at least one keynote speaker at the first WorldCALL conference (Davies 1998). While it is true that working with web-based interactivity currently entails a step backward in programming sophistication, it also entails large steps forward in universal accessibility, cross-platform compatibility and authentic materials availability. Added to this is the expectation that what cannot be done via the Web today may soon be possible as new technologies emerge and develop. This chapter will present a sampling of current approaches to interactive language learning on the Web, examine the relative potential and limitations of current and emerging tools for Web-based interactivity, and suggest possible directions for further exploration.

In this chapter, 'interactivity' will be defined as the programmed ability to allow user input and provide appropriate responses to that input. In addition, only pages designed explicitly as language learning tools will be examined as opposed to other interactive web pages that could be used as input for communicative tasks (see Mills 1998a for a simple example of this latter possibility). The potential of the following technologies will be explored roughly in the order of the frequency of their use for language learning: established technologies – Common Gateway Interfaces (CGIs) and JavaScript; less commonly used technologies – Java and Shockwave; minimally used technology – Dynamic HyperText Markup Language (DHTML); and emerging technology – XML.

Established technologies

CGIs

Certainly the most widely established interactive technologies on the Web for language learning purposes are Common Gateway Interfaces (CGIs) and JavaScript. CGI programs can be written in many different programming languages: Perl, C++, AppleScript, and others. What defines a particular software program as a CGI is its function. CGIs add functionality to web server software by receiving data from the server software, processing it in some way, and then passing the results back to the server software. In some cases, the CGI merely serves as a bridge between the server software and other software running on the server (e.g. database, email program, spreadsheet, etc.) to pass data back and forth; in other cases, the CGI itself processes the input and passes it back to the server software to be served to the browser (visitor counters are a well-known example of this type of interaction).

In contrast to most other interactive technologies, CGIs run on the server and so are independent of the browser software or computer the learner is using. This makes CGIs currently the most reliable technology for making interactive resources available to the broadest possible range of learners. In the world of online ESL resources, for example, perhaps none is so well known as *Dave's ESL Café* (Sperling 1995). This site makes extensive use of CGIs for a number of purposes, for example as a means of providing feedback to responses in language learning exercises. There are more efficient technologies for simply providing feedback, as will be noted below, but for a web site like the *ESL Café* with its broad appeal, the use of CGIs makes good sense – very few users will be excluded from the site on the basis of the browser or type of computer that they use.

Also, because CGIs run on the server, they are able to use, create and modify files on the server itself. One familiar example of this on the Web is the 'guestbook' type of application where visitors to a web site enter comments which then appear on a page at that site. The CGI processes the information submitted and appends it to an HTML file on the server. Of greater interest for language learning is the use of this capability for accessing large amounts of data stored on the server or for collecting data. One example of CGIs providing access to large amounts of data is from the University of Chicago *ARTFL* project and consists of a simple interface where a learner can type in any French verb, choose a tense and click on a button to see the verb conjugated for all persons in that tense (Olsen, no date). The University of Texas at Austin relies on CGIs for a similar purpose in the extensive set of grammar exercises that it offers as part of its web-based materials for first-year French (Blyth et al. 1997).

On the data collection side, the pen pal portion of the University of Illinois' *ExChange* project uses a database made accessible on the Web by a CGI to allow learners from around the world to register themselves for an email pen pal exchange and to search for pen pals with similar interests (Stegemoller et al. 1996). Similarly, Volker Hegelheimer (1998) used a web-accessible database to collect data for his research into enriched web-based reading environments. Although neither of these examples fit completely the definition of interactivity given above, it is not difficult to imagine using a web-accessible database to collect information about learners for analysis as they work and then provide exercises, item types, or error feedback more closely suited to their needs (Godwin-Jones 1998).

But CGIs also have limitations. Being server-based is an asset, but it is also a liability. First, using a CGI requires access to the server. For the developer this means dealing with often restrictive CGI policies intended to safeguard the security of the server. For learners this means the necessity of working online as opposed to the off-line interactive potential of JavaScript, for example. Furthermore, because CGIs run on the server, they must be scripted in a language compatible with the server platform and cannot automatically be ported from one server to another (though there are many varieties of Perl, for example, and Perl scripts can usually be adapted to run on other server platforms). Finally, because they are server-based, any inter-activity requires additional network traffic between the browser and the server. For example, when a learner fills in a quiz that relies on a CGI for feedback and then clicks to check the answers, the browser sends the answers to the server for evaluation by the CGI and then waits for the response from the server. This can be a slow and frustrating process.

In spite of these limitations, CGIs are good for providing web-based inter-activity when near-universal compatibility is an issue or when there is a need for data collection or file manipulation on the server. In addition, because they were the first widespread interactive technology available on the Web, there are many archives of ready-made CGIs available on the Internet and it is at least sometimes possible to find one that does what is needed and is compatible with the server platform in use.

JavaScript

According to Netscape, in April 1998 'more than 3.5 million Web pages included JavaScript' (Netscape Press Release 1998 – many of these would be rather trivial uses), and it is becoming more commonly used for interactive language learning as well. One factor in JavaScript's widespread and growing use is undoubtedly its accessibility to non-programmers. JavaScript is probably the easiest interactive technology to learn and use and, like CGIs, there are many helpful resources on the Web for learning JavaScript and archives of scripts available for use. Other strengths of JavaScript are based on the fact that, in contrast to CGIs, it runs on the client computer and so does not require special access to the server to make pages interactive. It works the same regardless of the server software or platform, and is not slowed down by network traffic once the web page is loaded on the client computer. In fact, JavaScript applications can be run without access to a network connection, off a disk for example. In addition, JavaScript can do some things that other interactive technologies cannot do, such as embedding user environment information directly in a web page, and can complement other interactive technologies, such as providing environment information to Java applets or preprocessing forms for CGIs.

These strengths make JavaScript ideal for providing fast error correction and feedback functions and, indeed, many language-learning sites have moved in this direction. One example of such a use is a practice exercise developed for advanced ESL learners in need of a verb form spelling review. Here the learners type short answers and then click a button for instant feedback as to which answers are correct and which are not. There is a link to a set of verb form spelling rules for review if needed, and learners who are really stuck can click a button to see all the answers (Salzmann & Mills 1997).

Another use of JavaScript in language learning is to provide vocabulary glosses. *The Bonjour de France* site features exercises where learners can move the cursor over certain linked vocabulary items in a reading text to see a gloss in a separate window (e.g. Pellerin 1998). For a one-window approach to the same feature, see Mills (1997) where the glosses appear in a text box on the same page. With longer texts it might be preferable to put the gloss in the status bar of the window, in a text box in a separate frame, or to use DHTML to pop up a new layer in the same window and make it disappear again (see below for more on DHTML).

Another functionality of JavaScript that has been used for language learning is its ability to swap and map images in a web page. In one portion of a very creative lesson on Spanish clothing vocabulary, Marlene Johnshoy capitalises on these abilities to allow learners to select a type of clothing they would like to learn vocabulary for and the image on the page is swapped to correspond to the learner's selection. Then the learner clicks on the various articles of clothing on the model to find out what they are called in Spanish. The image of the model is mapped using JavaScript so that the corresponding Spanish word is put into a text box (Johnshoy 1997). Another interesting page making use of these same image manipulation features uses a still life by Picasso to help learners learn the names of colours in Spanish (de Arana, no date). JavaScript is also useful in allowing control of and interaction with other multimedia resources, including QuickTime Virtual Reality (Duber 1998).

JavaScript is used frequently to control multiple frames simultaneously and can also provide random numbers. Both of these features can be seen in an online simulation project from the University of Illinois. *Imagination Voyages* provides ESL learners the information they need to work together and make decisions regarding a trip they are planning to the Grand Canyon. JavaScript controls multiple frames, provides random numbers as input for the simulation and keeps track of learner decisions and their status in the simulation; for example, how many days are still available to them and how much money they have left (Mills, in progress).

Of course, JavaScript also has limitations. JavaScript cannot send information from the browser to the server, so it cannot store results or student records on the server without help from a CGI, Java or email. Furthermore, because JavaScript is generally embedded directly into the HTML for a web page, it is not as secure as other technologies where source code is compiled and unreadable to most users. There are ways to work around this to protect sensitive data (the answers to a quiz, for example) by using .JS source files or browser cookies, but neither method is probably completely secure. In addition, JavaScript is not as powerful as CGIs or Java.

The greatest limitation of JavaScript, however, has been its extreme browser dependence: from the introduction of JavaScript in Netscape Navigator 2.0, each major release of Netscape's browser has supported a higher level of JavaScript, but often earlier versions would freeze if they encountered features implemented in later versions. Even though there are ways of avoiding this, the interactive page developer is faced with the decision of which level of JavaScript to write to (and consequently, which browser versions to exclude from interactivity on the page). And that is without Microsoft Internet Explorer's implementation, JScript, in the picture. JavaScript, unfortunately, has suffered from the browser battles and has been implemented somewhat differently between the two major browsers as they have sought to differentiate themselves (for more details on this, see Mills & Lindeman 1998:247–250). Fortunately a standard scripting protocol has been developed and approved by the European Computer Manufacturers Association (ECMA) and is now supported by current Netscape and Microsoft browsers. ECMAscript, as it is called, is 'based on several originating technologies, the most well-known being JavaScript (Netscape Communications) and JScript (Microsoft Corporation)' (European Computer Manufacturers Association 1998).

Of course, most browsers still in use do not fully support ECMAscript (support begins with Internet Explorer 4 and Netscape Navigator 4.5), so it will still be some time before a script can be written with confidence that it will execute properly and predictably on all major browsers in use. This fact leads to the conclusion that, currently and for some time into the future, it is important to know which browser(s) your primary intended audience uses in order to be able to write JavaScript or ECMAscript to the levels supported by their software. This is not a big problem when writing primarily for use by students in the laboratory, or across campus; it becomes more difficult if the primary targeted audience is learners from all over the world and this would be one reason to consider CGIs for interactivity.

If the developer is prepared to take into account the range of browsers the target audience uses, or is willing to work with those basic core elements of JavaScript that are supported by the maximum number of browsers and versions in use, JavaScript is a good technology for implementing any type of interactivity where tight security is not critical. When the browsers used by the targeted audience are known, then more advanced browser-specific features of JavaScript can be taken advantage of. For example, JavaScript 1.2 as implemented by Navigator 4+ supports a 'getSelection()' function which allows access to any text in a web document which has been highlighted by the learner. Such a function can be used to perform automatic online dictionary lookups of learner-selected words and phrases from any online text, given a creative implementation (Mills 1998b). Hopefully ECMAscript, which is very similar to

Netscape's JavaScript 1.1 with added support for Unicode (Hanrahan, no date), will continue to incorporate the best of the two browsers' idiosyncratic features so that an increasing number of them are supported by both browsers.

Less commonly used technologies

Java

Less commonly used than CGIs or JavaScript in web pages for language learners are Java and Shockwave. Java, Sun Microsystem's cross-platform programming language, is much more powerful than JavaScript, but also much less accessible to the non-programmer. This probably accounts for the slow rate at which it has found its way into language learning sites. With a growing number of increasingly user-friendly visually oriented Java editors, however, it will probably become more a part of the language learning scene on the Web over the next couple of years. Though it is more powerful than JavaScript, it shares in many of JavaScript's strengths since Java is also executed on the client computer after being downloaded from the server (see above). In addition, the Java technology has to a large degree minimised (though not yet completely eliminated) cross-browser and cross-platform compatibility problems.

Examples of Java in current use for interactive language learning on the Web include *Jonathan Revusky's Interactive English Grammar Pages* (Revusky 1997), where Java is used to create a traditional type of CALL interface to allow practice with English infinitives and gerunds through translation from a choice of Spanish or French sentences. Vocabulary help and hints are available as well as the ability to request the correct answer. The interface is not flashy, but it is functional. The same exercise could probably be done in JavaScript with the advantage that in JavaScript it would load faster under adverse network conditions and with the disadvantage that the Java version is more easily compatible with a broader range of browsers.

From the Helsinki University of Technology, there is an interesting project entitled the *Xercise Engine* developed by students under the oversight of Ruth Vilmi (1997). The *Xercise Engine* has the ability to create and run four types of online exercises: multiple choice, fill in the blank, matching and hangman. Again, this is fairly traditional CALL fare, but the *Xercise Engine* team also advocate and demonstrate the use of the various exercise types as part of an ongoing 'adventure' where the learner reads part of a story and then has to finish an exercise before being able to continue on with the story. More significantly though, the creators have incorporated centralised record keeping into the exercises that teachers can access to get an idea of how learners have used the materials and how well they have done with them. This online record-keeping is one of the areas where Java begins to distinguish itself from JavaScript.

Unfortunately, it is generally recognized that Java is not yet a fully mature programming language and experience bears out the fact that it is not without occasional inconsistencies in its performance. Indeed, few of the Java resources for language learning investigated for this study have proven to be 100% reliable, although all have worked at least part of the time. While Java has great potential for empowering language learning, any implementations done in Java should certainly be tested carefully to help identify and avoid (or at least anticipate and warn about) the inconsistencies that seem to come with this technology.

As Java matures and becomes more reliable, more robust error analysis, learner record-keeping and tailored feedback options should be possible. Of course, as the complexity grows, so does the download time necessary before the Java applet can start running. At the same time, the future also holds promise for increased network bandwidth so that larger files will download more quickly. Meanwhile, perhaps a good niche for Java that it does not yet seem to be filling would be in providing small, focused tools or templates to interactively guide learners in their use of authentic materials on the Web. Although not used to guide learner interaction with authentic materials, one very nicely focused example of Java for language learning (and one that has worked consistently) can be found at Robert Beard's (1996) pages illustrating various tenses and aspects of Russian verbs of motion. In the particular example cited here, Java is used to animate a group of people moving through a crowd in various ways. As they pass through, two people in the crowd have a dialogue (speech balloons with Russian text alternate above the two speakers' heads). Their use of the verbs of motion reflect the real-time progress of the group of people making their way through the crowd. Though this use is not 'interactive' as defined above, it is an excellent example of a relatively simple, focused use of Java to do one thing and do it well on a language learning web page.

Shockwave
Shockwave is a browser plug-in from MacroMedia which brings the power of the Director or Authorware authoring systems to the Web, and it is growing in popularity for use in language learning. The proprietary nature of the Shockwave plug-in, the steep learning curve associated with both Director and Authorware, and perhaps the cost of the authoring packages, are among the major disadvantages of this approach to web-based interactivity, but the plug-in is now being distributed automatically with Windows 95 and 98, Apple OS 8, Netscape Communicator 4, Internet Explorer 4 and the America

Online Browser (Macromedia 1998), so the need to download a third-party plug-in is no longer much of an obstacle. Using Shockwave makes especially good sense when there are existing materials or expertise in one of the authoring systems it supports, and although the download time of complex interactive multimedia material can be slow, as with Java, streaming is now available so that the application can begin working while the rest of the program finishes downloading.

Certainly one of the first sites to incorporate Shockwave into language learning materials was the *Cutting Edge CALL Demos* site of Jim Duber (1996). His site is experimental in nature and not really a full-blown language learning resource, but it deserves mention for the pioneering work with this technology in particular. Here there are Shockwave grammar and listening practice exercises; 'interactive animations' for preposition practice where learners follow directions to move an object in the window to its correct location according to their understanding of the preposition used; and some micro-listening discrimination activities focusing on the difference between minimal pairs such as 'the store's open' versus 'this door's open'.

Many of the Shockwave sites for language learning use it primarily to present animation, for example showing how to write Urdu script (Hisam 1996), or audio, for example introducing basic Japanese vocabulary (Sato et al. 1997). Some, like Duber (1996), use it to provide interactivity as well. Among these latter, Okanagan University College in British Columbia, Canada, has made prolific use of Shockwave to provide interactivity in their various online ESL resources. They offer a nice set of pronunciation resources including multi-item minimal pair practice and drill opportunities, tongue twisters, and interactive dictation exercises (Rhodes 1998). In addition, they use Shockwave in very impressive interactive multimedia TOEFL and TOEIC preparation materials and to deliver audio in a serialised listening/reading comprehension story called 'Takako's Great Adventure' (Rhodes 1997).

Although there are plug-ins available for other authoring systems, such as SuperCard and HyperCard, little or no work seems to have been done with these programs for language learning on the Web. At this point, Shockwave is by far the most common plug-in technology for language learning applications and, although Shockwave and Java offer similar capabilities (except that Java is able to send information back to the server whereas Shockwave is not), there seems to be more use of Shockwave than Java for language learning. Furthermore, at this point, the Shockwave materials are consistently more impressive and reliable.

Minimally used technology: DHTML

Dynamic HyperText Markup Language (DHTML) has a great deal of pedagogical potential, almost none of which has been exploited to assist language
learners thus far. Like JavaScript, DHTML, which was implemented in version 4 of both the Netscape and Microsoft browsers, has been implemented
differently by Netscape and Microsoft and so has not been as easy to work
with as it might have been. Apart from using a web page design tool such as
Macromedia's Dreamweaver which automatically generates DHTML compatible with user-specified browsers, creating DHTML pages for use with
both major browsers has been challenging. However, with the approval of
ECMAscript and the newly approved Document Object Model (DOM –
approved 1 October 1998 by the W3C – W3C Press Release 1998), this situation should soon be changing for the better. These two components, the
scripting language and the DOM, are at the heart of DHTML: the DOM
defines what objects the scripting language can act upon; the scripting language determines what happens and when. This means that almost any part
of a web page can be changed, moved, hidden or revealed after it has been
loaded without any further interaction with the server (see de Arana 1998 for
a beautiful literary application of this technology). Having core standards for
both the scripting language and the DOM supported by both of the major
browsers will make designing DHTML-based interactivity for language
learning an easier and more rewarding process.

And so, what exactly can DHTML do to enhance language learning? The
only current implementation of DHTML that I am aware of for language
learning has been done by Juan Ramón de Arana in his *Pronombres relativos*
page (1997). This page begins with sentences such as 'Viví con unos amigos
españoles muy simpáticos'. When the small arrow at the beginning of the
sentence is clicked, however, the preposition and relative pronoun 'con
quienes' moves up out of the appropriate place in the original sentence and
moves down to an empty line where the new sentence 'Los amigos españoles
con quienes viví eran muy simpáticos' forms around it – a very nice dynamic representation of adjective clause formation. This is followed by a practice
exercise in which the student clicks on the arrow next to the one of two choices for the form of the relative pronoun for a given sentence and, if the answer
is correct, is rewarded by seeing the relative pronoun drop into its proper
place in the sentence. Though this web page may be somewhat simple, it is
unarguably elegant and effective, especially considering the simple static
alternative in regular HTML.

DHTML could obviously be used to graphically demonstrate and present
practice material on motion-relevant grammatical points such as tense and
aspect, prepositions of direction or verbs of motion. A DHTML solution for
the Russian Verbs of Motion demonstration done in Java as described above

could probably accomplish the same thing with less download time. DHTML could be used for drag and drop word- or sentence-ordering exercises or other types of text manipulation and it could certainly provide a total physical response task as a response to a listening or reading comprehension task. In the 'interactive animation' preposition tasks implemented in Shockwave above, a DHTML solution would require less download time and would not require a plug-in. Of course, these DHTML activities will require that the browsers used support DHTML as implemented in the page, and the new standards will require another generation of browsers before they are fully implemented; so, for the present, it is important to have an idea of the browsers used by the targeted audience and to remain compatible with them. If the targeted audience is too broad, it will probably be necessary to wait for the widespread adoption of the next generation browsers before relying too heavily on DHTML.

Emerging technology: XML
The Extensible Mark-up Language (XML) W3C recommendation was finalised in February 1998 (Berners-Lee 1998) and has not yet appeared in the mainstream of the World Wide Web, but it is already supported to some extent by Microsoft Internet Explorer 4.x and the new 5.0 beta releases (Flynn 1998); likewise, it will be supported by Netscape Navigator 5.0 (Netscape Press Release 1998). The rumblings of expectation as to how XML will revolutionise the Web are building up to a low roar in various technology-related publications. Falling somewhere between Standard Generalised Markup Language (SGML) and HyperText Markup Language (HTML), which is a smaller and more limited subset of SGML, XML promises to provide a lot more power and flexibility to web documents, not to mention greater cross-browser compatibility and a usefulness to web documents beyond the Web itself:

- Authors and providers can design their own document types using XML, instead of being stuck with HTML. Document types can be explicitly tailored to an audience, so the cumbersome fudging that has to take place with HTML to achieve special effects should become a thing of the past: authors and designers will be free to invent their own markup elements.

- Information content can be richer and easier to use, because the hypertext linking abilities of XML are much greater than those of HTML.

- XML can provide more and better facilities for browser presentation and performance; ...

- Information will be more accessible and reusable, because the more flexible markup of XML can be used by any XML software instead of being restricted to specific manufacturers as has become the case with HTML.

• Valid XML files are kosher SGML, so they can be used outside the Web as well, in an SGML environment. (Flynn 1998)

With regard to empowering web-based language learning, one application of immediate potential interest is the ability to provide multiple presentations of the same content in the same document (Bosak 1997; Randall 1997), thereby allowing various learners to access the same material in the manner which best suits their own learning styles or linguistic backgrounds. For example, a reading passage could be marked up in such a way that a gloss of the difficult vocabulary items could be placed in the margin – or not – at the learner's discretion.

XML promises the power to individuals and/or industries to define their own markup tags for use in their profession (Randall 1997); one specialised application of XML that has already emerged is SMIL which allows for synchronisation of multimedia events and some degree of interactivity as well (Bouthilier 1998). There is already a web page entitled *XML for English Teachers* and on this page the author gives the example of creating tags for a reading passage as described above so that the browser will be able to identify target words and their glosses: '<v><w>word or lexical phrase </w><g>gloss</g></v>' (Fernquest 1998) where the opening and closing <v> tags define the unit, the <w> tags define the word or phrase and the <g> tags define the gloss. Then depending on the specific instructions passed to the XML browser by the Document Type Definition (DTD), the gloss could appear or not appear, appear only on demand, or the full text document could serve to output a simple vocabulary list with only the elements within the <v> tags appearing in the list with appropriate formatting.

It is likely that language professionals will be interested in the development of DTDs that would facilitate syntactic, pragmatic, conversational and other relevant types of markups of texts. In addition, language teachers might well be interested in seeing DTDs developed that would provide useful pedagogical handles on texts. The reading example above is one such example, as is perhaps some type of alternative choice options or embedded comprehension, or discussion questions for the creation of contextualised comprehension tasks. Then it might be advantageous to incorporate two or more relevant DTDs: one pedagogical, one linguistic (Flynn 1998) in order to create interactive online tasks of a new variety. Such specialised markup can only lead to greater finesse and efficiency in the design and implementation of interactive language learning tasks on the Web.

Conclusion and resources for further investigation

In this chapter we have taken a quick look at the promise and limitations of six current and emerging web-based interactive technologies, each with its own unique advantages and disadvantages. It should be clear that the choice of which technologies to pursue for the development of interactivity at any given web site is largely a question of the *available resources* (server platform? programming expertise? existing materials?), *target audience* (class using browsers on campus? as many learners as we can reach from all over the world?) and *purpose of the undertaking* (collectiong data? security?). Beyond these considerations, available and new tools should be considered. For example, a new development application to simplify the creation of XML documents, a new plug-in for a familiar authoring application, as well as any new technologies that are being standardised that might be useful.

Of course, it may well be that the ideal solution for a given need will be a combination of two or more of these technologies. Although this brief survey has looked at each one independently, clearly for many purposes they can be used profitably to complement one another. For example, in Volker Hegelheimer's research project, JavaScript was used to control the media (frames, audio and pop-up windows for glosses) and collect the data into hidden HTML form fields at the browser level, and then, when a user had completed a task and pushed the submit button, a CGI running on the server collected the data and stored it in a database (Hegelheimer 1998). It is hoped that this brief survey of the current and some of the emerging interactive technologies will serve to enable better decisions to be made on web page development. Also to that end, a list of relevant resources for further exploration of these and related topics has been made available online at <http://iei.lang.uiuc.edu/~dmills/WorldCALL/resources.html>.

References

Note: this list of references is also available online with clickable hyperlinks at <http://iei.lang.uiuc.edu/~dmills/WorldCALL/refs.html>.

Beard, R. (1996). *Russian Verbs of Motion*. Retrieved November 1998, URL <http://www.departments.bucknell.edu/russian/language/java/vesti.html> [Note: Click on the picture once it has finished loading. The URL for Dr Beard's main page is http://www.departments.bucknell.edu/russian/language/.]

Berners-Lee, T. (1998). *W3C Technical Reports & Publications*. Retrieved November 1998, URL <http://www.w3.org/TR/>

Blyth, C., Kelton, K., Munn, Y., Eubank, E. & Dickerson, G. (1997). *French Grammar Exercises*. Retrieved November 1998, URL <http://www2.sp.utexas.edu/fr/student.qry>

Bosak, J. (1997). *XML, Java, and the Future of the Web*. Web Review. Retrieved July 1998, URL <http://webreview.com/wr/pub/97/12/19/xml/index.html>

Bouthilier, L. (1998). Synchronized Multimedia on the Web: A New W3C Format Is All Smiles. *Web Techniques Magazine*. Retrieved November 1998, URL <http://www.webtechniques.com/features/1998/09/bouthillier/bouthillier.shtml>

Davies, G. (1998, July). *True creativity often starts where language ends*. Paper presented at WorldCALL, Melbourne.

De Arana, J. R. (1997). *Pronombres relativos*. Retrieved November 1998, URL <http://mld.ursinus.edu/~jarana/Ejercicios/Self-Check/relativos1.html>

De Arana, J. R. (1998). *Garcilaso de la Vega – Soneto XXIII*. Retrieved November 1998, URL <http://mld.ursinus.edu/~jarana/Ejercicios/SelfCheck/Garcilaso/xxiii.html# >

De Arana, J. R. (no date). *Color and objects*. Retrieved November 1998, URL <http://mld.ursinus.edu/~jarana/Ejercicios/Self-Check/Adjetivos.html>

Duber, J. (1996). *Cutting edge CALL demos*. URL <http://www-writing.berkeley.edu/chorus/call/cuttingedge.html>

Duber, J. (1998). *My apartment: The game*. Retrieved November 1998, URL <http://www-writing.berkeley.edu/chorus/call/cuttingedge/thegame/index.html

European Computer Manufacturers Association (1998). *Standard ECMA-262: ECMAScript Language Specification* (2nd ed.). Retrieved November 1998, URL <http://www.ecma.ch/stand/ecma-262.htm>

Fernquest, J. (1998). *XML for English teachers*. Retrieved November 1998, URL <http://www.geocities.com/SoHo/Square/3472/eslxml1.html>

Flynn, P. (1998). *Frequently asked questions about the Extensible Markup Language: The XML FAQ*. Retrieved November 1998, URL <http://www.ucc.ie/xml/>

Godwin-Jones, R. (1998). CGI: *Server-based Interactivity*. Retrieved November 1998, URL <http://www.fln.vcu.edu/cgi/4.html>

Hanrahan, S. (no date). *Item: JavaScript is dead ... long live the ECMA Scripting Language?* Retrieved November 1998, URL <http://www.sjhdesign.com/scrptwrx/obsrvr2.htm >

Hegelheimer, V. (1998). *Effects of textual glosses and sentence-level audio glosses on reading comprehension and vocabulary recall*. Unpublished doctoral dissertation. Department of Educational Psychology, College of Education, University of Illinois, Urbana, IL.

Hisam, A. (1996). *Urdu Quaida*. Retrieved November 1998, URL <http://www.pak-data.com/alif/quaida.htm>

Johnshoy, M. (1997). *La Ropa: Vocabulario*. Retrieved November 1998, URL <http://LanguageCenter.cla.umn.edu/lc/staff/marlene/final/vocab.htm>

Macromedia, Inc. (1998). *Macromedia Shockwave – Partners*. Retrieved November 1998, URL <http://www.macromedia.com/shockwave/productinfo/partners/>

Mills, D. & Lindeman, M. (1998). Beyond scrolling status bars: JavaScript for language learning. In P. Liddell (Ed.) *FLEAT III Foreign Language Education and Technology: Proceedings of the Third Conference* (pp. 243–54). Winnipeg: Printcrafters, Inc.

Mills, D. (1998a). *Greedy!* Retrieved November 1998,
URL <http://www.staff.uiuc.edu/~dmills/greedy.html> [note: requires Netscape Communicator 4 or better]

Mills, D. (1998b). *JavaScript Lookup.* Retrieved November 1998,
URL <http://deil.lang.uiuc.edu/JS4LL/experimental/JSLookup/>

Mills, D. (1997). *onMouseOver Gloss Template.* Retrieved November 1998,
URL <http://deil.lang.uiuc.edu/JS4LL/templates/MouseOverGloss.html>

Mills, D. (in progress). Imagination Voyages. Retrieved November 1998,
URL <http://deil.lang.uiuc.edu/travelsim/>

Netscape Press Release (1998). Netscape rallies content community around leading web development technologies of today and tomorrow – JavaScript, XML and RDF. Retrieved November 1998, URL
<http://www.netscape.com/newsref/pr/newsrelease599.html?cp=nws04flh2>

Olsen, M. (no date). *Verb conjugation.* Retrieved November 1998,
URL<http://humanities.uchicago.edu/forms_unrest/inflect.query.html>

Pellerin, V. (1998). *Légende bretonne. BonJour de France: le Français à votre portée.* Retrieved January 1999, URL
<http://www.bonjourdefrance.com/n1/qcm/a52t.htm >

Randall, N. (1997). XML: A second chance for Web markup. *PC Magazine,*
URL <http://www.zdnet.com/devhead/stories/articles/0,4413,1600301,00.html> accesed November 1998.

Revusky, J. (1997). *Jonathan Revusky's Interactive English Grammar Pages.* Retrieved November 1998, URL <http://web.jet.es/jrevusky/esl.html>

Rhodes, B. (1998). *English pronunciation.* Retrieved November 1998, URL
<http://www.faceweb.okanagan.bc.ca/pron/>

Rhodes, B. (1997). *Faculty of Adult and Continuing Education.* Retrieved November 1998, URL <http://www.faceweb.okanagan.bc.ca/f>

Salzmann, A. & Mills, D. (1997). *Verb Form spelling mini-quizzes.* Retrieved November 1998,
URL <http://deil.lang.uiuc.edu/class.pages/structure1/mini_quiz1a.html>

Sato, Y., Sato M., Takahashi, H. & Takahashi, M. (1997). *Nihongo Paku Paku.* Retrieved November 1998, URL <http://www.twics.com/~ysdrunka/>

Sperling, D. (1998). *Dave's ESL Café.* Retrieved November 1998,
URL <http://www.pacificnet.net/~sperling/eslcafe.html>

Stegemoller, W. J., Ahn, J., Choi, H. Tracewell, J. & Vedrashko, Y. (current Eds) (1996). *ExChange.* Retrieved November 1998,
URL <http://deil.lang.uiuc.edu/ExChange/>

Vilmi, R. (1997). *Xercise Engine.* Retrieved November 1998,
URL <http://law.cs.hut.fi/XE/>

W3C Press Release (1998). *The World Wide Web Consortium Issues DOM Level 1 as a W3C Recommendation: Interoperability for Dynamic Web Pages and XML Applications.* Retrieved November 1998,
URL <http://www.w3.org/Press/1998/DOM-REC>

8

CALL and the Development of Learner Autonomy

Françoise Blin
Dublin City University, Ireland

Introduction

The implementation of CALL (Computer-Assisted Language Learning) and TELL (Technology-Enhanced Language Learning) in the foreign language curriculum in third-level institutions generally derives from our views and beliefs on education, the role of technology in education, the language teaching and learning process, and language itself. The integration of these beliefs with practical considerations (such as local resources, staff expertise, socio-cultural background of both teacher and learners, educational policy of the institution concerned, etc.) leads to the establishment of language learning environments.

In many cases, learner autonomy – or at least one of its multiple representations – is the driving force behind the design and implementation of language learning environments which rely on the use of technology. But what is the relationship between CALL/TELL and learner autonomy? Can we identify whether, and to what extent, CALL/TELL contributes to the way in which learners move towards learner autonomy? Do learners need to be well engaged on the road towards autonomy before they can benefit from CALL/TELL and become autonomous users of the target language? At a time when the CALL community is searching for new research paradigms (see

Chapelle 1997; Garrett 1998), there is no simple answer to these questions and this chapter does not pretend to offer a definitive answer. Rather, its purpose is to briefly explore some of the issues at stake and to show how a learning environment has been designed to allow for both research and learning to inform each other.

Towards a definition of learner autonomy

The literature offers many representations of the concept of autonomy and its applications in foreign language education (see Blin 1998). One of these representations is often equated with the notion of learner independence or, to quote Brookfield (1986:56), with 'methodological expertise'. Learners will be *independent* to the extent that they will be capable of working on their own without help or direction from the teacher or tutor. Little (1996:23) defines autonomy as 'a capacity for self-direction'. According to him, 'this capacity is exercised in the planning, monitoring and evaluation of learning activities, and necessarily embraces both the content and the process of learning. Learners take their first step towards autonomy when they consciously accept responsibility for their own learning; and they develop their autonomy through a continuous effort to understand what they are learning, why, how, and with what degree of success'. Brookfield, however, argues that:

> It is quite possible to exhibit the methodological attributes of self-directed learning in terms of designing and executing learning projects but to do so within a framework of narrow and unchallenged assumptions, expectations, and goals (Brookfield 1986:57).

According to him, 'the most fully adult form of self-directed learning ... is one in which critical reflection on the contingent aspects of reality, the exploration of alternative perspectives and meaning systems, and the alteration of personal and social circumstances are all present' (1986:59). A broader definition of the concept of autonomy is therefore required. Autonomy also encompasses the concept of self-government which is 'the administration by a people or state of its own affairs without external direction or interference' (The Shorter Oxford English Dictionary). The development of learner autonomy involves more than the development of individual independence in relation to the setting of objectives and to ways of attaining these. It also involves the development of *interdependence* through which a group of learners and teacher will collaboratively take responsibility for and control of their learning/teaching environment.

Therefore, learner autonomy is here defined as an educational goal that can be promoted by an approach to education that will help learners to move from dependency – through counter-dependence – to independence and interdependence (Boud 1988). Autonomy is not restricted to an individualistic interpretation0 but it encompasses both individual and social features of notions such as control over events and responsibility over the learning process and outcome. The development of learner autonomy aims at enhancing the construction of knowledge and skills by learners as well as their creative potential, while acknowledging that not all students will demonstrate the same level of autonomy at any given time (Ellis 1994).

Such perspectives on the relationship between learner independence and interdependence on one hand, and between construction of knowledge and social interaction on the other would call for a discussion on constructivist theories of learning and instruction derived from the seminal works of Piaget (see Xypass 1997) and Vygotsky (1978). Such a discussion would, however, go far beyond the scope of this chapter. Running the risk to oversimplify a complex debate, we will suggest that both view collaboration as necessary for learning to take place, albeit for different reasons. For Piaget, it is through cooperation that children are able to verify the rules individually discovered while acting on objects within a rich educational environment. Furthermore, the concept of self-government in schools is central to his vision of education in general and of the development of 'moral' education in particular.

If 'Piaget has shown that cooperation provides the basis for the development of a child's moral judgement' Vygotsky (1978:90) argues that this can be applied to children's learning processes:

> We propose that an essential feature of learning is that it creates the zone of proximal development; that is, learning awakens a variety of internal developmental processes that are able to operate only when the child is interacting with people in his environment and in cooperation with his peers. Once these processes are internalised, they become part of the child's independent developmental achievement. (Vygotsky 1978:90)

Even though Vygotsky was primarily concerned with children, the Zone of Proximal Development, defined as 'the distance between the actual developmental level as determined by independent problem solving and the level of potential development as determined through problem solving under adult guidance or in collaboration with more capable peers' (1978:86), could be of significant importance for the development of autonomous language use and for the development of learner autonomy/independence (see Little & Brammerts 1996).

CALL and learner autonomy

If many representations of learner autonomy can be found in the literature, so can many claims about the role of Information and Communication

Technologies in relation to its development. Computers are said to offer ways of promoting learner independence and interdependence while facilitating the construction of knowledge about the target language and enhancing the development of language skills (see Wolff 1997, 1998). CALL is said to promote certain aspects of learner autonomy such as learning at one's own pace, freedom to choose materials and one's pedagogical path, and this argument has often been used to justify the establishment of self-access language centres.

Describing the potential of desktop-based Virtual Reality to support tandem learning, 'where two people with different native languages work together in pairs' (Brammerts 1996:10), Schwienhorst (1998:125) argues that 'multi-user VR can support firstly the development of the autonomous language user, because of the wealth of interactivity with the environment and the wealth of interaction with native speakers, and secondly the development of the autonomous language learner, because of their own production of meaningful learning material and the permanence and visibility of the written medium'.

However, in the same article Schwienhorst (1998:119) reminds us of the two principles on which tandem learning is based: reciprocity and learner autonomy. 'Reciprocity implies that both learners use both languages in equal amounts and support each other equally in the language learning process ... Learner autonomy insists on the responsibility for their own but also their partner's learning.' Learner autonomy, according to Little, is even a necessary condition if tandem learning is to be successful:

> Unless they are given a great deal of guidance and support, learners who have not already achieved a significant degree of autonomy are likely to find tandem-learning difficult to cope with and almost impossible to sustain (Little 1996:28).

One conclusion that could be derived from this one example is that some applications of Information and Communication Technology in language learning promote the development of learner autonomy, *provided* that learners are already significantly autonomous. Consequently, learner training is often seen as playing a decisive role. The literature offers a wide range of prescriptive measures whose purpose is to ensure that learners become self-directed (albeit the inherent danger stressed by Brookfield and recalled in the previous section). Advice is given on how to guide and support students, principles are derived in relation to self-instructional materials design. However, few studies, if any, give a thorough description of what learners *do* when they are in the process of becoming autonomous language learners, and fewer still give a detailed description of the development of learner autonomy in an environment supported by technology. Yet examples of the potential contribution of technology to the development or promotion of learner autonomy abound.

What seems to be missing here is yet another research paradigm. Chapelle (1997:21) argues that 'what is needed … is a perspective on CALL which provides appropriate empirical research methods for investigating the critical questions about how CALL can be used to improve instructed SLA'. I would further argue that what is also needed is a perspective on CALL which provides appropriate empirical research methods for investigating the critical questions about which type of CALL-supported environments will foster the development of learner autonomy for which type of learner (in terms of autonomy).

Despite the limitations of efficacy research as shown by Garrett (1998), the efficacy of CALL is still often questioned and examined in terms of control and interaction, both central to our conception of learner autonomy. If interaction and/or interactivity may often be reduced to the narrow interpretation of learner-computer interaction, Crookall, Coleman and Oxford (1992:100) argue that 'the learning environment can be pictured as a network of interactions, only part of which is that between the learner and the computer'. The increasing possibilities offered by telecommunication technologies have reinforced the importance of learner–learner and/or teacher–learner interaction in technology-supported language learning environments. Examining the potential relationship between different interactionist traditions (input, output and sociocultural perspectives) and computer-mediated communication, Warschauer (1998) concludes that 'computer-mediated interaction appears to have a promising potential that deserves more study'. Along the same lines, Chapelle (1997:27) emphasises the 'need for descriptive research documenting the nature of the interaction (learner–learner or computer–learner) that learners engage in within various CALL contexts'. Whereas she mainly focuses on the input–output perspective, Lamy and Goodfellow (1999:45) prefer to apply the social-interactionist view 'which offers an additional perspective to the input-output view … , and because it is also concerned with control in the interaction, it is relevant to our intention to consider the role in online learning of reflection and learner autonomy'.

However, the idea of control in relation to learner autonomy encompasses more than control in the interaction. Also, in relation to CALL in general, 'a fundamentally important difference exists between control over what comes up on the screen and control over the social situation in which one is learning' (Crookall, Coleman & Oxford 1992:99). According to these authors,

> … the learning potential in such areas as oral communication and social interaction skills would seem (intuitively) to be highest in the [Computer Assisted Environments] where the learners, rather than the

computer, have control over events, where inter-learner, rather than computer-learner, interaction predominates, where the main objective is involvement with the social dimensions of situations, and where language is seen as a tool for meaningful communication among humans (Crookall et al. 1992:105).

This brings in the issue of the social structure of the learning environment which may therefore influence the way the technology is used. New roles for teachers and learners are emerging, along with different patterns of interaction between them. Comparing the social structure of a classroom and of a computer lab, Schofield (1995) observes a shift both in teacher–student and in student–student interactions and argues that the use of technology in educational contexts transforms the social aspects of the classroom. She also argues, conversely, that the social context in which the technology is used will inform and shape its use. If we accept that control and interaction are core elements of the social structure of the classroom, their exercise within a technology-supported language learning environment needs to be thoroughly examined. It may even be possible to conceive them as defining the relationships between the various elements of the language curriculum designed to promote and foster learner autonomy.

In computerised environments, however, the role attributed to technology is also significant. Levy discusses at length the implications of the tutor and tool roles of the computer on language learning environments. More specifically, Levy (1997:199) argues that, in the case of the computer tutor, 'control is delegated to the computer to manage the learning, and in consequence, students will rely on its judgements'. Later on, he suggests that one strength of the computer tutor is that 'learner characteristics can be accommodated by the mechanisms in the computer program itself and through allowing the student control over pace, content, and learning styles' (1997:205). Furthermore, 'with a tutor, the computer can be relied upon to manage interactions, and, ideally at least, the program will adapt to the student's needs, level, and ability, then present material accordingly' (1997:211). This would suggest that learners have actually very little control over events. Learner autonomy may be restricted to its narrowest sense. The amount of control exercised by students will also depend on the course organisation and overall management. Where the use of CALL packages is prescriptive, it is doubtful that the computer tutor will enhance the development of learner autonomy. In the case of self-directed learning, learners who have not achieved a high degree of autonomy may find it very difficult to select appropriate materials, and to sustain a learning program. Learner training and guidance will have to play a significant role.

In contrast, Levy argues that '... the tool role of the computer is fundamentally non-directive. Tools are neutral, and how they are used is not pre-determined' (1997:181). Also, '... the computer is not managing the interactions ... ; the learner has the responsibility ...' (1997:200) and further on, 'the human is in direct control of the tool' (1997:208). Learners' responsibility and control over events are here emphasised and therefore one may conclude that the computer tool is more likely to promote learner autonomy, given that adequate learner training is essential if the tool is to be used appropriately.

However, the neutrality of the tool deserves to be looked at in more depth. Basing his discussion on Rabardel's (1995) model, Rézeau (1998:8) introduces the notion of instrument where 'the instrument is a dual entity, consisting on the one hand of what [Rabardel] calls the artefact (i.e. the tool) ... and, on the other hand, of the schemata of use developed by the designer as well as by the end-user'. He argues that the schemata of use developed by the learner will influence his/her learning strategies (1998:9). Following Rézeau's argument, we need to be attentive to the fact that the training provided in the use of the computer tool may not have the anticipated effects, depending on the conceptions that the learner will have forged in relation to tool and task. The gap between the intended use of the computer tool by the designer, the anticipated use by the teacher and the actual use by the learner may provide some valuable information on the level of autonomy achieved by both teacher and learner. Conversely, the level of autonomy achieved by learners, along with the opportunity given to them to exercise it, may influence the way they appropriate a tool so that their language learning experience and outcome are enhanced – or not.

This is not far away from Levy's (1997:222) point that 'technology precipitates changes, often in ways that can be difficult to predict' or from Schofield's (1995:226): '... using computers is likely to have unanticipated effects on students, teachers, and classrooms because in adopting the technology one is likely to be accepting, or more probably evolving, an entire set of unplanned changes as well as the planned technological ones'. These changes need to be explored, whether they concern the development of learner autonomy, the exercise of control over the learning environment and the learning strategies or the interactions, or whether it is the language learning process and outcomes that are to be investigated. I would also argue that if the function of the computer, whether tool or tutor, has implications on teachers' roles, the latter, in turn, has implications on the role that will be attributed to the computer. The way both teachers and learners perceive their respective roles will influence, if not shape, the use of technology in language learning environments. From the start, the language curriculum must therefore make explicit to all concerned the parameters that will define the type of control to be exercised by each actor, including the computer.

The next section will describe how a language learning environment supported by technology has been designed in attempt to foster the development of learner autonomy while making it possible to investigate its relationship with CALL.

Learner autonomy and CALL: A case study

In recent years, Dublin City University (DCU) lecturers in all faculties have expressed great concern over the transition from secondary to tertiary education. Spoon-fed and exam-driven students entering their first year in DCU show poor learning skills and generally seem ill prepared for their new learning environment. Also, in response to prospective employers' needs, the acquisition of transferable skills on all programs, and a move towards the development of learner autonomy, have become the focus of many groups and committees at all levels of the institution. Political and socio-economic representations of autonomy are therefore interacting here with educational and psychological representations. The following case study will, however, focus on the latter.

The above concerns have been taken on board by the School of Applied Language and Intercultural Studies (SALIS) which has been carrying out a number of pilot projects since 1993 (see Blin 1998) when the Semi Autonomous Language Learning Unit (SALLU) was established. The primary function of this unit was to support students of other disciplines taking some language modules as part of their program of study (for details of the initial design and implementation, see Blin 1996). Over the years, it has become an essential resource for all students and staff involved in language-related modules. SALLU accommodates multimedia workstations (stand-alone and networked), TV monitors, video recorders, and camcorders. Teaching and learning materials can be borrowed by all registered users, whether staff or students. It was initially set up as a self-access resource centre where students, advised and guided by their lecturers and supported by helpers (foreign and/or post-graduate students), could come and select activities and materials. However, it soon became apparent that the use of these facilities were depending, firstly, on the objectives and teaching methodologies described in the various language syllabi and, secondly, on teachers' attitudes towards learner autonomy and use of ICTs in relation to language learning (see Blin 1997, 1998). In subsequent years, as the provision of computer facilities on campus steadily increased, most students had gained access to state-of-the art equipment in their own faculty or school and to the Internet. Lack of space and resources in SALLU on one hand, and expanding facilities outside the unit on the other, led to consider a possible move towards a 'virtual' language learning resources centre accessible from everywhere, on and off campus, that would complement the existing structure. A revised IT-supported language learning environment, making use of a web-based course delivery system (TopClass®)[1] which integrates both the tutor and tool functions of the computer, was therefore designed. It is currently implemented and evaluated with Science and Engineering students and with students in their first year of the Applied Computational Linguistics program, all of whom take French as an integral part of their program of study. The choice of students was motivated by the fact that only a small number of students were involved: approximately 65 students in the four years of the BSc in Chemistry with French (CF), BSc in Physics with French (PF), BEng in Electronic Systems (ES), and 20 students in the first year of the BSc in Applied Computational Linguistics (ACL). This proved to be a manageable, and yet varied, group of students with whom different pilot modules could be delivered without requiring too demanding a technological infrastructure.

The language curriculum and learner autonomy

The above students are all required to spend a minimum of an academic year in a French university or *Grande Ecole*. This period of residence abroad usually takes place in the third year of the program. In the case of the BEng in Electronic Systems, students are required to spend the second semester of their third year in a French Engineer School. On successful completion of this semester and of a fourth year back in DCU, students are then offered the possibility to spend a further 12 months in their host institution with a view to obtain a dual qualification (Irish MEng and French *Diplôme d'Ingénieurs*). The French component on these programs is designed to prepare students for their year abroad and, in their final year in DCU, to prepare them for a professional or academic career involving the use of the language at an advanced level.

The language curriculum, therefore, adopts strong elements of LSP while aiming at developing learner autonomy and the acquisition of transferable skills. The curriculum is seen here as 'a way of organising what the learners want to do' (Kenny 1993:440). It provides both learners and teachers with a framework which will allow them to exercise autonomy individually, but also as a community of learners (e.g. teachers becoming learners of their students' specialism) who collaborate to carry out a defined task or project. Its ultimate aims are to bring students from teacher-dependence in their first semester to independence and interdependence at the end of their studies, to help them become autonomous language users so that they can function spontaneously and accurately in any situation, professional or otherwise, in which they may find themselves in the future.

Most importantly, however, the first two years of the program aim at enabling students to become autonomous learners with respect to their specialisation as well as the target language. Indeed, it has been shown in recent years that the major difficulty faced by science and engineering students during their period abroad relates to what I call their 'scientific' integration. Scientific education varies greatly between France and Ireland. Students soon find themselves in a situation where access to knowledge and learning become dependent on the acquisition of new computer skills and of different abstract representational systems. Failing to autonomously use different mathematical tools, for example, may result in students being isolated from their native peers, feeling lost and unable to cope with academic demands, and suffering from low self-esteem. Laurillard (1993:27–28) argues that 'in order to mediate knowledge, we must understand how students deal with the means of access to it, i.e. symbolic representations, the written code'. In the case of science students preparing for a period of residence abroad, I would further argue that students themselves need to understand how they deal with the symbolic representations, not only in the target culture but also in their own educational context. Learning physics through French certainly requires the ability to understand oral and written language but also the ability to understand and 'act on descriptions of the world' (Laurillard 1993) through a different set of mathematical representations than those learned in Ireland. Consequently, the objective of the LSP course is to bring students to reflect on the different representations of the same concept, to become aware of the way they themselves deal with these representations, and to develop strategies that would help them to express their difficulties and to interact with French lecturers and peers so that learning can actually take place. In order to achieve this rather ambitious objective, project-based learning was seen as a most promising approach: project work constitutes the core activity for nine out of the eleven French modules offered overall on these degree programs.

Examples of projects carried out by students over the last five years include: conducting, filming and presenting a scientific experiment, setting up a scientific and technological museum, designing (in collaboration with French Telecommunication students) a multimedia learning environment enabling synchronous communication, writing a text book which is to constitute a reference document for the written examination, giving a 'research paper' at a 'students conference', and more recently, designing a web site for French-speaking students wishing to study in Dublin City University.

The curriculum is designed in such a way that control over specific objectives, classroom management, assessment methods and criteria, and teaching and learning strategies are gradually transferred to students, within a framework providing global objectives. For example, while modules in the first year are very much teacher controlled, final year students negotiate the role of the teacher in collaboration with the latter (including timetable, level and nature of teacher intervention, etc.).

First year modules are centred around learner training. In the first semester, an introductory module focuses on the acquisition of language-learning skills and strategies and on the consolidation of language skills learned in secondary education. This is followed in the second semester by a module that emphasises collaborative and project work. During the first semester, students are required to keep a learner diary in the target language. In the second semester, the learner diary is replaced by individual and group reports detailing the various stages of the project, the methodology adopted by the team, the problems encountered and their solutions, the learning outcomes. In parallel, physics and chemistry students attend introductory French for science modules in each semester.

Integration of ICT in the language curriculum
The role attributed to the computer in the case of the introductory module is mainly that of 'tutor'. Students are encouraged to use various CALL packages to improve language skills and to complement what has been done in class. In all other modules, the 'tool' role is predominant. Electronic databases and the Web are extensively used to retrieve and organise information while students produce language in the form of oral and written presentations, web pages and scientific posters, using generic Windows applications. Domain-specific packages, such as *Chime*, *IsisDraw* and Microsoft *Equations*, allow students to produce symbolic expressions and diagrams. In the case of collaborative projects involving French and Irish students, videoconferencing is also used at regular intervals.

More recently, TopClass has been used not only to support the curriculum through the development and web-based distribution of teaching materials and to expand the opportunities for learner–learner and teacher–learner interaction, but also to generate data, through the system tracker, on students strategies and use of the system. Each learner is registered in one or more 'virtual' classrooms corresponding to the modules followed. Among the system features, the discussion lists are the most extensively used. Process-oriented materials have been developed by this author to assist First Year students in their collaborative and project work and in the use of the various packages. These course pages are seen as a complement to both classroom activities and to the tutorials taking place in the networked computer laboratory. In subsequent years, however, content-oriented materials will be generated by students and distributed via the system. So far, test facilities and the possibilities to customise learners' progression through the materials have not been exploited to a large extent, except for the purpose of eliciting information from students through closed and open-ended questionnaires.

As the only requirement for accessing the system is access to the World Wide Web, collaboration between students and teachers located on and off campus has been made possible. Virtual classes have therefore been created, firstly to support cross-cultural projects between France and Ireland and, secondly, to support exchanges between Irish students currently residing in France, students who have returned, and students preparing for their year abroad.

The development of learner autonomy and CALL: Preliminary observations

Given the space limitations, it is impossible to give here a detailed account of the observations and data generated by the overall environment described above. However, some preliminary observations deserve to be reported.

Firstly, regarding the development of learner autonomy, a systematic analysis of learner diaries enabled the construction of a methodology leading to a 'qualitative measurement' of autonomy achieved by learners by the end of their first semester in DCU. Five levels of autonomy have been so far identified which provide a detailed description of what students 'do' at different stages of their move towards autonomy. In relation to the use of the computer-tutor within a curriculum emphasising control over the setting up of objectives, and consequently over the choice of materials and activities, preliminary results would suggest that students, who have otherwise demonstrated the ability to make informed choices regarding the setting up of personal learning objectives and the selection of materials and learning activities, are more likely to make efficient use of CALL materials. However, even those students tend to show a lower level of autonomy regarding the use of CALL in comparison to other materials.

Secondly, unplanned changes in control mechanisms over the learning environment as a whole have been observed. For example, Electronic Systems students involved in a collaborative project with the *Institut National des Télécommunications* (Evry, France) gradually enjoyed an increased control over the technological infrastructure available to them. For the first time, to my knowledge, in the history of the university, undergraduate students have been given administrators' rights on a server, direct access to the Internet (i.e. bypassing the university proxy server), and the authority to monitor a students' discussion list whose access was strictly restricted to them (i.e. no teacher had access to the messages posted on the list). This, in my view, illustrates the process by which a learning environment, initially fostering learner autonomy, leads to a a situation where learners who, through the exercise of their autonomy, become more responsible users of the technology and learn to gain control over the environment. In this case, the increased control given to students unleashed their creativity and resulted in modified learner–learner and teacher–learner interactions that can now be investigated.

Thirdly, if the volume and quality of learner–learner interactions in a CMC environment can be analysed within an interactionist framework as briefly mentioned previously, attention must be given to the effect of the occurrence of such interactions on the development of learner autonomy and consequently on the development of autonomous language use. The discussion list open to students who have the experience of residing and studying abroad proved to be a lively forum. Using the classification of messages elaborated by Lamy and Goodfellow (1999), the messages posted mostly belong to the conversational type. Students engaged in social conversations ranging from the food available in their respective canteens to the forthcoming France–Ireland rugby match. A first examination of these messages, within an interactionist perspective, would suggest, as reported by Lamy and Goodfellow that such exchanges may not be conducive to learning. However, the impact of these 'conversations' on those students who are about to leave Ireland for France suggests otherwise. Students who are attentive passive contributors to the list (i.e. they are reading and reflecting on both content and form of the messages but not necessarily contributing) spontaneously bring their comments to their language class. Students have started to identify cultural aspects of life in France that they may find difficult to adjust to, and gaps between their own use of the target language and that of students abroad. Consequently, they have started to discuss learning objectives and strategies that would help them to benefit from their residence abroad. These objectives and strategies have, then, become the focus of learning tasks carried out individually or in groups.

Conclusion

The previous examples can only illustrate the argument presented here. They do not pretend to constitute a definitive answer to our initial question: What is the relationship between CALL and the development of learner autonomy? They suggest, however, empirical methods for investigating this relationship. Ethnographic and phenomenographic methods and longitudinal studies will be required in order to provide a full description of the context in which instructed language learning is taking place. Only then will we be able to investigate the type of language learning taking place in various types of language learning environments supported by technology.

Notes

[1] TopClass is distributed by WBT Systems, URL <http://www.wbtsystems.com/>.

References

Blin F. (1996). Integrating CALL in the language curriculum: The SALL Project. In B. Ruschoff & D. Wolff (Eds), *Technology-enhanced language learning in theory and practice* (pp. 50–63). Proceedings of Eurocall 94, Pädagogische Hochschule, Karlsruhe, Germany.

Blin F. (1997). CALL and the learner-centred curriculum: What about the teacher? In J. Kohn, B. Rüschoff & D. Wolff (Eds), *New Horizons in CALL, Proceedings of EUROCALL 96*, 119–137. Sombathely.

Blin, F. (1998). Les enjeux d'une formation autonomisante de l'apprenant en environnement multimédia. In T. Chanier & M. Pothier (Eds), *Apprentissage des langues et environnements informatiques hypermédia*. Etudes de Linguistique Appliquée, 111, 215–226.

Boud, D. (1988). Moving towards autonomy. In D. Boud (Ed.), *Developing student autonomy in learning* (2nd ed.) (pp. 17–39). London: Kogan Page.

Brammerts, H. (1996). Tandem language learning via the Internet and the International E-Mail Tandem Network. In D. Little & H. Brammerts (Eds), *A guide to language learning in tandem via the Internet*. CLCS Occasional Paper No. 46, 9–22. Dublin: Trinity College.

Brookfield, S. D. (1986). *Understanding and facilitating adult learning: A comprehensive analysis of principles and effective practices*. Buckingham: Open University Press.

Chapelle, C. (1997). CALL in the Year 2000: Still in search of research paradigms? *Language Learning & Technology 1*, 1, 19–43. URL<http://polyglot.cal.msu.edu//llt/vol1num1/chapelle/default.html> (retrieved on 26 April 1998).

Crookall, D., Coleman, D. W. & Oxford, R. L. (1992). Computer-mediated language learning environments: Prolegomenon to a research framework. *Computer Assisted Language Learning 5*, 1–2, 93–120.

Ellis, G. (1994). Pourquoi l'autonomie? Actes du 2ème colloque sur l'autonomie dans l'apprentissage des langues, *UPLEGESS*, 20–21 janvier 1994, 8–9.

Garrett, N. (1998). Where do research and practice meet? Developing a discipline. In F. Blin & J. Thompson (Eds), Where research and practice meet. Selected papers of EUROCALL 97 Conference, *ReCALL 10*, 1, 7–12, Hull: CTICML in association with EUROCALL.

Kenny, B. (1993). For more autonomy. *System 21*, 431–442.

Lamy, M.-N. & Goodfellow, R. (1999). 'Reflective conversation' in the virtual classroom. *Language Learning Technology 2*, 2, 43–46. URL <http://polyglot.cal.msu.edu/llt/vol2num2/article/index.html> (retrieved on 13 Feb. 1999).

Laurillard, D. (1993). *Rethinking university teaching*. London: Routledge.

Levy, M. (1997). *Computer-assisted language learning: Context and conceptualisation.* Oxford: Oxford University Press.

Little, D. (1996). Learner autonomy and learner counselling. In D. Little & H. Brammerts (Eds), *A guide to language learning in tandem via the Internet.* CLCS Occasional Paper No. 46. (pp. 23–34). Dublin: Trinity College.

Little, D. & Brammerts, H. (Eds) (1996). *A guide to language learning in tandem via the Internet.* CLCS Occasional Paper No. 46. Dublin: Trinity College.

Rabardel, P. (1995). *Les hommes et les technologies, Approche cognitive des instruments contemporains.* Paris: Armand Collin.

Rézeau, J. (1998). The learner, the teacher and the machine: Golden triangle or Bermuda triangle. *TELL & CALL* (CALL Austria Journal), Jan.

Schofield, J. W. (1995). *Computers and classroom culture.* Cambridge: Cambridge University Press.

Schwienhorst, K. (1998). The 'third place': Virtual reality applications for second language learning. In F. Blin & J. Thompson (Eds), Where research and practice meet. Selected papers of EUROCALL 97 Conference, *ReCALL 10*, 1, 118–126. Hull: CTICML in association with EUROCALL.

Vygotsky, L. S. (1978). *Mind in society: The development of higher psychological processes.* M. Cole, V. John-Steiner, S. Scribner, & E. Souberman (Eds & Trans). Cambridge, Mass.: Harvard University Press.

Warschauer, M. (1998). Interaction, negotiation and computer-mediated learning. In V. Darleguy, A. Ding, & M. Svensson (Eds), *Educational technology in language learning: Theoretical considerations and practical applications.* URL <http://www.insa-lyon.fr/Departments/CDRL/interaction.html> (retrieved on 26 April 1998).

Wolff, D. (1997). Computers and new technologies: will they change language learning and teaching? In J. Kohn, B. Rüschoff & D. Wolff (Eds), *New Horizons in CALL, Proceedings of EUROCALL 96*, 65–82. Sombathely.

Wolff, D. (1998). The use of e-mail in foreign language teaching. In V. Darleguy, A. Ding & M. Svensson (Eds), *Les Nouvelles Technologies Educatives dans l'apprentissage des langues vivantes: réflexion théorique et applications pratiques,* Lyon: INSA de Lyon. URL<http://www.insa-lyon.fr/Departements/CDRL/wolff.html/> (retrieved on 26 April 1998).

Xypass, C. (1997). *Piaget et l'éducation.* Paris: Presses Universitaires de France.

9

CALL-ing the Learner into Focus: Towards a Learner-Centred Model

Debra Hoven
University of Queensland, Australia

Introduction

Over the past several years, an increasing number of multimedia language-learning software packages have been developed and marketed while, to date, only preliminary attempts have been made to evaluate the effectiveness of such software in general, or of more specific features within the packages which may or may not contribute to improved learning (Brandl 1995; Liou 1995; Bradin 1996; 1998). Simultaneously, the proliferation of mechanisms for computer-mediated communication has emphasised the notion of the computer as an interlocutor in the communication process. Many administrators, teachers, researchers and users of computers in language learning have asked questions about the effectiveness of computers in the language learning process (Pederson 1987; Luff, Gilbert & Frohlich 1990; Dunkel 1987, 1991; Johnson 1991; Chapelle 1994). However, as Papert (1987) and Chapelle have pointed out, it is not so much the computer but the kinds of tasks and activities that learners do on the computer that can make the difference. As Chapelle comments:

> CALL texts are produced in any language learning context where the computer takes an interactive role. Such contexts may be comprised of learners working individually with a computer, of learners working in

pairs or larger groups with a computer or multiple connected computers, or of learners working with teachers or other experts. In each of
these cases, the participants – one of which is the computer – contribute to an emerging text which is affected by the nature of the context and which both affects and provides evidence for the quality of the
learning experience. (Chapelle 1994:38)

Chapelle draws on Halliday (1977) and Halliday and Hasan (1989) for her
extension of 'context' to include not only 'features of the activities, topics,
participants, and language that comprise the text and in which the text is
embedded' (Chapelle 1994:43), but also features outside of the computer program such as 'learners, their purposes, and the setting of the instruction'. In
addition, she mentions other features which are created by the instructor or
teacher. These include the 'types of CALL materials and the parameters for
using the materials' (1994:43), all of which influence, and are influenced by,
the learning environment.

Jonassen also stresses the point that:

Technologies do not directly mediate learning. That is, people do not
learn from computers, books, videos, or the other devices that were
developed to transmit information. Rather, learning is mediated by
thinking (mental processes). Thinking is activated by instructional
interventions, including technologies. Learning requires thinking by
the learner. In order to more directly affect the process, therefore, we
should concern ourselves less with the design of technologies of transmission and more with how learners are required to think in completing different tasks (Jonassen 1992:2)

These observations set the scene for the framing of learner-centred CALL
design in terms of a sociocultural methodology, by effectively highlighting
the importance of various features of context in creating the texts produced,
the negotiated, mediated, and interactive nature of the creation of these texts,
and the important role learners' cognition and mental processes play in the
language learning process. This incorporation of cognition in the design
model is exemplified by the potential for the learner to make decisions about
the content, mode, order, pace, level, and level of self-direction of the presentation of the package. In addition, it can also be taken to refer to the capacity a software package provides for the learner to interact with, interpret,
negotiate, and make meaning from the texts available, whether these are written, audio or audiovisual.

Features of learner-centredness for CALL

We now turn to a discussion of those features of a learner-centred CALL
model that bring the learner into focus. Given the current state of our

knowledge and research in instructional design, CALL and second language pedagogy, what are the essential characteristics of a model that embodies learner-centredness? The following five principles are proposed as a starting point:

- Sociocultural methodology provides an appropriate paradigm.
- Consideration of the critical features of learner-centredness includes the recognition of features that are less amenable to change, raising of awareness among learners of features somewhat amenable to change, and accommodation of the features more amenable to change.
- Allocation of control to learners needs to be accompanied by awareness-raising in how to manage this control.
- Task-based pedagogy provides a useful framework for the instructional design of the lesson material.
- Consideration of models of good practice from both mainstream second language pedagogy and CALL needs to be incorporated.

A sociocultural paradigm for CALL
Sociocultural methodology seems to be the most appropriate paradigm to use for the framework of the design of a learner-centred CALL model, as it incorporates negotiated, mediated creation of meaning among learners, between learners and teachers, and between learners and computers.

Further, the adoption of a sociocultural approach allows the inclusion of learning strategies in the instructional design and anticipated implementation of the model. As Jonassen (1992:2) stresses, investigating how learners acquire and use thought and mental processes helps to make the learning process more effective. How this can be achieved is best discussed in terms of the four major concepts of sociocultural theory. These are mediation, goal-oriented or situated learning, the Zone of Proximal Development (ZPD), sometimes termed 'apprenticeship learning' (Warshauer 1996), and the 'community of practice' proposed by Donato and McCormick (1994).

Mediation
Mediation, whether physical or symbolic, means the employment of some catalyst which allows connections to be made between humans and their own (internal) mental world, or the (external) physical world. In Vygotskian terms, the most important symbolic tool for this mediation process is language, which can be used to organise, plan and maintain the environment both internal and external to the individual.

Within this paradigm, communication strategies and social strategies, often excluded from language learning strategies by researchers within the interlanguage and psycholinguistic paradigms, can be incorporated as sets of language learning strategies. In other words, communication strategies are used to communicate, while at the same time improving communication. That is, the mediation process of employing communication and social strategies to communicate improves both the communication and the learning.

The level of success of communication can be judged by the learner on the basis of the appropriateness of the response to the learner's expectations. Thus learning is effected through communicative and social strategies since the language and strategies used are modified on the basis of response appropriateness. Unlike cognitive and social psychological theories, in which strategies in language learning are seen to be relatively static and generalisable from tasks and contexts, sociocultural theory focuses on the influence of language tasks and contexts in bringing about the dynamic emergence of strategic approaches in individual learners.

Goal-oriented or situated learning

Within this sociocultural paradigm, education or awareness-raising in the use of more desirable or effective strategies is achieved through the mediation of situated activities that allow learners to model, appropriate and achieve self-mediated processing, rather than by direct instruction. However, as Gillette (1990) reminds us, it is important that strategies implemented in the classroom culture are actually directed towards language learning goals.

Similarly, Donato and McCormick (1994) stress that these strategies are situated in the higher levels of mental processing, which are not uniformly developed. Their 1994 study, in fact, shows that a sociocultural approach encourages a more strategic task orientation, where 'strategic activity is seen as inherently goal embedded' (Stone 1989:36). This reinforces the point made by Gillette above that, because the one strategy may be employed with several (and possibly conflicting) goals in mind, it is important to focus on constructing strategic tasks which provide the context for, and foster the use of, higher level mental processes – the metacognitive and higher cognitive strategies of researchers in other paradigms (O'Malley & Chamot 1990; Victori & Lockhart 1995).

In a CALL context, this implies that in order for a software package or program to foster in learners the development of higher mental processes, it must provide an environment based on making available a range of strategic tasks, while also providing information on the purposes of these tasks, to encourage self-reflection and new strategic orientations in learners' actions. Ideally, learners using such a package should be able to choose their own tasks on the basis of information provided about them, on the basis of their own language learning (and other) goals in using the materials. In other words, the choices they make mediate their interaction with the materials. They should thereby be able to identify for themselves those areas in which they need more practice. This perspective on strategy development would allow learners to take an 'active task approach', identified by Naiman and his colleagues (1978) as one of the characteristics of a good language learner.

The Zone of Proximal Development

Within a sociocultural paradigm, selection of, or access to, progressively more detailed feedback or help within a CALL package can also be framed in terms of the Zone of Proximal Development (ZPD) proposed by Vygotsky (1978). In an interesting study to investigate the role of negative feedback on regulation and second language learning in the ZPD, Aljaafreh and Lantolf (1994:468) identified three characteristics of effective intervention mechanisms. They found that intervention should be *graduated*, *contingent* (offered only when needed), and *dialogic*, or negotiated between the expert and the novice. Thus, the help is offered by a more experienced member of the joint activity, and begins at a highly implicit level. It is subsequently *graduated* down to the level of specificity needed by the novice member.

This help is also *contingent* in that, as the novice becomes more able to function independently, the level of directiveness and specificity in the help is progressively reduced. This progressive assessment of the learner's needs, and tailoring of help to meet them, is only possible through the *dialogic* activity that unfolds between more capable and less capable individuals. Thus, the process of learning as exemplified through the concept of the ZPD can also be described as 'scaffolding', in which, as learners become progressively more adept, the expert or mentor is able to dismantle the scaffolded environment. This is possible because the learners themselves have already internalised the necessary problem-solving processes (Donato 1994:41).

Implications of these findings for feedback in CALL packages are supportive of the notion of self-managed access to the help and feedback facilities, and a 'layered' construction of these features. By this is meant that individual learners (the novices) need to be able to determine when they want to have access to any of a range of help facilities available, and that these facilities are designed as successive layers, the deeper and more extensive or explicit help only being accessible from the layer above. Thus, at the top level, a learner may only need access to whether an answer is correct, or to the meaning of a word, while more comprehensive help such as transcripts or grammar notes may be provided at a deeper level.

The 'community of practice'

As a final note towards the sociocultural framework for the development of a CALL model, it is useful to review the concept of interactivity as employed in this paradigm as the 'community of practice'. In a study by Platt and Brooks (1994), for example, on the validity of the term 'acquisition-rich environment', it was found that the learner's interaction with the language and the dynamic creation process are just as important as the language itself. It is these strategies of interaction with the target language and creation of meaning that enable learners to participate in the target language culture. In their study of on- and off-task language of learners participating in problem-solving tasks, they found that learners were not so much '*in* an acquisition-rich environment' as 'they *created* or *constructed* a context through their *use* of the target language to solve a problem' (1994:504).

For the purposes of an instructional design framework within the socio-cultural paradigm, the concept of learners creating and constructing meaning implies that learner choice and self-management of activity is critical, both in the tasks to be done, and in the navigation through the feedback and help facilities. On another level, since 'learners need opportunities to engage in analogous kinds of problem-solving tasks in order to become better at doing them' (Platt & Brookes 1994:509), it is important to provide several tasks of each kind at each level for learners to use.

Features internal to the learner

Numerous studies have shown that individual learners differ in their approach to language learning in numerous ways, including their preferred channels of perception, the learning processes they activate, their background experience and education, their aptitude and motivation for language learning or learning in general, and their age and level of maturity (Skehan 1989; Larson-Freeman & Long 1991). These differences in turn affect choices made by both learners and their teachers as to which materials, resources, teaching and learning approaches, and forms of interaction are most effective for language learning to proceed.

Broadly speaking, these differences can be classified as being either internal or external to the learner, though there are areas of obvious cross-over such as learning styles where external features of tasks, for example, can influence features of perception which are essentially internal to learners. The extent to which learner choices and differences can be accommodated within a learning environment has a critical influence on the level of success in language learning that individual learners achieve.

Individual differences can be defined as those features or factors within learners which influence differential success in language learning or which can be identified as accounting for such differences. As will be discussed in more detail below, some of these features can be changed, modified or developed through instruction and awareness-raising, whereas others are less amenable to change. Furthermore, in order for learners to take advantage of multiple channels of perception, they need to be aware of their preferred styles of perception, the extent to which the available media correspond to these, and how best to exploit this correspondence.

Features less amenable to change

The aspects of individual difference listed below have been identified in the literature as being unchangeable or less amenable to change (Larson-Freeman & Long 1991; Hoven 1997). The factors or characteristics referred to here are specific to individual learners, and include age and maturity, developmental features, sex, aptitude for language, hemispheric processing orientation, previous language learning experience, and L1 proficiency.

It is necessary for us to be aware of the existence of these factors and the influence they have in order to choose more appropriate materials, or to direct learners to make use of available materials in certain ways. In addition, through education and awareness-raising in a range of learning strategies, it is possible to help learners compensate for less desirable or less effective characteristics which they may have. However, within learning materials themselves, and within a program of instruction or learning, little change can be effected in learners with regard to these features. A learner may, for example, be beyond an age when language learning can easily be achieved through the use of certain techniques, but they can be made aware of, and encouraged to employ, other techniques or strategies which have been shown to be more effective for older learners.

Features somewhat amenable to change

Certain other individual characteristics are discussed in the literature as sometimes or under certain conditions, being amenable to change. These include:

- personality (introversion/extroversion, self-esteem, anxiety, risk-taking, sensitivity to rejection, empathy, inhibition, and tolerance of ambiguity);
- socio-psychological factors (motivation and attitude);
- learning style and cognitive style;
- sense modality preference; and
- sociological preference (preferred level of social interaction – pair/group etc.).

Proposals have been made by teachers and researchers about the desirability of matching teaching style and the nature of classroom interaction with the personality characteristics of individual learners. While it is proposed that such matches will promote learning, little evidence has been provided for any consistency in the findings (Hamayan et al. 1977; Wong-Fillmore 1982).

In addition, personality and aptitude are both features which are relatively difficult to influence or change (Skehan 1989:38–39, 71–72) within a language program. Nevertheless, despite these difficulties, studies of personality and aptitude provide us with valuable information about the range of influencing features in the learning process, and which characteristics might be more desirable in the promotion of learning than others, particularly as they relate to individual learning. This information then enables us to make provision in language-learning programs and materials for the range of characteristics that learners bring to them.

Cognitive styles, learning styles and strategies: Changeable or not?
In order to determine whether, or to what extent, changes can be effected in the cognitive styles, learning styles and learning strategies of learners, it is first necessary to understand what these terms mean. Cognitive style, for example, has been defined as:

> ... general characteristics of intellectual functioning that influence how one approaches a learning task (Brown 1987); the manner in which people perceive, conceptualize, organize and recall information (Ellis 1986). (Wenden 1991:36)

Learning style, however, includes:

> ... cognitive, affective and physiological behaviors that indicate learners' characteristic and consistent way of perceiving, interacting with and responding to the learning environment; more concrete than cognitive style (Willing 1988). (Wenden 1991:36)

It is important that learning or cognitive *styles*, which refer to 'the student's preferred way of tackling learning tasks in general', be distinguished from learning *strategies* which 'concern the way a student elects to tackle a particular learning task' (Watkins 1982:78). Learning or cognitive styles, therefore, while they can be varied somewhat by learners, are not easily influenced by external factors such as learning materials. Learners can, nevertheless, be made aware of their own preferred styles, and some more sophisticated learners are also able consciously to modify their style according to the tasks they encounter (Brumby 1982).

As Scarcella and Oxford comment:

> ... when left to their own devices, and if not overly pressured by their environment to use a certain set of strategies, students typically use learning strategies that reflect their basic learning style (Ehrman & Oxford 1989). They can, however, learn to develop additional learning strategies and test the value of ones they already use. (Scarcella & Oxford 1992:63–4)

To reframe this discussion of individual differences within a sociocultural framework, it is also useful to consider the reflection of Peirce (1995), that individuals differ, not only from one another, but also within themselves from one point in time to another, and from one context to another.

Three critical elements which emerge from this wide-ranging discussion are summarised as follows:

- Learners can be assisted in compensating for characteristics less appropriate to successful language learning through help in developing stronger characteristics in other areas.
- Learners need to move out of their individual 'comfort zones' in order to participate productively and effectively in the learning process, and to carry the learning beyond the immediate task to novel situations.
- Learners need information, support, and the infrastructure to negotiate this development; they need not only to be given control, but also to be provided with the means by which to take control on their own terms.

The last of these elements above brings us to a discussion of the third principle of a learner-centred model introduced at the beginning of this section – the issue of control.

Allocation of learner control: Control of what?
An essential issue in the design of a learner-centred CALL model is the allocation of control of both the navigation through the software, and the learning engendered in the software. In order to make the most of control in a CALL context, learners need to understand their own learning processes, to be able to make informed choices about the paths their learning takes, and to be pro-active in managing and directing their own learning. All of these facets of allocation of control to the learner revolve around learners being able to use, and develop within themselves, effective language learning strategies. In the design of a learner- and learning-centred CALL package, the software interface and instructional design also need to provide support and information for learners to assist them in the development of the necessary strategies. It becomes clear, therefore, that the central goals of learner-centred design are to help learners both to recognise their own uniqueness and to realise their full language learning potential (Ely & Pease-Alvarez 1996:5).

In addition, the integration of new media, such as multimedia, into our existing teaching and learning programs, needs to remain modelled on existing principles of good practice in the use of other media. As Bickel and Truscello have recently emphasised:

> The use of technology does indeed require gathering new and different kinds of resources, but our roles do not change qualitatively. We remain facilitators, guides, counselors, and information providers. The materials and pathways onto which we guide our students simply become electronic. (Bickel & Truscello 1996:16)

Claims for the advantages of using computers frequently include the capacity of computers to allow learners to work at their own pace, and in their own time. A corollary to these advantages is that learners often work in a self-access context, and that this entails the need for learners to be able to manage or direct their own learning. In addition, in a learning environment incorporating the use of CALL software, learner differences in the area of preferred modes of perception (visual, aural or kinesic) need to be catered for. This latter can be achieved by designing tasks to exploit different modes, through the provision of a wide variety of text and media types, and by the use of a variety of navigation modes. There is also evidence that learners can be trained to use different and more effective strategies through awareness-raising in their use in specific circumstances (Brett 1994; Liou 1995; Hoven 1997). However, most learners still need guidance and guided practice in acquiring the skills and strategies involved in managing their own learning (Wenden 1995; Victori & Lockhart 1995).

As part of his report for the Council of Europe entitled *Autonomy and Foreign Language Learning*, Holec (1979:3) defined autonomy in language learning as '*the ability to take charge of one's own learning*', where an ability was 'a power or capacity to do something' (in contrast to a 'behaviour') and taking charge of this entailed 'to have, and to hold, the responsibility for all the decisions concerning all aspects of this learning' (1979). For Holec, self-directed learners on the road to autonomy need to be informed of language needs in society as a whole, the results of research into second language acquisition processes, and dimensions of verbal communication, if they are going to be able to formulate their own objectives and become users of learning strategies. In other words, learners need to know how to make these decisions strategically, but at the same time the infrastructure of the learning institution must allow for these decisions to be made by the individual learners concerned. This process of acquiring autonomy requires a *gradual deconditioning* of learners from the previously held judgements and prejudices about both the target language and the language learning and teaching process. It also requires *gradual acquisition* of knowledge and skills in using the range of tools and resources available, including such internal mental resources as self-evaluation and monitoring, and external resources like teachers or native speakers.

As proposed here, a sociocultural approach focuses on language in use: how meaning is extracted, negotiated and maintained in interactions between learners, contexts and texts, whether these texts are spoken, written, monologues, conversations, visual or graphic representations, or conveyed by means of a computer. In fact, in a sociocultural perspective on strategic language learning, computers are recognised as a mediation tool for transforming 'natural, spontaneous impulses into higher mental processes, including strategic orientations to problem solving' (Donato & McCormick 1994:456). When CALL is used in a self-access or private practice context, it is the learners' interaction with, and therefore management of, the learning environment that determines the learner-centred or humanistic nature of language learning. The incorporation of the development of learning strategies into CALL program design, including those implicated in the exploitation of paralinguistic features of language as well as metacognitive and cognitive strategies, is therefore critical in the provision of a learner-centred CALL environment which helps learners gain more control over their own learning.

In a discussion of learners' management of their own learning, Holec considers to what extent learners are ready to take this management role. He urges teachers to observe their learners to determine whether they are managing their learning or merely 'managing to learn' (1987:145). Here he is highlighting the importance of allowing learners to 'have the choice between taking full responsibility for the process or simply submitting to it' (1987:147).

Holec goes on to propose the role of 'the good studier' as being the focus of learning as a management process. In this sense, he diverges from other language learning studies discussed here, by separating language proficiency level and language achievement from the strategic decisions that need to be made by learners on objectives, content, techniques and methods, and assessment. Several important points that emerge from the Centre de Recherches et d'Applications Pédagogiques en Langues (CRAPEL) studies in which Holec has been involved are that: learners can improve their ability to manage their own learning, their increase in competence is variable, and there is no necessary causal relationship between knowing how to self-direct and implementing this knowledge in practical ways. The analogy that Holec draws is that of 'someone who knows how to drive a car [who] may sometimes prefer to be driven' (1987:156).

In his commentary on the changing face of CALL, Stevens (1992) notes three positive contributions of humanistic principles to teaching and learning practices: the provision of environments conducive to learning; the move from teaching-centredness to learning- or learner-centredness; and a reemphasis on the worth of individual learners, and learners as individuals. He sees the obvious product of these influences as being the focus, in modern software design, on the development and fostering of learner autonomy as exemplified in exploratory CALL such as multimedia applications, and problem-solving software such as adventure games. As an earlier study has shown (Stevens 1984), 'learning is enhanced when choice and control are in the hands of the learner' (Stevens 1992:23). However, bearing in mind the cautions of Holec, Robinson (1991:158) in the CALL context also warns of the dangers of putting learners in charge of their own learning when they have not yet developed the skills to be in control, or to succeed at a language task.

These considerations lead us to the hypothesis that computers can best be incorporated into language learning by allowing learners to make their own choices about the texts they work on, the paths they take through these texts, and the kinds of tasks and tools they use to access these texts. However, this availability of choice by no means precludes a learner's choice to allocate control of their learning paths to the teacher/designer of the instructional package. This flexibility in the level of control also entails the provision of explicit information to learners on how to make the choice about the level of control at which to work, as well as information on how to make efficient use of this control in terms of both navigation through the package and material on which to work. We now turn to an examination of the characteristics of task and instructional design that facilitate learners' acquiring these skills and strategies.

Task-based pedagogy and good practice in CALL
Kumaravadivelu advocates a learning-centred, task-based pedagogy for language teaching and learning on the grounds that it provides a comprehensiveness that other pedagogies do not. This approach entails that the design of tasks:

> has to take into consideration minimally, the following psycholinguistic principles: language learning is a developmental process; it is a decision-making process; it is a process of negotiation; it is not linear and additive; it is primarily incidental; it is largely a subconscious activity; and it is a meaning-focused activity. (Kumaravadivelu 1993:81)

If we examine the principles Kumaravadivelu lists here, we find several areas of correspondence with the principles of a sociocultural methodology discussed earlier.

In other literature on task design and interaction, several features can be identified among the various aspects of the classroom implementation of tasks which contribute positively to second language acquisition. With regard to the nature of the tasks themselves, the following have been found:

- Problem-solving (closed/convergent) tasks produce more questions in total, more questions per subject, and more confirmation checks and referential questions in total than debate (open/divergent) tasks (Duff 1986; Long 1989).
- Information exchange (closed/convergent) tasks produce comprehension and confirmation checks, clarification requests, repairs, preventive moves, reactions, and self/other repetition (Doughty & Pica 1986).

- Modifying language input of tasks is better done through interaction and negotiation than by pre-modification to decrease complexity and increase quantity and redundancy (Pica et al. 1986, 1987; Ross et al. 1991).
- Negotiation of input and output on tasks seems greatest on larger semantic units, with little negotiation occurring in relation to syntactic elements such as time and aspect (Ashton 1986).
- Two-way ('jigsaw') tasks produce more and better negotiation work than 1-way tasks (Long 1980; Doughty & Pica 1986; Pica et al. 1989; Long 1992).
- Decontextualised tasks produce more negotiation than contextualised ones (Snow 1989; Long 1992).
- 'There-and-then' (temporally and spatially removed) tasks produce more negotiation than 'here-and-now' (local in time and place) tasks (Snow 1989; Long 1992).
- More negotiation occurs when a feedback option is provided than when it is not (Loschky & Bley-Vroman 1990; Tomasello & Herron 1988, 1989).

With reference to computer-enhanced listening and viewing comprehension, it would seem, therefore, that tasks need to be designed to incorporate some elements of negotiation of the texts (perhaps in the form of feedback and assistance available as part of the software package), and that these texts need to be authentic and possibly decontextualised. In addition, feedback needs to be provided, and there should be elements of problem-solving and induction involved in the task demands. Within a CALL environment, these criteria should therefore be met, in order to provide tasks that promote the processes of negotiation, and that encourage learners to develop negotiation skills with the activities and facilities of a CALL software package.

Models of good practice: Strategies for taking control
In a learning environment involving CALL, learner resistance to self-managed learning can be addressed by providing learners with exposure to awareness-raising activities across all parts of their language-learning program, including in the CALL software. In the initial stages, highly structured (teacher-centred) materials need to be available to cater for the needs of those learners with a strong dependence on teacher direction. However, to cater for differentially rapid development in the direction of autonomy, it is also necessary to provide the means whereby learners can take more control if they feel capable. As alluded to earlier, this can be achieved by writing into the design of a CALL software package several levels of entry, or several modes of interaction based on varying levels of learner control.

Thus, for example, novice learners or learners new to self-managed learning would choose to work at the most structured lesson level. Learners with
some experience could work with more flexibility at a level where they
choose the kinds of tasks and texts to work on. Finally, more sophisticated or
more confident self-managed or self-directed learners could choose to work
at the least structured level. Here, they are able to browse texts of different
types, explore and compare the language and paralinguistic features used,
and call on the various background and help facilities.

In order to achieve the level of control proposed here, learners need to
gain an understanding of the strategies that are available to them, and the
interaction among them, the framework within which this interaction occurs,
as well as to practise using effective strategies in context. The literature of
both general learning and language learning is informative here in formulating a comprehensive model. Of the lists and inventories of strategies examined, Oxford's (1990) classification of language learning strategies seems the
most comprehensive, and the most suitable for modification to the CALL
context. However, this classification still lacks sufficient emphasis on paralinguistic strategies that are intrinsic to a multimedia CALL package. It is,
therefore, necessary to modify the framework of Oxford's classification to
include a paralinguistic category (Hoven 1997).

In addition, Oxford's distinction between Direct and Indirect strategies,
even with a paralinguistic category, is inadequate for a sociocultural paradigm. In order to take better account of the role of interaction in the dynamic nature of the construction of meaning in language learning processes,
Oxford's framework needs further reconceptualisation into three levels which
are progressively more outwardly directed: metalinguistic (internal to the
learner), processing (both internal and externally influenced), and interactional (more externally influenced than internal to the learner). This new
framework can then be incorporated into our model in three ways (see Hoven
(1997) for an exemplification of such a software package).

Firstly, less self-directed learners who choose to work at the most structured level are presented with an overview of the framework, with connections to tasks that practise the various strategies listed. Secondly, tasks are
designed such that the more effective strategies are incorporated into the
working of the tasks. Thirdly, to assist with the development of metacognitive strategies, tasks are labelled with their cognitive level and classification,
and learners can go at any time to the overviews of both the cognitive taxonomy and the strategy overview.

As discussed earlier, individual differences among learners, variations
among texts, contexts and tasks, and the nature of learner interaction with the
software all contribute significantly to differential learner success in language
learning mediated by computers. In the model proposed here, meaning is

constructed by learners through their interaction with the tools and resources available in the CALL software. At the same time that learners are negotiating meaning through a listening and viewing comprehension task and the associated help tools, they are also co-creating with the software their own individual learning paths. Another essential element of the realisation of a sociocultural paradigm through the software is allocation of control to the learner using it. With the understanding that different learners need and desire different levels of control and structure, the three-layered model allows learners to take control in an informed and staged or 'scaffolded' manner. The location and function of navigation tools, the content and design of tasks, and the whole instructional design concept are all grounded in this understanding.

However, such a software package should not be used in isolation. It is envisaged as being used as just one tool in a complete learning environment (Hoven 1992). In such an environment, the incorporation of awareness-raising in language learning strategies and a task-based approach reappear in other components of the teaching and learning process.

Another essential feature of the flexibility of this model to cater for individual differences is realised through the inclusion of tools and tasks in the package which highlight visual, aural and kinesic modes of perception and learning. At the task level, for example, some tasks require simple yes/no decision-making implemented by a mouse-click. Other tasks, however, allow more kinesic learners to use their preferred mode by picking up objects with the mouse and moving them to the appropriate locations.

Conclusion

Some learners naturally prefer to manage their own learning; others can come to prefer it when they have sufficient understanding of how to do it; while yet others may never feel comfortable or successful when required to manage their own learning. These findings point to the need in self-access CALL packages for a flexibility of approach that caters for this range of learner capacity for managing their own learning. As we have seen, there is also the need to incorporate information that helps learners increase their awareness of their own learning and their understanding of strategies and approaches to improve this.

We conclude, therefore, that the help and feedback components of a CALL package are critical in a sociocultural model for learner-centred CALL, and that the help should include information on learning styles and strategies, and some context or background information on the texts available, as well as the more common language- or task-specific help. In addition, the design of tasks needs to incorporate practice in the use of those strategies that have been shown to be effective in language learning, and particularly in self-managed learning. In terms of the interface design, the navigation elements similarly should allocate to learners control over their paths through the package. The three-layered approach to learner access suggested in the model represents one practical approach to the implementation of the sociocultural paradigm in a learner-centred CALL software package based on multimedia texts.

References

Aljaafreh, A. & Lantolf, J.P. (1994). Negative feedback as regulation and second language learning in the zone of proximal development. *The Modern Language Journal 78*, 465–483.

Ashton, G. (1986). Trouble-shooting in interaction with learners: The more the merrier? *Applied Linguistics 7*, 128–143.

Bickel, B. & Truscello, D. (1996). New opportunities for learning: styles and strategies for computers. *TESOL Journal 6*, 15–19.

Bradin, C. (1998). Utilisation of input in CALL: A research study. In J. Gassin, M. Smith & D. Cunningham (Eds) *Proceedings of the 1998 WorldCALL Conference* (pp. 21–23). Melbourne: The Horwood Language Centre, University of Melbourne.

Brett, P. 1995. Multimedia for listening comprehension: The design of a multimedia-based resource for developing listening skills. *System 23, 1*, 77–85.

Bradin, C. (1996). How second language learners utilize input in CALL. In F.L. Borchardt, C.L. Bradin, E.M.T. Johnson, & L. Rhodes (Eds), *Proceedings of the Computer Assisted Language Instruction Consortium 1996 Annual Symposium: 'Distance Learning'* (pp. 17–21). Durham, Nth. Carolina: Duke University.

Brandl, K.K. (1995). Strong and weak students' preferences for feedback options and responses. *The Modern Language Journal 79*, 194–211.

Brumby, M. (1982). Consistent differences in cognitive styles shown for qualitative biological problem-solving. *British Journal of Educational Psychology 52*, 244–257.

Chapelle, C.A. (1994). CALL activities: Are they all the same? *System 22*, 33–45.

Donato, R. (1994). Collective scaffolding in second language learning. In J.P. Lantolf & G. Appel (Eds), *Vygotskian approaches to second language research* (pp. 33–56). Norwood, NJ: Ablex Publishing Corporation.

Donato, R. & McCormick, D. (1994). A sociocultural perspective on language learning strategies: The role of mediation. *The Modern Language Journal 78*, 453–464.

Doughty, C. & Pica, T. (1986). Information-gap tasks: Do they facilitate second language acquisition? *TESOL Quarterly 20, 2*, 305–325.

Duff, P. (1986). Another look at interlanguage talk: Taking task to task. In R.R. Day, (Ed.) *Talking to learn: Conversation in second language acquisition* (pp.147–181). Rowley, Mass.: Newbury House.

Dunkel, P. (1987). The effectiveness literature on CAI/CALL and computing: Implications of the research for limited English proficient learners. *TESOL Quarterly 21*, 2, 367–372.

Dunkel, P. (1991). The effectiveness research on computer-assisted instruction and computer-assisted language learning. In P. Dunkel (Ed.), *Computer-assisted language learning and testing*. New York: Newbury House.

Ely, C. M. & Pease-Alvarez, L. (1996). Learning styles and strategies in ESOL: Introduction to the special issue. *TESOL Journal 6*, 1, 5.

Gillette, B.K. (1990). *Beyond learning strategies: A whole-person approach to language learning*. Newark: Unpublished doctoral dissertation, University of Delaware.

Halliday, M.A.K. (1977). *Explorations in the functions of language*. New York: Elsevier, North Holland.

Halliday, M.A.K. & Hasan, R. (Eds) (1989) *Language, context, and text: Aspects of language in a social-semiotic perspective*. Oxford: Oxford University Press.

Hamayan, E., Genesee, F. & Tucker, G. (1977). Affective factors and language. *Language Learning 27*, 225–241.

Holec, H. (1979). *Autonomy and foreign language learning*. Oxford: Council of Europe/Pergamon Press.

Holec, H. (1987). The learner as manager: Managing learning or managing to learn. In A. Wenden, & J. Rubin (Eds), *Learner strategies in language learning* (pp. 145–157). Englewood Cliffs, NJ: Prentice-Hall.

Hoven, D. (1992). CALL in a language learning environment. *CÆLL Journal 3*,2, 19–27.

Hoven, D. (1997). *Improving the management of flow of control in computer-assisted listening comprehension tasks for second and foreign language learners*. Unpublished doctoral dissertation, University of Queensland.

Johnson, D. (1991). Second language and content learning with computers: Research in the role of social factors. In P. Dunkel (Ed.), *Computer-assisted language learning and testing* (pp. 61–83). New York: Newbury House.

Jonassen, D. (1992). What are cognitive tools? In P.A.M. Kommers, D.H. Jonassen, & J.T. Mayes (Eds), *Cognitive tools for learning* (pp. 1–6). Berlin: Springer-Verlag.

Kumaravadivelu, B. (1993). The name of the task and the task of naming: Methodological aspects of task-based pedagogy. In G. Crookes & S.M. Gass (Eds) *Tasks and language learning: Integrating theory and practice* (pp. 69–96). Clevedon, England: Multilingual Matters Ltd.

Larson-Freeman, D. & Long, M.H. (1991). *An introduction to second language acquisition research*. Essex, England: Longman Group UK Limited.

Liou, H-C. (1995). Evaluation of interactive videodisc courseware: Effects of strategy training and collaborative learning. In F.L. Borchardt, & E.M.T. Johnson (Eds), *Proceedings of the Computer assisted Language Instruction Consortium 1995 Annual Symposium 'Computers and Collaborative Learning'* (pp. 112–115). Durham, Nth. Carolina: Heinle & Heinle Publishers.

Long, D.R. (1989). Second language listening comprehension: A schema-theoretic perspective. *The Modern Language Journal 73*,1, 32–40.

Long, M.H. (1992). *Input, focus on form, and second language acquisition.* Paper delivered at the PacSLRF Conference, Sydney, July.

Loschky, L. & Bley-Vroman, R. (990). Creating structure-based communication tasks for second language development. *University of Hawai'i Working Papers in ESL 9*, 1, 161–212.

Luff, P., Gilbert, N. & Frohlich, D. (Eds) (1990). *Computers and conversation.* London: Academic Press.

Naiman, N., Frohlich, M., Stern, H.H. & Todesco, A. (1978). *The good language learner.* Research in Education Series 7. Toronto: The Ontario Institute for Studies in Education.

O'Malley, J.M. & Chamot, A.U. (1990). *Learning strategies in second language acquisition.* Cambridge: Cambridge University Press.

Oxford, R.L. (1990). *Language learning strategies: What every teacher should know.* Boston, Mass.: Heinle & Heinle Publishers.

Papert, S. (1987). Computer criticism vs. technocentric thinking. *Educational Researcher*, January–February, 22–27.

Pederson, K.M. (1987). Research on CALL. In W.F. Smith (Ed.), *Modern media in foreign language education: Theory and implementation* (pp. 99–131). Lincolnwood, Ill.: National Textbook Company.

Peirce, B.N. (1995). Social identity, investment, and language learning. *TESOL Quarterly 29*,1, 9–31.

Platt, E. & Brookes, F.B. (1994). The 'acquisition-rich environment' revisited. *The Modern Language Journal 78*, 497–511.

Robinson, G.L. (1991). Effective feedback strategies in CALL. In P. Dunkel (Ed.), *Computer-assisted language learning and testing* (pp. 155–167). New York: Newbury House.

Ross, S., Long, M.H. & Yano Y. (1991). Simplification or elaboration? The effects of two types of text modifocations on foreign language reading comprehension. *University of Hawai'i Working Papers in ESL 10*, 2, 1–32.

Scarcella, R.C. & Oxford, R.L. (1992). *The tapestry of language learning.* Boston, Mass.: Heinle & Heinle.

Skehan, P. (1989). *Individual differences in second-language learning.* London: Edward Arnold.

Snow, C.E. (1989). Beyond conversation: Second language learners' acquisition of description and explanation. In J.P. Lantolf & A. Labarca (Eds) 1989. *Research in second language learning: Focus on the classroom* (pp. 3–16). Norwood, N.J.: Ablex Publishing Corporation.

Stevens, V. (1984). Implications of research and theory concerning the influence of control on the effectiveness of CALL. *CALICO Journal 2*, 1, 28–33, 48.

Stevens, V. (1992). Humanism and CALL: A coming of age. In M.C. Pennington & V. Stevens (Eds): (pp. 11–38).

Stone, A.C. (1989). Improving the effectiveness of strategy training for learning disabled students: The role of communicative dynamics. *Remedial and Special Education 10*, 35–42.

Tomasello, M. & Herron, C. (1988). Down the garden path: Inducing and correcting overgeneralization errors in the foreign language classroom. *Applied Psycholinguistics 9*, 237–246.

Vygotsky, L. S. (1978). *Mind in society: The development of higher psychological processes*. M. Cole, V. John-Steiner, S. Scribner, & E. Souberman (Eds & Trans). Cambridge, Mass.: Harvard University Press.

Warschauer, M. (1996). Sociocultural learning theory and computer-mediated communication. In F.L. Borchardt, C.L. Bradin, E.M.T. Johnson & L. Rhodes (Eds), *Proceedings of the Computer Assisted Language Instruction Consortium 1996 Annual Symposium: 'Distance Learning'* (pp. 265–269). Durham, Nth. Carolina: Duke University.

Watkins, D. (1982). Identifying the study process dimensions of Australian university students. *The Australian Journal of Education 26*,1, 76–85.

Wenden, A.L. (1995). Learner training in context: A knowledge-based approach. *System 23*, 2, 183–194.

Wong-Fillmore, L. (1982). Instructional language as linguistic input: Second language learning in classrooms. In L. Wilkinson (Ed.) *Communicating in the classroom*. New York: Academic Press.

Victori, M. & Lockhart, W. (1995). Enhancing metacognition in self-directed language learning. *System 23*,2, 223–234.

10

Improving EFL Learning Environment through Networking

Peiya Gu & Zhe Xu
Suzhou University, China

Introduction

In China, where English proficiency is achieved mainly in the situation of formal teaching, classroom environment plays an important role in determining the learning results. However, for many years, the effort of Chinese teachers of English to improve the classroom environment has been generally not very successful. This is largely due to the EFL context and various practical restrictions.

First, genuine interactions are difficult to bring about in EFL classrooms. Without authentic communicative needs, students often display resentment when asked to interact with their classmates. On the other hand, the language competence problem of many Chinese teachers discourages them to initiate meaningful teacher–student interaction. Second, due to pressure from students and school authorities to pass national exams that measure linguistic ability on a discrete point basis, the test-oriented approach becomes a prior choice. Accordingly, drill and grammar-based exercises take precedence over authentic tasks that foster students' overall communicative competence. Third, rigid curricula and scheduling are at odds with teachers' attempts to make innovations. To strike a balance between the duties imposed on them and the changes they hope to bring about is an awesome challenge, even to those strong advocates for reform. Fourth, teachers' enthusiasm to apply communicative approaches is often dampened by classroom realities such as large class sizes and restricted access to materials and technology. Finally, the teacher-centred approach, though not conducive to a motivating classroom atmosphere, is widely accepted by both teachers and students. One possible explanation may be that the tradition of Chinese culture tends to lay great emphasis on the importance of teachers as knowledge givers, and questioning of them would be viewed as challenging authority. Therefore, any changes in prevailing teaching practices would meet with resistance.

All the constraints mentioned above are closely related to the sociocultural background of China, especially the highly centralised education system. Fortunately, the past decade witnessed some educational reforms in areas such as English proficiency measurement, secondary school English curricula, and higher education decentralisation (Shih 1996). But the impact of these changes is not profound and far-reaching enough to respond to the pressing need of China's economic growth, which is demanding an increasing work force with both adequate English proficiency and computer literacy. Also, networking as an educational tool no longer is an impossibility in China. Today over 400 universities throughout the country have been linked together by China's Education and Research Network (CERNET), one of the four basic national networks set up since 1996 that provide direct access to the Internet. Numerous provincial, institutional networks as well as academic community intranets have also been emerging. The fact is that some universities already have the necessary hardware conditions for carrying out networking projects.

Related literature

While grappling with all the difficulties to find solutions to ELT in China, Chinese teachers may find it beneficial to draw on the experience of their international colleagues with the latest educational tool of computer networks. In some countries, networks within classrooms or labs and across schools (termed 'intranets') or across national boundaries (the Internet) have been serving a variety of purposes for language teaching, such as holding electronic discussions, conducting collaborative writing projects, and organising cross-cultural exchanges. Current literature on networking has reported success in various respects of optimising language learning conditions. For example, networking is seen as fostering authentic communication. Based on a study of the language output of university German students, Chun (1994) argues that the use of computer networks facilitates the acquisition of interactive competence by providing learners with opportunities to generate and initiate different kinds of discourse. Warschauer, Turbee and Roberts (1996) offer another perspective toward the potential of networking. Through studying a comprehensive amount of research reports examining the effects of networking on student empowerment, they arrive at the conclusion that networking, if appropriately used, can help enhance student autonomy, promote equal participation, and develop learning skills and critical learning perspective. There are other reported benefits of networking, such as increased motivation (Frizler 1995; Berge & Collins 1995; Warschauer 1996), emergence of multicultural awareness and global understanding (Sayers 1993; Berge & Collins 1995; Singhal 1997) and access to a rich source of authentic language (Singhal 1997; Meloni 1998).

Research design

Research questions

Proponents of networking seem to have presented a convincing argument that the new technology has the potential to provide an optimal environment in which effective language learning may take place. But does this also ring true for ELT in China? To answer this question, it seems we should first have a clear idea about what constitutes a good language learning environment. Through a careful study of SLA and ESL literature, Egbert and Jessup (1996:2–5) presented a model of four conditions most widely researched and supported (for a more thorough overview, see Egbert 1993). These are:

Condition 1: Opportunities for learners to interact and negotiate meaning with an authentic audience.

Condition 2: Learners involved in authentic tasks which promote exposure to and production of varied and creative language.

Condition 3: Learners have opportunities to formulate ideas and thoughts and intentional cognition is promoted.

Condition 4: An atmosphere with ideal stress/anxiety level in a learner-centred classroom.

For convenience of observation and analysis, these four environmental conditions were further developed into eight constructs: (1) opportunities for learners to interact and to negotiate meaning (Interaction); (2) an authentic audience (Audience); (3) authentic tasks (Task); (4) opportunities for exposure to and production of varied language (Sources); (5) enough time and feedback for formulating ideas and thoughts (Help); (6) learner intentional cognition (Cognition); (7) an ideal-anxiety atmosphere (Atmosphere); (8) and learner control (Control) (see Egbert & Jessup 1996:7–8). Apparently, China's EFL context and various practical restrictions have posed great difficulty in providing these conditions. Now networking technology seems to have offered a new avenue for these endeavours.

However, actual classroom applications and research on the use of networking in ELT in China has been sparse, despite the increase of the number of net-linked computers in schools. In an effort to make better use of the available technology and gain some understanding toward the potential impact of networking on the classroom language learning environment, a small-scale study was conducted at Suzhou University in the spring semester of 1998. The research questions were as follows:

RQ1: Does networking have an optimising impact on the conditions for an ideal language learning environment?

RQ2: How do students perceive their network-supported learning environment?

RQ3: How might networking improve EFL learning environment?

Subjects
The subjects of this study were 11 junior English majors from a regular Suzhou University Comprehensive English class (traditionally named Intensive Reading). They were randomly selected from almost half of the class (45 in total) who made the choice of their participation in this networking project among other extra-curricular projects for practicing English outside the classroom. Like the rest of their classmates, 10% of their final course grade was based on their performance in one of the projects. A demographic information survey showed these 11 participants had an average of eight years of English learning history and had fairly good typing ability. Their knowledge of computers before participation was rated 'poor' for five and 'fair' for six. Five students had computers at home. Their computers were mostly used for practicing typing, playing CD-ROM music and games. None of them had the experience of using email, the Web, or other Internet functions.

The setting and tasks
The project was done in a multimedia computer language lab newly set up in the School of Foreign Languages with one graduate student as tutor. The research plan was based on the lab's hardware conditions, and the available network access. The lab is connected to the university's network centre that is linked to the Internet through CERNET mentioned above. With the help of a lab technician, 25 multimedia Pentium/100 PCs in the lab have been linked

together by Microsoft Exchange software to form an intranet that enables in-class mail exchange and electronic discussion. This intranet also has a function of sharing information through a public folder which contains useful language learning resources downloaded from the Web by the teacher. Due to cost concern and slow transmission, students' access to the Internet was controlled so that most of the time they could only visit some selected web sites in the public folder. But through the Intranet, they could send out email messages directly from their terminals. Their incoming messages were forwarded to the lab's email address (the only account for the lab) and distributed by the tutor through the intranet. Considering the unpredictability of technical conditions, which might cause unforeseeable obstacles, we had our research loosely structured to allow flexibility. However, the bottom line was all the same: to make cost-effective use of all available technological tools for providing students with maximum experience of learning through networking.

A variety of online tasks were assigned to achieve this goal. For example, students first signed up for the 'Cities Project', an online student communication project organised by an American professor in New York. They used email and a Web board to 'talk' with teachers and ESL/EFL students from Washington DC, New York, Honolulu, California, Paris and Khmelnitskiy. During the process, they also visited some university web sites developed by the 'Cities Project' groups, and the famous *Dave's ESL CAFE*. From April to June, a collaborative writing exchange activity was conducted with an ESL/EFL intermediate writing class from Drexel University in the US. Each student was paired with a writing partner and was required to exchange through email two pieces of writing on anything of their own interest for peer comment and discussion. In addition to tasks that required the entire group participation, small group and individual tasks were also assigned. Students were divided into three groups and each was required to design and finish a group project for final presentation. Meanwhile, every student was asked to keep a weekly learning journal and participate in in-class electronic discussions.

The tutor and the students met at the lab two afternoons a week regularly (three hours for each), while the teacher paid occasional visits providing guidance and help when necessary. The lab was also open during regular office hours in the daytime and on three evenings a week.

Data collection
The use of both the Internet and intranet seemed to have created a new learning environment. To assess the impact of networking on this environment, quantitative data was collected through a record of the participants' email exchanges as well as an end-of-project survey. Then a statistical analysis was conducted to measure the degree to which it satisfied the optimal language

learning conditions. Meanwhile, to gain an insight into the process, qualitative data such as the tutor's observation notes and students' writings was also used for detailed analysis. In the section below, some major instruments and procedures are described briefly.

Survey

By the end of the project, a survey was conducted that questioned the participants about their perceptions of the network-supported learning environment. It was administered in English and consisted of two parts. The first part contained self-designed 35 items to be answered on a five-point Likert scale, with number 5 being the highest score. It was based on the eight constructs mentioned previously. Students' responses to the first part of the survey were calculated to get an overall mean score for all students, for all 35 questions. Then the mean Likert score on each question for the 11 students was calculated and compared to a hypothesised mean of 3 (representing a neutral score) using two-tailed t-tests. This procedure was done to determine which questions generated positive or negative responses at a greater than chance level. The significance level was set at $p < .05$. The second part asked five open-ended questions related to the students' overall evaluation of the project and the benefits and limitations as they perceived. Detailed notes were taken on common voices as reference for later discussion (for the full survey, see Appendix).

Students' writings

Students were required to save their writings on a disk, including their learning journals, their email correspondence via the Internet, and their internal exchanges with both the teacher, the tutor and classmates. This source of data helps develop a good understanding of students' attitudes toward using the computer networks to learn English. It also reflects their progress in developing computer skills, writing ability and communicative competence.

Tutor's observation notes and email correspondence

Throughout the project, the tutor kept notes about major events, impressions and observations. This helps reveal the tutor's perceptions of the changes in student motivation and ability in conducting various tasks. In addition, the tutor kept a frequent email contact with the teacher and other teachers of the collaboration projects, which serves as another information source for this study.

Findings and discussion

Statistical results

The overall mean score for all students on all questions was 4.060, significantly higher than a hypothetical neutral score. All 35 mean scores of the questions were higher than neutral, 31 significantly so. Among the individual questions, the most positive response was given to Q9. Next highest were Q4, Q13, Q1 and Q25 (see figure 1).

Figure 1: Questions with the highest mean scores

Q9:	The teacher and my classmates are always available when I need help	4.636
Q4:	The activities I do help me learn English effectively.	4.455
Q13:	The learning atmosphere is cooperative and supportive.	4.455
Q1:	I have chances to use English for real communication.	4.364
Q25:	I can get immediate feedback from the teacher to my thoughts, ideas, and performance	4.364

To understand how the network-supported learning environment under the study meets the essential requirements for an optimal model, the questions were grouped together under the eight constructs on the basis of which they were initially designed. The overall means and standard deviations of the eight constructs were then calculated and listed in figure 2. They were all significantly greater than the hypothetical neutral score with the highest mean of 4.27 given to the Task construct.

Figure 2: Overall means and standard deviations of eight constructs

Constructs	Mean	SD
Task	4.27	0.13
Interaction	4.24	0.14
Help	4.20	0.39
Atmosphere	4.15	0.31
Audience	4.00	0.39
Cognition	4.00	0.27
Sources	3.95	0.23
Control	3.80	0.28

By the end of the project, the record of the students' email exchanges was also collected and analysed to show the quantity of language input and output through both in-class and out-of-class email correspondence. Figure 3 is a summary of the results.

Figure 3: Total, monthly and weekly language input and output

	Incoming messages	Outgoing messages	Word count for outgoing messages
Total/11 students	464	536	120,353
Av. monthly/each	12	14	3,126
Av. weekly/each	3	3.5	782

Detailed analysis

From all the data collected (both quantitative and qualitative), five themes seem to emerge, revealing the students' overall positive perceptions of the network-supported learning environment as well as their tremendous effort made in the process. In this section, these five themes will be discussed and illustrated with examples from the available sources accumulated throughout the project.

Authentic written interaction with a variety of audience

This theme first comes from the statistical fact of the second highest mean for the construct Interaction (4.24) and the fifth place of the construct Audience (4.0). It is made clearer by the high mean scores for the relevant questions, such as Q1 'I have chances to use English for real communication' (4.364), Q2 'I have chances to exchange ideas with other learners of English' (4.273), and Q3 'I have chances to discuss problems and difficulties with the teacher' (4.273).

Students also reported benefits from the authentic interaction with a different audience through the intranet within the lab and the Internet with the outside world. First, the intranet seems to have enhanced student–teacher and student–student interaction by providing authentic needs for communication. In a conventional classroom, large class sizes and the highly structured environment limit the opportunity for free interaction. In addition, the lack of real communicative needs makes it difficult to elicit meaningful social interaction. As one student reflected in her learning journal, 'Although I am an English major, I did not have many chances to really use my English. Instead, I just have to attend various activities organised by classes or schools. More often than not, they are not true communication …'. But the intranet seems to have the potential to generate a truly interactive classroom discourse. The same student went on, '… when doing this project, I usually write something purposefully, for example asking for some information and giving some explanations. Thus, I can see the usage (use) of English as a tool, which really arouses my interest'.

Second, with the Internet connection, the teacher and students are not the only audience that students can interact with. Global communication with a variety of audience becomes an appealing possibility. Through email contacts with people from 22 countries and regions in five continents, students obtained rich experiences of interacting with people from different cultures for different purposes. They commented on it as 'a fascinating experience' to have direct communication with native English speakers. This is the kind of opportunity that Chinese learners of English have been longing for, but are not sufficiently given. Today's new technology seems to offer an inexpensive solution to the problem. However, at this stage not all the learners (including teachers) could use this new tool efficiently due to lack of training, language barriers, and electronic and cross-cultural communication complexities. In this project, five of the 11 students were able to keep regular contacts with native speakers (mostly English teachers), while the rest had some such contacts, but not regularly. This accounts for the second lowest mean (3.455) and the highest standard deviation (1.128) for Q18 'I have chances to communicate with native English speakers'.

Tasks mutually designed for more language exposure and language output

Among the eight constructs, Task generated the highest mean of 4.27, which is echoed by the second highest mean for Q4 'the activities I do help me learn English effectively', and other high means for the related questions. Students showed great enthusiasm toward various networking activities. In the 'Cities Project', they eagerly absorbed information about life in the outside world and at the same time proudly introduced Suzhou, a famous 'Garden City' in China, to their key pals. In order to get more accurate cultural and historical information about the city, they checked related national web sites and even did some library research on their own. The writing exchange activity, for another instance, provided a rare chance for students to share their writing with other EFL/ESL learners. Through peer comment, they also developed a critical perspective toward the writing process. Apart from organised activities, networking engaged students in self-assigned individual tasks to suit their personal needs. With the convenience of email, students were free to find their own key pals for less focused communication. They could also read downloaded articles at their own convenience and use the intranet for self-initiated interaction with classmates.

All these activities paved the way for the final group project students developed themselves. One of the groups created a web page named 'Suzhou Glories', introducing Suzhou from different perspectives. This product was the most exemplary of how students' creativity can be enhanced by the use of the new technology. Despite their ignorance about web page design, they learned to use *Frontpage* software to create hypermedia texts and graphics. For the content of their web pages, they wrote articles themselves, called for contributions from their classmates and schoolmates, and interviewed foreign teachers, business people and even passing overseas tourists in the streets. Then they edited all the materials and organised them into four columns: Indoor Boast, Kaleidoscope, Tea-house, and First Impressions. They even wrote a special page to conclude their learning experience with a proud voice: 'You can never guess how much we have gained through this project!!!'

It is obvious that while completing all kinds of tasks, students expanded their language exposure through a variety of sources, such as the Web, the teacher, classmates, and overseas email partners. Email correspondence, in particular, proves an effective way to stimulate language output (see statistics in figure 3). All the participants were surprised to find that they had read and written at least three times more than their classmates who were not in this project. 'Really I've never imagined that we've done so much!' one said.

However, the quality of both the exposure and the output depends in part on the email partners' knowledge and language proficiency. Our analysis of students' incoming email shows that native speakers tend to write longer messages, offer more information, and know better how to encourage student expression. Similarly, students' discourse with those native speakers is of greater length and develops more complex and sophisticated English than that with other ESL/EFL students. Take one student for example: she wrote an average of 503 words for each exchange with a Californian teacher, while her email to other ESL students averaged 210 words only. There were complaints that some ESL/EFL email partners wrote poor English and provided little useful information. That accounts for a mean of 3.545 for Q7 ('I get to know a lot of interesting and new things through my key pals' email messages'). Despite the problem, students commonly agreed the mere presence of a real audience urged them not only to get their message conveyed, but to convey it precisely, coherently and appropriately.

Improved written feedback even with limited network access

One feature of computer-mediated communication (CMC) is time- and place-independence (Warschauer 1996a). It offers students flexibility to do their work at any time of the day from any computer connected to the Internet. However, none of the 11 students had the Internet connection at home and could not access the networks elsewhere but in the lab. Besides, their tight schedule for exams and other courses prevented them from coming to the lab as often as they wished. Some students complained about not having enough time to keep up with the activities and the group tasks. This was truthfully reflected by the comparatively low mean score of 3.727 for Q26 ('I have enough time to complete the tasks').

It is worth noting, however, that questions related to feedback obtained high mean scores which may be the explanation for the third highest mean of 4.20 for the Help construct. One of the questions, Q9 ('The teacher and my classmates are always available when I need help'), got the highest mean of 4.636. Feedback, as a facilitator of students' idea and thought formulation, is a critical component of the optimal learning conditions. Throughout the project, feedback giving was a continuous process. It came in various forms: written and verbal, formal and informal, group and individual. It played an important role in assisting students in effective email writing and offering help in completing group tasks. As networking freed the teacher from the lecture-style instruction, more time for individualised oral and written help was allowed. But it is the written form of feedback that seemed particularly facilitated by networking.

First, the process of giving feedback becomes more interactive in a networking context. When the teacher gives comment to the students on their performance, students would respond to present their own opinions. Thus, the initial feedback elicited more interactions, which in turn developed language and thought. Second, networking eases the process of group editing and commenting. Students' work could be freely sent to many recipients for comment. This convenient way of file sharing helped students get more feedback and ideas they could build on. Third, networking expands the source of feedback. In a conventional classroom, students get feedback mainly from their teacher or classmates. But the long distance capability of CMC makes overseas email partners an additional source of feedback, and students can have choices concerning from whom they receive assessment and advice.

Enhanced motivation and engaged learning

The intranet makes it easy for the teacher to encourage discussion of learning problems, experiences and strategies, and to provide a certain degree of metacognitive guidance whenever suitable. To promote students' engagement in learning, it is also important that they become highly motivated to take the opportunities presented to them and to be cognitively engaged in their learning process. The motivating effect in the network-supported learning environment is the most significant observation throughout the project.

The instrumental benefits of learning computer skills and using email and the Internet proved to be an important motivation factor. In their responses to the open-ended Q1, all of the students commented that these skills were important for their future career. Meanwhile, intrinsic motivation for learning English was kept high as students engaged themselves in real communication. As one student remarked, 'I used to consider English as a means to get a job. Only when I have taken part in this project did I really feel the great communicative power of English. This illumination will surely spur on to fresh efforts'. To them, 'Writing is no longer an assignment from the teacher but a way to express our ideas and exchange information'. Obviously, the use of networking enhanced student enjoyment of, interest in, and attention to the learning activities.

Collaborative atmosphere and learner autonomy

In a learning environment where students are busy working on their computers, the teacher's role must undergo a significant shift from a knowledge giver to a facilitator. Accordingly, the students in this project were given much independence and responsibility for their own learning. They chose their own group tasks, decided their own way of accomplishing the tasks, and negotiated with each other for any major decisions. As two students commented: 'Most of time we depend on ourselves. We become the master of ourselves in this process'; 'To be frank, the project is the best teaching pattern that I've ever experienced ... In these activities, we play a more active role which made us feel happy and had a desire to learn more'.

Compared with the Internet tools, such as the Web which was strictly controlled due to practical restrictions, the intranet seemed more at the students' own disposal. In fact, this supportive network helped the emergence of a learning community in which the teacher was not the only source of knowledge. Students learned from each other, shared what they knew and worked together toward their common goals. Collaboration, not competition, and communication, not isolation, was set as the tone from the start of the project. As expressed by a student, 'The intranet links everyone together as a whole unit. Whenever someone has difficulties, others will offer suggestion and kindly help out. The cooperative spirit formed in this activity is just what we lack in a conventional class'.

The learning atmosphere was also characterised by a low-stress and high-attention level. Student performance was assessed not by a single exam but by an integrative approach that took into account their overall performance throughout the project. This alleviated exam-related anxiety made them pay more attention to the learning process itself. However, it is interesting to note that Q31 ('I'm afraid to make mistakes') does not have statistical significance with the second highest standard deviation of 1.120. It is found that networking may cause a new kind of anxiety related to the use of technological tools. Sometimes user errors cause loss of files and disappearance of message being composed. Spelling mistakes in email addresses also result in mail bounce-back which in turn led to delay of receiving response. For some students these may cause frustration and new anxiety when operating the computer.

Implications

This study is an early attempt in unravelling the potential impact of networking on the EFL learning environment in China. Although the generally positive results seem to have confirmed its educational value in supporting the teaching–learning process and optimising the environment, the small group size, loose research structure and the fact that the participants were volunteers leave the results open for question and further research.

Meanwhile, it should be noted that technology does not offer ready-made solutions to all the problems we meet with in the classroom. Despite its various advantages, network-supported communication is basically a written form of communication and cannot substitute face-to-face human interaction. Furthermore, applying networking to English learning in China is very demanding for both the teacher and students. The study has offered us some useful implications:

1 *Changes in teachers' roles and challenges of their old educational beliefs*
A networking classroom demands a new social dynamic. Students are no longer passive learners to be filled with knowledge transmitted by the teacher. They become more independent of the teacher as they have access to other sources of knowledge. This requires that teachers rethink their traditional educational beliefs and step down from the podium to students' computer stations; they need to foster a more balanced relationship with students, and reestablish their role as a facilitator, guide and helper.

2 *Student training in basic computer skills before participation*
Some students have little knowledge about operating a computer. This puts them at a disadvantage both technically and psychologically. At the start, a great deal of their time may be spent struggling with the computer. It takes some time before they gain their confidence and acquire a sense of accomplishment. Therefore, to get students well prepared for any networking tasks, prior training is necessary, so that they can focus on what they are going to do with the computer rather than how to do it.

3 *Continuous administrative and technical support*
Support from school leaders is essential to the success of any networking project. It is with this kind of support that we were able to offer students maximal access to computers and the Internet technology within

limits. Technical assistance is another indispensable condition. Throughout the project, we were frequently hassled by technical glitches such as machine breakdowns and connection problems. If it was not for our dedicated technician who provided continuous troubleshooting, little progress could have been made.

To conclude, networking in China's ELT offers a broad field for exploration. We hope more investment and endeavours can be made and a 'win–win' situation can be finally created. But to make this come true, teachers and educators in China must first recognise the potential impact that networking can have on the English language learning environment.

References

Berge, Z. & Collins, M. (1995). *Computer-mediated communication and the online classroom in distance learning.* Cresskill, NJ: Hampton Press.
Chun, D. (1994). Using computer networks to facilitate the acquisition of interactive competence. *System 22*, 1, 17–31.
Egbert, J. (1993). Learner perceptions of computer-supported language learning environments: Analytic and systemic analysis. Unpublished doctoral dissertation. Tucson: University of Arizona.
Egbert, J. L. & Jessup, L. M. (1996). Analytic and systemic analyses of computer-supported language learning environments. *TESL-EJ 2*, 2, 2–5.
    URL <http://www.kyoto-su.ac.jp/information/tesl-ej/ej06/al.html>
Frizler, K. (1995). *The Internet as an educational tool in ESOL writing instruction.*
    URL <http://thecity.sfsu.edu/~funweb/thesis.htm>
Meloni C. (1998). The Internet in the classroom: A valuable tool and resource for ESL/EFL teachers. *ESL Magazine 1*, 1, 10–16.
Sayers, D. (1993). Distance team teaching and computer learning networks. *TESOL Journal 3*, 1, 19–23.
Shih, M. (1996). English teaching in China in an era of reform: Some effects of changing policies. *TESOL Matters 6*, 4, 1–24.
Singhal, M. (1997). The Internet and foreign language education: Benefits and challenges. *The Internet TESL Journal 3*,6.
    URL <http://www.aitech.ac.jp/~iteslj/Articles/Singhal-Internet.html>
Warschauer, M. (1996a). Computer-mediated collaborative learning: Theory and practice (Research Note No. 17). Honolulu, Hawaii: University of Hawaii, Second Language Teaching & Curriculum Centre.
Warschauer, M. (1996b). Motivational aspects of using computers for writing and communication. In M. Warschauer (Ed.), *Telecollaboration in foreign language learning: Proceedings of the Hawaii symposium.* (Technical Report #12) (pp. 29–46). Honolulu, Hawaii: University of Hawaii, Second Language Teaching & Curriculum Centre.
Warschauer, M., Turbee, L. & Roberts, B. (1996). Computer learning networks and student empowerment. *System 24*, 1, 1–14.

Appendix

Survey: Student perceptions of the network-supported learning environment*

Part I
For each of the following questions, please write a number (1–5) on the left margin:
1 = strongly disagree, 2 = disagree, 3 = neutral, 4 = agree, 5 = strongly agree

1. I have chances to use English for real communication. (4.364**)
2. I have chances to exchange ideas with other learners of English. (4.273**)
3. I have chances to discuss problems and difficulties with the teacher. (4.273**)
4. The activities I do help me learn English effectively. (4.455**)
5. I have great interest in taking part in the various problem-solving activities. (4.273**)
6. I have chances to read English written by real people that I communicate with. (4.000**)
7. I get to know a lot of interesting and new things through my key pals' email messages. (3.545)
8. I can have the teacher's individual attention. (4.091**)
9. The teacher and my classmates are always available when I need help. (4.636**)
10. I have time and chances to reflect on my learning experience. (4.091**)
11. I pay attention when doing my work. (4.273**)
12 I know how well I'm doing. (3.636**)
13. The learning atmosphere is cooperative and supportive. (4.455**)
14. I feel comfortable working with my classmates and the teacher. (4.273**)
15 I'm given more responsibility for my own learning. (4.000**)
16 I decide my own pace of learning. (3.727**)
17. My opinions and suggestions are neglected. (4.091**when reverse coded)
18. I have chances to communicate with native English speakers. (3.455)
19. I have chances to share my feelings and thoughts with my classmates. (4.000**)
20. This project offers us a variety of activities that encourage me to use English meaningfully. (4.182**)
21. The ways we use English for different purposes while completing different tasks reflect our future needs. (4.182**)
22. I have chances to be exposed to the real language used in daily life. (4.091**)
23. The Internet provides us with a variety of authentic language learning materials. (4.000**)
24. I use English in many ways (e.g. to express my opinion, to look for relevant information, to discuss issues, etc.) (4.091**)

25. I can get immediate feedback from the teacher on my thoughts, ideas, and performance. (4.364**)
26. I have enough time to complete the tasks. (3.727**)
27. I think carefully about the things I do in the lab. (3.818**)
28. I get more involved in doing tasks in the lab than in a traditional classroom. (4.182**)
29. I feel I'm in an environment that encourages my free expression. (4.273**)
30. I feel I'm part of a community. (4.091**)
31. I'm afraid to make mistakes. (3.636 when reverse coded)
32. I can do what suits my own way of learning. (3.364)
33. I help to decide on topics for discussion and writing. (3.818**)
34. The project satisfies my needs to talk with others with a clear purpose. (4.273**)
35. I'm engaged in activities that encourage me to negotiate meaning with others in English. (4.091**)

Overall mean score for all students, all 35 questions: 4.060
* Means of responses are listed in parentheses
** Significantly better than a hypothetically neutral score of 3 at $p<.05$

Part II
1. What do you benefit from most in this project?
2. What are some other benefits you can think of?
3. How does this project affect your attitude toward English language learning?
4. What are the limitations of this project?
5. What kind of advice would you give when we conduct a similar project in future?

11

Outcomes-Based Learning and the Role of CALL in South Africa

Gudrun Oberprieler
University of Cape Town, South Africa

Introduction

'Outcomes-based education' (OBE) is the new watchword in the current overhaul of the education system in South Africa.[1] It is being prescribed to schools by the Education Department to replace decades of rote learning and an overemphasis on examinations and traditional testing methods. Despite the fact that this new direction is welcomed in principle by educationists, many have serious doubts whether the school system with its great shortage of teachers and the most basic facilities, the lack of training in teachers, and huge classes, can produce the desired results. Higher education institutions are making efforts to follow suit and introduce OBE. This is a result of government policies, global and national trends, and due to pedagogical insights, to external pressures brought about by dwindling financial resources, changing economic and job market realities, and to growing demands of feeder communities for accountability.

The debate around language policy and the role and status of indigenous and foreign languages in South Africa gained momentum after 1994 with the declaration of all 11 South African languages as official languages under the new Constitution, which awards all citizens equal language rights.[2] The government supports multilingualism, and the Education Department promotes 'additive bilingualism' (the learning of two other languages besides the home language) in the education system. Higher education institutions are called upon to formulate institutional language policies, which will impact on the awarding of government funding.

Current language policy in South Africa

The new Constitution explicitly commits the state to taking 'positive measures to elevate the status and advance the use of [indigenous] languages', the development of which was purposefully neglected under the apartheid government. The Constitution furthermore guarantees equal status and 'parity of esteem' to all official languages, and it also supports the development of the Khoi, Nama and San languages, and sign language. Other languages used by minority groups in South Africa,[3] as well as languages used for religious purposes,[4] are guaranteed promotion and respect under the Constitution (1996:5). The new government established the so-called Pan South African Language Board to oversee the implementation of the national language policy.

The Language In Education Policy of July 1997 subscribes to the national language policy as spelt out in the Constitution and strongly supports multilingual education. The education system promotes additive bilingualism as an underlying principle of education. In other words, it supports maintaining home languages while also aiming at providing access to and supporting the acquisition of at least another two languages by all citizens. Among the main aims of the Ministry of Education for supporting multilingualism is 'to promote full participation in society and the economy through equitable and meaningful access to education', and 'to counter disadvantages resulting from different kinds of mismatches between home languages and languages of learning and teaching' (Language In Education Policy 1997:6). The new Constitution grants South African citizens the fundamental right to receive education in the official language or languages of their choice in public educational institutions, where practicable.[5]

Language learning at South African universities

Despite the new policy outlined above, the reality is that there is currently a striking discrepancy between sociopolitical developments in South Africa in terms of a national language policy which promotes multilingualism, and the value attributed to language skills under the new dispensation on the one hand, and the desperate situation of many language departments at higher education institutions on the other. Many language departments at universities, especially the foreign language departments, have shrunk considerably over the past few years; some have been amalgamated, others have been closed.

Many students for whom English or Afrikaans are a second, third or fourth language are severely disadvantaged at higher education institutions, because the language of instruction at all universities and technikons is either English or dual medium (English and Afrikaans[6]), while the tuition of these languages at school level is often inadequate. There is currently not a single tertiary education institution in South Africa that uses an African language as medium of instruction. Despite the new language policy, it is also highly unlikely that any university or technikon will declare an African language its sole medium of instruction. The resources in terms of staff and funding are simply not available, and such a decision is also very unlikely to receive much support from feeder communities, as English is seen by most as the gateway to education, employment and a better standard of living. It is more likely that some of the African languages will be used as languages of communication in teaching and learning alongside English or Afrikaans.

In spite of the recognition of South Africa as a multilingual country both by the Constitution and the South African Schools Act of 1996, there is at this stage 'no national policy framework within which the higher education institutions could establish their own institutional language policies and programs' (A Programme for the Transformation of Higher Education 1997). The Ministry plans to create a Council for Higher Education which will, among other tasks, investigate the language situation in higher education institutions and, together with the Pan South African Language Board, advise the Minister of Education on the development of a national language framework for higher education (1997:2.77, 2.78). This framework will have to address questions like medium of instruction; language(s) of communication; the development of all South African languages; the training of language teachers, interpreters and translators; the promotion of the language-based arts; and effective communication with the rest of Africa and the world in the areas of culture, diplomacy, science and business (1997:2.79).

Despite the current absence of such a national policy framework, public higher education institutions are now required by law to determine their institutional language policy, and to publish it and make it available on request (Higher Education Act 1997:27.2). Although higher education institutions are given the freedom to formulate their own internal language policy, the Ministry makes it quite clear that institutional policies will in future have to be in line with the national education language policy framework, and that government funding will be directly affected by institutional decisions (A Programme for the Transformation of Higher Education 1997:2.80, 2.81).

On the one hand, there is considerable pressure from the government, in particular the Education Department, on higher education institutions to deliver their part in the implementation of the vision of a truly multilingual society and multilingual individuals, as spelt out in the Constitution. On the other hand, language teaching both at school level and in tertiary education is not in a healthy state. In schools, English is compulsory in all schools, Afrikaans still in some, and the learning of African languages has increased. But often the teaching is bad and methods outdated, due to lack of teacher training.

Foreign language teaching in secondary schools and at higher education institutions in South Africa has been in crisis for many years now.[7] Issues such as dwindling student numbers in the language departments, the decline in numbers of mother-tongue speakers who go on to study their home language and literature at university level, the increasing dilemma of what to teach *ab initio* learners within the three short years of undergraduate studies, the perceived decline of preparedness of students for university study generally, the question what could be done to make foreign language learning more attractive – all these issues have received attention at national conferences of professional associations for many years. Nevertheless, the decline of foreign language learning could not be halted. There are now far fewer schools than a couple of years ago that offer languages other than the 11 official ones, and at university level there are hardly any autonomous foreign language departments left. In most cases, changes are accompanied by cuts in teaching staff. Foreign language units also have to fit in with institutional and national language and educational policies and trends such as interdisciplinary program development. As a result, literature is increasingly taught in English translation. On the positive side, in some cases this has led to the development of interesting new comparative literature courses. The formerly unthinkable often becomes possible now in South Africa. The merger in 1999 of the Departments of Afrikaans and Nederlands and African Languages at the University of Cape Town – initiated by the two departments themselves – is an indication that the negative pressures of dwindling funds and student numbers do not necessarily spell doom and gloom in all cases.

Not only the European language departments are under siege. Due to the political changes, Afrikaans has lost its status as one of the two official languages besides English. This has resulted in a dramatic drop in student numbers in the Afrikaans and Nederlands departments especially at the English medium universities. Much more surprising is the fact that the African language departments are not really flourishing either, although no university would probably think of dispensing with its African language department altogether, given the sociopolitical developments of the immediate past and the present. The reasons for the stagnation are manifold, but African language departments must also now try and recruit more customers by assessing and addressing students' needs.[8]

The only language departments which are not under threat are the English departments, because despite the fact that under the new national language policy all 11 languages have equal status, English is clearly dominant and the importance of English language skills in all areas of public life is growing rapidly. Nevertheless, the English departments at South African universities have traditionally given very little attention to language teaching and concentrated rather on literature, as their students were either mother-tongue speakers or could be assumed to have studied English at school for many years. Now there are many more students for whom English is at least a second if not a third or fourth language, and whose language skills are often very inadequate to cope with English as language of instruction in an academic environment. But it is mostly Academic Development Programs and Applied English Language Studies departments who deal with these language problems.

The demand for outcomes in education

The Education Department has set up a so-called 'South African Qualifications Authority' (SAQA) which has worked out a new National Qualifications Framework (NQF). The NQF presents a revised school curriculum, guidelines for tertiary education (universities, colleges, technikons), for adult learning and on-the-job training, and new national qualifications that will allow for standardisation, greater mobility and recognition of prior learning. The reasoning behind this is that the economy and the changed sociopolitical scenario in South Africa need citizens with new and different skills.

In the schools, 1998 has seen the start of the much-publicised 'Curriculum 2005' which will be phased in up to the year 2005. The underlying paradigm shift is that from a content-based curriculum to an outcomes-based one. Decades of rote-learning, exam-oriented, teacher-centred and textbook-bound teaching is to be replaced with a learner-centred approach, aiming at guiding learners towards critical thinking, reflection and action, and on-going assessment and guidance by the teacher. The focus is meant to shift from what is taught, to what is learnt and how. Although the new school curriculum is widely welcomed by educationists in principle, there are serious concerns whether the new system can and will succeed in the way it is intended. Fifty years of apartheid education and the consequent unequal distribution of facilities and resources, a grave shortage of teachers, huge classes, a serious lack of training in teachers, let alone immense social problems resulting from poverty and malnutrition, are clearly not conducive to the fast success of an outcomes-based curriculum (see Jansen 1997).

Although universities have much more autonomy over their structures and curricula than schools, there is a lot of pressure for change in higher educa-tion as well, most of which is directly related to what is happening in South African schools. At tertiary level, the main pressures are increasing massifi-cation of higher education, simultaneous drastic cuts in state funding, the demand for greater accountability to various stakeholders (including the State, tax-payers, employers, students and their parents), and the need for course structures and curricula to reflect national and world-wide sociopolit-ical changes. The demand for greater accountability of higher education insti-tutions to the communities they serve is directly related to the call for quali-ty assurance of qualifications, and to the need, after decades of gross inequalities, for equity and redress in student access and chances of success, employment and training of staff, and institutional development.

The University of Cape Town, as an example, has revised its broad edu-cational outcomes to subscribe to the Department of Education's view of 'synergy between scholarship and society', by committing itself to outcomes-based rather than knowledge-based education, and to the merger of studying a discipline and training for a career (Strategic Planning Framework 1997:2). The University's mission documents declare the following desired generic learning outcomes: effective literacy, effective numeracy, computer literacy, the ability for communication, problem-solving and information handling, critical thought and reasoning, and rigour and precision of language (SPF 1997:9). The goal is a to achieve a level of 'graduateness' in students, 'a sound balance between depth and breadth of learning and between subject knowledge and appropriate generic skills, on providing students with broad preparation for engaging positively with the social and economic realities of the contemporary world, on rigour and internationally recognised qualifica-tion standards, and on offering a strong foundation for lifelong learning' (Centre for Higher Education Development 1998:7).

Envisaged outcomes of language learning in South Africa

The Constitution and government policy documents such as the Language in Education Policy (1997) place great emphasis on the positive role of lan-guage in bringing about the envisaged new social order. There are high expectations of the positive influence that the recognition of all 11 languages and the promotion of language learning will have on the process of reconcil-iation and the building of a multilingual, multicultural and 'non-racial nation in South Africa', and in countering 'any particularistic ethnic chauvinism or separatism through mutual understanding' (Language in Education Policy 1997, Par. A 2, 4). The role of languages in education is therefore seen to be closely linked to national interests and what one might call desired 'socio-political outcomes'. The promotion of multilingualism and additive biling-ualism in the Language in Education Policy are especially meant to serve the intended broad educational outcomes of developing the nine African lan-guages, and redressing past linguistic and racial discrimination by ensuring access of previously disadvantaged learners to education and their success within the educational system.

In schools, African language speakers often wish to be taught in their mother tongue, at least at primary school level. But there is no accepted stan-dard for these languages, so standardisation and development in many areas is necessary. There is also a need for more learning of African languages at formerly white schools where this had only happened on a very limited scale. The biggest need, however, is for the teaching of English. Many African par-ents want their children educated in English, as this is seen as the only way to a good education and a decent standard of living. White and 'coloured' (of mixed race) parents choose either English or Afrikaans as medium of instruc-tion, depending on their home language.

Although universities will officially not admit students with no or extremely poor skills in the language of instruction, especially in the case of English, there are many students who struggle with the linguistic level required for academic discourse and need intervention in this area. Many do not succeed in their studies because of the language barrier. Academic English and especially discipline-specific jargon is a big obstacle. The University of Cape Town is considering introducing an English language pro-ficiency test for admittance. But, on the other hand, it cannot afford to be seen to exclude intellectually capable students because of language restrictions. The English language issue has to be addressed more rigorously.

There is now also a real urgency to address the increasing demand for skills in African languages. This is especially true for professionals in the fields of health care and social work who increasingly need at least a basic level of proficiency in an African language. Traditionally, they have relied on interpreters, which was often problematic and is becoming less acceptable under the new dispensation. In future, there will probably also be an increas-ing demand among academic staff at universities for learning African lan-guages in order to communicate more effectively in an academic context with students, if not only as a sign of goodwill and reconciliation. Furthermore, there is a growing demand for trained translators and interpreters in all sec-tors of society. Expanding trade links with the rest of Africa have created a market, albeit small, for French and Portuguese language skills.

In the light of the current emphasis on outcomes-based education, it can be argued that in the Western world language teaching and learning has been orientated towards the outcomes of its endeavours for a very long time, probably much more so than many other disciplines. Language students, especially in tertiary and adult education, mostly engage in their studies with a clear picture of the desired outcomes of their efforts, be it communicative competency or the ability to read texts or to write in the target language. Language course designers and teachers are almost always under pressure to spell out clearly what students can expect to have learnt by the end of a course or module, and what level of competency they will have reached. At the end of many language courses there is a competency examination and a certification process. Language teaching, especially in adult education, has become a service industry with considerable costs involved for learners who want a good product and visible proof of their learning outcomes.

Furthermore, it can be claimed that the paradigm shift in teaching and learning methods now proclaimed by the education authorities in South Africa has already taken place in Foreign Language Teaching over the past twenty years or so. Although classroom practice does most likely not match the theory in all cases, teaching and learning methods in language studies have changed dramatically over the last two decades. Contemporary methods involve communicative and cooperative language learning, emphasis on the autonomy of the learner and learner-oriented teaching, inclusion of existing knowledge of learners, context-based and project-based learning, authenticity of materials, differentiation of skills into four categories (listening, speaking, reading and writing), the integration of skills training, and intercultural communication.

In the South African education system, especially in the school sector, the theory of language teaching now at last seems to move in the direction of modern pedagogical principles. However, in spite of changes in national policy, some provincial education departments are often very reluctant to follow suit. There are studies that claim that this has resulted directly in a decline in pupil numbers in some provinces (e.g. Struckmann 1997). It is also no secret that in spite of more enlightened policies in some of the provinces, reality in many instances has a long way to go to catch up with the theory. Although there are exceptions, especially in better equipped schools, many language teachers resort to antiquated teaching methods which they are familiar with and have experienced themselves as learners, due to lack of training and time for creative thinking in very stressful circumstances. The situation in the language departments at universities generally is a lot better.

The signs are there that language learning will become a much bigger issue in the future. However, the question as to who will foot the bill for developing African languages and teaching them more widely in schools, at university and in adult education has yet to be answered. Who will pay for training students in the health care professions and other areas of social service at all tertiary institutions in communicative skills in African languages? Where will the language teachers and the resources for facilities come from? How will more opportunities be created for people to learn English or improve their skills? And how will a high standard of language teaching and learning be ensured and address the needs of learners? Can computers and information technology play an important part in this, or is money spent on CALL a waste of resources?

Potential roles of CALL in the South African education system

As a *sine qua non*, CALL requires computers. There are many private and probably quite a number of public schools with computer facilities, although for the majority of schools this is still an unimaginable luxury. Most universities now seem to have computer labs that are used either exclusively for language teaching or are shared facilities for a variety of purposes.

But, overall, CALL is neither widely practised nor much promoted in South Africa. There are a number of reasons for this. Firstly, predictably, there is often a lack of funding for facilities (including electricity at many schools), space, maintenance and security, and language software. There is also hardly any training available in computer-based education (CBE) in general or in CALL in particular for either teachers or lecturers. Due to the crisis situation in schools and massive retrenchment of teachers, and to the shrinkage of language departments at universities, especially foreign language departments, there is less and less training of language teachers happening nationally. The teaching profession is not seen to be attractive due to lack of future prospects and low pay. Very often there is a lack of structures within which CBE and CALL could be promoted and furthered. CBE is a collaborative enterprise, as Patrikis (1997) rightly points out, and it often does not happen in a beneficial way because of lack of cooperation at institutions. Another reason for CALL not being used widely to address the language learning needs in South Africa, is the lack of computer software for African languages, in fact the lack of good teaching materials overall.[9]

This is not to say, however, that nothing is happening. But all efforts are on quite a small scale. A few examples are the externally funded Multimedia Education Group (MEG) at the University of Cape Town which has developed software for English for Academic Purposes (also for history and archaeology), and a multimedia package for Xhosa, authored by a lecturer from the Department of African Languages in collaboration with MEG, that was recently released. The package is already being used successfully by students and is being marketed. At the University of the Witwatersrand, a collaborative effort between a lecturer from the Department of African Languages and a professor of modern languages from McMaster University in Canada, who is a specialist in language software development, has produced a package of learning materials for Zulu which include exercises on disk. A CD-ROM with listening exercises is currently in the making. The publisher has initiated the production of a version of the package in Xhosa. Apparently, there is also a project at the University of Natal to produce some software for Zulu. Although there might be some other internal software development initiatives at other institutions in the country, the publishers of teaching materials are unlikely to be interested in anything else but the three major African languages in South Africa – Zulu, Xhosa and Sotho. The market for the other six is so limited that sales would probably not even cover the production costs.

However, computer-assisted language teaching and learning does no longer only mean having a laboratory full of expensive multimedia computers available, and a library with multiple copies of equally pricey (in South African currency at least) software packages. In the beginning of computer-assisted learning, the machines were hailed mainly for their aptness to address aspects of learning that group teaching had never been able to offer, and which support the now widely acknowledged paradigms of autonomous learning. Computers can support individualised learning, they can help learners to engage in the learning process at their own pace based on their individual background and needs, they can encourage autonomous or at least semi-autonomous (Schulze-Lefert & Weiland 1989) learning and so on. There is now an extensive literature on the successes and problems encountered in projects making use of computers in an 'agentive' way in the learning process (Debski 1997a, 1997b; Patrikis 1997). The use of computers as agents for individualised learning still has a very important role to play, especially in facilities such as language centres that are set up for self-study. In South Africa, it would be of great benefit in the education system if more such learning centres for languages and many other areas could be set up – at educational institutions, in businesses, at NGOs, and in community centres. Language-learning activities with Windows or even DOS-based software, or with multimedia CDs if these are affordable, would address the needs of many learners, despite justified concerns about the pedagogic and technical quality of many products (e.g. Patrikis 1997; Rösler 1998).

However, technological progress has now made it possible to move beyond individuals hacking away at grammar exercises on their own PC. The advent of the Internet with email and the World Wide Web is opening up a whole new range of opportunities for language teaching and learning, and more and more language teachers are engaging with this new medium in very creative ways. It is most interesting to observe how pedagogy is moving along with developments in technology.[10] The computer is no longer only an agent for more individualised learning, it can now also be used as an instrument for new communicative forms of teaching and learning. In fact, the Internet brings us back again from individualisation to new social forms of learning, it takes us from an 'agentive' to an 'instrumental' way of using computers (Debski 1997a, 1997b; Patrikis 1997; Rösler 1998), it enables what has been coined 'social computing' (Debski, Gassin & Smith 1997). The key words are no longer *autonomy* and *individualisation* of the learner, but instead *utilisation* of the computer for learning in an interactive way through email, teleconferencing and the Web, which is putting the emphasis on the process of learning, creativity, social interaction, project-based learning, activity, goal-oriented exploration and connection (Barson 1997; Collombet-Sankey 1997; Debski 1997b; Jung & Vanderplank 1994; Mozzon-Mcpherson 1996; Patrikis 1997; Rösler 1998; Shneiderman 1997; St John & Cash 1995).

One should not read into this a move away from autonomous learning practices, but rather see this development as an opportunity to bring back the results of individual learning endeavours to a level of social interaction. This is, after all, where the need for language learning arises – in human communication. The Internet offers new forms of communication for language learners, that is, global communication with other speakers by way of technology (see also Debski 1997).

It seems to me that the Internet may offer more possibilities of introducing CALL to the language learner in South Africa than the multimedia computer with the CD-ROM. Computing as a social activity can be less expensive than catering for the individual needs of learners by setting up facilities with large numbers of computers. This would still be desirable of course, but in an imperfect world a single computer with Internet access at a school can be used to introduce dozens of students to the global information network. One multimedia computer with Internet access and some basic software costs less than R10 000. Equipping a whole laboratory costs hundreds of thousands of rands which are not available. Classes, including language classes, could engage in project work in groups who had to surf the net for information. They could link up with classes or individuals anywhere else in the world via email, for example, to improve their English language skills or for projects in tandem learning. If it can be done by individuals, it can also be done with groups. In this way, pupils and students alike could be engaged in learning activities in creative, collaborative and active ways. Their learning process would include social interaction and exploration. If an institution has only two computers, students in a language class could be divided into two groups, send each other messages, create exercises and tasks for each other and so on. Creative teachers, and students, could no doubt come up with many exciting tasks. And many of these tasks would be possible in any language, without depending on the expensive development of software.

Students would, even on a limited basis, gain subject knowledge as well as computer skills. Teachers would be able to shift their traditional roles from knowledge-providers to facilitators. All of this is very much within the parameters and the aims of the proclaimed outcomes-based education principles. CBE would promote these goals and implement them in new and exciting ways. Of course, teachers still have to be trained, there are security and maintenance issues, and technology cannot be used without electricity. And teachers, school buildings, desks and chairs and books are needed, before one would buy a computer. But at least some exposure to information technology could certainly be possible to more children than is currently the case. Tertiary institutions that are generally better equipped than schools could engage in exciting projects.

Conclusion

The question must be asked whether one can afford to introduce information technology in education on a large scale in South Africa, or in any other developing country with similar social challenges for that matter. Computers are costly, they become outdated much more quickly than textbooks or other educational materials. Given the scale of poverty, homelessness, lack of health care, unemployment and the education crisis, should one therefore aim at making them a common commodity wherever possible? And against the background of the dire educational situation in South Africa, can one really take the high aims of outcomes-based education seriously, and especially make sophisticated projects possible through what has come to be called 'social computing'? (Debski, Gassin & Smith 1997). Jansen (1997) and other educators in South Africa have expressed serious doubts even about the pedagogic desirability of such enterprises at this point in time. Will OBE bring about a renewed over-emphasis on evaluation and results instead of the process and the content of learning endeavours? Will the desired outcomes of today be less desirable tomorrow and date as quickly as the latest computer model or this season's fashion? Is it perhaps justified to be as cynical as the school teacher who, after the umpteenth meeting on the subject, declared that the faster we come out of outcomes-based education the better?

On the other hand, one could also put the somewhat over-used counter question: can we afford not to have computers in educational institutions, for CALL and for other subjects? And, in the light of very unequally equipped schools and universities in South Africa, if not all can have it, at least for now, does that mean that nobody should have it? It is unconvincing to argue that equal deprivation of educational institutions will create a better chance for things to improve, although redress for historically deprived schools and universities understandably comes under discussion on a regular basis. Computer literacy is now indispensable on the job market, especially for graduates. Using computers for teaching and learning confers not only subject knowledge, but also develops IT competencies, essential social skills and different learning styles. Although a computer does not turn a poor teacher into a more competent one – nor does it substitute teachers altogether as authorities still often hope will happen – there is little doubt that the creative use of information technology for educational purposes can make a real contribution to achieving desired learning outcomes, be it of a social nature or in terms of skills and knowledge. In fact, the versatility and broad scope of facilities like email and the Web as educational tools might even prevent students turning into well-programmed and outcomes-orientated human *doings*, instead of them developing into balanced human *beings* as one would hope.

There is a parallel in the tale of Babacar Fall, a Senegalese journalist and communications specialist who was appointed by UNESCO to revive the Pan African News Agency (PANA) in the early 1990s. Fall's dream of a wired Africa began to be realised when in 1992 a Dakar-based French research company provided PANA with a basic Internet link. Fall is convinced that the reason for the many expensive failures of aid projects on the African continent are due to the dismal state of African communications, which makes the continent largely invisible to world media. 'We can leapfrog', he argues, 'Africa doesn't have to go from drums to telegraphs to telex. We can go right to satellites, electronic media, and a computerised newsroom.' And he makes a revolutionary statement:

> For years ... the main obstacle to real development has been the statement, "We have to feed the people first". After all, who can withhold food? But if you want the people to feed themselves, you have to have a different view. ... Say you go to a small village. People are hungry. Is the priority an electronic mailbox ... or 100 kilograms of corn? ... What we've learned, over the past twenty years, is that the mailbox may well be the priority (Greenwald 1995).

Acknowlegments

Financial assistance from the University of Cape Town and the Centre for Science Development (CSD) for my attendance at the WorldCALL Conference is gratefully acknowledged.

Notes

[1] The emphasis in this article is on tertiary education. However, the entire education system in South Africa is currently undergoing major changes, so that many of the topical issues at universities are directly related to what happens at school level. The article will therefore also refer to the situation in secondary education wherever necessary.

[2] The official languages of South Africa are: Sepedi, Sesotho, Setswana, siSwati, Tshivenda, Xitsonga, Afrikaans, English, isiNdebele, isiXhosa and isiZulu (Constitution of the Republic of South Africa 1996:5).

[3] Languages such as German, Greek, Gujarati, Hindi, Portuguese, Tamil, Telegu and Urdu.

[4] Languages such as Arabic, Hebrew and Sanskrit.

[5] Section 29(2) of the Constitution.

[6] Traditional Afrikaans medium universities have all recognized the signs of the time and now offer many of their courses in English as well.

[7] European languages such as French, Italian, German and Portuguese, and languages such as Hebrew and Arabic.

[8] Some of the reasons for the stagnation of African language departments are the shortage of methodologically trained language teachers in African languages, and consequently the use of outdated teaching methods, and the perceived unattractiveness of course contents in many instances. But there are also others: the fact that relatively few white adults are eager to learn African languages; that those who do mostly only want a communicative competency for professional reasons (the pressure in this area is increasing), and the courses offered by university departments do not really cater for this; the fact that most black South Africans tend to learn languages more in an informal rather than a formal way and do not flock to university departments to study them.

[9] The reason for this is historic. Under the apartheid government, Afrikaans was especially promoted and large sums spent on its development, while the development of African languages was purposefully neglected.

[10] Debski (1997a) draws an interesting comparison between shifts in language pedagogy and shifts in social perceptions as portrayed in Sherry Turkle's much-quoted book *Life on the Screen: Identity in the Age of the Internet* (1995, London: Weidenfeld & Nicholson).

References

A Programme for the Transformation of Higher Education (1997). Education White Paper 3. July. Pretoria.

Academic Planning Framework (1996). University of Cape Town.

Balla, J. & Boyle, P. (1994). Assessment of student performance: A framework for improving practice. *Assessment & Evaluation in Higher Education 19, 1*, 17–28.

Barson, J. (1997). Space, time and form in the project-based foreign language class-room. In R. Debski, J. Gassin & M. Smith (Eds), *Language learning through social computing* (pp. 1–37). Applied Linguistics Association of Australia Occasional Papers 16. Melbourne: ALAA & The Horwood Language Centre.

Boud, E. (1990). Assessment and the promotion of academic values. *Studies in Higher Education 15*, 1, 101–111.

Centre for Higher Education Development: High Level Plan (Draft) (1998). University of Cape Town.

Collombet-Sankey, N. (1997). Surfing the net to acquire communicative competence and cultural knowledge. In R. Debski, J. Gassin & M. Smith (Eds), *Language learning through social computing* (pp. 141–158). Applied Linguistics Association of Australia Occasional Papers 16. Melbourne: ALAA & The Horwood Language Centre.

Constitution of the Republic of South Africa (1996). Pretoria.

Curriculum 2005 (1997). [Information Brochure]. Pretoria.

Curriculum 2005 (1997). Orientation Program Teachers' Notes. Pretoria.

Debski, R. (1997a). From individualisation to socialisation: An essay on CALL with reflections on Sherry Turkle's *Life on the Screen*. In R. Debski, J. Gassin & M. Smith (Eds), *Language learning through social computing* (pp. 201–219). Applied Linguistics Association of Australia Occasional Papers 16. Melbourne: ALAA & The Horwood Language Centre.

Debski, R. (1997b). Support of creativity and collaboration in the language class-room: A new role for technology. In R. Debski, J. Gassin & M. Smith (Eds), *Language learning through social computing* (pp. 39–65). Applied Linguistics Association of Australia Occasional Papers 16. Melbourne: ALAA & The Horwood Language Centre.

Debski, R., Gassin J. & Smith M. (Eds) (1997). *Language learning through social computing*. Applied Linguistics Association of Australia Occasional Papers 16 (pp. 39–65). ALAA & The Horwood Language Centre.

Draft Statement on the National Curriculum for Grades 1–9 (1997). Pretoria.

Eisner, E. W. (1993). Reshaping Assessment in Education: Some criteria in search of practice. *Curriculum Studies 25*, 3, 219–233.

Greenwald, J. (1995). Wiring Africa. *America Online*.

Higher Education Act (1997). Pretoria.

Jansen, J. (1997). Why OBE will fail. Forthcoming: *Cambridge Journal of Education,* special issue on South African education.

Jung, H. & Vanderplank, R. (Eds) (1994). *Barriers and bridges: Media technology in language learning*. Proceedings of the 1993 CETaLL Symposium on the Occasion of the 10th AILA World Congress in Amsterdam. Frankfurt am Main/Bern/New York/Paris: Peter Lang.

Language in Education Policy (1997). Pretoria.

Moore, R. (1997). *Quality, skills and performance indicators: Assessing the gaps*. Unpublished.

Moore, R. (1998). *Towards quality programmes: A guideline for program planners at UCT*. Discussion document.

Mozzon-Mcpherson, M. (1996). Italian via email: From an online project of learning and teaching towards the development of a multi-cultural discourse community. *Alt-J (Association for Learning Technology Journal) 4*, 1, 40–50.

Patrikis, P.C. (1997). The evolution of computer technology in foreign language teaching and learning. In R. Debski, J. Gassin & M. Smith (Eds), *Language learning through social computing* (pp. 159–178). Applied Linguistics Association of Australia Occasional Papers 16. Melbourne: ALAA & The Horwood Language Centre.

Rösler, D. (1998). Autonomes Lernen? Neue Medien und 'altes' Fremdsprachenlernen. *InfoDaf 25*, 1, 3–20.

Schulze-Lefert, P. & Weiland, K. (1989). Der halbautonome Lernweg. Gruppenunterricht – Mediothek – Individuelles Lernen. Ein Erfahrungsbericht. In M. Müller et al. (Eds), *Autonomes und partnerschaftliches Lernen. Modelle und Beispiele aus dem Fremdsprachenunterricht* (pp. 131–144). Berlin: Langenscheidt.

Shneiderman, B. (1997). Foreword to R. Debski, J. Gassin & M. Smith (Eds), *Language learning through social computing* (pp. v–viii). Applied Linguistics Association of Australia Occasional Papers 16. Melbourne: ALAA & The Horwood Language Centre.

St John, E. & Cash, D. (1995). German language learning via email: A case study. *ReCALL 7*, 2, 47–51.

Strategic Planning Framework 1997–2000 (1997). University of Cape Town.

Struckmann, H.E. (1997). Assessment in foreign language teaching: Is a paradigm shift required? *Journal of Educational Evaluation 5*, 64–68.

12

Changing the Research Paradigm: Qualitative Research Methodology and the CALL Classroom[1]

Gary Motteram
University of Manchester, UK

The debate about how we research the CALL classroom is not a particularly new one, but it has perhaps become more focussed as we approach the millennium and as CALL is seen by many to have come of age. This chapter is going to look at a number of issues concerned with researching the CALL classroom. It is going to present these ideas against a background of the continuous advances of technology and their seemingly relentless impact on education and life in general. It is also going to consider more general issues in Second Language Acquisition (SLA) and English Language Teaching (ELT) and talk of additional models of research for the new millennium.

In the early days, things seemed quite clear-cut. Computers were limited in what they could do and interested researchers observed usually carefully constructed small groups interacting around computers. Researchers attempted to show that computers could improve discrete parts of language acquisition. They used empirical research methods and the aim ultimately was to show that the increasingly heavy investment in computers was value for money where language improvement was concerned. More recently it has been proposed that we should be following the particular methods of SLA when we conduct research. Here we would wish to argue that research into

CALL should take a much broader approach. Developing a true theory of CALL means looking at qualitative research methods in the first instance and including teachers as researchers into our research endeavours to give us a more grounded theory.

As a supervisor of Master's dissertations and PhD theses, one of my tasks is to help students to select appropriate research methods to apply to a range of different projects. Some of these projects are concerned with looking at how existing software is being used in classrooms (taking both software and classrooms in their widest possible interpretations). Some are to do with the creation of new software as a way of examining particular issues in language learning, for example the teaching of listening skills. Some are concerned with the implementation of new schemes within a particular educational context. Some are to do with the examination of how technology is being used by teachers.

What tends to happen is that, despite the diversity of projects, most students do their initial literature review in the field of CALL and find a good many articles that take an empirical view and so, despite my best efforts to direct them to general literature on research methodology, think that this is the most useful (perhaps the only) paradigm for their own research. If you look at the progression of survey articles over time, you can see that this trend is constantly reinforced. Useful early and more recent articles to follow up include Higgins (1985), Kenning (1990), Lonergan (1991), Levy and Green (1995) and more recently Warschauer and Healey (1998).

The principal aim of this chapter is to look more broadly at research methodology to see what is happening elsewhere in classroom research and to see how other methods can broaden the data that is reported to give us a better overall picture of the CALL field. In the end, this broader picture may help us achieve the ultimate goal of providing us a broad theory of CALL. This chapter is not arguing that one approach should necessarily exclude others, but that the chosen approach should reflect the requirements of what is being researched. As Salomon (1991:15) quoting Shulman (1988) points out, it is the *question* that should dictate the *type* of study. So, if we are looking at one piece of software and comparing it with another, one approach is taken; if we are trying to find out how the computers are being used in schools in a particular context, another type of study should be undertaken.

Two recent articles on research practices in CALL will help us to understand why my students tend to pick particular paths for their research rather than others. Chapelle argues strongly that the way forward for CALL is to follow the research methods and questions favoured by SLA researchers:

> ... if progress is to be made in CALL, it seems necessary to shift from general approaches such as those of psychology, computational linguistics, and educational technology to the specific questions and

methods of researchers who investigate instructed SLA. (Chapelle 1997:28)

Her idea here is that, although we can look further afield for suitable mechanisms, we ought to focus on an area that appears to have resonance in the CALL field. See also Chapelle (1990, 1994) for further discussion of issues in CALL research. My view would be that along with SLA methodologies we should be looking at recent trends in educational and ELT research, so that the most appropriate type of research can be conducted and reported. In presentations at the WorldCALL conference, Garrett (1998), amongst others, expressed similar views to Chapelle. I have some sympathy with this view, and will come back to it below.

An article by Garrett (1998) makes a number of additional points. She argues that now the technology has come of age for language learning, and that if CALL is not to be high-jacked by administrators as a way of delivering language learning cheaply and at a distance and without teachers, we need to harness the technology itself to help us to gather data. By doing this, educators who regularly use technology will be able to help non computer-using colleagues to understand the power that the technology has for enhancing language learning. She says:

> We have to use our practice – our day-to-day integration of technology, our understanding of the necessary design links between pedagogical goals and technological implementation – to drive the definition of language teaching as a whole in ways that are both valid and acceptable to teachers. (Garrett 1998:9)

I am very happy with her perspective on teaching and the role that teachers should play, but am worried about her ways of including teachers in the research that is going on. Another quotation from the same article gives us a clearer insight into the proposed research methodology.

> A researcher working with the teacher would collect a wide variety of data from students in the classes to track all the variables that could be controlled for. (Garrett 1998:12)

The concept of research expressed here is one where the researcher is the outsider and teachers' views are not necessarily being taken into account. Also, it makes the assumption that in classrooms variables can and should be controlled. Teachers and learners are observed doing activities and then what they do is analysed and reported. The teacher's role is as the consumer of the research (see the discussion of Ellis below), and the teacher is at a distance from where and when research is reported. Freeman characterises the feelings of teachers about this kind of research in the following ways:

> ... an awkward silence has grown up between teacher and researcher; in it has flourished a gulf between what teachers know about practice

through doing it and what research can say about teaching and learning. (Freeman 1996:88)

... the dominant conception of the relationship between research and classroom practice has been one of implied transmission. (Freeman 1996:89)

Whereas the methodologies that Chapelle (1997) and Garrett (1998) describe are valid for certain kinds of controlled investigations, it is the intention of this chapter to look at the impact that CALL is having in less rigorously controlled classroom environments. It is also concerned to include teachers more centrally into the development of CALL theory.

Little describes a symposium on CALL research that took place at the 1997 EuroCALL Conference. He describes this event as a lively debate in which a number of participants point out that research into CALL should, amongst other things, include:

Action research in order to ensure that our research enterprise is not a linear but a cyclical process, leading back into the teaching/learning situation. (Little 1998:128)

In the world of FLT education, Wallace (1991) has proposed that along with other disciplines FL teachers adopt a reflective approach. His ideas are based on those of Schön, a general educational theorist, and the core rationale for Wallace's view is to make teacher education an experience that is more teacher- and classroom-centred. To do this, Wallace has included classroom-based action research as a central part of his teacher education methodology.

Interestingly, in recent articles and books and at conferences, Ellis has argued that SLA research should make more effort to include the teacher. He argues (1997, 1998) that there are three ways of modelling teaching and research in SLA:

*   teacher as consumer
*   teacher as informant – teachers supply researchers with information
*   teacher/researcher collaboration

Surprisingly, given all the empirical research that he has undertaken over the years, Ellis seems more recently to be advocating building up a picture of theory from practice, something that Wallace has been arguing for some time now and which is best summarised in his recent book on action research for language teachers (Wallace 1998). Action research does not exclude empirical research, but the increasing trend, in my opinion, is towards qualitative methodologies as being most appropriate for classroom investigations. We have also seen, more recently, agitation in mainstream applied linguistics journals like *TESOL Quarterly* and *Applied Linguistics* for a qualitative paradigm with a special issue on qualitative research in *TESOL Quarterly* (1995) and a recent article by Edge and Richards (1998) in *Applied Linguistics*, in which they argue strongly for such methodologies. However, Chapelle (1997) is advocating the research methods of SLA researchers; yet SLA researchers like Ellis are now saying that there is something missing from that research paradigm. Is there a problem here?

CALL is not alone in needing discussion of whether it ought to make additions to, or change its research paradigm. In other related fields there has been a lot of soul searching. Mel Ainscow, a professor of special educational needs at Manchester University, describes the work that he is doing in very similar terms to the way that Wallace (1998), Bailey and Nunan (1996) and others have argued in area of ELT. Ainscow (1998) describes the way in which research in special education has generally 'been influenced by theories derived from psychology and biology'. He also describes courses that teachers attend where they 'learn about theories derived from such research in order that they can then use these to inform the development of their practice' The pattern is clearly very similar to ELT where there have been influences from psychology, sociology and linguistics and CALL where, as Levy (1997) has pointed out, there have been influences from a whole raft of disciplines. Ainscow's paper goes on to argue for the methodology which he terms 'practitioner-based enquiry' to be more widely accepted in his own profession, so that instead of having the situation that we all recognise where theory does not become practice, theory *comes out of* practice as has been advocated above. Practitioner-based enquiry aims to be inclusive of the teacher and usually takes place in a classroom or school. It would generally be qualitative in terms of its data and methods. What do I mean by this?

Crossley and Vulliamy provide a useful description of qualitative research that sits well with my own views and helps us clarify the term:

> [Qualitative research] … provides descriptions and accounts of the processes and social interactions in 'natural' settings, usually based upon a combination of observation and interviewing of participants in order to understand their perspectives. Culture, meanings and processes are emphasised, rather than variables, outcomes and products. Instead of testing pre-conceived hypotheses, much qualitative research aims to generate theories and hypotheses from the data that emerge, in an attempt to avoid the imposition of a previous, and possibly inappropriate, frame of reference on the subjects of the research. (Crossley & Vulliamy 1997:6)

A qualitative methodology can allow CALL to begin to develop its own theory rather than relying on the methodologies of other disciplines which may be flawed, as we have seen above. Teachers are encouraged to report what is happening in their own classrooms. They are given the necessary research training that allows them to collect data in their own environments and to report it to a wider audience, or are encouraged to work with experienced researchers as mentors. This allows a broader picture to build up.

According to Ertmer (cited in Leedy 1997:156), there are four key types of qualitative research. These come out of various discipline traditions, respectively anthropology, law, philosophy and sociology. They are:

- case study
- ethnography
- phenomenology
- grounded theory.

It is not the aim of this contribution to go into great detail about these approaches, as there is an ever-growing literature on research in the ELT world (e.g. Cumming 1994; Davis 1995; Lazaraton 1995; McDonough & McDonough 1997; or Wallace 1998). However, table 1 contains a handy summary from Ertmer (in Leedy 1997:166), which is useful in understanding qualitative research methodology.

Table 1: Qualitative research methodology

Case study	'To understand a single 'case' in-depth in order to understand the person or phenomenon'
Ethnography	'To understand the relationship between behaviour and 'culture''
Phenomenology	'To describe the experience from the participants' point of view'
Grounded Theory	'To derive a theory that links participants' perspectives to general social science theories'

This approach helps us to see the range of methodologies that we can use to look into the context of CALL. It puts the emphasis on the people who are involved in using computers, both the teachers and the learners. It gives us a way for teachers to look at their own practices alongside their day-to-day work. It may also help to give us information about institutional, regional, or country-wide initiatives.

Let us look at what this alternative view of research might add to our knowledge about CALL. Interestingly I found only two articles that mention some of the methodology that I am advocating here. The first one comes from Mercer and Scrimshaw who say the following about this kind of research:

Teachers' accounts of their classroom experiences … are usually in the form of a narrative, which includes the teacher's own feelings and intentions as well as an account of what took place, as they saw it.

They may also contain some evaluation of the results or the process, examples from children's work, comments by children on these activity [sic] extracts from curriculum plans and so forth. (Mercer & Scrimshaw 1993:188)

However, they go on to reject this particular approach for pragmatic reasons and prefer to adopt an approach that brings the teacher and the researcher into partnership, so that researchers can contribute their skills and the teacher theirs. There is also a descriptive article by Chapelle, Jamieson and Park (1996). This reviews four different methodologies and finishes with ethnography. Revealingly, they only describe one piece of research that takes a fully ethnographic approach. They do not mention the other types of qualitative research described in the table above.

Why then should teachers and PhD candidates be encouraged to do more practitioner-based, classroom research? To help support this view, I would like to offer four more quotations from Freeman:

> ... teaching is a complex, messy business of knowing what to do in the classroom.

> The process we call research must become more open and accessible to teachers.

> The more usual forms of telling associated with research are impoverished. (Freeman 1996:109)

> Questions of what teaching is and of what people know in order to teach are absolutely central; to avoid them is folly for everyone concerned with education ... And the findings of researchers and others concerned with understanding education ought to viewed with scepticism if these people do not seriously entertain the central issue of what teaching is and of what people know in order to do it. (Freeman 1996:110)

These words carry a resonance about what we try to do with our teachers on courses at Manchester University and in local schools that we visit as part of our ongoing research.

Lastly, I want to describe two research projects undertaken in the Manchester area where a practitioner-based approach has been used and this has helped not only to yield interesting data which helps to push forward the theory debate, but has also helped to get the teachers involved in research at the same time.

The first one took place at a school in Oldham (a former mill town near Manchester) and involved three teachers: the class teacher, a language support teacher and myself, also working as a support teacher.[2] The project lasted a year and was linked to the process of me getting what is called recent and relevant experience.[3] The school had just bought a new cluster of computers and was interested in ways that they might get best practice from the use of these machines. They were also interested in focussing attention on a particular class who were perceived as underachieving and for whom this was the last two years of compulsory schooling. Throughout the year, we worked with this particular group of children, some with behaviour difficulties and some who for various reasons needed language support. The class was a mainstream English class and was starting the two years of study that lead up to GCSEs (school-leaving exams in the UK). Everything that they did throughout these two years would have an impact on what their final English marks would be, so the aim was to record what happened as we worked with the children. Recording of data was done through diaries kept by the three teachers. We also had regular weekly meetings to discuss how the project was going.

In a situation like this the number of variables is enormous. Even if we had wanted to do some kind of controlled experiment, it would not have worked anyway. In terms of the school context, breaking up an established group would also not have been a good idea, nor would it have been feasible to have another class as a control group, as other similar classes did not exist in the school. Other possibilities, like using observation techniques, were also rejected as being too distant from the teaching and the pupils. As one of the participating teachers, I gained insights that I would have never got as an observer. The situation was already strange for the children, as I was new to the school. They were going to have to cope with having me in the class for starters and that was going to take some getting used to. Although I spent a lot of time at the school, I was not going to be fully in residence, I was clearly different.

Technology in general (we also made use of video), but computers in particular, were a focal point for these children throughout the school year. We used word processing as an initial starting point and followed a process approach to writing development (see Pennington 1996). We made use of a simple HyperCard database to help the learners keep track of their ideas and used a simple program to help teach them about narrative structure. Printouts from their writing featured in class displays and Open Days. As the children's skills developed, their confidence with the technology grew and we found that the pupils were giving informal lessons to their friends and other teachers, showing off their new-found skills. There were some very positive outcomes from this project (I rang the school recently to find that one of the children from that group is now doing a degree in IT at a local university, which, considering the group that he was in at the time, is quite an achievement.) Here are some of the other highlights:

- The pupils got a good grounding in IT with particular emphasis on skills associated with language development.

- The children when interviewed felt that the work that they had done with the computers had benefited their language skills. Their regular classroom teacher felt that there had been improvements, too.
- One child (not the one described above) started to make significant improvements in other subject areas because of a general increase of confidence in his own abilities and in his self-esteem.
- One child, who had been a regular truant, started to attend classes regularly and would come in to do extra work in the lunch-time sessions that we held.
- A number of children felt that they were finally benefiting from a school system that they had felt in the past had not been too helpful to them.

This is what is called a case study. It is of a particular classroom over one year. The researcher acts as a catalyst for desired pupil achievement. The other school teachers played a major role in the project, they provided ideas, skills, kept journals, wrote project reports. They grew along with the project. The researcher does not come in and 'take away' the results, he or she works in close collaboration with the classroom teachers and the school and then together they disseminate the findings to various local groups encouraging similar work to take place. Both the regular teachers, the pupils and the researcher are involved in the developing narrative that is part of the project.

The second study, which is current now and led by a colleague at Manchester, started by looking at the role email can play in facilitating language development for bilingual children in local secondary schools (Slaouti 1998). The project has grown from there. It is now in its third year and started as a request from a school where a colleague of ours works who had an interest in developing CALL with his pupils. The new project started as a link between the local school and trainees on our Diploma in TESOL course at Manchester University. The positive data is building up. In the first year the trainee teachers and the pupils exchanged a number of messages and Web pages were designed and put up. There were some difficulties with access to the Internet for the school and there was only one group email address; however, the children were clearly attracted by the project and were very pleased to see their efforts on the Web.

The project clearly had an impact on all concerned, and made the trainee teachers involved reflect hard on the some of the issues discussed in the literature on the use of email to enhance the teaching of writing. Slaouti (forthcoming) herself speculates on the role that email should play in the teaching of writing and quotes one of the trainees' messages:

Attempts to encourage final proof-reading also drew sentiments of discomfort from the teachers themselves.

From: 'Sian Etherington'

To: slaouti@fs1.ed.man.ac.uk

Date sent: Thu, 1 May 1997 11:58:37 BST

Subject: Ducie

Hi Diane,

I have just written to Maizorig asking him to correct some problems with his description of himself. However, I am dissatisfied with the way I've done this. I targeted the obvious errors and gave him a list of problems to check: this looked a bit dispiriting (a list of 8 >mistakes) and didn't give any guidance on what the problems were. I want to see how much he can do for himself before giving specific pointers, but is this asking too much? My other worry is that I haven't looked at more overall quality of the writing (cohesion/ flow of ideas etc.) although I think that what he wrote was mostly OK in this respect. If I were talking to Maizorig about his work I'm sure that I would do this differently – on E-mail it seems very impersonal and back to being very teacher-like. a bit of a shock for him after all this personal communication.? Well, those are my fairly muddled thoughts. Sian

The very nature of email and its potential for dynamic interchange allowed for very meaningful development of ideas but appeared less conducive either to more formal feedback about error or to the learners picking up on any attempts at reformulation (Slaouti, forthcoming).

Various claims (see Kroonenberg 1995; Warschauer 1996; Warschauer, Turbee and Roberts 1996) have been made for the use of email in the teaching of writing and thinking skills, here we see a trainee teacher reflecting on the process and a researcher able to draw a conclusion.

In the second year a new school joined us. This contact came through a colleague at the University who is involved in initial teacher education. This second school is much better set up technologically and the project was easier over the second year. The work is continuing in that school and research funding is being sought. The continuation involves more teachers within the school and has become more general than language support. This is beginning to be a network of schools that are involved in related projects and so, as a result, the findings from the research become increasingly powerful.

The data that has been collected so far includes observations and reflections from the teachers, trainees and children. There is also the email data itself, the exchanges that took place between the participants. This range of data helps us see the multi-layered nature of the project. The data can be analysed in a number of ways both quantitatively and qualitatively, but here the numbers are used to support the qualitative observations. It is also a project that has changed over the three years that it has been running. It is organic and without the broad range of data it would not be possible to see all the elements that are involved and how they interact. The story is a continuing one. The data has helped provide insights into:

- highs and lows in motivation
- a role for email which allows learners to 'rehearse' ideas
- how we can overcome the constraints of technology that exist in real school settings.

All of this is going on against the introduction of the National Grid for Learning in the UK, a government initiative to get schools online and teachers up to speed with Information and Communications Technology (ICT), so a great deal of useful information is being generated. What can we do with our 'findings'? To start with, we can feed them directly back into our own teacher education courses. We can facilitate other schools to set up similar projects. Our narratives are there, nothing is hidden, other teachers can see what is involved, but can also see what advantages there are for learning for their own pupils. Teachers can judge things for themselves as to whether they want to be involved in such research.

The second project has enabled us to test our hypotheses about technology for language support in schools. It has also shown the way that technology can work throughout the school to support the National Curriculum, but it is not experimental in nature, it is helping to provide a real solution for the school. The children were enabled to do real things with the technology, they did everything themselves, including the Web authoring. The teachers made decisions from week to week, prepared supplementary materials in response to the learners' needs and saw whether the technology could do what they wanted it to.

As you can see from the discussions of the two projects, to paraphrase Freeman (1996), the reports contain discussions of issues that are messy, but they do have a richness about them that appeals to other teachers. They are also well grounded in the schools where the teaching goes on and the teachers themselves are fully involved and committed to what they are doing.

Conclusion

This chapter has been an attempt to suggest that a more context-embedded research tradition might help to move our field of CALL forward. It would help to provide practitioners with insights into other classrooms around the world where CALL is being used. It does not attempt to say that other research traditions have got it wrong, it merely suggests that a broadening of the type of research that we do might help to persuade practitioners that

CALL is something to try in their own classrooms. Teachers' voices are as important in the debate as anyone else's and that by building a body of class-room-based research we can strengthen our developing theory of CALL.

Notes

[1] My thanks go to all of the people and organisations that helped me produce this paper. I particularly want to thank the International Association of Teachers of English as a Foreign Language, Tony Williams of Wida Software, and Manchester University for providing me with the funds to go to WorldCALL. I would also like to thank Mel Ainscow, Mike Beaumont and Diane Slaouti who put aside time in their busy lives to read and comment on early drafts of this chapter.

[2] Language support teachers work in schools with bilingual children, not as main-stream class teachers, but in support of the children's language development.

[3] The aim of recent and relevant experience was to encourage teacher trainers to go back into the real classroom on a regular basis.

References

Ainscow, M (1998). Would it work in theory? Arguments for practitioner research in the special needs field. In C. Clark, A. Dyson & A. Millward, *Theorising special education.* London: Routledge.

Bailey, K. M. & Nunan, D. (1996). *Voices from the language classroom.* Cambridge University Press.

Chapelle, C. (1990). The discourse of CALL: Toward a context for descriptive research. *TESOL Quarterly 24,* 2, 199–225.

Chapelle, C. (1994). CALL activities: Are they all the same? *System 22,* 1, 33–45.

Chapelle, C. (1997). CALL in the year 2000: Still in search of research paradigms. *Language Learning and Technology 1,* 1.

Chapelle, C., Jamieson, J. & Park, Y. (1996). Second language classroom research traditions: How does CALL fit? In Pennington, M., *The Power of CALL.* Houston: Athelstan.

Crossley, M. & Vulliamy, G. (1997). *Qualitative educational research in developing countries: Current perspectives.* London: Garland.

Cumming, A. (Ed.) (1994). Alternatives in TESOL research: Descriptive, interpreta-tive, and ideological orientations. *TESOL Quarterly 29,* 1, 673–699.

Davis, K. A. (1995). Qualitative theory and methods in applied linguistics research. *TESOL Quarterly 29,* 3, 427–452.

Edge, J. & Richards, K. (1998). 'May I see your warrant, please?': Justifying out-comes in qualitative research. *Applied Linguistics 19,* 3, 334–356.

Ellis, R. (1997). *SLA research and language teaching.* Oxford: OUP.

Ellis, R. (1998). *Second language acquisition research: What's in it for teachers?* Paper given at the 32nd IATEFL Conference at UMIST, Manchester, UK.

Ertmer, P. A. (1997). Common qualitative research designs. In Leedy, *Practical research: Planning and design*. New Jersey: Merrill.

Freeman, D. (1996). Redefining the relationship between research and what teachers know. In K. M. Bailey & D. Nunan, *Voices from the language classroom*. Cambridge: Cambridge University Press.

Garrett, N. (1998). Where do research and practice meet? Developing a discipline. *ReCALL 10*, 1, 1–12.

Higgins, J. (1985). Computer assisted language learning. In V. Kinsella, *Cambridge Language Teaching Surveys 3*. Cambridge: Cambridge University Press.

Kenning, M-M. (1990). Computer assisted language learning. *Language Learning*, April, 67–6.

Kroonenberg, N. (1995). Developing communicative and thinking skills via e-mail. *TESOL Journal 4*, 2, 24–27.

Lazaraton, A. (1995). Qualitative research in applied linguistics: A progress report. *TESOL Quarterly 29*, 3.

Leedy. P.D. (1997). *Practical research: Planning and design* (6th ed.). New Jersey: Merrill.

Levy, M. & Green, A (1995). CALL bibliography for postgraduate study. *System 23*, 1, 87–106.

Levy, M. (1997). *CALL: Context and conceptualisation*. Oxford: Clarendon.

Little, D. (1998). Seminar on research in CALL. *ReCALL 10*, 1, 127–128.

Lonergan, J. (1991). A decade of development: educational technology and language learning. *Language Teaching*, January, 1–10.

Mercer, N. & Scrimshaw, P. (1993). Researching the electronic classroom. In P. Scrimshaw (Ed.), *Language, classrooms and computers*. London: Routledge.

McDonough, J. & McDonough, S. (1997). *Research methods for language teachers*. London: Arnold.

Pennington, M. (1996). Writing the natural way. *CALL 9*, 2–3, 125–142.

Salomon, G. (1991). Transcending the qualitative–quantitative debate: the analytic and systemic approaches to educational research. *Educational Researcher*, Aug–Sep, 10–18.

Slaouti, D. (1998). Motivating learners to write: A role for email. *CALL Review*, January, 9–13.

Slaouti, D. (forthcoming). *Developing writing skills: A role for email*. Selected Proceedings of the BAAL Conference 1998.

Wallace, M. (1991). *Training foreign language teachers: A reflective approach*. Cambridge: CUP.

Wallace, M. (1998). *Action research for language teachers*. Cambridge: CUP.

Warschauer, M. (1996). *Motivational aspects of using computers for writing and communication*. Second Language Teaching and Curriculum Centre: University of Hawaii. URL<http://www.lll.hawaii.edu/nflrc/NetWorks/NW1.html>

Warschauer, M, Turbee, L. & Roberts, B. (1996). Computer learning networks and student empowerment. *System 24*, 1, 1–14.

Warschauer, M. & Healey, D. (1998). Computers and language learning: An overview. *Language Teaching 31*, 57–71.

13

A Methodology for Designing Student-Centred Hypermedia CALL

Dominique Hémard
London Guildhall University, UK

Introduction

Trends

Current research in Computer-Assisted Language Learning (CALL), and hypermedia CALL in particular, has generally focused on teaching and learning theories and strategies best suited to computer-based delivery, as well as on relevant learning outcomes in terms of applications, benefits and achievements. To this end, studies have compared CALL deliveries with traditional classroom learning, and gauged computed language material in an attempt to measure learning efficiency and improvement as well as evaluate CALL instructional design qualities. As a result, the main tenet and principal objective of basic CALL research has been and still is to a large extent to 'discover something about the way students best learn a second language' (Pederson 1988:110). However, if the 'learning task' is the subject of particular research attention, far less consideration is given to the other two important variables in mediated instruction referred to by Salomon (1979) as 'the learner' and 'the coding elements'. This is particularly evident in critical studies seeking evidence of student requirements and user interface design considerations within the confines of hypermedia CALL design in higher education (HE). What is striking in research focusing on the 'learner' variable is that students are often simply perceived as a readily available user population, which can be turned into convenient 'guinea pigs', sampled and conditioned to perform specific comparative tasks for the purpose of pedagogically based research. Interestingly, whilst CALL practitioners still debate and argue about the learning potential, value and use of authored applications, it is widely assumed that students are naturally attracted by technologically enhanced learning deliveries and, therefore, willing to participate in such experiments, convinced of the usefulness of the proposed exercises and approach. Thus, aside from general statistical figures regarding numbers involved, levels, contexts and, at times, characteristics such as age and gender, little is known about actual students' views and needs. As for the third variable, concerns regarding the design of the interface are still largely ignored, or not sufficiently integrated as a necessary prerogative within the design process, due to a lack of expertise, time and resources.

Impact on design
Problematically, this historical imbalance and narrow focus in research is an important factor impacting on the creative dimension of hypermedia CALL and CALL systems in general, in terms of design, development and use. This is all the more so since the authoring process is still essentially empirical and contextual in approach, and represents a serious design challenge in view of the complex and interactive nature of its language base. If such a process is influenced by the predominance of technologically led design choices and affected by ill-defined instructional boundaries, it is also particularly exacerbated by the prevalent adoption of a task-based, bottom-up, 'practitioner-led' approach (Levy 1997:158). It is this poor fit between research and design which has marred CALL development by creating an intractable design difficulty stemming from the lack of clear and measurable design objectives. Firstly, a pragmatic authoring mode tends to generate low-level and fragmented instructional goals within a curriculum environment, thereby focusing on specific design problems to be solved. Secondly, theory-driven design goals, when defined, cannot be satisfactorily evaluated due to inadequate feedback created by a lack of identified student requirements against which to measure them. Ultimately, the CALL interface remains an adjunct to the language curriculum, and the students a largely unknown quantity beyond their passive representations.

Repercussions
Consequences generated by this dearth of qualitative data regarding such a 'captured', therefore easily targeted, but also equally misjudged, user group

are numerous. Not only is this detrimental to a satisfactory authoring process and output as previously mentioned, but also, it has, by default, created a design vacuum between authors and users. Worse still, it has led to an ill-founded design illusion based on false assumptions and *idées reçues* concerning students' cognitive processes and capabilities including experience, ICT (Information and Communication Technology) expertise, confidence, interests and motivations. Furthermore, the lack of student/author exchange has generated a negative, counter-productive attitude on the part of students who have, rightly, felt alienated from the design process, the resulting user interface and its subsequent interaction. Indeed, this unfortunate disposition can often be witnessed in classroom teaching contexts when students are required to interact with a CALL package as part of their language program. Such a state of play cannot, in any way, be conducive to generating initiatives on the part of students and innovations on the part of teachers, since they could hardly be further apart.

The need for a rapprochement
Ironically, what is currently being observed is reminiscent of a dialogue of the deaf. For, if students, as interested parties, express the need to be heard, if only to improve the interactive outcome they will be subjected to, authors, likewise, seem to be particularly keen to find out what these prospective users have to say for precisely the same basic reason, albeit rather unsuccessfully. This message was unequivocally clear during the WorldCALL conference, not only at the level of design, but also in the context of novel forms of user interaction, as well as staff and student involvement within the learning process. On this basis, the first principle in user-centred design, 'know the user', is especially pertinent and topical. (See for instance Dix et al. 1993; Preece et al. 1994; Shneiderman 1998.)[1] However, beyond the immediacy and simplicity of the message, getting to know users' characteristics as well as their specific requirements can be deceptively difficult. Not only do preconceived ideas have to be resisted, but also students cannot necessarily articulate their opinions easily and elucidate what their needs are in an area where they themselves have little experience and, more importantly, where they have seldom been directly implicated.

Given the current design stalemate observed in CALL, this chapter proposes a methodology combining both a contextualised approach and techniques developed in Human Computer Interaction (HCI), designed to involve students and provide them with the necessary context and support to generate valuable feedback and clearly enunciated requirements. The description of the method is followed by a case study in hypermedia CALL designed to illustrate the approach and further highlight its potential.

Methodology

The proposed method derives from the lack of existing data on students and the need to ascertain student requirements as part of research in hypermedia CALL (Hémard 1998b). Indeed, if language students are regularly exposed to CALL activities as an integral part of their language curriculum, little is known about their experience, their attitudes towards it and their requirements aside from superficial answers given to token CALL questions in existing language unit questionnaires. Therefore, the rationale for this approach was to initiate a more conducive evaluation culture within CALL, concentrating on the interface as a separate entity in isolation from its language learning environment. The aims of the approach were essentially fourfold; it sought to:

1 sketch out an overall student profile in order to select a representative group of students for the experiment;
2 provide a progressive, interactive exposure to hypermedia to help the students familiarise themselves with the given environment;
3 facilitate the adoption of an evaluative role with an appropriate structure based on design criteria; and
4 generate critical feedback on the strength of their experience.

Whilst the main objective was to extract student requirements, the approach similarly attempted to show that, given the empirical hallmark of CALL development, summative evaluations of existing applications could and should play a quintessential role in informing new, formative design projects. Finally, it was felt that the success of the method rested on its practicality and applicability focusing on an identified student population whilst seeking to stimulate interaction with, and trigger reaction from, existing CALL applications.

A four-stage approach

The adopted method comprised four discrete and sequential parts. Its first stage focused on establishing an adequate and manageable student representation. It sought to identify an overall student profile delimited by a finite number of adopted *global descriptors* (Ohlsson 1993:204) based on context, interest and objectives, which were administered by means of questionnaires. These descriptors related to hypermedia CALL, and centred on ICT and multimedia experience as well as degrees of confidence and motivation, and attempted to identify potential variations across levels of language study in higher education (refer to the case study later in this chapter). Moreover, as the approach specifically focused on the CALL interface and was purposefully removed from the known classroom environment, it was important to introduce and explain its aims and objectives as well as highlighting its potential and originality. Finally, this stage sought to enlist volunteers or, at the very least, students willing to participate as interested parties, and who fitted the identified profile. Efforts were made to ensure that findings were as little corrupted as possible by coerced or remote interaction, as in fixed experiments.

The second stage concerned the organisation and implementation of user walkthrough sessions designed to provide a structured setting for the gradual introduction of interactive sessions as well as to capture impressions, reactions and reflections in the form of mental models elicited from the students' interaction and behaviour (Hémard 1998). These customised user walkthroughs designed to record verbal protocols (Bainbridge 1990; Polson et al. 1992; Preece et al. 1994) provided a flexible framework giving students complete freedom of action within manageable interactive briefs under a simple rule consisting of thinking aloud and commenting on actions and related computer responses. The verbal protocols were recorded rather traditionally with recording sheets, supporting an informal and highly flexible setting.[2] This arrangement brought together experimenter, students and interface on a regular basis over a protracted period of time to simply 'look at and comment' on some relevant software. The time element here was important as it helped shape a new design space, and develop a novel and much welcome collaboration with and between students. As a result, this stage was perceived as the mainstay of the approach and its most rewarding phase, as it was instrumental in facilitating a student–computer interaction. It also prepared the ground for a summative evaluation by providing a useful initiation into the yet unexplored area of critical software evaluation. In this respect, user walkthroughs provided exploratory and task-based sessions, which were particularly useful for providing interactive experience and confidence, as well as allowing students to develop a sharper critical analysis. Furthermore, by recording student actions, outcomes and observations, these verbal protocols were similarly invaluable to CALL authors as they could help detect design flaws and problems when discrepancies arose between actions and their outcome, referred to as *gulf of execution* by Norman (1988: 51). Last but not least, recordings of observations shed some interesting light on students' attitudes and thoughts when comparing, associating and relating the CALL interface with their own structural, or '*how-it-works*', models, and functional, '*how-to-use-it*', models (Preece et al. 1994:134).

The third phase dovetailed into user walkthroughs and attempted to crystallise the critical, but only verbally expressed, stance adopted by students by leading them through a systematic summative evaluation of the software using customised audits (Ravden & Johnson 1989). Whilst verbal protocols highlighted student perceptions and predisposition as well as raising interface design considerations, they were also valid and particularly relevant as hands-on sessions providing students with a practical and visual support for their own evaluation. It was very much this initial and protracted interactive experience which subsequently needed to be channelled into a customised evaluation framework based on a checklist of design criteria, with a view to providing finer, more focused evaluation data. Therefore, following practical sessions, the students were able to reminisce over their interactive experience, and express their views on the strengths and weaknesses of the given applications on the basis of a list of selected evaluation criteria (Ravden & Johnson 1989). This approach was adopted as a useful and practical vehicle for conveying how students themselves related to the importance and relevance of these criteria in relation to specific interfaces. In so doing, the checklist was conceived as a kind of photographic developer, primarily setting design pointers for students to focus on, whilst interacting with the software to trigger recall factors, or to support and prove their case. Above all, this analysis attempted to prioritise and highlight the critical nature of students' verdicts in order to identify how their concerns, their awareness of design inadequacies, or their sheer indifference to aspects of the interface expressed themselves. In turn, the audit stage of the experiment was also instrumental in attempting to provide students with an evaluation support, as well as an embryonic expertise allowing them greater objectivity and focus in the formulation of their personal requirements. One audit was organised for each group of students and for each application undergoing the evaluation process. All design criteria were discussed orally, assessed and entered by the experimenter. Not unexpectedly, experienced students were, generally, more articulate than their inexperienced counterparts, who often did not feel sufficiently competent to openly criticise a piece of software when the poor interaction was linked to personal inadequacies rather than identified design flaws. Indeed, this feeling of incompetence was somewhat reinforced by a noticeable and recurrent inability to fully understand and relate to the questions in the checklist which were often criticised for being too jargonistic. The checklist, adapted from Ravden and Johnson (1989), was revised to make it more appropriately concise for students, and also to incorporate new multimedia and language learning issues, particularly relevant to this experiment. For reference, the checklist was divided into three sections. The first section comprised questions related to all identified aspects of the interface, themselves separated into ten subsections covering the following design criteria: (a) Visual Clarity, (b) Consistency (c) Adaptability, (d) Informative Feedback, (e) Explicitness, (f) Appropriate Functionality, (g) Flexibility and Control, (h) Multimedia Extensions, (i) Applicability for Language Learning, (j) Error Prevention and Correction and, finally, (k) Student Guidance and Support. The second section was designed to highlight major and minor usability problems found in the hypermedia CALL applications. The final section concentrated on eliciting general comments related to the usability of the application.

The fourth and final stage was based on structured focus groups within which discussions revolved round the elaboration of students' own requirements in hypermedia CALL established on the strength of their new competence. Therefore, the focus group sessions could be seen to fulfil a dual function. On the one hand, they were strategically placed at the end of the experiment, facilitating the recall, summing up and the bringing together of the various strands of the students' interactive experience with the help of the visual display and relevant audits of all the CALL interfaces interacted with. On the other hand, these sessions were particularly important as they were instrumental in delivering, probably for the first time, well-thought-out, properly discussed, argued and largely agreed student requirements for future CALL design.

Strengths and weaknesses of the approach
As can be seen, the approach was voluntarily gradual, progressing through selection, interaction, recognition, identification and deliberation so as to provide the students ultimately with the appropriate experience, support, and confidence to find themselves in a position to describe their thoughts on the chosen interface. This progressive approach was probably one of the method's greater strengths as it created a much sought-after student involvement, generated an unshackled interaction, and yielded valuable data related to student perceptions, reflections and claims from known, but as yet unheard, stakeholders. However, ironically, its greatest feature could possibly rest on its practicability and feasibility. After all, it simply tapped a recognisable and easily reached target student population using existing and clearly identified resources in terms of available hardware facilities and hypermedia and hypermedia-related software. In this respect, it felt as though CALL could hugely benefit from its collective expertise and experiential development whilst capitalising on the inherent flaws and weaknesses still undermining its future prospects.

Equally, and inevitably, weak aspects of the method can also be pinpointed. Not least of these was the difficulty encountered when initially trying to convince prospective students of the opportunity, merit, value and realisable potential of the exercise in order to enlist them in a free working partnership. The students who agreed to participate did so willingly, if somewhat warily for some, knowing that there were no strings attached apart from simply adhering to the rules of the user walkthroughs. Naturally, non-assessed, extra-curricular activities are, by nature, far more problematic to organise and implement than assessed experiments integrated into a specific program of language studies. However, extra efforts to coax yet not to coerce students into joining the project were considered a necessary price to pay for achieving valuable, uncorrupted results especially when studying student attitudes, interest and motivation. Consequently, although the student volunteers managed to reasonably match the identified global student profile, in terms of combinations of characteristics, the number of students who undertook and completed the experiment was, not unexpectedly, low and subsequent data therefore open to distortion. The choice of software was also perceived as another potential source of weakness. Since the hypermedia CALL packages played a pivotal role throughout the experiment, as they came under the scrutiny of students and triggered interaction and reactions, their choice impacted on the outcome. Even if the selection was carefully considered, comprising as it did interactive video, multimedia and hypermedia interaction, their availability was also an important factor. Additionally, as students were allowed, even encouraged, to be as critical and outspoken as they wished, it felt as though the selected software was callously and unfairly singled out, taken apart, judged and condemned without any means of redress or right of appeal granted to other relevant interested parties.

Case study

As previously mooted, the proposed methodology stemmed from a research study in hypermedia CALL authoring leading to a number of key findings at the level of student characteristics, mental models and student requirements (Hémard 1998b). It sought information on four important but largely unknown student characteristics in French in higher education related to computer skills, ICT confidence, multimedia interest and experience. This student profile, established on the basis of a questionnaire (Hémard 1998b), whilst interesting in its own right, was particularly instrumental in selecting a representative group of students for the project.

Not surprisingly, the response from students was mixed, showing two extremes, from reluctance and resistance to participation in the exercise by most students to some enthusiasm on the part of a minority. Worthy of mention was the minority of agreeable, but also, experienced and confident students, found from the final year intake. In the final analysis, these characteristics suggested that students could almost be separated into two distinct groups identified by their degree of ICT experience and confidence. Interestingly, the majority of students approached for this general profile indirectly conveyed a dismissive attitude, possibly in an attempt to shun further involvement in the project or, simply, to conceal their own apprehension or lack of interest. Moreover, the commonly held view that new generations of students are, by nature or default, pre-conditioned and pre-disposed towards computers, multimedia or computer assisted learning environments was, in this particular instance, disproved. On this basis, the experience/confidence axis was used to select and pair students for the experiment. In all, 12 students completed the experiment: six experienced Level 3 students, four Level 2 students of mixed ICT ability, and two inexperienced Level 1 students (Hémard 1998a).

CALL applications were selected according to their type, which was limited or suited to hypermedia CALL software on CD-ROM in the French language accommodating a sufficiently wide range of different platforms. These were: *Télé-Textes,* presented as a video-based interactive application; *Up to standard,* categorised as a multimedia application; *A la recherche d'un emploi* and *France InterActive* representing two hypermedia packages. This selection of software, whilst inevitably affected by availability and resources, was nevertheless thought to be particularly representative of developments in hypermedia CALL design. Moreover, the noticeable scope of potential user interaction provided by these platforms was seen as beneficial to the breadth and depth of the summative evaluation.

User walkthroughs facilitated the student interaction, and they equally elicited and captured actions, reactions and reflections in verbal protocols, which were analysed to identify design problems and discern mental models, themselves the object of an in-depth study (Hémard 1998a). For example, proficient students were almost always in a position to form functional models, which made them responsive, but similarly very sensitive, to a number of design aspects of the interface. These ranged from colour schemes, the quality of graphics, visual displays, references, online supports to limitations of the functionality. Interestingly therefore, the interface design was seen as primordial to sustain both motivation and interaction, suggesting a strong duality between identification and stimulation. Conversely, unconfident students, being all too often overwhelmed by confusing functional models and burdened by a heavier cognitive load, were generally oblivious of such design considerations whilst cautiously and uncritically interacting with an accepted, albeit complex, interface. At a different level of interaction, all students made personal references to their known learning environment. For instance, confident students would often try to identify the learning potential of hypermedia by challenging a system with a view to establishing its legitimacy, validity, authority and authenticity as a *bona fide* learning platform. Blurred distinctions between pedagogical goals and expected interactions similarly impacted on the interactive approach, be it peripheral browsing or sustained, systematic exploration leading to varying performances and achievements. Students with little confidence were more likely to adopt inculcated models of good learning practices, generating parallels with functional models such as the language laboratory whilst preferring a linear, systematic task-based progression. Finally, structural models, though fewer than functional ones, by virtue of being largely elicited by the more confident students, were also interesting in that they often suggested the students were more advanced or enthusiastic than authors when navigating in a spatial language environment.

If verbal protocols recorded and analysed the student comments, audits were designed to provide an initiation and a simulation to help students familiarise themselves with the very process of summative evaluation, hence enabling them to be more proactive in formulating their views. Ultimately, this approach encouraged them to focus on and discuss design aspects of the interface, which led them to articulate their own requirements seen against their interactive experience. In this respect, student requirements must be perceived as essential qualitative and evaluative data with the potential to generate a greater understanding and a more precise representation of student views and needs. The resulting data were particularly interesting inasmuch as they provided a new critical dimension to attitudes and reactions. For instance, experienced students tended to focus more on screen design and the interactive potential of the interface, which had come under sustained criticism during the experiment. Conversely, inexperienced students, feeling more diffident, concentrated rather on language learning and practical design issues linked to interactive predicaments they had encountered. If the screen display was used as a filter, in the first instance, the initial requirement set the general tone: *Produce a good, professionally designed screen display*, suggesting that hypermedia CALL was still marred by 'in-house' amateurism and resulting design weaknesses. Summing these up, they ranged from inconsistencies, cluttered screens, instability, and unreliability, to choice of colour schemes, as well as poorly interactive, unattractive and irrelevant displays of material. If design choices came under criticism, so did the type and quality of the functionality perceived as being poorly mastered by authors, especially in complex, interactive, multimedia displays. Requirements varied from *Make exercises relevant and realistic,* and *The functionality must be adequate and appropriate, but not overwhelmingly complex* to *There must be complete compatibility between the design of the expected functionality and its technological delivery.* Convoluted actions and a proliferation of buttons were specially targeted as in the case of simulations.

Strikingly, students were particularly exercised by the function fulfilled by the computer within the language learning process. On the one hand, they clearly identified the role played by the hypermedia applications with that of the computed representation of the teachers authority, whilst on the other, they resented such a role, not only because of traditional preferences and political motives, but also on the grounds that the computer was not comparable to the teacher. This student position, which is at the very core of the present theoretical debate in CALL (Levy 1997) infiltrated requirements with requests such as *The students must be allowed unrestricted movement,* or *The students must be given full control over their interaction* to more personal ones such as *Treat students like normal human beings* or *Do not attempt to design an interface with a view to making the computer look and respond like a human* or even *Ensure errors or bugs do not creep in if you want to retain teaching status and credibility.* However, in spite of such a resistant mental model linking the computer with instructional powers, students strove to liken the user interface to a self-sufficient, fully interactive language learning support. A number of requirements reflected this dichotomy or, indeed, contradiction, not only at the level of language teaching and learning aims but at the level of objectives in terms of student interaction and personal output. So whilst seeking full control, requirements ranged from *A hypermedia system must be a completely self-sufficient learning platform,* or *State clearly the adopted learning strategy. State clearly the expected learning outcomes* to *Increase the learning potential* and *Provide introductory suggestions of language learning approaches with their recommended access.*

Obviously, these are simply indicative of the kind of requirements formulated by the students on the strength of their interactive experience but, hopefully, this selection, based on ubiquity and consensus, can illustrate the potential they convey in terms of qualitative data. Student requirements are instrumental in shaping the functionality and usability features of the user interface to be designed, and play a pivotal role in establishing usability goals, which, with appropriate support such as design guidelines, help to lead to design solutions. Reciprocally, a conceived design solution should encapsulate and fulfil identified requirements. As a result, the design solution is essentially predicated upon the proper design interpretations and implementation of usability goals through the use of satisfactory design guideline recommendations. Therefore, usability goals and, by extension, user requirements, by addressing various aspects of the interface design, can provide early and valuable guidance and a focus for future evaluation work (Christie & Gardiner 1990).

Admittedly, the broad range of requirements produced by virtue of being general or generic whilst still software-specific, are more easily and readily appreciated as representing advice or guidelines leading to design considerations, as opposed to specific design solutions. Furthermore, different students and a different software selection might have produced a differing set of results. Additionally, the lengthy process which was felt to be needed to arrive at valid and relevant student requirements can also be perceived as an obstacle or corrupting factor in the collection of authentic qualitative data. But this was and still is a promising start, which led to a fulfilling and gratifying experiment, during which the students were often challenged, questioned, keen and responsive. Unwittingly, unnoticeably even, they also interacted within different French environments in a way which would have been inconceivable in an open access mode, or even in a classroom situation.

Conclusion

The overall aim of the experiment was to get to know the students, establish a different form of interaction and communication with the targeted student population, as well as to focus on student requirements *per se*. Indeed, the point is made that requirement identification must be seen as an important factor in the pre-design context, since the performance and success of the interface design will be conditional upon its precise targeting and ensuing usability, matching skills, needs, and achievements (Foley 1983).

However, perhaps the most important message is that students, as targeted users, need to be far more involved in the creative process in order to redefine not only the authoring brief and the quality of the CALL interface, but also the role of the computer in language learning, and the nature of the interaction within the wider language learning environment. On this premise, an improved user interface design based on applicability and usability is a necessity if students are to be attracted and inspired by its potential and willing to play an interactive part in promoting its use. In this respect, language students as well as teachers and authors need to work together both to generate team projects and the production of language material and, critically, to regain the design initiative to enable hypermedia CALL to become a valid and credible interactive proposition worthy of interest. Therefore, beyond the provision of student requirements, seen as the logical outcome of this protracted data gathering exercise, it is the very nature and modalities of the student interaction as well as the teacher/student interrelation, which must be redefined and capitalised upon. In the final analysis, hypermedia CALL authoring can adopt a more dynamic approach, increase its pedagogic scope and output and, by dint of concentrating on conceptual design, find itself a more focused role within the overall design process.

Notes

[1] See also references concerning related usability, learnability and flexibility factors within existing design guidelines in, for example, Brown 1988; Gaines & Shaw 1984; Hardman & Sharratt 1990; Hémard 1997; Marshall et al. 1987; Smith & Mosier 1986.

[2] More efficient and accurate means exist such as the tape recorder and the video camera aided by electronic tracking devices. The choice can depend on resources but also, tellingly, on logistics and objectives as managing student availability, technical equipment and room allocation.

References

Bainbridge, L. (1990). Verbal protocol analysis. In J.R. Wilson & E.N. Corlett (Eds), *Evaluation of human work: A practical ergonomics methodology* (pp. 161–179). London: Taylor & Francis.

Brown, C.M. (1988). *Human–computer interface design guidelines*. New York: Ablex Publishing.

Christie, B. & Gardiner, M.M. (1990). Evaluation of the human–computer interface. In J.R. Wilson & E. Nigel Corlett (Eds), *Evaluation of the human work: A practical ergonomics methodology* (pp. 271–320). London: Taylor & Francis.

Dix, A., Finlay, J., Abowd, G. & Beale, R. (1993). *Human–computer interaction*, Hemel Hempstead: Prentice–Hall International.

Foley, J.D. (1983). Managing the design of user–computer interfaces. *Computer Graphics World 12*, 47–54.

Gaines, B.R. & Shaw, M.L.G. (1984). *The art of computer conversation: A new medium for communication*. Englewood Cliffs, New Jersey: Prentice Hall.

Hardman, L & Sharratt, B. (1990). User–centred hypertext design: The application of HCI design principles and guidelines. In R. McAleese & C. Green (Eds), *Hypertext: State of the art* (pp. 252–259). Oxford: Intellect.

Hémard, D. (1997). Design principles and guidelines for authoring hypermedia language learning applications. *System 25*, 1, 9–27.

Hémard, D. (1998a). Knowledge representations in hypermedia call authoring: Conception and evaluation. *Computer Assisted Language Learning 11*, 3, 247–264.

Hémard, D. (1998b). *Theoretical framework for authoring hypermedia for language learning*. Unpublished doctoral dissertation, London Guildhall University.

Levy, M. (1997). *Computer–assisted language learning: Context and conceptualization*. Oxford: Clarendon Press.

Levy, M. (1998). *Design processes in CALL: Integrating theory, research and evaluation*. Unpublished.

Marshall, C., Nelson, C. & Gardiner, M.M. (1987). Design guidelines. In M.M. Gardiner & B. Christie (Eds), *Applying cognitive psychology to user–interface design* (pp. 221–278). Chichester: John Wiley and Sons Ltd.

Norman, D.A. (1988). *The psychology of everyday things*. New York: Basic Books Inc.

Ohlsson, S. (1993). Impact of cognitive theory on the practice of courseware authoring. *Journal of Computer Assisted Learning 9*, 194–221.

Pederson, K.M. (1988). Research on CALL. In Wm. Flint Smith (Ed.), *Modern media in foreign language education: Theory and implementation*. Lincolnwood, IL: National Textbook Company.

Polson, P.G., Lewis, C., Rieman, J. & Wharton, C. (1992). Cognitive walkthroughs: A method for theory-based evaluation of user interfaces, *International Journal of Man-Machine Studies 36*, 741–773.

Preece, J., Rogers, Y., Sharp, H., Benyon, D., Holland, S. & Carey, T. (1994). *Human–computer interaction*. Wokingham, England: Addison–Wesley.

Ravden, S. & Johnson, G. (1989). *Evaluating usability of human–computer interfaces: A practical method*. Chichester: Ellis Horwood Limited.

Salomon, G. (1979). Media and symbol systems as related to cognition and learning. *Journal of Educational Psychology 71*, 2, 131–148.

Shneiderman, B. (1998). *Designing the user interface: Strategies for effective human–computer interaction*. Addison–Wesley.

Smith, S.L. & Mosier, J.N. (1986). *Guidelines for designing user interface software*. Report ESD-TR-86-278, Electronic Systems Division, the MITRE Corporation, Bedford.

14

Constructing Learning in a Virtual Immersion Bath: LOTE Teacher Education through Audiographics[1]

Tony Erben
Central Queensland University, Australia

Introduction

Of the many so-called innovations which have occurred in the language education industry over the past 30 years, only two innovations have been credited with providing a *unique* contribution to the field. One is immersion pedagogy (Krashen 1984) and the other is computer-mediated online learning (Warschauer 1997). However, while the benefits of immersion education and the uses of technology in education have been well documented, research into computer-mediated communication and computer-mediated pedagogy in immersion settings remain at best scant. Sociocultural theory offers a means to capture how students through computer-mediated interaction become self-regulated; in other words, how students first learn to use and then learn through electronic technologies.

The aim of this paper is (a) to provide a contextualised account of the linguistic and pedagogic changes which occur in a university teacher education immersion classroom when instruction is networked through the medium of one particular online technology, namely audiographics, and (b) to characterise the linguistics and pedagogic adaptations in the classroom, as student-teachers develop from other- to self-regulated activity. While audiographic technology used in immersion settings has the potential to enhance meaningful second language self-regulation as well as to promote student-teachers' own professional development, its creative applications have tended to be minimalised because it remains under-researched and under-theorised.

The context of the study: The LACITEP speech community

The immersion context referred to above is a four-year Bachelor of Education (LOTE) degree program called the Languages and Cultures Initial Teacher Education Program (LACITEP) at Central Queensland University, in which up to 80% of the curriculum is delivered through the medium of Japanese.

LACITEP became the first initial teacher education program delivered through Japanese immersion (see figure 1). In effect, language immersion (Japanese) was employed as a means to produce qualified multiskilled teachers, specialised and proficient in the areas of generalist elementary, foreign language, Japanese, and immersion education.

While immersion education has spread to many countries over the past 30 years, it is primarily employed in elementary and secondary schools. Immersion at the tertiary level, on the other hand, is still basically in its infancy.[2]

A second aspect of context relevant to this study is the need to educate student-teachers to teach in remote areas. In the Queensland schooling system, the major challenge is to provide language education for students distributed across an area approximately the size of Western Europe. In Central Queensland, the population density ratio is approximately 1.8 persons/km^2 (cf. US 27/km^2; UK 235/km^2; and Korea 437/km^2) where 61% of schools are in rural areas and 40% of these have a student population under 100. In direct response to this situation, one of the requisite skill-based competencies to be acquired by students in the LACITEP program is the effective use of electronic media for distance education purposes. As a result, a number of subjects incorporate the use of a range of electronic technologies including the use of audiographics.

Figure 1 illustrates the levels of use of a range of electronic media, including email, video conferencing, audiographics etc., used in the LACITEP degree program. The inclusion of such technologies within specific subjects is based on the principle that 'through doing comes learning'. In other words, teachers learn best how to use technologies for educational purposes if their own learning takes place through such technologies.

Figure 1: Delivery of total curriculum through immersion and use of electronic media as a percentage of subject contact time

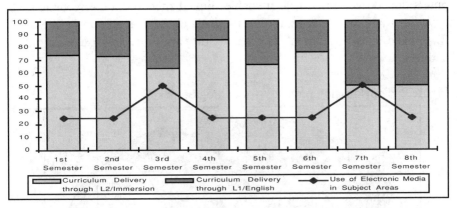

Immersion and second language learning

The nature of immersion education itself, as well as the pedagogical and linguistic processes involved, provide opportunities for student participation in activities that lend themselves to the facilitation of second language learning. One of the most fundamental ideas behind immersion is the 'linguistic bath' principle; that is, to impart to majority language speakers a mainstream curriculum through the medium of a second language (L2) in order to foster the acquisition of that L2. Krashen (1984) describes language immersion classrooms as 'input-rich environments', leading to his proposition that the singular most important contributory factor in the immersion success story is a direct result of the provision of ample *comprehensible input*. As a direct result of employing the linguistic bath principle, students are provided with *increased L2 contact time*, opportunities for *output* (Swain 1985) as well as opportunities to engage in *meaningful L2 interaction* (Pica 1987). More importantly, collaborative interaction in immersion settings may be viewed as both a means for communication as well as a cognitive tool for linguistic and professional development (Swain & Lapkin 1998).

In the next section, the types of technologies-in-use in language education, in a context of adopted technologies in Australian universities, are outlined, with a view to providing further description of the technology adopted in this study: audiographics.

Audiographics

Audiographic technology is a network-based media tool that facilitates multimedia, data, and visual-conferencing in the classroom by providing a two-way audio and two-way virtual–visual computer link. It allows users to learn interactively, to store and/or send images and information from separate computers linked over a network. It enables linked sites to share screens in such a way that any typed information is immediately seen at all remote sites (fig. 2). Linked sites are thus able to share software tools and use these interactively.[3]

Figure 2: Transmission pathways of audiographics

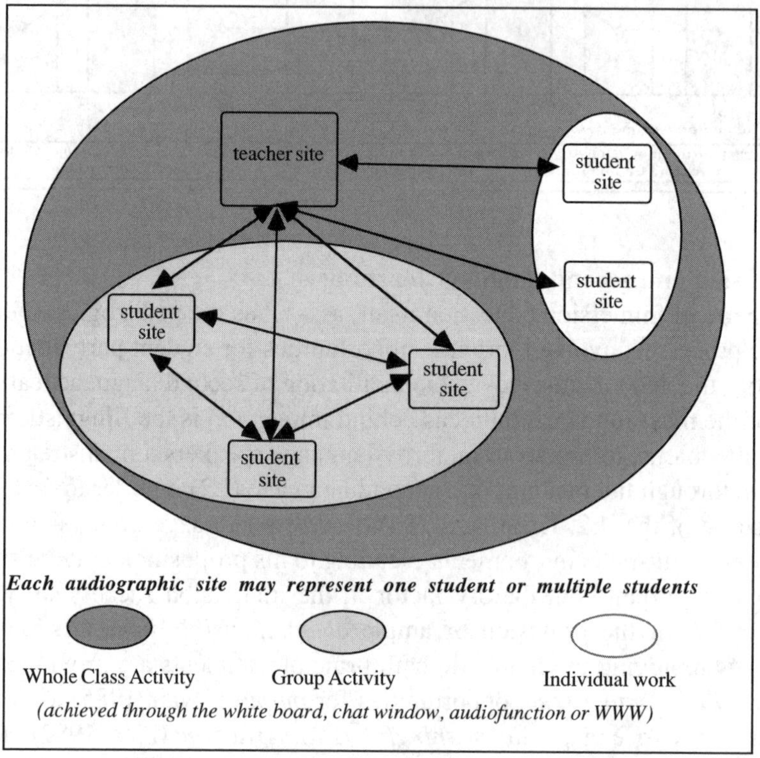
teacher site
student site
student site
student site
student site
student site
Each audiographic site may represent one student or multiple students
Whole Class Activity
Group Activity
Individual work
(achieved through the white board, chat window, audiofunction or WWW)

Immersion through audiographics: Research questions

As one cannot readily take for granted that face-to-face and electronically networked immersion classes are the same, the following questions are posed: 'How are linguistic and pedagogic processes (re)constructed in an immersion setting when instruction is networked through audiographics?' Specifically, (1) 'How is interaction mediated through audiographics and what implications does this have in terms of the professional development of student teachers?' and (2) 'In what ways is student–teacher self-regulation facilitated or constrained in a context where instruction through language immersion in a teacher education setting takes place through networked audiographic technology?'

Framework

In order to make sense of the instructional activities of student-teachers in a teacher education program and simultaneously capture the 'situatedness' of the individual and organisational nature of what student teachers do, a range of ideas need to be amalgamated into a framework of concepts that would allow one to explain adequately how instructional processes are constructed in a networked immersion environment.

Within this study, immersion pedagogy and interaction is framed by Vygotskian sociocultural notions which view learning as 'situated'. This rationale revolves around the view that learning is inherent in activity that is culturally derived and mediated by various tools/texts (Vygotsky 1978). While SLA researchers have focussed on the types of interactions which facilitate second language learning, such studies do not explain how students collaborate to become literate members of particular speech or knowledge communities. A sociocultural perspective provides a means to link concepts of interaction and learning with activity and as such provides a useful framework to explore processes of pedagogy, language and computer-mediated communication in a networked immersion setting (Warschauer 1997:472).

'The history of technology illustrates how it may first be developed to enhance an activity, then to extend that activity and finally to transform the activity' (NBEET 1996:9). In line with this notion, Postman (1992:16) describes how technology does not ultimately add or subtract anything, but that it changes everything; 'we need to know in what ways it [computers] is altering our conception of learning ... and how it undermines the old idea of school'. In terms of interaction, we need to consider the many ways in which things interact, not all of which have to do with language. Interaction may occur between people, but also between people and the artefacts they create and use. The products of such interaction can in turn recreate and reconstruct the very discourses themselves. Vygotsky called such interaction mediated. For Vygotsky, the essence of interaction resides in its mediation by tools and signs and that these signs are to be viewed as the catalysts for restructuring human actions (Cole 1985:148). In other words, forms of mediation are not viewed as simply facilitating activity that would otherwise take place, but are viewed as fundamentally shaping and defining it (Wertsch 1990:114).

Language is conceived as an integral component of as well as a tool of social interaction. Good classroom interaction makes possible good conditions for effective instructions. Both constitute pedagogy. However, for the purposes of analysis, discussion and presentation, this study focuses more on the conditions of pedagogy in as much as they relate to interactive practices (verbal and non-verbal) in an audiographic immersion setting. By conceptualising instruction not just as 'delivery' but as the full gambit of pedagogic practices, it is hoped to blur the distinction between teaching and learning, and so attend to the dialogic relation between interaction and learning as well as pedagogy and the construction of language knowledge.

Recent research (Erben & Bartlett 1998) has provided only exploratory analyses of the instructional implications of immersion education through synchronous technologies. Chun (1994:17) speaks of computer networking as generating a variety of discourses as well as allowing 'students to play a greater role in managing the discourse'. Parr (1995), however, indicates that different electronic media support education pedagogy in different ways, implying that specific forms of network-based instructional media may in fact accentuate particular kinds of educational practices and discourses.

Methodology

The methodology of the study was conceived within the broad framework of the case study method (Bartlett, Kemmis & Gillard 1983). The unit of analysis was the *critical incident,* the commonplace or typical event that occurs in routine professional practice which is problematised through analysis (Tripp 1993). The method involved the observation and description of the event with explanation for its meaning in the immediate context of its occurrence. Both observation and interview techniques were used in the study with the latter following upon this initial analysis. Data consisted of networked communication between LACITEP-related sites. In all cases, observation centred on the pedagogic and linguistic behaviours of participants at each site with a focus on the bilateral influence of teacher–student and student–student interactions. Two teacher educators, three teacher-assistants and twenty student-teachers were engaged in this phase of the project. Transcripts and computerised audio and video evidence were analysed and categorised for linguistic and pedagogical processes and practices within critical incidents.

The study

This study was broken down into two components. Firstly, LACITEP teachers were observed teaching face-to-face in classes. These classes were videotaped and then viewed by the same teachers. The teachers were asked to reflect on the processes of their own teaching based on what they observed and guided by the question: 'In what ways is instruction in my immersion class constructed in terms of planning, organisation, communication, motivation and control?'. The discussions were taped and the collected data was collated and categorised into issues of instructional practices. These practices were subdivided into pedagogical processes and linguistic processes. This data became our base-line information (though not *a priori* categories) which enabled the researchers to explain how the immersion learning environment is maintained and/or reconstructed through audiographics; in other words, how student-teachers' self-regulation is facilitated or constrained through changes in the pedagogical and linguistic processes occurring in the mediated audiographic immersion classroom.

The second component of the project consisted of tracking one third-year LACITEP class over a seven-week period where (1) student-teachers were taught a unit (six hours in total divided into 30-minute segments and delivered over a three-week period) from the subject 'Teaching, Learning & Planning' through audiographics with the class being in 'line-of-sight', and where (2) the same student-teachers were taught a subsequent unit from the subject 'Teaching, Learning & Planning' (eight hours in total divided into 30-minute segments and delivered over a four-week period) where delivery was networked through audiographics and delivered over different sites. Classes were observed and videotaped and both the teacher and student-teachers were interviewed at various stages throughout the study. The data was collated in terms of critical incidences of instruction and analysed for their significance and effects on linguistic and pedagogical processes.

Results and discussion

In adopting audiographics, student-teachers are required to learn not only how to become immersion teachers, but they are also learning to become literate in the use of electronic media. In this way, student-teachers develop proficiency in utilising flexible learning tools in preparation for the time when they themselves are placed in Queensland schools and may have to teach LOTE through distance education. Thus electronic technology in an immersion context is not taught as an 'object' but through its functional use in context-embedded, experiential situations. For LACITEP student-teachers, there is both an instrumental and integrative motivation to use the audiographic technology.

Table 1 illustrates the issues raised as a result of the first component of the study (see above). While the researcher admits that it is neither comprehensive nor complete, it does serve to flag issues which are critical to understanding instruction in a teacher education immersion setting. Throughout the workshop teachers insisted on the necessity of maintaining the two tenets of LACITEP, which in turn came to frame teachers' pedagogic practices, namely, to deliver the content of a teacher education program through Japanese to English majority speakers in such a way that (1) LACITEP students would be able to comprehend and engage with the curriculum at university level and

(2) the Queensland-based teacher education curriculum would make sense culturally and linguistically when negotiated and delivered through Japanese.

Table 1: Pedagogical and linguistic issues characterising language immersion

Instructional issues *Pedagogic issues*	Linguistic issues
• analytical/experiential teaching • student-centred teaching/learning activities; class/group/pair/individual-based tasks • immersion in: L1/L2 cultural practices content knowledges **curriculum continuity** • techniques/strategies; demonstration, modelling, use of realia, • constructing contexts for learning; orientation, enhancement & synthesising activities **classroom routines** • teacher control (pace, seating, social organisation) • engagement/motivation (on-off task)	• use of simplified & elaborated input/output • interaction/negotiation • authentic L2 talk~teacher talk • sociolinguistic patterns of teacher-professional discourse • naturalistic SLA/formal SLA • context-embedded/context-reduced L2 • classroom communication (public/private) • classroom scripts
Instructional issues traversing boundaries	
• mode of transmission of subject matter & L2 • scaffolding • resources • feedback	

Teachers indicated that point (2) was not always possible; that the curriculum had to be renegotiated at all times because of the fact that, as students were specialising as Japanese teachers, content needed to be infused with Japan-specific subject matter. Concomitant with this is the problematic of the sociocultural loading and semantic meaning given to curriculum content when delivered through Japanese. As a result, it was felt that the linguistic-cultural tension, though subsumed, drives as well as guides all instructional processes.

It was identified that this linguistic-cultural tension needed to be managed in so far that all aspects of the program, from the degree level to the curriculum level had to be, above all else, carefully planned. As a result of the planning phase, matters pertaining to organisation, communication, motivation and control would take shape and ultimately determine the nature of pedagogical and linguistic activities in the classroom. In an audiographic immersion context, activities are enabled through the multiple facilities of audiographics which include an interactive whiteboard, email, Chat window, slide show, two-way virtual, visual and audio facilities.

Interaction mediated through audiographics

Interactions may be grouped according to the nature of the relationships among participants. The presence of the hardware technology changes the nature of the interaction, so that it becomes mediated.

Mediated interaction allows information or symbolic content (such as language) to be transmitted to individuals who are remote in time, and/or space. The inclusion of contextual information then becomes an issue for teachers and learners because there is no mutual sharing of the same spatial–temporal reference system. There is also a narrowing of the range of symbolic cues available to participants (gestures, intonation etc.) while other symbolic cues such as writing are often accentuated. There is increased probability of ambiguity; it is in this respect that some instructional practices will be 'amplified', 'reduced' or 'reconstructed' in order to minimise real and potential ambiguity. Finally, as the range of these cues is narrowed, student-teachers have to fall back on their own resources and this is where one may observe the development of pedagogical or linguistic practices to deal with the specifics of a situation; for example, in communicating with others or with content through audiographics.

Mediated activity through audiographics

It was noted that there was a narrowing of the range of symbolic cues in mediated interaction. This means that the degree of reciprocity and interpersonal exchange was less than one would observe in face-to-face interactions. There was diminished access to forms of communication often described, for example, as non-verbal: gestures, intonations, visible facial expressions and so forth. Classroom participants were linked together in a process of communication and symbolic exchange, particularly through the verbal and written forms of text. Because there was no face-to-face access to a wider range of symbolic cues and reference systems that are known, learned and understood due to physical presence or context, teachers and student-teachers had to 'work' to produce cues (pedagogic and/or linguistic) that required *amplification* and/or *reduction*. Table 2 illustrates the types of pedagogic and linguistic reductions, amplifications and reconstructions that occurred in audiographic immersion classes vis-à-vis those identified as being utilised in face-to-face immersion education.

Amplification refers to those classroom discursive practices which, because of the nature of the mediated interaction at a distance, participants need to modify – in terms of increasing the production, frequency and/or intensity of cues, signs, and behaviours – in order to achieve the same desired effect as if the same cue, sign or behaviour was produced in a face-to-face classroom. On the other hand, reduction refers to cues, signs and other discursive practices which are, due to their mediation through audiographics, diminished, abridged or shortened in production, intensity or frequency when compared with the same practice in a regular face-to-face classroom.

Table 2: Immersion through audiographics: A reconstructed and virtual linguistic bath

Immersion in face-to-face contexts		Immersion in mediated contexts (Amplifications, reductions and/or reconstructions)	
Pedagogic characteristics	Linguistic characteristics	Pedagogic characteristics	Linguistic characteristics
• provision of analytical/ experiential teaching-learning experiences, • provision of class / group / pair / individual activities, • co-construction of contexts for learning between teacher and learners, • establishment of enquiry, discovery and constructivist-based teaching-learning in the classroom, • organisation of an amalgam of self-paced, learner-centred and teacher-led scaffolding curricula activities.	• opportunities for increased contact time with the L2, • provision of ample comprehensible input/output, • opportunity to engage in meaningful content-based interaction/negotiation, • provision of authentic, simplified and/or elaborated L2 discourse, • provision of opportunity for extended patterns of interaction (e.g. open/close questioning), • provision of context-embedded L2 activities.	• amplification of teacher-led activities, however, as students become familiar with the functions of the software teacher-centred activities reduced leading to reconstruction of the nature of class / group / pair and individual work, • number of potential physical and electronic learning sites increased resulting in amplification of student–student initiated constructions & reconstructions of contexts for learning, • texts for learning are reconstructed, • reconstruction of classroom routines, • reduction of teacher control (pace, seating, socialorganisation, environment).	• amplification of private classroom communication, • reconstruction of public (nature, processes) classroom communication, • nature of contact with the L2 is more in the hands of the student, • classroom scripts are reconstructed when interaction is mediated, • interaction does not have to occur between two people, • the teacher does not remain the sole provider of synchronous L2 discourse, • repetitions, redundancies, circumlocutions, and elaborations/ simplifications are amplified, • language is seen by students as something which is constructed, rather than just transmitted.

Examples of amplification include the necessity for teachers to increase question wait time due to the fact that delayed transmissions from site to site may occur depending on the power of telephone lines. If the audiographic lesson takes place across two 'sites', where the teacher is at one site and the students sit in front of an audiographic machine at the other, it becomes necessary for the teacher to organise one of the students to operate the audiographic equipment; in other words, a go-between who acts as the human component of the technology and who becomes the human interface between the teacher and the rest of the students in the classroom. This student then acts as a facilitator through which the work output of the students is channelled back to the teacher. Other aspects of classroom behaviour which are amplified are the volume of student off-task talk and on-task talk, much in the same way that students tend to increase their voice modulation and intonation. In audiographic sessions students tend to talk more openly and overtly with each other when conversing about their work. Due to the fact that more students are interacting more with other students in the classroom, it is necessary for the teachers to introduce communication protocols, so that they can organise turn-taking, as well as know who is talking. One simple example of this would be the use of saying '10-4' after each conversational turn. Teacher-talk in audiographic classrooms contain far more repetitions, redundancies, confirmation checks and elaborations than teacher-talk face-to-face situations. Other aspects of classroom practices that are enhanced are peer tutoring and 'speak-writing'.

Examples of reductions occur in situations when audiographics is first introduced into the classroom; a reduction in the intensity of interaction between teacher and learner is noticeable as both try to familiarise themselves with the technology. A concomitant effect of the diminishing of classroom interaction is a reduction in work output. Other reductions include a decrease in manual capabilities (e.g. paper, books and notes become less used as the technology appropriates the functions of these). There seems to be a reduction in the use of other electronic media with an increase in audiographic application use (e.g. video, OHP, tape recorder). Similarly, there is a reduction in activities which are experiential and/or inquiry-based which need to be teacher-directed or modelled (e.g. demonstration lessons such as physical education and science). The distribution time for materials (worksheets) sent through the post to students is reduced, as these can now be sent electronically. Lastly, when audiographics is introduced technical hiccups can and do occur. The loss of learning opportunities through such technical hiccups, where the connection between sites may freeze or where one of the audiographic applications goes off-line can stop the pace of the lesson. In the beginning, the teacher tended to concentrate on overcoming the technical hiccup rather than just readjusting the lesson with fallback activities.

There is, however, another element to consider when educational processes are mediated through a new technology such as audiographics. This concerns the fact that the amplification and reduction processes themselves can contribute to a change in discursive practices per se. In other words, amplifications and reductions can warp 'given' instructional processes to such an extent that new processes are created or old practices do not suffice. The technology allows for multiple focus points through the use of different applications. Also, collaborative and multilevel learning is reconstructed through the use of email, chat windows and interactive whiteboards. Another example of this may be seen when students take control of the technology; they feel as if they are taking control of knowledge and the lesson itself by appropriating classroom procedures and routines; for example, the teacher becomes much more of a facilitator with regard to what happens at the other 'sites' of learning, the students become far more proactive in deciding how their own learning will unfold.

Table 3 is an overview of the types of linguistic and pedagogical amplifications, reductions, collapses and reconstructions which were noted over the course of this study.

Table 3: Linguistic and pedagogical amplifications, reductions, collapses and reconstructions

Amplification	Reduction	Collapse & reconstruction
• increased wait time (delayed responses which may be due to echoes or group think time or extra use of repetitions and redundancies by the teacher), • extended support of a facilitator (a go-between who acts as the human component of the technology and who becomes the human interface between teacher and student), • appropriation of additional physical space of the classroom (private actions), • more noticeable, proactive physical set up of the classroom (seats, lighting) • quiet time (students in limbo) • students engage in activities unrelated to formal learning, • increase need for immersion students to attend to and concentrate on the content, • pressure on students to work in certain spaces (in front of the computer), • planning (subject units that can be audiographiked >need for prevideo taping and editing in planning phase) • increased emphasis on peer tutoring, • greater number and diversity of multiple displays /multilevel learning/multiple focus points. • increased volume of public/private talk, • enhanced use of communication protocols, • increased voice modulation, • increased use of repetition, redundancies, confirmation checks and elaborations, • enhanced focus on written language in terms of 'speak-writing'.	• production of work diminishes, • decreased manual capabilities (for example, paper, books and notes become less used as the technology appropriates the functions of these), • reduction in use of other electronic media with increase in audiographic application use (eg; video, OHP, tape recorder) • reduction in activities which are experiential /discovery/inquiry learning-based needing a teacher to be physically present: (demonstration lessons such as PE and Science) • decrease in anxiety with increase in technoliteracy development (eventually the establishment of routines speeds up organisational and learning time), • distribution time for materials (worksheets): send> print> copy rather than just hand out • loss of learning opportunities through technical hiccups which stop the pace of the lesson become more noticeable as the teacher needs more time to rectify (in the beginning the teacher concentrates on overcoming the technical hiccup rather than just readjusting the lesson with a fallback activity • intensity of interaction is less, • reduced usage of the second language when audiographics first utilised with a class group, • decreased use of appropriate L2 forms until more students become familiar with technology (word coinages).	• some amplifications and reductions warp 'given' management processes to such an extent that new processes are created especially when 'given' or old practices do not suffice (the technology allows for multiple focus points through the use of different applications; collaborative and multilevel learning is reconstructed through the use of email, chat windows, interactive white boards), • students take control of technology ; they feel as if they are taking control of knowledge and the lesson itself by appropriating classroom procedures and routines (the teacher becomes much more of a facilitator with regard to what happens at the other 'sites' of learning, the students become far more proactive in deciding their learning unfolds), • modelling cultural practices; eg bowing in lessons leads to the use of different verbal cues or picture icons, • not teacher fronted lesson but audiographic fronted, • peripherals of classroom (such as wall posters) become centred on peripherals in the 'machine', • need for technical support (other people become involved in the teachering-studenting process). • the development not of foreigner talk (FT), not of teacher talk (TT), but of computer mediated communication talk (CMC) (the customisation of the second language specifically and classroom interaction in general.

Over the seven-week period in which student-teachers were observed, discursive practices did not remain constant. In the beginning, many more instances of amplifications and reductions occurred due to the fact that classroom participants attempted to adjust *known* classroom practices and routines to the requirements of engaging in learning and interaction through Japanese immersion mediated through audiographics. However, as classroom participants adapted to the use of audiographics, instructional processes came to be increasingly reconstructed in ways which represented a substantive shift away from how these processes occurred in face-to-face immersion classrooms. Interestingly, as instantiations of these reconstructions increased, the number of amplifications and reductions decreased over the seven-week period (figure 3).

Figure 3: Weekly instances of pedagogical and linguistic amplifications and reductions over a seven-week period

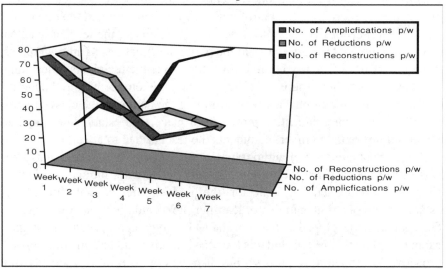

Finally, figure 3 is useful in as much as it allows one to differentiate the kinds of instructional practices involved in various instructional situations. Moreover, it shows that different types of discursive practices arise due to the different ways in which recipients both appropriate and receive symbolic cues.

Student-teacher self-regulation through audiographics
Even before students are able to interact with any new form of technology, they are often socialised into thinking that technology is alienating: the discourses surrounding technology are often strange and user unfriendly. This leads to instances where students resist interfacing with new technology. Some students switch off, do not participate, do not try to 'play around with the technology in order to get a feel for it'.

However, as students familiarise themselves with audiographics, a process of appropriation may be observed. Students 'play' with it, they investigate its limitations, they challenge its uses, they try to adapt it to the existing realities of learning. Once the new technology becomes embedded in the discursive routines of classroom participants, it ceases to be an 'add-on', a 'new toy' and becomes an uncontested routine in everyday classroom practices. The potential risk is that if the technology is appropriated into classroom routines, it may run the risk of eventually being viewed as something neutral, in much the same way as the curriculum is constructed by the discursive practices of the dominant sections of society as being neutral. Of course, neither are.

Student-teachers underwent an observable developmental process. Initially, in order to manage learners at another site, the teacher tended to initialise only one function of the audiographic software. By only having to organise instruction through one function of the software, the teacher was able to devote more time to controlling what was happening at the other site. As the functions of the technology became internalised, the teacher adapted their management techniques to suit the particular functions of audiographics as they were used. The teacher relaxed control over the recipients of teaching to allow ever smaller groups of self-directed learners to form. Initial patterns of control consisted of physically determining the nature of the class's distribution, putting communicative protocols in place, and establishing facilitators to minimise the number of students the teacher had to attend to.

For students, the use of audiographics was somewhat collectivising. This was due to the fact that the technology only permitted a limited number of sites to be established. The reflector (the hardware device that allowed the establishment of a finite number of learning sites) could only carry eight sites. Once students developed a 'feel' for the technology, appropriation strategies came into play: that is, the students took the initiative and became much more proactive in the learning process, but also generally in taking and making decisions about classroom social dynamics (open on-task private communication, making decisions about what part of the technology to use within different groupings, making decisions about who types, who talks, who facilitates).

A consequence of participating in mediated audiographic interaction was that student-teachers also went through ever-increasing self-regulatory learning activity. In order to make sense of this, Aljaafreh and Lantolf's (1994:470) five general levels of transition toward self-regulation was adopted. Self-regulated activity was measured against instances of student-teachers' linguistic and pedagogic practices vis-à-vis the following behaviour, (1) intervention, noting errors, correcting: (2) reliance on tutor/lecturer for managing mechanical/technical operations of audiographics: and (3) signs of improvement in level of interaction of participants. It was evident that over the course of the seven weeks of observation, student-teachers not only engaged in reconstructed pedagogical and linguistic behaviour unique to the audiographic immersion environment but also clearly became more self-regulated in doing so (see figure 4).

Immersion education through audiographics: Implications and issues for the professional development of student-teachers
Mediated interactions occurred between a range of participants and objects in the audiographic language immersion classroom. These included: learner–teacher, learner–learner, learner–content and learner–interface technology interactions.

Each student-teacher was obliged to manage all four interactions in order to guarantee their inclusion in each lesson and thus to appropriately engage with the process of professional development. It was evident in the study that, for the immersion teacher the learner–interface technology and learner–content interactions were more frequent, more intense and longer in duration. With respect to student-teachers per se, all four were important, but there was an observed tendency to focus more intensely and for longer periods on learner–learner and learner–interface technology interactions.

Immersion teachers tended to manage processes that were more distributive and related to direct instruction or transmission of learning content. For student-teachers, the focus on learner–learner interactions led to observable diversity in the formation and re–formation of learning in social groupings.

Figure 4: Weekly instances of other- and self-regulated activity

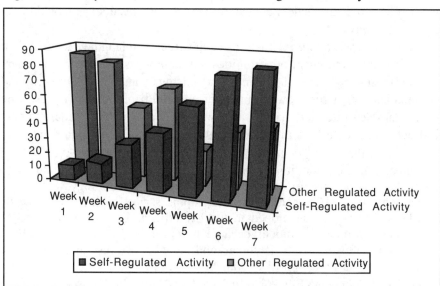

Much of the observed learning indicated that students engaged primarily in self-managed learning with the 'other'; that is, principally with other learners, but also with objects (e.g. the computer), spaces and events. In addition, the management process was characterised by disruption and discontinuity with an amplification and/or reduction of students' strategies to manage their learning. The nature of these discontinuities, rather than inhibiting or reducing the opportunity to learn, often 'worked' strategically and effectively to enhance professional development opportunities.

A second emerging issue in this study related to the interface of learner–technology interactions. One aspect of the study was the ways in which student-teachers engaged the technology and appropriated its qualities to support language learning as they became more technoliterate, and subsequently reconstructed their own practices. Initially, the participants were 'confronted' by the technology and amplification and reduction was evident. There were disruptions and discontinuities in the instruction process, many of which not only had to be managed by the teacher and the student-teachers, but also were used to allow them to make sporadic 'learning leaps' with language content. A related aspect of the study was the discontinuity in positioning between what the teacher wanted students to do or manage and what the students themselves wanted to do or manage.

Third, in observing the mediated interaction, it was clear that interactions were complex in nature. For example, there appeared to be ebbs and flows in the nature of synchronicity of interactions, with some at various points in time being asynchronous and at other points in time being synchronous. These contributed to disruptions in learning and were largely about the participants' capacity to receive and/or appropriate symbolic cues. In managing instruction, student-teachers appeared to cope with resultant interactions in ambivalent ways.

Multiple synchronous interactions to construct, and language learning and professional development opportunities, ultimately assisted student-teachers to internalise new ways of planning, organising, managing, delivering and communicating in their own multilevel and multi-proficient classes. One clear example of this internalised ability by student-teachers to adapt to new instructional situations is illustrated by the following teacher statement:

> ... when the audiographic software was first used in the LACITEP immersion classroom it soon became apparent that the design features of the software used to enable the audiographic technology was not particularly suited for use with ideographic scripts such as Japanese (the software was developed in the United States). As a result, the Japanese immersion model became compromised (use of English medium software, icons, keyboard and menubars). This situation initially led to a reduction of overall L2 use in the classroom, however student-teachers soon realised that they were able to access Japanese

WWW sites and interact with authentic Japanese documents and at the same time communicate in chat rooms. This eventually led to an amplification of the number of native speakers students could interact with in any one lesson. This development in turn led eventually to virtual talk-sites being integrated into the content of the lesson.

Conclusion

The institutionalisation of audiographic technology is ongoing at Central Queensland University. It is represented by such activities as the integration of technology into specific subject units, and the building of research programs around the application of audiographics to immersion education. However, this process is still fragile in the sense that audiographics is only used within LACITEP; it has not been publicly available for mainstream students. It is not yet privileged institutionally, and staff would need to undergo professional development.

The study indicates that an immersion education through audiographic technology is not only possible but highly facilitative of instructional practices that promote the negotiation of content through language immersion and the professional development of student teachers in the area of technoliteracy. Networked immersion education can be seen as a mediated linguistic bath; one in which the student is far more active in regulating a range of pedagogical and linguistic processes compared with face-to-face immersion education contexts. In trying to become self-regulated the student comes to actively influence these processes in terms of the intensity, duration, frequency, direction, outcomes and mode of each mediated activity. It may be observed that, combined, these factors positively contribute to the overall professional development of the LOTE student-teacher for eventual teaching service in Queensland, Australia.

Notes

[1] This paper is drawn from data collected from a project funded through the Committee for the Advancement of University Teaching. The project entitled 'Audiographic Language Delivery Through Instructional Management' was jointly conducted by Tony Erben and Leo Bartlett. I acknowledge Leo Bartlett for his collaboration in the construction of jointly authored papers (1997, 1998) as well as his insights and constructive input in the overall CAUT project which ultimately led to the genesis of this paper.

[2] St Lambert commenced as an educational experiment in Canada where the school's primary curriculum was to be provided through the medium of a second language. This linguistic bath came to be known as immersion education.

[3] See Appendix for examples of screen dumps illustrating the various audiographic facilities.

References

Bartlett, L., Kemmis, S. & Gillard, G. (Eds) (1983). *Readings in case study method* (vols 1–8). Geelong, Vic.: Deakin University.

Chun, D.M. (1994). Using computer networking to facilitate the acquisition of interactive competence. *System 22*, 1, 17–31.

Cole, M. (1985). The zone of proximal development: Where culture and cognition create each other. In J. V. Wertsch (Ed.) *Culture, communication, and cognition.* Cambridge: Cambridge University Press.

Erben, T. & Bartlett, L. (1998). Managing Japanese immersion through audiographics: Teachers networking instruction in an initial teacher education LOTE program. Volume 1 & 2. A Commonwealth curricula project for the Committee for the Advancement of University Teaching (CAUT). Canberra: DEETYA.

Krashen, S. (1984) Immersion: Why it works and what it has taught us. In *Language and Society,* Special Issue, No. 12. Ottawa: Commissioner of Official Languages.

National Board of Employment, Education & Training (NBEET) (1996). *The implications of technology for language teaching.* Commissioned Report No. 52. Canberra: AGPS.

Parr, A.J. (1995). *A study of instructional techniques used with interactive television.* MEd Thesis, Faculty of Education, CQU.

Pica, T. (1987). Second language acquisition, social interaction and the classroom. *Applied Linguistics 8,* 1, 3–21.

Postman, N. (1992). Deus machina. *Technos 1,* 4,16–19

Swain, M. (1985). Communicative competence: Some roles of comprehensible input and comprehensible output in its development. In S. Gass and C. Madden (Eds) *Input in second language acquisition.* Rowley, Mass.: Newbury House.

Swain, M. & Lapkin, S. (1998). Interaction and second language learning: Two adolescent French immersion students working together. In the *Modern Language Review 82*, 3, 320–337.

Tripp, D. (1993). *Critical incidents in teaching.* London: Routledge.

Vygotsky, L. (1978). *Mind in society.* Cambridge: Harvard University Press.

Warschauer, M. (1997). Computer-mediated collaborative learning: Theory and practice. In *The Modern Language Journal 81*, 4, 470–481.

Wertsch, J.V. (1990). The voice of rationality in a sociocultural approach to mind. In L.C. Moll (Ed.) *Vygotsky and education: Instructional implications and applications of sociohistorical psychology.* Cambridge: Cambridge University Press.

Appendix

Screen dumps of audiographic lessons

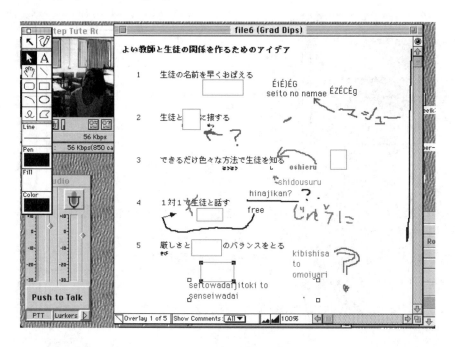

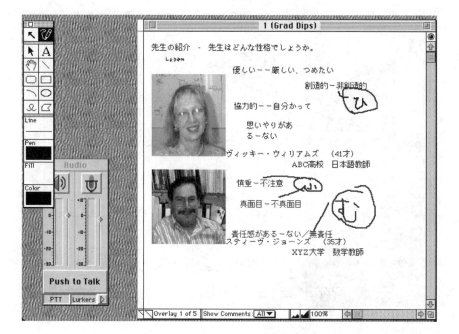

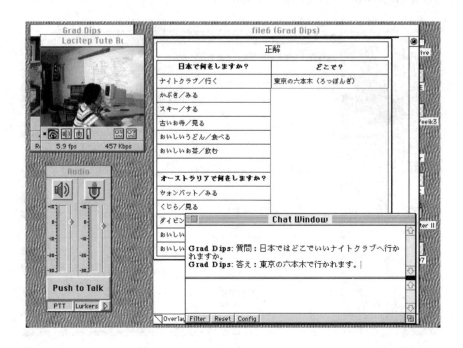

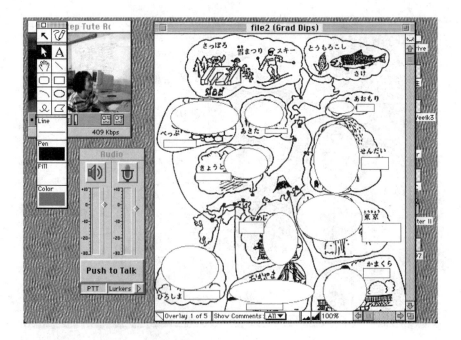

15

CALL and Online Journals

Vera Paiva
UFMG, Brazil

Classroom discourse

Numerous studies have tried to show the complexity of second language classroom interaction. Bellack et al. (cited in Allwright & Bailey 1991), Flanders (cited in Coulthard 1985) and Coulthard (1985) describe classroom interaction structure; Hatch (1978) emphasises the role of interaction in second language acquisition; Allwright (1980) analyses patterns of participation – turns, topics and tasks – in language learning and teaching; Seliger (1983) demonstrates that students who initiate more turns get better results in proficiency tests; Ellis (1984) studies the development of second language in the classroom; Slimani (in Allwright and Bailey 1991) finds that there is a relationship between interaction and proficiency; Chaudron (1988) points out the importance of instruction and interaction in second language learning; Tsui (1995) discusses classroom interaction and its effects on participation and learning; Atkinson (1995), and Majer and Majer (1996) study teacher talk. These studies and others make it clear that there are two main factors in learning a foreign language: input and student interaction. The studies, which describe classroom interaction structure, point out that teachers are responsible for most of the turns and that students share a small part of the classroom discourse.

Bellack et al. (in Allwright & Bailey 1991:98) describe classroom inter-action as being made up of four moves. Following their model, we can present the following example:

1 *Structuring*: Christmas is coming.
2 *Soliciting*: What are you going to do, Mary?
3 *Responding*: I will buy some gifts.
4 *Reacting*: You'll buy some gifts. Good!

Flanders (1970, in Coulthard 1985:95), proposes an interaction system which comprises ten categories: seven for teacher talk, two for student talk, and one for 'silence or confusion' and Sinclair et al. in Coulthard (1985:102) describe the macro-structure of a lesson as made up of transactions which are divided into exchanges. Exchanges are made up of moves which consist of one or more acts.

Unlike spontaneous conversation, which is generally made up of adjacency pairs, classroom interaction usually consists of three moves: initiation, response and follow-up (IRF). Let us look at some examples by McCarthy (1993:16):

MOVE	EXCHANGE 1	EXCHANGE 2	EXCHANGE 3
Initiation	A: What time is it?	A: Tim's coming tomorrow.	A: Here, hold this.
Response	B: Six–thirty	B: Oh, yeah.	B: (takes the box)
Follow-up	A: Thanks.	A: Yes.	A: Thanks

Thornbury (1996:01) says that, 'IRF sequences especially where the F consists of feedback on form rather than content – i.e. the standard "eliciting" technique – have been blamed for constraining the development of authentic discourse in classrooms'. Van Lier (in Thornbury 1996:1) states that this kind of sequence 'makes it unattractive and unmotivating for students to participate in classroom interaction, since the responses may be evaluated or examined publicly, rather than accepted and appreciated as part of a joint conversation'.

Several research reports indicate that the teacher dominates the classroom discourse. Musemeci (1996), for instance, observed three 50-minute lessons, conducted by three different teachers, in the 13th week of a 15-week course using a content-based instructional approach. She found that the teachers dominated classroom talk, speaking 33, 35 and 36 minutes out of 50; that is, 66 to 72% of the available class time. The small amount of time devoted to students' speech may be explained by the teachers' control of the turns. Johnson (1995:114) reminds us that 'despite the fact that student–student interaction allows students to interact with one another, more often than not, teachers still maintain a certain amount of control over the structure and sometimes, even the content of student–student interaction'.

Allwright (1980:170), using audiotaped data from two parallel UCLA low-level ESL classes, concluded that, as we might expect, teachers have 'a vastly disproportionate number of turns overall compared with other participants' and that most of them have the function of 'discourse maintenance', that is, taking an unsolicited turn, when a turn is available. He adds that 'the teacher also does almost all the interrupting, and is even among those guilty of turn stealing'.

This phenomenon might be partly explained by teachers' intolerance of silence. Teachers usually solicit a response and if students do not take the turn in a few seconds the teacher takes the turn again. Other studies demonstrate that if teachers increase their wait time the quality and quantity of students' participation will also increase.[1] Van Lier (1989:66) says that preliminary results of a study conducted by Long et al. 'indicate that increasing wait time has a beneficial effect on the quality of learner responses. The issue of wait time is also very relevant to the investigation of repair and correction in L2 classrooms, where it can be shown that longer wait time increases opportunities of self-repair'.

A great number of teachers' turns are in the form of display questions; that is, a question to which the questioner knows the answer, in contrast to spontaneous conversation where referential questions are the ones more likely to appear. According to Nunan (1989:29–30), 'several recent studies have looked at teachers' use of display and referential questions'. Nunan quotes Brock's investigation on the effect of referential questions on ESL classroom discourse. Brock (1986) found out that 'the learners in the groups in which more referential questions were asked gave significantly longer and more syntactically complex responses'. We can, therefore, conclude that more authenticity in classroom interaction increases learning opportunities. Slimani also found:

> ... an intriguing complex relationship between proficiency, interaction, and uptake. In her study the most proficient learners interacted more frequently than their less proficient classmates, and apparently participation was relatively profitable for them: roughly 50 per cent of what they claimed to have learned was derived form episodes of classroom interaction they had personally taken part in. Basically, for the less proficient learners it appeared that listening to other learners was more profitable than participating verbally themselves. (Slimani cited in Allwright & Bailey 1991:133)

All these studies make us realise that one of the roles of second or foreign language teachers is to provide contexts which make interaction possible and that we must be aware that the traditional classroom seems to be characterised by a series of factors which prevent students from talking.

Spontaneous conversation and classroom interaction

A comparison between spontaneous conversation and traditional classroom interaction (see table 1) brings to light the inferior position of students in this kind of speech event since teachers are more proficient and have the power to select topics, control the turns, and interrupt.

Table 1: Comparison between spontaneous conversation and classroom interaction

SPONTANEOUS CONVERSATION	TRADITIONAL EFL CLASSROOM INTERACTION
Language is the means	Language is the means and the content
Participants are equally proficient in the language	The teacher is more competent/students' competence is variable
Participants select the topics	The teacher selects the topics
Initiation of exchanges is at random	The teacher usually initiates the exchanges
Turn distribution is made by participants	The teacher distributes the turns and holds most of the floor
Moderate interruption	The teacher is always interrupting
Nobody needs permission to speak	Students usually need permission to speak
Questions are asked for information	Answers are usually known
Answers are not usually repeated	The teacher usually repeats the answers
All the participants can ask questions.	The teacher usually asks more questions
Self-corrections are made	Most of the corrections are initiated by the teacher

Hardly ever does a student make an attempt to interrupt the teacher or to introduce a topic in the classroom. It is not uncommon to see students who remain silent although they have unsolved doubts. According to Musumeci (1996:286), 'students prefer to verbally request help only in small groups or one-to-one interactions with the teacher'. According to Tsui (1995:81), getting students to respond to their questions, raise questions, offer ideas and make comments is a problem most teachers face. According to her, research has shown that 'students' talk accounts for an average of less than 30 per cent of talk in teacher-fronted classrooms'. Tsui argues that 'studies on language and learning have shown that the children not only learn to talk, but they also talk to learn' and quotes Swain (1985) who points out that 'the production of comprehensible output is also essential to the acquisition of the target language'.

In FL contexts, teachers are always concerned with the lack of opportunities for real interaction as the contact of the learners with the target language is largely restricted to the classroom and hardly ever does that kind of environment offer ideal conditions for real interaction. Most of the situations are simulations, which are affected by negative affective and social factors such as inhibition and playing a social role not adequate to the learner's personality or culture.

Virtual interaction

As we have already discussed, the classroom poses many constraints to learners' interaction such as teachers dominating the classroom talk, interrupting the students, stealing their turns, giving feedback usually on form, asking display questions and showing intolerance of silence. It seems, however, that virtual classroom interaction can offer an environment free from most of those restrictions. According to Hoffman:

> Computer networks can broaden interaction among learners and teachers by providing them a channel of communication free from the restrictions of time and distance. Learners can access a wider variety of teachers – and other learners, both native and non-native speakers of the target language – throughout the world. (Hoffman 1996:55)

In fact, opportunities for interaction through computers, using either email or Chat, may be broadened not only in terms of time and space, but also in terms of partners. We can bring into the classroom, at least virtually, not only learners and teachers, but also native speakers and topics we would have never imagined before. As the students are motivated to interact with people outside the classroom, they have the chance to select topics that were not supposed to be part of a language class. The most important characteristic of this new kind of interaction is the decrease of face-threatening situations, for example problems with pronunciation, inability to take the turn or not being selected by the teacher, no chance to introduce topics, no permission to talk with a classmate during the class, and last but not least, the risk of making a mistake and being corrected in front of the whole class.

Writing activities using email become real communication as an authentic use of the language is achieved. Learners communicate because they feel like interacting and not because they are told to.

Hoffman (1996:72) adds that 'the "information gap" that promotes real communication is widened in network communication by the perceived distance – the physical gap – between the learners and by the lack of visual and aural cues'. In fact, some classroom activities, such as physical or classroom description, which are highly artificial, become meaningful when done by email. Another interesting point is that email has some of the characteristics of oral discourse. Martin (1997:4) says that 'email lies somewhere between the formality of writing a letter or report, and engaging in informal oral conversation'. For Basallote:

email generally reduces aspects of static social context such as gender, race, handicaps and status, and reduces physical communication cues (frowning, hesitating, intonation, etc.). It favors more equal participation by those who are often excluded or discriminated against: shy students, students with unusual learning styles, students who are apprehensive about writing, etc. (Basallote 1997:10)

In email, we do not have physical communication cues, but another feature of this new genre is the use of *emoticons*[2] which, in a certain way, replace some of the cues given by intonation and face expressions.

Traditional classroom interaction and email interaction

Computer interaction, as opposed to traditional classroom interaction, seems to minimise a series of factors, which contribute to inhibiting students' participation. According to Ortega (1997:84), oral interaction constraints, such as fear of interrupting or of being interrupted, the need to manage the floor and the transfer of speakership, and the need for interlocutors to co-orient the production of sequentially relevant discourse, are reduced in electronic discussions. In the context of foreign language learning, pronunciation difficulties and the need for constant monitoring disappear. Ortega (1997:85) quotes several studies that demonstrate that electronic interaction is performed 'without the dangers of being interrupted, making interlocutors become bored or impatient, receiving physical or verbal evaluative signs from the audience, or forgetting one's own ideas while waiting for an opportunity to take the floor' (Ortega 1997:91). Table 2 illustrates traditional classroom interaction and email interaction.

Although a number of positive aspects of email interaction have been listed, certain negative ones that might interfere with the learning/teaching process must be acknowledged (see table 3).

Contrary to general expectations, electronic interaction appears warmer than that usually found in the traditional classroom. Hoffman states that:

the students see the teachers' use of the network connection as evidence of a concern for their individual needs and a willingness to become personally involved with them. Students find that the "faceless" medium of network communication makes it emotionally easier for them to ask questions ... A number of students have reported that their teachers' helpful attitude in email communication made them more inclined to interact comfortably on a face-to-face basis. (Hoffman 1996:67)

As Robb (1996:6) reminds us, 'don't be surprised to find some students exchanging snail-mail addresses with their keypals, turning a virtual friendship into an actual one'.

Table 2: Comparison between traditional classroom interaction and
   email interaction

Traditional classroom interaction	Email interaction
Face to face	Distance interaction
One student may get more attention	Students do not feel ignored
Turns are allocated by the teacher	Everybody can send a message
Some students 'steal' others' turns	All the students have the same opportunities
The teacher often initiates the turns	The student initiates the turns
The teacher is an authority	The teacher is a participant
More face threatening	Less face threatening
Impersonal relationship	Personal relationship
Does not facilitate dialogue between the teacher and the students	Facilitates dialogue between the teacher and the students
Artificial interaction	Real interaction
Fictional audience	Real audience
Participation is coordinated by the teacher	Students participate according to their own pace and will
Timed interaction	No time constraint
Simultaneous monitoring	Message can be corrected before being sent
Absent students cannot participate	Students can always participate
Interaction in the classroom only	Possibility of interaction with the world
Natural desire to interact is repressed	Natural desire to interact is stimulated
Students are afraid of running risks and experimenting	Students are less afraid of running risks and experimenting
Focus on form	Focus on meaning

Table 3: Negative aspects of classroom and email interaction

Traditional classroom interaction	Email interaction
No problems with equipment	Problems with connection and equipment
Number of students is limited	Number of students may represent increased work hours for the teacher
Access to teacher usually limited to classroom	The teacher can be contacted before and after the class which might represent overwork
Intruders are not allowed	Vulnerable to intruders

The research

In Brazil, the Federal Government has been encouraging schools to use computers in the classroom and, in 1997, a multimedia lab was set up in our university.[3] It has 29 computers linked to the Internet and students can be found there from morning to evening. The lab has been a great aid to the introduction of new methodologies and for minimising the negative interference of social and affective factors in foreign language learning. The teachers/researchers involved in the lab project believe that Internet resources, such as email, discussion lists, and Chat can decrease the affective filter as the students interact in a more relaxed way.[4] Having that in mind, English courses for the development of reading and writing skills using email and web-based tasks have been offered. Although all the students go to the lab at the same time, twice a week, under the teacher's supervision, all the communication process is conducted via email. The students interact with the teacher, with their classmates and with students and people abroad.

The underlying principles of the course are based on the communicative approach, enhanced by some constructivist principles. The teacher provides the necessary support for the students to develop their language skills and supplies different contexts for real interaction. In this way, the students develop projects, that is, they write about topics they have researched on the net and solve problems searching for data in the Web. They do individual and group tasks, and have partners in the classroom and abroad. They also write online journals and send the entries to their teachers every week, reporting what they have done during the week, talking about their difficulties and their feelings towards the course, evaluating their progress and pointing out the strong and weak points of the course and of the methodology. Journals seem to be a motivating tool to foster interaction between students and teachers. Students introduce topics and, besides talking about their personal experience in the course, they also talk about their personal life and their feelings, thus using the computer to keep a closer relationship with the teacher.

In order to find out the characteristics of email interaction in the classroom, I collected data during the second semester of 1997. There were 22 students in the classroom and the data consisted of email messages which were sent to the teacher, together with some copies of messages sent to their classmates or keypals abroad.

Findings

Drawing on the classroom discourse theory, the data was analysed to make a comparison between traditional classroom interaction and email interaction. It is evident that the teachers' dominance in email interaction decreases, as the medium does not allow them to interrupt the students, take unsolicited turns or steal the turns. It is also evident that all the questions raised during the course were referential ones and most of the feedback was on content and not on form. The students initiated many exchanges and, although students sometimes failed to send messages, which can be interpreted as a kind of 'silence', the teacher tried to urge the students to participate instead of feeling responsible for doing all the 'talking'. Twelve characteristics of email inter-action were particularly evident, and will be discussed below.

1 Written text with some oral features

Written communication assisted by computers has an intimate relation with oral discourse. According to Levy (1997:223), 'the ways in which students write also changes when email is the tool that is employed. Written commu-nication mediated via computer in this way is reminiscent of spoken dia-logue'. The use of the verb *talking* in the example below symbolises the stu-dent's feeling of actually talking to her classmate when using email. This feeling might be caused by the fact that email is a means of communication almost as fast as the telephone.

(1) *Mary[5], I'm so glad I have finally gotten my code. I can't believe that for the first time in my life, I'm talking to someone, using a computer ...*

2 More opportunities for learners to negotiate meaning

In the next example, we can see one positive aspect of electronic chat. 'Conversation' is managed in a more natural way and instead of the usual teacher initiated repairs, the student, according to her report, makes herself understood by means of paraphrase in an attempt to negotiate meaning. In traditional classrooms, the students are seldom asked to paraphrase what they are saying. The teacher usually corrects the form instead of giving the stu-dents another opportunity to make themselves understood. Besides that, stu-dents can understand each other, at least in foreign language learning con-texts, because all of them speak the same interlanguage. When our students have the chance to enter a chat session with foreigners they experiment with different situations. Sometimes they interact with native or more proficient speakers and have to make an effort to make themselves understood. On other occasions, they are the more proficient ones and have to select simple language and easier vocabulary to make the 'conversation' succeed.

(2) *... I think chat improves english because as you said last class it's interactive and if we make a mistake wich the person couldn't under-stand we have to say it another way ... this make us behave like a dictionary because we have to translate one word but in the same language!!!*

3 Email makes asynchronous dialogue possible

The next example shows one teacher and a student evaluating the course. The students had had problems with the school server and the teacher advised them all to find a free email account (www.hotmail.com or www.rocket-mail.com). When the student replies, she keeps part of the previous messages and the result is a blending of three different messages. The final version of the message assumes the form of a dialogue.

(3) *Hi Vera!*

>Fortunately, we got rid of FALE addresses and the problems with the system administrator. Are you enjoying internet?

Yes, I just love it! I always have a good time when I am in the lab.

>Do you think it can help you learn more English? I hope so.

Sure! I feel I improved a lot my English, specially my writing. Besides my vocabulary has increased and I'm not afraid of mistakes anymore.

Well, I've heard it was your Birthday last Friday. I'm sorry but I couldn't sent you a message or a card. Anyway ... Congratulations! Even late. ;o)

Kisses

X

4 More opportunities to use various language functions

Studies such as the ones carried out by Haas (1987) and Wang (1993), according to Levy (1997:223), demonstrate that 'in writing dialogue journals using email, ESL students wrote more, asked more questions, and used different language functions more frequently compared with pen and paper'. It is interesting to observe in example (3), that the student, besides answering the teacher's question, also introduces another topic (see the discourse marker 'well' used to change topics) – the teacher's birthday – and uses other functions not expected by the teacher. The student informs the teacher about something in the past, apologises and greets. Such dialogue would not be expected in a traditional classroom interaction in a context in which the teacher asks the student to evaluate their course.

5 Negotiated interaction with the teacher

The next excerpt shows a student apologising for being late with an assignment. The teacher gives her more time because as students work at their own pace, it will not interfere with the class rhythm. The negotiation is private, without any witnesses, and the other students do not take part in the 'conversation'. The same thing would hardly ever happen in the traditional classroom. The dialogue itself is not supposed to happen in a traditional course. As we can see, the teacher reminds the student that there are other tasks to be performed, the student makes it clear that she has time available for them, and wishes the teacher a good trip as she is travelling for a conference. In the teacher's absence, the students will go on working and wherever she is, she can be in touch with them. This dialogue would not probably occur in a traditional classroom. In the Brazilian context, the student would probably look for the teacher after class and talk with her in Portuguese. The teacher would probably say that if she postponed that assignment she would have to do the same for the whole class in order to be fair.

(4) >*Hi x,*
>>*my assignments but I had one of the busiest weeks of my life. Sorry for being late.*
>>*Bye,*
>>*X*

>*Never mind as far as you have enough time for the other two projects.*
>*Cheers,*
>*Vera*

Hi Vera,
I hope you enjoy your trip. I'll have time for all the projects. Don't worry. Bye.
X

6 Space for individual needs and interests

Students generally find little space for their interests and individual needs in traditional classrooms. All the students are expected to perform the same tasks at the same time and place and within a limited span of time. In virtual courses, where each learner works at their own pace, it is possible to care for individual needs. In example (5), a student who is an Internet expert talks about his individual objectives and asks for more tasks to develop vocabulary. On the other hand, in example (6), another student says he needs more time to learn how to use the Internet. The teacher sent the first student some links where he could find resources to develop vocabulary and gave special attention to the other student who needed help to learn more about the net.

(5) *(...) My main goal is to improve my vocabulary by learning every word, expression and term I can from Internet, so I'd like to suggest we develop any task so that we can do it.*

(6) *(...) I can't deal with Internet well up to now, but I've learned to work with email.*

7 Space and time constraints are overcome

The examples below illustrate the increase in learning opportunities. The learning environment is no longer confined to a classroom controlled by a teacher who follows a single plan for all the students. In example (7), the student says that he has interacted with people from different parts of the world, overcoming space barriers; in (8), a second student says she cannot go to the lab at the appointed time, but asks for suggestions for her project, overcoming time constraints; in (9), a third student comments she had been working in the lab during lunch time; and in (10) a fourth student tries to contact a student who has been absent from the class.

> (7) *Dear Vera,*
>
> *I'm finding a new world with this class. Last week I told with people from Australia, New Zealand, USA and England. It was very interesting, I'm impressed how the world become small with computers.*
>
> (8) *(...) I couldn't come to class this morning but I'm answering your message now!*
>
> *I have something to ask you! Do you have any suggestion for the personal project??? I'm lost! About the dream tour I'd like to know if I can include some London history on it!*
>
> (9) *I always go to the lab in the lunch time (I don't have luch anymore and I'm losting weight!) and have a pleasure time. I go to chat and learn a lot of things. New people and mainly new vocabulary. I learn about other countries and cities.*
>
> (10) *X!!!*
>
> *Where are you???*
> *Why have you lost many class?*
> *I miss you. I got email of chinese students.*
> *See you.*

8 The teacher is not the main actor in the learning process

The teacher's physical presence is not a necessary condition for the learning process. The students are responsible for their own learning and can work according to their own rhythm. The teacher is not the one who knows everything, but the one who guides and stimulates curiosity and interaction. In example (11), the student teases the teacher because she missed one class.[6] Nevertheless, we can see that her absence did not prevent students from working.

> (11) *Hi Vera,*
>
> *You've missed the class, er... So bad! :)*
>
> *I haven't started my Internet Guide yet. I gonna start it on this week. Thanks for the ideas to the Tour Guide. My suggestion is on my last week report. It is not so good as I wanted, but it can help.*

9 External feedback may occur

Feedback has an essential role in FL learning. Its importance grows when a native speaker or someone from outside the classroom provides it. In the examples (12) and (13), the students show their satisfaction with the positive reinforcement they received from native speakers.

> (12) *Dear Vera,*
>
> *I'd like to tell you how I'm glad to take this course. I've learning a lot how to deal with Internet and also improving my English. Cleo, the farmer in USA, told me that my wrinting is good and there's not many erros to correct. She's very kind. When I'm chating in EARTHWEB, some people tell me the same. I just have to learn how to use some abreviations in order to save time.*
>
> *Kisses,*

> (13) *Hi Vera,*
>
> *(...) I know that I have to improve my englihs but in the room chat, basic english, I really received congratulations: "you speak good englihs", said one. I really like it because I could be well understood by English and American ones!!!*

10 Personal topics may be introduced

In example (14), I reproduce part of a student's comment about her sadness for being at the end of her university course. She points out that she is going to miss her classmates and the university environment.[7] It is almost improbable that topics like that one, so personal, would appear spontaneously in traditional classroom interactions.

> (14) *(...) Sorry for make you my psychologist, but i needed to talk to someone who know what I'm feeling now.*

11 The teacher can also be a learner

Sometimes the teacher does not know any more about the new technologies than some of the learners. The students can share their knowledge with the teacher and with their classmates. In the example below, the student reveals her amazement at her teacher's lack of knowledge and the inversion of their roles. The student teaches and asks the teacher to acknowledge whether she has got it.

> (15) *I'm very surprised to hear that you don't how to deal with hotmail. You are an expert in internet! Anyway it's too easy and for free. You have to dial: (www.hotmail.com) and sign up and then you have your free email and don't need a private provider.*
>
> *Well, I tried to help you... Tell me later if I got it.*
>
> *Kisses,*
>
> *X*

12 Interaction after the course is over

In classes using email, students can go on interacting with the teacher after the course is over. The messages below were sent to the teacher after the course was over. In example (16), the student asks the teacher to go on sending her interesting links and also her final grades. She explained she was not able to attend the last class when the students were told about their grades. In example (17), the student abandons the English language and sends a message in Portuguese and suggests they can exchange information from then on. The teacher is no longer the authority. Now she is a friend with whom the student feels like interacting even though the course is over.

(16) *Please keep on sending us interesting address, they are very helpful. I'll try to do the same. Sorry for didn't come to the last class. I had to work on Friday morning. So it was not possible to come. Could you send me a message telling my grades? If not, don't worry.*

(17) *Estava aqui terminando o trabalho e pensando como foi legal as aulas ter conhecido e trocado emails com pessoas do mundo inteiro é o que é mais legal nisso tudo é que tornamos amigos e depois das aulas ainda continuaremos amigos e eu espero Vera que continuemos a trocar mails e qualquer bom endereço que eu descobrir comunico a você assim como qualquer novidade na rede!*[8]

Conclusion

All the excerpts listed above exemplify how the use of the English language became a means of actual communication. The students produced natural utterances and the teacher did not make any judgement about the form of the messages. By avoiding explicit corrections and by changing the focus from form to content, the teacher provided a context for more spontaneous and less threatening interactions. Some students' initial fear of technology immediately changed into pleasure and desire to use the computer to practise the language.

This contribution has demonstrated that computer-assisted foreign language learning provides the students contexts for more meaningful language use, increases learning opportunities, motivates autonomous learning, opens space for different rhythms and needs, makes the access to authentic material possible, and transcends the classroom walls as the contact with people all over the world becomes possible.[9] As Meloni points out,

Many students love computers. Unlike some teachers, students feel comfortable with computers and are very receptive to any learning activities that involve the computer. Increased motivation leads to increased language use which leads to improved proficiency. Meloni (1998:10)

The use of online journals, associated with the new technologies, helped the teacher and the students to reflect on the teaching and learning processes. The students developed reading and writing skills in a relaxed environment and felt motivated to go to the lab at different times not pre-determined by the school. The teacher had the chance to care for individual differences, to analyse the suggestions and to redefine the course objectives.

We can conclude that computers can humanise the classroom, decreasing the distance between teachers and their students. An investment in 'technology literacy', which will be highly beneficial for education as a whole, is hence necessary. There is no reason to fear that computers will replace teachers, but some experts agree that teachers who use technology will surely replace those who do not. Knowing how to deal with machines is not sufficient because it is always possible to reproduce in a computerised environment the teaching models where the teachers' authority prevents the learners from being autonomous and responsible for their own learning. The computer is just a means; the way we use it is what can bring a new dimension into the learning process.

Notes

[1] Rowe (1969), Holley & King (1974), cited in Allwright & Bailey (1991), and Long et al., cited in van Lier (1989).

[2] An emoticon (also known as a 'smiley') is a symbol composed of a few text characters, and used as a kind of emotional shorthand to add meaning.

[3] The lab was sponsored by CAPES, a Brazilian governmental agency that gives support to university education.

[4] As used by Krashen (1985:3) 'the affective filter' is a mental block that prevents acquirers from fully utilizing the comprehensible input they receive for language acquisition.

[5] The students' real names were changed and their messages were not edited.

[6] The course used virtual resources but was part of a traditional program with a fixed schedule for the classes. The teacher and the students were expected to go to the lab twice a week for one hour and 40 minutes.

[7] The new technologies will allow former students to go on 'living' in the university through virtual spaces through discussion lists, news groups, or distance learning and continuing education projects.

[8] I was here finishing my paper and thinking how I enjoyed our classes. I enjoyed having exchanged emails with people all over the world and the best of all was that

we have become friends and that after the course is over we will still be friends. I hope we will go on exchanging addresses. I will send you any good address I find and also any new information about the net. [author's translation]

[9] Besides that, the new technology decreases the use of paper and helps to preserve the environment.

References

Allwright, R.L. (1980). Turns, topics, and tasks: Patterns of participation in language learning and teaching. In D. Larsen-Freeman, *Discourse analysis in second language research*. Rowley: Newbury House.

Allwright, R.L. & Bailey, M. (1991). *Focus on language classroom*. Cambridge: Cambridge University Press

Atkinson, D. (1995). English only in the classroom: Why do we do it? *Polish Teacher Trainer 3*,1. URL <http://cksr.ac.bialystok.pl/flattic/ptt/feb95/8.html>

Basallote, Y.S. (1997). Email in class? You can do it, too. *English Teaching Professional 5*, 10–11.

Brock, C. (1986). The effect of referential questions on ESL classroom discoursse. *TESOL Quarterly 20*, 1.

Chaudron, C. (1988). *Second language classrooms*. Cambridge: Cambridge University Press.

Coulthard, M. (1985). *An introduction to discourse analysis*. Hong Kong: Longman.

Ellis, R. (1984). *Classroom second language development*. Oxford: Pergamon Press.

Haas, C. (1987). *Seeing it on the screen isn't really seeing it: Reading problems of writers using word processing*. Pittsburgh: Carnegie Mellon University.

Hatch, E. (1978). Discourse analysis and second language acquisition. In E. Hatch (Ed.), *Second language acquisition* (pp. 401–35). Howley, Massachusetts: Newbury House.

Hoffman, R. (1996). Computer networks: Webs of communication for language teaching. In M. Pennington (Ed.), *The power of CALL*. Houston: Athelstan.

Holley, F. & King, J.K. (1974). Imitation and correction in foreign language learning. In J.H. Schumann & N. Stenson (Eds), *New Frontiers in second language learning* (pp. 81–89). Rowley MA: Newbury House.

Johnson, K. (1995).*Understanding communication in second language classrooms*. New York: Cambridge University Press.

Krashen, S. (1985). *The input hypothesis: Issues and implication*. Harlow: Longman.

Levy, M. (1997). *Computer-assisted language learning*. Oxford: Clarendon Press.

Majer, H. & Majer, J. (1996). Teacher talk: Theory and classroom realities. In J. Field, A. Graham & M. Peacock (pp. 13–22), *Insights 1*. Kent: IATEFL.

Meloni, C. (1998). *The Internet in the classroom: A valuable tool and resource for ESL/EFL teachers*. URL <http:/www.eslmag.com/Article.htm>

Martin, G. (1997). Getting personal through impersonal means: Using electronic mail to gain insight into student teachers'perceptions. *Research and Reflection 3*, 1, May. URL <http://www.soe.gonzaga.edu/rr/v3n1/martin.html>

McCarthy, M. (1993). *Discourse analysis for language teachers*. Cambridge: Cambridge University Press.

Musumeci, D. (1996). Teacher-learner negotiation in content-based instruction: Communication at cross-purposes. *Applied Linguistics 17*,3, 286–325.

Nunan, D. (1989). *Understanding language classroom*. New York: Prentice Hall.

Ortega, L. (1997). Processes and outcomes in networked classroom interaction: Defining the research agenda for L2 computer-assisted classroom discussion. *Language Learning & Technology 1*,1, 82–93. URL <ttp://polygrot.cal.msu.edu/llt>

Robb, T. (1996). Email keypals for language fluency. *Foreign Language Notes* (Foreign Language Educators of New Jersey) *38*, 3, 8–10. URL <http://www.kyoto-su.ac.jp/people/teacher/trobb/keyplas.html>

Rowe, M.B. (1969). Silence, silence and sanctions. *Science and children 6*, 6, 12–13.

Seliger, H. (1983). *Learner interaction in the classroom and its effects on language acquisition*. Rowley: Newbury House.

Swain, M. (1985). Communicative competence: Some roles of comprehensible input and comprehensible output in its development. In S. Gass & C. Madden (Eds), *Input in second language acquisition*. Rowley, Mass.: Newbury House.

Thornbury, S. (1996). *Teachers research teacher talk*. Paper presented at UCLES Diploma TEFLA Conference, London. URL <ttp://www.ihes.com/Diploma/ttalkdip.html>

Tsui, A. (1995). *Introducing classroom interaction*. London: Penguin.

van Lier, L. (1989). *The classroom and the language learner*. London & New York: Longman.

Wnag, Y.M. (1993). *E-mail journalism in an EL reading and writing classroom*. Unpublished doctoral dissertation. Eugene: University of Oregon.

16

Building an Online Open and Distance Language Learning Environment

Robin Goodfellow, Patricia Manning &
Marie-Noëlle Lamy
Open University, UK

The open and distance language learning environment

The UK Open University (OU) has approximately 8000 students studying languages at a distance. For most of these learners the dominant feature of the learning environment is the limited contact they have with teachers or fellow learners. This, of course, is normal in distance learning. But in language learning, distance learning almost seems a contradiction – language is communication, how can you learn it in isolation? Despite the apparent paradox, in the current climate of technology-inspired educational change and the movement towards independent lifelong learning (European Year of Lifelong Learning 1996[1]), open and distance learning (ODL) seems to be becoming not only a viable alternative to the language classroom, but almost a preferred mode of learning. This chapter looks at some of the requirements for an online environment to support ODL in language learning. Also, it describes and evaluates an attempt to build such an environment, and points to the kind of research that is needed to ensure we are using the technology appropriately.

The design of materials for conventional ODL

Open University learning materials are designed for active learning in the absence of face-to-face communication. This is normally achieved via the promotion of an 'internal didactic conversation' (Holmberg 1989) which learners have with themselves, concerning both course content and learning strategy. This can be an extremely effective and convenient way for adults to learn (Lockwood 1995). However, an additional challenge for the language course teams has been to find ways to help their students externalise the process, so that the development of automaticity and accuracy in production can be addressed as well. This requirement has inspired a number of subject-specific modifications to the generic OU approach. For example, in order to practise speaking in the absence of live interlocutors, students may be asked in some exercises to tape-record target-language conversations with themselves, taking up two roles in a scenario, for instance. The problem is that they cannot get immediate feedback on their performance. So learners are asked instead to take time to review what they have done and consider not only how they performed, but also how they felt about their achievement (Stevens 1995). In effect, the learners are asked to reflect, not only on the meaning of the learning material, but on the different strategies for comprehension, memorisation and self-assessment that they bring to their interaction with it.

The role of new technology

The limitations of conventional media such as print, video, audio tape and so on, for supporting productive aspects of language learning, have led to the investigation of new technologies, such as computer-mediated-communication (CMC) for use in ODL environments. The expectation has been that CMC would effectively take the distance out of ODL, by providing the opportunity for communicative interaction, including feedback.[2] However, in the event analysed in this chapter, learners' use and perceptions of electronic communication have proved to be more complex than anticipated. Whilst there is plenty of activity on the Internet involving younger language learners and their teachers in project and resource-based work (e.g. HUT writing project web site[3]), the independent use of CMC for communicative practice by adult distance learners is not so developed. If we look, for example, at the work of the Tandem Email Network,[4] we find that, whilst the approach promises the development of a highly effective pedagogy for learner independence, it has not unleashed the language learner's drive to communicate with native speakers in a way that might have been expected. In a recent program at Sheffield University, for example, a term's work produced an average of only six email messages to French and German partners per student (Lewis 1998). There is also evidence from a small-scale in-depth study of learner attitudes to this technology as a platform for more interaction, carried out at the OU in 1997 (Goodfellow 1997), suggesting that there is a view amongst some who regard themselves as learning under pressure, that email interaction with other learners or native speakers would not necessarily assist them in the goal of passing the exam and could create extra demands on their time. It is clear that, whilst technology has the capability to emancipate the distance language learner, much still depends on that learner's own view of what is worth the effort.

So CMC has not yet become the natural home of the distance language learner, as was once hoped. Some of the reasons for this can be found in the nature of the medium itself. In its most widely used form, it is still largely written and asynchronous, it is socially opaque, and it is still technically unreliable. But we should recognise also that communicativeness itself is now less of an all-inclusive goal for language pedagogy than it once was. In Little's (1997) view, the 'dominant form' of the communicative approach (by which he means a focus on spoken communication at the expense of both writing and grammatical knowledge) fails to develop any kind of language awareness and does not foster learner autonomy. The lesson we take from this, and from our observations of the problems that CMC presents to independent language learners, is that the technology needs to support a range of learning activity, not simply increased opportunity for communication. This includes both productive activity intended to increase learners' facility with the target language, and reflective activities designed to develop their language awareness.

Reflection in language learning

Reflection can be understood as a generic term for those intellectual and affective activities in which individuals engage to explore their experiences in order to lead to new understandings and appreciations (Boud, Keogh & Walker 1985, quoted in Holmberg 1989:45). In the general literature on learning, it is usually related to Kolb's (1984) theory of experiential learning, wherein reflection plays a role in defining one of four 'types' of learning, that is, reflective observation (the others are concrete experience, abstract conceptualisation and active experimentation). Reflection has been applied to the support of self-organised learning through the concept of a 'learning conversation' – a form of dialogue about the learning experience concerned with bringing to a level of conscious awareness the learning strategies and values which were previously implicit – with a view to putting students in a position to modify them (Thomas & Harri-Augstein 1977, quoted in Holmberg 1989:51). Generating an effective learning conversation initially requires the assistance of a teacher, but eventually it becomes an internalised process and contributes to the development of 'the fully functioning man or woman' (Thomas & Harri-Augstein, in Holmberg 1989). Reflective practice of this kind is thus closely linked to the growth of learner autonomy.

In the literature on language learning, the concept of reflection has sometimes been subsumed in the discussion of metacognitive strategy (e.g. O'Malley & Charnot 1990), and defined as the self-management of learning through processes such as planning, monitoring and evaluation, as distinguished from the actual mental operations used to process linguistic content (cognitive strategy), or the ways that learners interact with other learners or native speakers (social strategy). Ellis (1994) has reviewed some teaching approaches which employ reflection in order to bring cognitive and social strategy into the metacognitive arena, and thus make them amenable to conscious development. Reflection on individual errors may be involved, for example, in facilitating the learner's 'noticing' of formal features in language input (1994:361). Reflection on the outcome of conversation may help to raise the learner's consciousness of how communication in the target language functions (1994:643). Reflection on success or failure at classroom tasks may bring out the learner's knowledge about how they plan, monitor and evaluate their learning (1994:538). The last example, however, implies that reflection may be too generic a concept to be classed simply as a metacognitive strategy alongside planning and evaluation. Some writers, particularly those who are interested in the currently topical issue of learner autonomy, have argued that learners need to reflect not only to be mentally active and self-directed (i.e. to use cognitive and metacognitive strategies), but also to be aware at the critical level, that is, 'Why should I do this task ?' as well as 'What skills and knowledge do I need?' (Wenden 1995, quoted in Carpenter 1996). This view gains strong support from the field of Language Awareness studies. Little (1997), for example, argues that a pedagogy which involves learners in 'negotiating and evaluating the learning process' through reflective writing tasks carried out in the target language enables learners to develop a high degree of autonomy both as language learners and as language users. Van Lier (1997) further argues that reflective processes, by which he means 'deliberate and purposeful engagement in actions', exist at a higher level of consciousness than metacognition ('knowledge about mental processes'). He also associates this level of mindfulness with increasing social interactivity and a pedagogy which focuses on the connection between language awareness and the development of self and social identity. The links that this kind of holistic thinking about language learning have with the learning conversations described by Holmberg (above) are made explicit by Broady:

Making such "learning conversations" a feature of the language class should help learners, on the one hand, value their own learning judgments and on the other, compare them with different points of view ... it is through such (explicit) reflection that learners can be encouraged to become more aware of the part they play in determining their learning and gradually offset expectations that the teacher and the class will provide all the necessary ingredients for language learning.
(Broady 1996)

These, then, are the principles behind the design of our online environment for distance language learning. We wish to engage students in a learning conversation, first with themselves and then with their tutors and peers, in which they consider critically how language functions and how they operate as learners. We want to promote reflective thinking about the learning process, which is expressed in conversational interaction through CMC. We want to use this interaction as a springboard for the development of autonomous strategies of language exploration and practice.

Reflecting on vocabulary learning

The learning conversations we seek to promote involve learners in reviewing activities which have both a practical and a technical dimension. These are van Lier's (1997) terms to describe the distinct forms of metalinguistic knowledge that are evident in the using and in the analysing. In the past, technical discussion about language has usually focused on grammatical structure, but we believe that there is a 'cultural' problem attending learners' perception of grammar. As other writers have pointed out, conventional teaching has done a lot to turn students away from any engagement with grammar (e.g. Metcalfe 1992). However, the same prejudices do not necessarily apply to the study of vocabulary. Writers such as Owen (1993), Johns (1991), and McCarthy (1990) have argued that vocabulary is the principle 'learning burden' on the way to proficiency, and that lexical relations are as influential in the generation of text as are syntactical ones. Others have suggested that lexical structure, because it is associational, might better typify the 'way our minds work' than do conventional rule-based grammars (Aitchison 1987). Some also hold that a 'lexical approach', which addresses issues of what it is to know a word – including its use, associations and denotations, collocations, syntax and phonology – is as principled a pedagogy as is a more conventional grammar-based approach (M. Lewis 1993). Perhaps even more importantly, for our purposes of reflective practice, these ideas seem to strike a chord with learners, who have long been obsessed with making sense of input that contains unfamiliar words, and with memorising these words for their own productive use.

It has been demonstrated elsewhere that computer-based strategies for vocabulary learning have the scope to engage learners in deep (i.e. structure-perceiving) approaches to their learning (Goodfellow 1994, 1995, 1998) and argued that these strategies can provide a sound basis for computer-mediated reflective learning conversations (Lamy & Goodfellow 1999 forthcoming). This chapter goes on to describe the environment we have developed, based on these principles, and to discuss the work that learners have engaged in and the nature of the computer-mediated learning conversations that they have generated.

Components of the environment: Lexica Vocab and Lexica Online

The core of the environment is Lexica Vocab (Goodfellow 1994, 1998), a stand-alone program which has been designed to support students in finding lexical structure in a mass of text, and in using these insights to enlarge their vocabulary. The program engages learners in activities which address the structure of lexical items in and out of context. Two examples of such activities are grouping words together by criteria of similarity in meaning or form, and searching for collocations. Results with learners using the program autonomously have suggested that there is a correlation between performance and deep learning approaches (Goodfellow 1994, 1998). Some students, however, do not make sufficient use of the program features most closely associated with deep approaches, for example the keyword-in-context concordancer and the structure-apprehending (i.e. investigating the linguistic data presented by the program environment) but are instead relying on old and often ineffective ones. These students have demonstrated the need for help from tutors or peers in altering their study habits to take advantage of the functions that the technology offers (Ebbrell & Goodfellow 1997).

In order to address this need, and to make the program more suited to teaching and learning in the ODL environment, an online discussion facility has been created in which distance learning students can be supported in using the program and in developing reflective practices in the management of their own learning. The combination of Lexica Vocab with this online discussion has been called Lexica Online (Goodfellow & Lamy 1998, Lamy & Goodfellow 1999, forthcoming).

The Lexica Online projects

The Lexica Online environment has been used to conduct two short courses for OU learners of French. These courses, Lexica 1 and Lexica 2, were a voluntary supplement to study on a mainstream OU course on French language and culture.

Structure of the courses

Participants were asked to commit themselves to a minimum number of hours of work over the period of the course (ten hours in six weeks for Lexica 1, 15 hours in eight weeks for Lexica 2). The work was divided between three core computer-based activities:

1 Students were to use Lexica Vocab plus an electronic dictionary to study a selection of texts from the mainstream course, and to extract, look up and learn a number of vocabulary items of their own choice. Lexica Vocab and the course texts were provided on disk, together with a larger corpus of general French text (approximately 50 000 words). Students' work was logged electronically by the program and they were asked to return the log files at the end of the course. A dictionary (Collins French–English) was provided on CD-ROM.

   The objective was to give the students the experience of using a variety of processing strategies on a list of vocabulary items selected for themselves. In earlier studies of stand-alone use of Lexica Vocab, targets were set at 50 words or phrases to be studied over five or six sessions, and it was found that this was rarely exceeded. If the study strategies adopted by the students include self-testing, which Lexica Vocab supports, then it is possible to use the incidence of successfully remembered items to work out a rough measure of effectiveness for the study, expressed as items successfully retrieved per hour of study.

   A second objective was to increase the learners' awareness of the nature and effectiveness of their own strategies for vocabulary learning. The strategies supported by Lexica Vocab include selecting items from context, inferring meaning from context, translation and paraphrase (using dictionary and concordancer), grouping words into categories, and self-testing in a variety of formats. These strategies are deployed by the learner in whatever order and degree they choose (although, logically, selection has to come first). In both the courses an attempt was made to structure this activity by setting tasks; for example, asking them to select ten new items and discuss the reasons for this selection, or asking them to suggest groupings for items taken from a particular text. Effectiveness in the use of these strategies is partially indicated by the program's performance measures, but the students' reflections on their work are hidden unless they express them publicly in online discussion.

2 Students were to spend time logged on to the Lexica web site, reading the course documentation (study guide, guide to Lexica Vocab, glossary of French technical terms, guide to the Francophone Web), and contributing to a computer conference which involved all other participants in the course, including tutors. The conference used a Bulletin Board System (Stratfold 1997[5]) in which messages were posted as replies to other messages and the developing discussion was represented as a series of 'threads' showing who was talking to whom. Figure 1 shows the introductory message and subsequent threads from the Lexica 1 forum. The underlined words are the subject headings of messages. Viewers can read the actual messages by clicking on them.

Figure 1: Lexica 1 forum

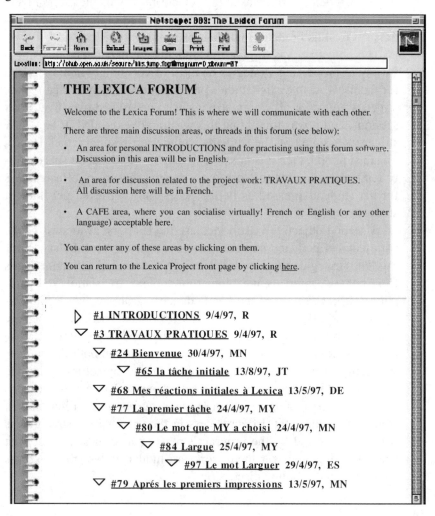

Apart from getting the learners to externalise their reflections, the aim was to develop their ability to 'talk in print' about French, in French. This involved developing an understanding of the interface itself, but also, and more subtly, it involved learning to 'discuss' in a manner which was constructive for other participants as well as themselves. Analysis of some of the discourse of the Lexica 1 forum, for example, has shown that students vary, not only in the accuracy of the French they use, but also in the competence with which they initiate and develop topics, so that they became sustained conversations (Lamy & Goodfellow 1999, forthcoming).

The initial subject of discussion was intended to be the work done in activities (1) above and (3) below, and issues arising from it. To facilitate this, a structure was imposed on the discussion consisting of, first, a period in which people were invited to introduce themselves; second, two practical 'tasks' in which they had to report on specific aspects of their use of Lexica Vocab; and third, a task in which they had to utilise the guide to the Francophone Web to find further texts with which to continue their vocabulary learning. As it was expected that the students would want to use the forum for social interaction as well as course work, a 'cafe' area was provided to be used in any way they wished.

3   Students were to explore the French web sites suggested, and other sites of their choice, looking for texts which were suitable to be downloaded and incorporated into the Lexica Vocab corpus for further vocabulary study. The objective of this activity was to help them widen their knowledge of the Francophone Web, and to give them a means of integrating this knowledge with their explicit vocabulary learning. A 'gateway' to the French Web was provided, consisting of a list of recommended sites, and a task was developed requiring them to locate a suitable text on the internet, download it into Lexica Vocab and process it for vocabulary.

Outcomes

The two Lexica Online courses were separated by 12 months, during which time data from the first one was analysed and a framework for evaluating the quality of online discussion was developed.

There were three main differences in the tutorial design between Lexica 1 and Lexica 2:

*   In Lexica 2 an explicit model was given of the Lexica Vocab activity which deals with the grouping of vocabulary items according to categories of similarity. Students were shown an example text and

asked to identify words in it which could be classified together under the heading 'human behaviour'.

- In Lexica 2 the reflective topic 'learning a language' was explicitly introduced as a subject for general discussion early in the course.
- Lexica 2 was extended from ten hours study over six weeks, to 15 hours over eight weeks, and scaled up from ten to 30 students, and from three tutor/moderators to four.

Quantifiable outcomes

The first set of outcomes considered here are the quantitative measures of student activity; for example, time spent, words studied, messages written etc. The estimated study times and averages from the work with Lexica Vocab shown in table 1, are from all nine of the Lexica 1 participants, and from 12 of the 26 active Lexica 2 participants.

Table 1: Lexica 1 and Lexica 2 compared

Times	Lexica 1	Lexica 2
Period of course:	10 hours over 6 weeks	15 hours over 8 weeks
Active students:	9	26
Tutors/moderators:	3	4
Average study times estimated by students on each activity:		
	hours	*hours*
Lexica Vocab:	8	10
Discussion forum:	4	12
Exploring the Web:	3	4
Work with Lexica Vocab:		
average items studied:	62	97
average % correct:	60	74
average items per hour:	5.7	3.3
average groupings	3	7.5
Web tasks completed:	6	14
Messages sent to forum:	*9 students*	*26 students*
Total	210	820
To tutorial areas:		
Students	48	168
Tutors	26	218

In both courses, student estimates of the time they spent considerably exceeded the minimum commitment. The average 11 extra hours spent on Lexica 2 was mainly accounted for by reading and writing messages on the course forum. In table 1, a distinction has been made between the total number of messages sent to the forum during each course, and the number sent to the 'tutorial areas', which were those parts of the conference delineated as areas for discussion of the set tasks (i.e. they exclude the 'introductions', and 'help' threads, and also the student social 'cafes'). Lexica 2 clearly generated proportionately more messaging activity, both in social and tutorial areas, though quite a lot of the latter is due to increased tutor and moderator contributions.

Lexica 2 also shows a different profile for the work with Lexica Vocab. Although Lexica 2 learners used the program on average only two hours longer than their counterparts in Lexica 1, they studied 35% more items, were correct 14% more often in their testing, and did more than twice as much word grouping. Lexica 1 students, on the other hand, had a much higher items per hour rate. These outcomes tend to suggest different strategic approaches to the work, which may have been affected by the tutorial design. The explicit discussion of grouping strategy in Lexica 2, for example, may have been responsible for the extra work in grouping that these learners did.

More of the Lexica 2 learners, approximately 50%, failed to complete the third stage of the course, the Web task. This may have been due to the extra time they spent on earlier stages, or on the fact that the extra length of this course resulted in a clash with an assignment due in the mainstream course that was going on in parallel. However, most of those who did complete the third stage continued to engage in online discussion for some time after the course was officially over.

Overall, the comparison shows that the attempt to scale up Lexica 1 did not result in a simple increase in activity, but instead produced a number of differences in type of activity and general approach. The greater intensity of Lexica 2 work on the Vocab program, the greater 'tail-off' between the Lexica Vocab work and the Web task, the lower proportion of student messages to the work areas and higher proportion of tutor messages, all indicate a difference between the pedagogical activity in the first course and the second. Some of this can be put down to organisational and technical problems, which were amplified by the increased number of students. But much of it must be due to the ways that individuals interpreted the course tasks. This suggests that there was considerable individual difference in the learning experience at the private level, and that there should be a lot of scope for individual contribution to reflective conversation about learning issues. The extent to which this is true is discussed below.

Qualitative analysis of forum interaction
    Another paper on Lexica 1 (Lamy & Goodfellow 1999, forthcoming) discusses categories of contribution to forum, according to their apparent effectiveness in optimising opportunities for reflection in the discussion, and their compatibility with theories of social interaction (van Lier 1997) and input

processing (Warschauer 1998). It identifies three main categories of contribution: monologue-type messages, social conversations, and reflective conversations, and argues that it is only in the latter that we would expect to find all the conditions for optimal learning conversations. For the purposes of the present comparison between the two Lexica courses, a fourth category of exchange has been identified, the 'classroom management' exchange, which is concerned with ensuring that students know what the tasks are, and helping them with any technical or general procedural difficulties they are having.

Monologue-type messages are typically posted by teachers, or in response to formal tasks or questions posed by teachers. They are characterised by (a) reflectiveness on the task in hand, or on some aspect of performing it, (b) low reciprocity, that is a lack of discourse features which are likely to stimulate comment or response from other learners, and (c) predictability arising from the context in which they occur. In the example from Lexica 2 (figure 2), the monologue consists of three messages listing expressions and their translations (message nos. #64, #66, #68). We can see from the text of message #64 that the student is reflecting on the difficulty of translation, but the sheer length of the list contained in the three messages, the lack of specificity in the invitation to other students to respond ('I'm sure you can find better translations'), and the predictability of the message as a report on a set task, ensures that the only response comes from a tutor (messages #71, #73).

Figure 2: A monologue-type message

```
#18 Le Travail 3/5/98, JD
    #27 LE TRAVAIL 12/5/98/, PM
#36 premier travail par E. - un travail abruti 17/5/98, E
    #39 mots feminins 19/5/98 ES
#64 Mon deuxiéme travail par E. 7/6/98 E
#66 Mon deuxiéme travail par E cont. 7/6/98 E
#68 Mon deuxiéme travail par E. 2nd cont 7/6/98 E
    #71 Travail trés riche! 7/6/98, ES
    #73 Barabara 9/6/98, ES
```

J'ai maintanant su l'occcasion d'étudier l'article au suject de BARBARA en grands détail, Je trouvais cet article très interessant grâce aux grandes quantités de phrases figurées. En conséquance j'ai decidé d'isoler ces phrases pour rendre une traduction. Parce que j'ai trouvé qu'il est impossible de traduire des mots hors de context. Pourtant je suis sûr que vous trouverez des meilleurs traductions.

I've had a chance to look at the article called BARBARA in detail...I found it very interesting because of the large number of figurative expressions...I decided to take these expressions out and translate them...because I've found it's not possible to translate words out of context...I'm sure you can find better translations.

Only 1% of the messages posted to the tutorial area of the Lexica 1 forum were messages from students of this type. In Lexica 2 this proportion rose to 16% (table 2).

Social conversations consist of interrelated messages, sent as comments or replies by tutors or students and characterised by a high degree of reciprocity and a low degree of reflectiveness. Because of their reciprocal nature, contributions to social conversations often elicit replies and, in the course of the development of a 'thread' (a chain of messages and replies), responses may gain in unpredictability (basically, people go off at tangents), giving the exchange a degree of contingency. It is this contingency which gives such interaction an intrinsic value for language learning (van Lier 1997), but because of the tendency of social topics to be non-reflective, they are less likely to promote conscious attention to linguistic form or learning strategy. In the Lexica forums, specific areas were designated for social 'chat', so there is a low incidence of such exchanges in the tutorial areas. Only 1% of messages are contributions of this type from students in the Lexica 1 forum. This rises to 5% in Lexica 2 (table 2).

Where some of the features of contingency and reciprocity find their way into exchanges which have an explicitly reflective focus, a type of conversation is generated in which language learning is both the topic and, hopefully, the observable outcome of the interaction. We have called this type of exchange 'reflective conversation'. An example from Lexica 2 is shown in figure 3.

Three messages are shown in figure 3 from a conversation taking place over a four-week period. Reflection on the meaning of the word 'sideral' (relating to the stars) is at the centre of it, although the thread actually begins (message #59) with a question about the English word 'marl'. Message #74 opens out the discussion on 'sideral'. The appeal to 'scientists or engineers' is a specific invitation to others on the course to respond, a clear intention to create reciprocity. From the response (message #78), a new topic is developed. The exchange is also characterised by the use of first names and by the employment of a hotlink to a site on the World Wide Web (message #78), whereby the topic could be further developed in a contingent manner.

Analysis of interaction in the tutorial areas of Lexica 1 forum shows that 36% of messages were student contributions to this kind of reflective conversation. Most of the successful reflective topics were concerned with meaning and translation, and arose from the Web task. But, earlier in the course, there were examples of conversation around the functions of Lexica Vocab, and later one or two students attempted to take on more formal issues, such as the behaviour of affixes. The changes in the tutorial design implemented in Lexica 2 were intended to generate more explicit discussion of the kind of insight into lexical structure that Lexica Vocab intends to promote (e.g. an

Figure 3: A reflective conversation from Lexica 2

#55 le deuxième travail 28/5/98. AE
#59 Marl 30/5/98, E
#74 mouchoirs et etoiles 4/6/98, C
#75 L' espace intersidéral!! 5/6/98, P
#78 Sideral 7/6/98, E
#79 Distribution des échelles de temps 7/698, E
#80 Que je sois dans le ruisseau, je regarde les étoiles 7/6/98, C
#106 Etoiles et rêveries!!! 24/6/98, P

La phrase, 'mis un mouchoir' m'intéresse aussi et j'aime bien ton explication, A. J'ai 'obscure' ou mieux, 'fudge' pour mon explication.

Je ne peux guère me rappeler ce que j'ai appris dans l'école, mais je pense que 'sideral' a quelque chose à voir avec les étoiles, c'est-à-dire, l'astronomie. Peut-être il est associé avec le temps et le mouvement. Je suis certaine qu'il y a des scientifiques ou des ingénieurs qui le sauront plus mieux que moi!

Amitiés

The sentence, "mis un mouchoir" reminds me of what I have learnt at school, but I think that 'sideral' has something to do with stars, in other words with astronomy. Perhaps it is associates with time and movement. I am sure that the scientists or engineers should know better than me

(mes excuses a Oscar Wilde!)
Merci, E! Selon moi, une explication parfaite. Maintenant, je me souviens tout!

Amities

(my apologies to Oscar Wilde!)
Thanks E...! It is a perfect explanation for me. Now, I remember it all!

Comme scientifique, j'essayerai d'expliquer le mot sidéral. En anglais, sidéréal veut dire "des étoiles". Si on parle de temps, il y a quelques moyens de définir la tempe, ou un jour par exemple. En utilisant le temps solaire, une joue est la longueur qu'il prend pour la terre faire une révolution sur l'axis. Mais, ce n'est pas assez précis pour les astronomes en calculant les positions des étoiles. Ils employant le temps sidéral, qui utilise la position de deux observations mériidionales de la premiére point de la constellation Aires pour définir un jour sidéral. Un jour sidéral est un peu plus court qu'un jour solaire, d'ou viens la nécessité pour avoir une année bonde dans une dans quatre pour réassigner le temps solaire avec le temps sidéral. Allez voir

SiderealDay.html (malheureusement en angliais) pour une explication meilleure.

As a scientist, I ll try and explain the word' sideral". In english, 'sideral' means "of the stars'. If one talks about time, there are ways of defining time, or a day for example. If we use solar time, a day is the time it takes for the earth to make one revolution on its axis. But this measurement is not precise enough for astronomers to ca;lculate the position of stars. They use sideral time, which uses two points south of the aries constellation to define a sideral day. A sideral day is sslightly horter than a solar day, which explains the need to add a leap year every four year to realign solar time with sideral time. Go and see

eww6n/astro/ SiderealDay.html (unfortunately in English) for a better explanation

awareness of different kinds of synonymy, or of the way words are related in the roots, or the existence of unsuspected collocations etc.). In fact, the proportion of student contribution to reflective conversation fell to 21% (table 2), with most of the discussion focusing on general issues of meaning and translation, as in Lexica 1. However, although Lexica 2 did not succeed in optimising the amount of student reflective conversation, it did produce a higher degree of student reflective monologue, and a greater variety of topics for reflection, including form-focused discussion (such as a consideration of the meaning of the root 'dic' in the term 'dicible') and the specifically reflective discussion topic 'language learning', which started early in the course and continued for 16 days.

Table 2: Lexica 1 and Lexica 2 compared for message types

	Lex 1		Lex 2	total
	students	tutors	students	tutors
Total messages in work areas	28	46	168	218
Class management msgs	14%	12%	1%	26%
Monologues	1%	11%	16%	2%
Social conversation	1%	3%	5%	6%
Reflective conversation	36%	22%	21%	23%

Discussion
The outcome data show that learners in both courses engaged in a lot of private learning activity, some of which, for example the Lexica Vocab work, would have involved them in reflecting on what they were learning and how they were going about it. The extent and precise nature of this reflective activity is, however, hidden to us. The performance profiles for the Lexica 2 group – the greater number of items studied and correctly tested and the increased grouping activity – might indicate a more technical (in van Lier's sense) kind of awareness under development. This was certainly one of the intentions of the more explicit tutorial input provided for Lexica 2, but the connection between input and performance here can only be speculative. Students also engaged in public online discussion, in the case of the Lexica 2 group to a far greater extent than expected. The analysis was expected to give a much better idea of how the reflective processes were developing. The data therefore shows that the changes in tutorial design did not have the effect of increasing the amount of reflective conversation. Rather, there was a decline in the overall percentage of reflective conversation, in favour of an increase in the amount of student monologue (table 2).

Monologues, as we have suggested, are often associated with responses to the set tasks. We might take the evidence of increased student monologues in Lexica 2 as being partly a result of the extra focus that the setting up of formal tasks was given in the second course. Whilst these messages do usually contain reflective content, their failure to generate sustained interaction reduces their value for the learning experience. The tension between the control that is exercised in the design of tasks intended to focus attention on the formal 'syllabus', and the flexibility needed to generate contingent interaction between learners is thus shown to be as acute in the CMC context as it is in the face-to-face equivalent (e.g. Kumaravadivelu 1993)

The influence of the tutor may also have helped to determine the discourse profile of individual groups. The lowest incidence of student reflective conversation and reflective monologue was found in the group with the lowest number of active students (Group 2 in table 3). This group also had the highest percentage of tutor class management messages. There may be a connection between the degree of organising of conversation that teachers attempt online, and the likelihood of sustained student–student interaction. This is not a straightforward matter of teacher-talking-time (Group 3's tutor posted nearly three times as many messages as all her ten students), but this does not appear to have significantly affected the percentages of reflective and monologue-type contributions the students made.

Table 3: Lexica 2 tutorial groups compared

Lexica 2 Tutorial Groups	Gp1		Gp2		Gp3	
	10 sts	tuts	6 sts	tuts	10 sts	tuts
Total messages	46	55	27	43	48	120
Class management	0%	21%	7%	36%	0%	26%
Monologues	17%	1%	19%	7%	15%	2%
Social conversation	4%	1%	3%	0%	7%	8%
Reflective conversation	25%	31%	10%	18%	22%	20%

Summary and future research

This chapter has argued for an approach to the design of online environments for distance language learners which focuses on critical reflection on learning practices as a key topic of communicative interaction amongst learners. It has described a design based around a study of French vocabulary, and reported on the outcomes of two pilot projects. The main conclusion has been that, whilst the design managed to engage the learners to the extent and in the different ways intended, the relation between their public and private reflective activity is unclear. More reflective work in the private arena did not necessarily produce more public learning conversation. In fact, aspects of the tutorial design introduced with the intention of fostering more learning conversation resulted in more student monologue.

Whilst we hold to the principles on which this design and our pedagogical practice has been based, it is clear that there is much that we do not understand about online interaction and the part that it plays in externalising private reflection. Future research needs to look for evidence relating to the ways that the following key processes work:

- Language acquisition via CMC. Can an online environment substitute in any way for a real world one, in the development of a learner's interlanguage?

- Technology-based strategies for language learning. Are there characteristics of the 'good online language learner' which are different from those of the 'good language learner' per se?

- The social construction of language knowledge. What factors constrain the development of new knowledge and skills in a virtual language learning community?

Candlin and Byrnes (1994) describe an 'open curriculum' in distance language education as one in which 'learners can develop their abilities to move beyond the prescribed subject-matter and prescribed ways of studying, and to collaborate in an open curriculum where the responsibility for the direction of their own learning lies within the learning network or learning web that has been facilitated'. Whilst the OU is committed in the long term to exactly this kind of autonomy, experience in the short term suggests that CMC by itself will not bring about an open curriculum. To get beyond the need for structured subject matter and ways of studying will require pedagogical as well as technological inspiration.

Notes

[1] 1996 The European Year of Lifelong Learning.
URL <http://europa.eu.int/en/comm/dg22/eyinet.html>

[2] It is worth noting that, although, at the time of writing, interaction via video and audio is feasible, fully-developed technologies for this kind of 'high-bandwidth' communication are still too expensive for mass use. Most use of CMC at the moment involves written text, and is likely to go on doing so for the foreseeable future.

[3] Helsinki University of Technology Writing Projects.

[4] International Tandem Email Network.
  URL <http://www.slf.ruhr-uni-bochum.de/email/infen.html>

[5] The EBBS system.
  URL<http://trout.open.ac.uk/bbs.html>

References

Aitchison, J. (1987). *Words in the mind.* London: Blackwell.

Boud, D., Keogh, R. & Walker, D. (1985). What is reflection in learning? In D. Boud, R. Keogh and D. Walker (Eds), *Reflection: Turning experiences into learning.* London: Kogan Page.

Broady, E. & Kenning, M-M. (Eds) (1996). *Promoting learner autonomy in university language teaching.* AFLS/CILT.

Candlin C. & Byrnes F. (1994). Designing for open language learning: Teaching roles and learning strategies. In Gollin (Ed.), *Language in Distance Education, how far can we go?* National Centre for English Language Teaching and Research, Macquarie University.

Carpenter, C. (1996). Peer-teaching: A new approach to advanced level language learning. In E. Broady & M-M. Kenning (Eds), *Promoting learner autonomy in university language teaching* (pp. 23–38). AFLS/CILT.

Ebbrell, D. & Goodfellow, R. (1997). Learner, teacher and computer: A mutual support system. In J. Kohn, B. Ruschoff & D. Wolff. (Eds), *New Horizons in CALL – Proceedings of Eurocall 96* (pp. 207–221), Hungary: Szombatheley.

Ellis, R. (1994). *The study of second language acquisition.* Oxford: Oxford University Press.

Goodfellow, R. (1994). *A computer-based strategy for foreign language vocabulary learning.* Unpublished PhD thesis, Institute of Educational Technology, Open University.

Goodfellow, R. (1995). A review of the types of CALL programs for vocabulary instruction. *Computer-Assisted Language Learning 8,* 2–3, 205–226

Goodfellow R. (1997). Needs analysis of eight students studying French with the OU. In *TELOS User Scenario Analysis and Functional Requirements Specification.* EU TELOS project ET3005 Deliverable D4.1

Goodfellow, R. (1998). Evaluating performance, approach and outcome in the design of CALL. In K. Cameron (Ed.), *CALL: Media, Design & Applications.* Lisse, Netherlands: Swets & Zeitlinger.

Goodfellow, R. & Lamy, M-N. (1998). Learning to learn a language: At home and on the Web. Proceedings of Eurocall 97, *ReCALL 10,*1, 68–78.

Holmberg, B. (1989). *The theory and practice of distance education.* London: Routledge.

Johns, T. (1991). From printout to handout: Grammar and vocabulary teaching in the context of data-driven learning. *ELR Journal 4,* 27–45.

Kolb, D. (1984). *Experiential learning experience as the source of learning and development.* Englewood Cliffs, NJ: Prentice Hall.

Kumaravadivelu, B. (1993). The name of the task and the task of naming: Methodological aspects of task-based pedagogy. In G. Crookes & S.M. Gass (Eds), *Tasks in a pedagogical context* (p. 83). Clevedon, Phil: Multilingual Matters.

Lamy, M-N., Goodfellow, R. (1999, forthcoming). Reflective conversation in the virtual language classroom. *Language learning and technology*, January. URL <http://polyglot.cal.msu.edu/llt>

Lewis M. (1993). *The lexical approach.* Hove: Language Teaching Publications.

Lewis T. (1998). *Tandem email – principles and practice.* Unpublished report for Open University POLLO program.

Little, D. (1997). Linguistic awareness and writing: Exploring the relationship with language awareness. *Language Awareness 6*, 2 & 3, 95–104.

Lockwood, F. (Ed.) (1995). *Open and distance learning today.* London: Routledge.

McCarthy, M. (1990). *Vocabulary.* Oxford: Oxford University Press.

Metcalfe, P. (1992). CALL, the foreign-language undergraduate and the teaching of grammar: A linguistic and political battlefield. *ReCALL 7*, 3–5.

O'Malley, J. & Charnot, A. (1990). *Learning strategies in second language acquisition.* Cambridge: Cambridge University Press.

Owen C. (1993). Corpus-based grammar and the Heineken effect: Lexico-grammatical description for language learners. *Applied Linguistics 14*, 2, 167–187.

Stevens, A. (1995). Issues in distance teaching in languages. *ReCALL 7*, 1, 12–19.

Thomas, L. & Harri-Augstein, E. (1977). Learning to learn: The personal construction and exchange of meaning. In M. Howe (Ed.), *Adult learning: psychological research and applications*, London: Wiley.

van Lier, L. (1996). *Interaction in the language curriculum: Awareness, autonomy & authenticity.* London: Longman.

van Lier, L. (1997). The relationship between consciousness, interaction and language learning. *Language Awareness 6*, 2 & 3, 128–145.

Warschauer, M. (1998). Interaction, negotiation and computer-mediated learning. In Darleguy, Ding, Svensson (Eds), *Educational technology in language learning: Theoretical considerations and practical applications.*
URL < http://www.insa-lyon.fr/Departements/CDRL/interaction.html>

Wenden, A. (1995). Learner training in context: A knowledge-based approach, *System 23*, 2, 183–194.

17

Technology and the Second Language Learner: How Does it Work Best?

Jane D. Tchaïcha
Bentley College, USA

Introduction

In the past two decades, computer-assisted language learning (CALL) has received a mixed reaction from practitioners and theorists involved in second language (SL) teaching and learning (Dunkel 1990; Garrett 1991:74–96; Pederson 1987; Williams & Brown 1991:26–46). 'Supporters' of CALL praise this technology as a means of enhancing the acquisition of a second language. Contrarily, 'non–supporters' of CALL have argued that its impact on students' progress in learning a second language is meagre. The varied reactions among these professionals may come from the way the research community has approached CALL research and SL acquisition (Dunkel 1990; Meich, Nave & Mosteller 1995:64–84). A large body of research on CALL has attempted to examine the effect of CALL on a particular language skill, such as listening comprehension, or on the integration of a particular grammar point into the students' knowledge base of the target language (Chun 1994:17–31; Stenson et al. 1992:5–19). Often, these studies have narrowed their focus by using one or two software programs. Other studies have concentrated on how certain design features in CALL promote more immediate learning than others (Borras & Lafayette 1994:61–75; Garza 1991:239–257; Hermann 1992; Nagata 1993:330–339). Still other studies have considered how important the appeal factor of the program plays in influencing students' use of CALL which, in turn, might affect how much benefit in terms of language acquisition is derived from its use (Fischer 1989:527–534; Hsu, Chapelle & Thompson 1993:1–15). In the latter studies, the user or student is more often the focus of the study than the software.

Initially, one could argue that the diverse findings that have emerged from these earlier studies threaten the future of CALL and its potential to play an integral role in SL teaching and learning – hence the mixed reception from members of the SL community. Yet these same studies have been essential in gaining an understanding about how technology, in particular CALL, can influence the learning of a second language. Learning about what CALL can feature and the kinds of skill areas that might or might not benefit from CALL use is a very logical first step towards gaining a better understanding of how this technology works for the SL learner. At the same time, however, to restrict the research focus today to a single program, design feature or particular skill, without examining other external factors that might contribute or mediate CALL's effect on language acquisition, seems too narrow a research approach.

The increasingly widespread use of CALL in language curricula strongly suggests that the research paradigm should be broadened as well. Just as computers and technology are complex and ever-changing, so are our students and their learning environments. The variation in learning environments, in how CALL is used, and who the learners are call for research paradigms that can accommodate an investigation of multiple factors simultaneously. Such a paradigm may seem like an impossible task, but herein may lie a valuable opportunity to sow new seeds of creativity in CALL research as the next millennium draws near. Finding new, comprehensive ways to evaluate the impact of CALL seeks a creative approach: one that allows for testing thoughtful hypotheses and using varied research methodologies to answer the multifaceted use of CALL.

In an attempt to consider a broader approach to CALL research than has been adopted thus far, the study that follows investigates the use of CALL to supplement language curriculum in a particular academic environment, along with other language activities. Indeed, the study is narrowly defined by its setting – a small business school in New England – but broadened by its attempt, through multivariate analysis, to explore other factors that may work in concert with CALL to enhance the acquisition of a target language. The other language activities include the traditional use of audio tapes (analog) and conversation practice with native speakers of the target language, supplementary services made available through the college's Modern Language Learning Center and common features of many language centres in the US. The decision to investigate the impact of supplementary language activities beyond the mandated three hours of classroom exposure to the target language was based on SL research showing that multiple and repetitive types of language input in a target language are important in developing SL competency (Leow 1998:49–64). In this study, the concept of multiple input was captured by monitoring how often students used the three forms of supplementary language activities. The principal research question addressed was:

> Do services/facilities at a language centre at the post-secondary level, including technology (audio tapes/CALL software) and conversation practice with native speakers of the target language, contribute to students' overall oral and written performances in elementary language courses?

The study also attempted to investigate several non-technical factors that have shown to be important contributors to students' SL acquisition over the years, in particular, the importance of students' aptitude and motivation for learning a second language (Curren & Kirk 1986:107–113, Skehan 1991:275–298; Sparks, Ganschow & Patton 1995:638–655; Spolsky 1989). In this study, grade point average (GPA) was used as a measure of academic motivation, and the Modern Language Aptitude Test (Sapon & Carroll 1959) was used as a measure of students' aptitude for learning a modern language. The possibility of these learner-centred factors mediating the potential effects of technical factors was also considered. All three question predictors – multiple language input, academic motivation, and students' SL aptitude – were examined separately and in concert with one another as they affected the outcomes variables – oral and written performance – as illustrated in figure 1.

Figure 1: Research paradigm

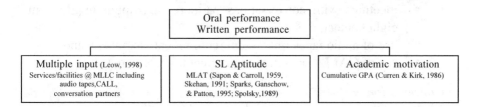

Method

Sample

One hundred and fifteen students (male = 59, female = 56) participated in the study in autumn 1997. All were enrolled in elementary language courses across five languages at Bentley College, a small business school in New

England. Among these students, 20 were enrolled in French I, 21 in Italian I, 25 in Spanish I, 10 in Spanish I (sequence 2), 29 in Japanese I, 10 in Chinese I. At the beginning of the semester, students registered at the Modern Language Learning Center (MLLC) where they provided specific information: their course, section, and student identification numbers for tracking purposes, information about previous academic training in the target language, background in English (native speaker, bilingual, ESL), major or intended major, and date of birth.

The average age of the participants was 20 years 3 months. The youngest participant was 18 and the oldest 34. Of the participants, 73% had studied one year or less of the target language prior to their college course. Among this sub-group, over half had never studied the target language. Eighteen per cent of the sample studied two to five years while 9% had not reported their previous academic training. Fifty-one per cent of the participants reported that they were native speakers of English; 33% reported they were bilingual (speaking two languages at home since childhood or residing in a non-English speaking country and attending English speaking schools); and 16% declared they were speakers of English as a second language (ESL), having five years or less of English and identified by Bentley College Admissions as needing additional ESL training provided by the college during the freshman year.

Data collection
Four waves of student data were collected for this study.

Wave one: Frequency of use of facilities/services at MLLC
   The facilities/services at the MLLC included

- meetings with conversations partners (maximum requirement: eight contacts),
- use of audio tapes (maximum requirement: six tapes); and
- use of CALL (maximum requirement: six lessons).

Conversation partners
Contact with native speakers of the target language consisted of conversations on specific functional topics, developed by the faculty, that emphasise practice in pronunciation, vocabulary and simple grammar structures. The conversation practice was scheduled by appointment (20-minute minimum); the number of required contacts varied from five to eight per lecturer. Students could also make appointments with conversation partners for extra help or more practice in the target language. Whatever the reason, the total number of contacts were counted for each student. On average, students had 3.72 contacts with a native speaker; the fewest number of contacts was one and the highest seven.

Audio tapes
Students enrolled in Spanish, Italian, Japanese and Chinese used audio tapes accompanying their text books and were expected to complete six tapes, respectively. Spanish students used the *Encuentros* series (Spinelli & Rosso-O'Laughlin 1997). Italian students used *Oggi in Italia* (Merlonghi 1994). Japanese students used *Learn Japanese* (Young & Nakajima-Okano 1985), and Chinese students used *College Chinese* (Lin 1993). French students did not use audio tapes distributed by the publisher of their text, *Vous y êtes* (St Onge & Terry 1990). Instead, these students used audio tapes specially designed by the French faculty to accompany the content of the first six chapters of *Vous y êtes*. Students used less than two audio tapes on average (mean = 1.3, low = 0 and high = 6).

CALL programs
Students enrolled in French, Italian and Japanese were required to complete a series of computer assignments, created in MacLang, Super MacLang and/or Hypercard. (The Spanish and Chinese faculty had not yet incorporated CALL as a course requirement, although similar programs are available for these languages in the Modern Language Learning Center). MacLang and Super MacLang (an updated version of MacLang) are two authoring programs that provide lecturers with easy computer tools to develop their own computer exercises. Their assigned exercises consisted of beginning grammar and vocabulary-based content using various practice formats that elicited a student's written input. The programs evaluated student responses, and, if incorrect, provided students with immediate feedback, including short written explanations and the option to let students re-enter another response. The Hypercard programs, which incorporate sound and text files simultaneously, also presented elementary language use, but emphasised oral/aural practice. Both software programs were created by members of the Modern Language Department at Bentley College to complement their particular curriculum and texts. Computer contacts among students required to use CALL approached three on average (mean = 2.84, low = 0 and high = 6).

Wave two: Students' aptitude for learning a second language as measured by the Modern Language Aptitude Test (Sapon & Carroll 1959)
Students in all elementary language courses took the long version of the Modern Language Aptitude Test (MLAT) during one class period between the fourth and sixth week of the autumn semester. Each of the five sections of the test (number recognition, phonetic scripting, spelling clues, words in sentences and paired associates) was hand-scored by the MLLC staff using

the key provided by the Psychological Corporation. Individual section scores and a total raw score were calculated for each participant. Students who were absent on the day of the test were excluded from the final analysis of the study. On average, students scored 104.49 (maximum score = 195) on the MLAT, with a low of 54 and a high of 154. Students tended to do better on average on sections testing phonetic aptitude and rote memory than on grammatical sensitivity.

Wave three: Academic motivation

Students' cumulative GPA (through the autumn semester 1997) was used as a measure of students' motivation. This information was obtained by the MLLC director (and principal researcher for this study) from the school's administrative database. On average, students had an 82.68 GPA.

Wave four: Student performance in the target language

Final grades on the oral and written assessments in their course were used as the measure of students' success in the target language. Lecturers were provided with special grading sheets to record students' grades on these measures and asked to submit them according to student identification numbers. Students' final grades were not used as the indicator of their performance to prevent possible collinearity with frequency of use variables. Since assessment included 10 to 15% of students' work in the Modern Language Learning Center, including the number of conversation partner contacts and completed audio and computer lessons, this work could be feasibly counted twice. On average, students performed slightly better on the oral assessment (mean = 88.42) than on the written assessment (mean = 81.04).

Data analysis

Initially, step-wise multiple regression analysis was to be conducted on one set of data. However, two sets of data naturally emerged after t-tests showed a significance difference in frequency of use of CALL, depending on course requirement, t = 2.13 p< .05. Students enrolled in Spanish and Chinese were not required to use CALL. Following this discovery, it was thought that for the non-CALL users practice with conversation partners and audio tapes could have a different impact on their performance in the target language than for CALL users. The best way to address this possible difference and obtain as accurate picture as possible regarding the influence of each of the question predictors (use of CALL, audio tapes and conversation partners) on the outcome variables (oral and written performance) was to develop a series of base models for non-CALL and CALL users against which the same two hypotheses were tested.

H1

Frequency of use of conversation partners, audio tapes, and/or CALL software (CALL users only) improves the prediction of oral and/or written performances of college students enrolled in elementary modern language courses, controlling for academic motivation and SL aptitude.

H2

Frequency of use of conversation partners, audio tapes, and/or CALL software (CALL users only) is mediated by students' academic motivation and/or SL aptitude when predicting oral and/or written performance in elementary language courses.

Each base model included students' GPA and MLAT total score and phonetic scripting score (MLATP – Section II of the MLAT). Previous research (Curren & Kirk 1986:107–113; Gardener, Tremblay & Masgoret 1997:344–362; Goodman, Freed & McManus 1990:131–141; Sparks et al. 1997:349–561; Sparks, Ganschow & Patton 1995:638–655; (Spolsky 1989) and results from simple correlations among *question predictors* and *outcome variables* in this study guided this choice.

Result

General findings: Base model

Oral performance

Results from the fitted multiple regression models for CALL users and non-CALL users show that the amount of variation in oral performance explained by academic motivation and SL aptitude differed for CALL users (15%) and non-CALL users (30%) (see table 1). Additionally, GPA had predictive value for both groups; MLATP had predictive value only for CALL users.

Table 1: Comparison of base models for oral performance for CALL and non-CALL users

	Intercept	Base Predictors-Main Effect			R^2	dfE
Model						
		GPA	MLATP	MLATT		
C 1	47.0552**	.3696*	.6467*	-.0480	.1536*	62
NC 1	30.0498*	.7170***	.2309	-.0678	.2960**	41

Fitted multiple regression models include control variables – Grade Point Average, Students' Score on Modern Language Aptitude Test Section II (phonetic scripting), and Students' Raw Total Score on Modern Language Aptitude Test

~$p \leq .10$	$p \leq .05$	**$p \leq .01$	***$p \leq .001$

C1 = CALL users; NC1 = non-CALL users
C1 = CALL users; NC1 = non-CALL users

Written performance

For written performance, the amount of variation explained by academic motivation and SL aptitude was approximately the same (32%) for both groups (see table 2). GPA continued to have predictive value for both groups; MLATP did not.

Table 2: Comparison of base models for written performance for CALL and non-CALL users

Fitted multiple regression models include control variables – Grade Point Average, Students' Score on Modern Language Aptitude Test Section II (phonetic scripting), and Students' Raw Total Score on Modern Language Aptitude Test.						
	Intercept	Base Predictors - Main Effect			R^2	dfE
Model						
		GPA	MLATP	MLATT		
C 1	-35.1219	1.2564***	.4758	-.0097	.3239***	62
NC 1	-13.4493	1.0697***	.8082	-.1164	.3242***	41

~$p \leq .10$	$p \leq .05$	**$p \leq .01$	***$p \leq .001$

C1 = CALL users; NC1 = non-CALL users

Hypothesis testing

To determine if each of the question predictors made a difference in either oral or written performance in the target language, each question predictor was added to the appropriate base model singularly and in concert with one another. As expected, the estimated R^2 statistic increased. However, a series

Table 3: The amount of variation (estimated R2) in oral performance by the addition of a question predictor(s)

The amount of variation (estimated R2) in oral performance by the addition of a question predictor(s)to the base model for oral performance, indicating if such an addition improves the prediction of oral performance significantly for both CALL and non-CALL users.			
	Question Predictor	R^2	Increment to R^2
Model			
non-CALL users			
NC 1 (base Model)		.2920**	
NC 2	tape	.3623***	4.42*
NC 3	tutor	.3135**	1.22
NC 4	tape, tutor	.3685***	2.36
CALL Users			
C 1 (base model)		.1536*	
C 2	tape	.2265**	5.74*
C 3	tutor	.1912*	2.84~
C 4	computer	.1538*	0.01
C 5	tape, tutor	.2401**	3.41*
C 6	tape, computer	.2277**	2.88~
C 7	tutor, computer	.1919*	1.42
C 8	tape, tutor, computer	.2431**	0.12

~$p \leq .10$	*$p \leq .05$	**$p \leq .01$	***$p \leq .001$

of F-tests were conducted to determine if these increases were significant. In most cases, they were not.

Oral performance

Only one question predictor – tape use singularly and in combination with conversation partners – was found to improve the prediction of oral perfor-mance for both users groups (see table 3). However, negative coefficients for tape use in the fitted regression models for both groups significant at the .05-level appeared, suggesting that students on average performed better orally using fewer audio tapes (see Appendix: Tables 5–6).

Written performance

None of the question predictors improved the prediction of written perfor-mance, controlling for academic motivation and SL aptitude (see table 4).

Table 4:   The amount of variation (estimated R2) in written performance by the addition of a question predictor

The amount of variation (estimated R2) in written performance by the addition of a question predictor to the base model for written performance, indicating if such an addition improves the prediction of written performance significantly for both CALL and non-CALL users.

Model	Question Predictor	R^2	Increment to R^2
non-CALL users			
NC 1 (base Model)		.3342***	
NC 2	tape	.3730***	2.47
NC 3	tutor	.3363***	0.00
NC 4	tape, tutor	.3813***	0.15
CALL Users			
C 1 (base model)		.3239***	
C 2	tape	.3244***	0.05
C 3	tutor	.3240***	0.01
C 4	computer	.3255***	0.14
C 5	tape, tutor	.3244***	0.03
C 6	tape, computer	.3257***	0.80
C 7	tutor, computer	.3255***	0.07
C 8	tape, tutor, computer	.3257***	0.53

~$p \leq .10$ *$p \leq .05$ **$p \leq .01$ ***$p \leq .001$

Mediating effects of learner-centred factors

In continuing the analysis and testing H2 regarding the mediating effects of academic motivation on tape use for oral performance, a series of interactions were introduced and showed that academic motivation did not mediate the effects of tape use or conversation partner contact, controlling for academic motivation and SL aptitude. Nor was there an effect of group membership based on gender or on type of language speaker, that is native English speaker, bilingual or ESL.

However, an interaction between tape use and phonetic aptitude was found, which may help to explain the somewhat disconcerting negative coefficient for tape use already mentioned (see figure 2).

Figure 2: Interaction: Phonetic aptitude and tape use

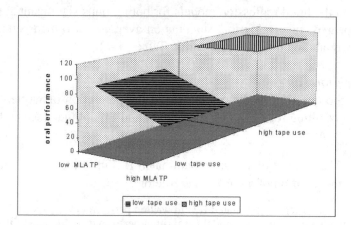

The interaction in figure 2 shows that the influence of tape use on oral performance was greater for students with lower phonetic aptitude than those with higher phonetic aptitude (which was pretty flat) and this gap increases as students show higher phonetic aptitude. Additionally, those students with low tape use and low phonetic aptitude seemed to do better on oral performance than their counterparts with high phonetic aptitude. The students at risk seem to be those students who have a fairly good phonetic aptitude and do not bother to use the tapes – they are the ones who do most poorly on the oral assessment. We also see this same trend when examining the interaction of phonetic aptitude and tape/tutor use (see figure 3).

Figure 3: Interaction: Phonetic attitude with tape–tutor use

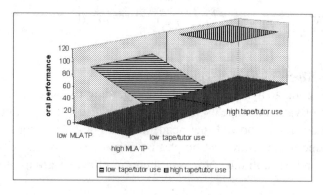

Discussion

What do these findings offer professionals avidly supporting use of technology in second language learning? While the findings from this study appear to suggest that students in elementary language courses do not reap a great deal of benefit from using certain types of technology separately or in concert with other language practice/input, one must recognize the parameters and assumptions underlying the investigation.

First, this study by design examined the *complementary role* that technology might play in students' performance. Therefore, the finding that none of the technologies had a major effect on learning outcomes should not be surprising. However, this same logic does not help to explain why the contribution of technology, when analysed from the angle of incremental impact, was negligible. Additional investigations in similar academic settings with similar curriculum and use of technology need to be conducted to see if such findings continue to emerge.

Second, this study examines the quantity of technology use; it does not consider time on task using such technology. This factor has proved important in previous studies (Leow 1998:49–64) and should be considered in future studies of this kind.

Third, specific types of CALL software were used. The research paradigm used in this kind of study would benefit from more studies that continue to include the same variables, but that assign students randomly to groups that use different CALL programs and in different ways.

Finally, only one level of language – elementary – was considered for this study. What about students in intermediate and advanced levels? Does technology contribute to their performance in the same way?

Indeed, this study seems to raise additional questions and suggests different combinations of predictor variables. At the same time, certain results from this study do support those of more recent investigations in SL. For example:

- Academic motivation appears to predict how well students perform in elementary language courses, supporting Curran and Kirk's previous research (1986).
- In some cases, particularly oral performance, phonetic aptitude (as measured by the MLAT test) appears to predict students' performance. While all parts of the MLAT appear to contribute to students' performance, the total MLAT score did not have predictive value. This finding challenges the most recent studies of Sparks et al. (1995, 1997), which attribute as much as 60% of students' performance to SL aptitude, but the nature of our type of language teaching methodology

and emphasis, based on the communicative approach, may influence the finding in this study.

Other results offer insights into how students are using technology:

- Students' use of CALL in this study differed significantly depending on whether or not lecturers made such language practice a course requirement. Lecturers might need to reconsider their strategy of making technology use optional, expecting to see some learning benefit.
- Tape use was more important for some students than others, depending on their phonetic aptitude. If we as technologists seek to encourage the use of CALL programs which increasingly use digitised audio, we also need to consider ways to attract even those students who demonstrate high phonetic skills but rarely seek out additional oral practice, because they seem to benefit the least. In sum, we need to find ways to encourage students to use technology more, even if they do not seem to need the practice.

Conclusion

Although not providing promising news as to CALL's positive effect on learning outcomes for beginning students of a modern language, this study offers a new direction for how the research community might examine technology and learning outcomes in second language learning. For the first time, learner-centred factors as well as technology factors are examined together in the same study. Indeed, the research paradigm used in the investigation represents only one way to consider these factors. Other investigative approaches, including interviewing and field observation, would also be informative and offer a more thorough picture of how technology works for the second language learner.

References

Borras, I. & Lafayette, R. (1994). Effects of multi-media courseware subtitling on the speaking performance of college students of French. *The Modern Language Journal 78*, 61–75.

Chun, D.M. (1994). Using computer networking to facilitate the acquisition of interactive competence. *System 22*, 17–31.

Curran, R. & Kirk, R. (1986). Predicting success in intensive foreign language courses. *Modern Language Journal 86*, 107–113.

Dunkel, P. (Ed.) (1991). *Computer-assisted language learning and testing: Research issues and practice* (pp. 5–36). New York: Newbury House.

Fischer, R. (1989). Instructional computing in French: The student view. *Foreign Language Annals 26*, 527–534.

Gardener, R.C., Tremblay, P. & Masgoret, A-M. (1997). Towards a full model of second language learning: An empirical investigation. *The Modern Language Journal 81*, 344–362.

Garrett, N. (1991). Technology in the service of learning: Trends and issues. *Modern Language Journal 75*, 74–96.

Garza, T. (1991). Evaluating the use of captional video materials in advanced language learning. *Foreign Language Annals 24*, 239–257.

Goodman, J. Freed, B. & McManus, W. (1990). Determining exemptions from foreign language requirements: Use of the Modern Language Aptitude Test. *Contemporary Educational Psychology 15*, 131–141.

Hermann, F. (1992). *Instrumental and agentive uses of the computer: Their role in learning French as a foreign language*. San Francisco: Mellen Research University Press.

Hsu, J.-F., Chapelle, C. & Thompson, A. (1993). Exploratory learning environments: What are they and what do students explore? *Journal of Educational Computing Research 9*, 1–15.

Lin, S. (1993). *College Chinese, volume 1*. Boston, Massachusetts: Cheng & Tsui.

Leow, R. (1998). The effects of amount and type of exposure on adult learners' L2 development in SLA. *Modern Language Journal 82*, 49–68.

Meich, E., Nave, W. & Mosteller, F. (1996). On CALL: A review of computer-assisted language learning in U.S. colleges and universities. In *Educational Media and Technology Yearbook, volume 22*. Littleton, CO: Libraries Unlimited, 61–84.

Merlonghi, F. C., Merlonghi, F. & Tursi, J. (1987). *Oggi in Italia* (3rd ed.). Boston, Massachusetts: Houghton Mifflin.

Nagato, N. (1993). Intelligent computer feedback for second language instruction. *The Modern Language Journal 77*, 330–339.

Pederson, K. (1987). Research on CALL. In Wm. Smith (Ed.) *Modern media in foreign language education: Theory and implementation* (pp. 99–131). Lincolnwood, IL: National Textbook Company.

Sapon, S. & Carroll, J. (1959). *The modern language aptitude test*. San Antonio, Texas: The Psychological Association.

Skehan, P. (1991). Individual differences in second language learning. *Studies in Second Language Acquisition 13*, 275–298.

Sparks, R, Ganschow, L. & Patton, J. (1995). Prediction of performance in first-year foreign language courses: Connections between native and foreign language learning. *Journal in Educational Psychology 87*, 638–655.

Sparks, R., Artzer, M., Ganschow, L., Patton, J., Siebenhar, D. & Plageman, M. (1997). Prediction of foreign language proficiency. *Journal of Educational Psychology 89*, 349–561.

Spinelli, E. & Rosso-O'Laughlin, M. (1997). *Encuentros*. New York: Holt-Rinehart, and Winston.

Spolsky, B. (1989). *The conditions for second language learning: Introduction to a general theory*. Oxford, England: Oxford University Press.

St Onge, S. & Terry, R. (1990). *Vous y Êtes*. Boston, Massachusetts: Heinle & Heinle.

Stenson, N., Downing, B., Smith, J. & Smith, K. (1992). The effectiveness of computer-assisted pronunciation training. *CALICO Journal*, Summer issue 5–19.

Williams, C. & Brown, S. (1991). A review of the research for use of computer-related technologies for instruction: An agenda research. In B. Branyan-Broadbent & K. Wood (Eds), *Education Media and Technology Yearbook – 1991* (pp. 26–46). Englewood, CO: Libraries Unlimited.

Young, J. & Nakajima-Okano, K. (1985). *Learn Japanese, volume 1*. Honolulu, Hawaii: University of Hawaii Press.

Appendix

Fitted multiple regression models for oral performance

Table 5: Adding the question prediction tape use to the base model for oral performance for non-CALL users

Model	Intercept	Base Predictors – Main Effects			Question Predictor	R^2	dfE
		GPA	MLATP	MLATT	TAPE		
NC 1	30.0498*	.7170***	.2309	-.0678		.2960**	41
NC 2	30.8631*	.7350***	.2470	-.0773	-1.6565*	.3623***	40

~$p \leq .10$ $p \leq .05$ **$p \leq .01$ ***$p \leq .001$

The fitted multiple regression model shows that the addition of students' tape use improves the prediction of oral performance in elementary language courses, controlling for students' grade point average (GPA) and language aptitude as measured by the Modern Language Aptitude Test, section 2 (phonetic scripting) and total raw score.

Table 6: Adding the question prediction tape use to the base model for oral performance for CALL users

Model	Intercept	Base Predictors – Main Effects			Question Predictor	R^2	dfE
		GPA	MLATP	MLATT	TAPE		
C 1	47.0552**	.3696*	.6467*	-.4080		.1536*	62
C 2	51.2889***	.3308*	.6695*	-.0773	-1.2689*	.2265***	60

~$p \leq .10$ $p \leq .05$ **$p \leq .01$ ***$p \leq .001$

The fitted multiple regression model shows that the addition of students' tape use improves the prediction (GPA) and language aptitude as measured by the Modern Language Aptitude Test, section 2 (phonetic scripting) and total raw score.

Table 7: Adding the question prediction conversation partner use to the base model for oral performance for non-CALL users

Model	Intercept	Base Predictors – Main Effects			Question Predictor	R^2	dfE
		GPA	MLATP	MLATT	Partner		
NC 1	30.0498*	.7170**	.2309	-.0678		.2960**	41
NC 3	29.3798	.6548**	.2626	-.0433	.6363	.3135*	40

~$p \leq .10$ $p \leq .05$ **$p \leq .01$ ***$p \leq .001$

The fitted multiple regression model shows that the addition of students' tape use improves the prediction of oral performance in elementary language courses, controlling for students' grade point average (GPA) and language aptitude as measured by the Modern Language Aptitude Test, section 2 (phonetic scripting) and total raw score.

Table 8: Adding the question prediction conversation partner use to the base
model for oral performance for CALL users.

Model	Intercept	Base Predictors – Main Effects			Question Predictor	R^2	dfE
		GPA	MLATP	MLATT	Partner		
C 1	47.0552**	.3696*	.6467*	-.408		.1536*	62
C 3	46.2709**	.4276*	.6783*	-.0562	-1.0975	.1912*	61

The fitted multiple regression model shows that the addition of students' tape use improves the prediction of oral performance in elementary language courses, controlling for students' grade point average (GPA) and language aptitude as measured by the Modern Language Aptitude Test, section 2 (phonetic scripting) and total raw score.

Table 9: Adding the question prediction CALL use to the base model for oral
performance for CALL users.

Model	Intercept	Base Predictors – Main Effects			Question Predictor	R^2	dfE
		GPA	MLATP	MLATT	CALL		
C 1	47.0552**	.3696*	.6467*	-.408		.1536*	62
C 4	47.0239**	.3712*	0.6387	-.0454	-.0666	.1538*	61
$\sim p \leq .10$		$p \leq .05$		$**p \leq .01$		$***p \leq .001$	

The fitted multiple regression model shows that the addition of students' tape use improves the prediction of oral performance in elementary language courses, controlling for students' grade point average and language aptitude as measured by the Modern Language Aptitude Test, section 2 (phonetic scripting) and total raw score.

18

Language Awareness and the Support Role of Technology

Margaret Allan
James Cook University, Australia

Introduction

This chapter focuses on the theoretical basis for work in progress to develop a network-based environment in support of academic writing. The overall aim of the project is to establish ways in which a web site on the campus network could contribute to existing English for Academic Purposes (EAP) provision, which consists a mix of the forms of support traditionally found within many universities. These include EAP language classes provided by an English Language Centre, one-on-one tutorial support provided largely by an Academic Counselling Service and, within one discipline area, individual and group support by a small, discipline-specific unit. Problems which have been expressed about such provision include:

- difficulties in finding suitable times for students with heavy workloads to attend classes;
- problems in providing appropriate content for mixed discipline classes;
- concern that one-on-one sessions to discuss individual assignments may have limited generalisability;
- problems of staff/student ratios; and
- awareness that disparate forms of support lack cohesion.

The project addressed the general question of designing a web site which could supplement existing provisions, and which could be used and developed in different ways by the different language support groups referred to above. The focus of the initial stage of the project was on the identification of roles for the technology in scaffolding EAP students in academic writing. In the broader context, the project seeks to take account of new perspectives on language and language learning which are being shaped by research in corpus linguistics and work in task-based learning.

Changing perspectives on language learning

The current project is taking place at a time when perspectives on language learning are discussed in terms of a shift away from the dominant paradigm of the presentation, practice, production (PPP) model (Woodward 1996). The behaviourist belief that learners will learn what is taught in the order in which it is taught is now largely discredited (Skehan 1996:18) and is giving way to recognition that language learning is a long-term, internal process which is best facilitated by exposure to natural use of the language. It is argued that this exposure gives learners opportunities to make inferences, hypotheses and generalisations about the language system as a whole (see, for example, Lewis 1996).

In a detailed working of an alternative to the PPP model, Willis (1996) describes a task cycle of 'task–plan–report' in which the task, undertaken in pairs or small groups, is an activity which replicates real-world communication in that it is an activity with a real outcome. Examples from a general English program (Willis & Willis 1988) include conducting a survey of a group for opinions or information, carrying out a problem-solving game or an information gap task. These are all tasks which produce a result which can be reported back to the wider whole class audience. It is important to note that throughout the cycle the focus is on use of language for meaningful outcomes, and not on learning about language as a system. The teacher acts to facilitate the doing of the task but makes no attempt to teach language that might be needed (for a detailed rationale, see Willis 1990). At the planning stage, when learners prepare to report back their findings, the teacher acts as informant when learners seek assistance, but it is not until the post-task stage that teachers finally turn to a more analytical focus on language form and function. This, then, is a framework for task-based learning which centres on communicative tasks, but also provides a principled place for an explicit focus on language, which comes at the end of the process rather than at the beginning, as it does in the PPP paradigm. Another important feature is that the language which furnishes examples for analysis is drawn from language the learner has already processed for meaning in communicative use. This is done through the creation of a learner's corpus of texts produced by native speakers undertaking the same communicative tasks.

Willis discusses her model in terms of general purpose English teaching and learning, but in my view it provides a context that is equally relevant to the EAP context of postgraduate students, which is the immediate focus of the present project. EAP students who have to write papers or assignments replicate the task cycle in that they have a real-world communication task (to research, do field work, or review a field) and writing the paper is similar to the report back stage, when they need to exercise all the control they have in order to write appropriately for the academic genres of their discipline. Their preparation of a paper is equivalent to the planning stage of the task cycle, and this is when they seek help. The help they need at this drafting stage is for specific information to meet immediate needs, usually met in one-on-one sessions with a language teacher. The task cycle model is a reminder that the completion of a report is not an appropriate end to the process, but rather the point where it is important to introduce generalisations about the form and function of the language that has been used. In the EAP context, the equivalent of the learners' corpus could be taken, for example, from journals in the appropriate discipline.

So far I have argued that the academic support teacher's job should not end with the linguistic proofreading of the student's essay. Given concerns about the labour-intensive nature of the editing session, it may seem unrealistic to suggest that it should be taken as the starting point for language awareness work. However, I shall suggest ways in which technology could contribute to this aspect of EAP work. First, I turn to a discussion of the methodology and content of language awareness work.

Language awareness

Accompanying an acceptance of the value of communicative tasks in providing learning opportunities to experience and use language, there is a redefinition of the goals of L2 teaching away from mastery of discrete structural items towards the less ambitious, less definable goal of raising awareness of language (Ellis 1992).

Language Awareness (LA) is broadly defined as 'a person's sensitivity to and conscious awareness of the nature of language and its role in human life' (Donmall 1985, in James & Garrett 1991:4). The Donmall report which produced this definition grew out of mother tongue teaching in the UK, and encompassed affective and social parameters as well as cognitive ones. The latter is the main area of focus in work associated with different labels:

consciousness-raising (CR), knowledge about language (KAL), as well as LA, reflecting the different sectors of English teaching/learning that, as Carter (1993:12–13) describes it, share a concern to 'create more effective language learning environments by making conscious knowledge about language an integral part of language learning'. The assumption within a Language Awareness approach is that the facilitation of conscious attention to language will encourage learners to notice and compare in ways that may have a delayed effect (Ellis 1992:239). There is a strong emphasis here on inductive learning with the aim of going beyond grammar, in its traditional sense of prescriptive rules, and in methodology of going beyond the mechanical 'rules-then-practice' of grammar translation methodology. In other words, the focus on conscious, explicit knowledge about language is combined with a concern that the methodology of LA should be task-based, rule-seeking and participant-centred (Wright & Bolitho 1993; Borg 1994).

Changing perspectives on language

LA work is most often taken to mean a focus on grammar, but it also increasingly means a focus on lexis, idioms, key words and collocations – reflecting the changing views of language which result from research in corpus linguistics. This research is providing information about the English language that is generating powerful arguments for a lexical approach to the selection of content in language courses (Sinclair & Renouf 1988; Willis 1990; Lewis 1993, 1997). This encourages a shift away from a primary emphasis in the PPP model on the controlled learning of structures (usually verb group structures) to a search for ways to take account of very different kinds of information about the frequency of occurrence and collocation patterns of lexical items (Sinclair 1991). For example, the word *give* is featured in language textbooks as a ditransitive verb with its 'core' meaning of *offer*, as in 'he gave me a book'. However, *give* is more frequently used as a delexical verb, which takes its meaning from the collocate, as in 'give a smile', 'give a sigh', 'give advice', 'give a warning'. As with other common English verbs, the most common use of *give* is delexical, but this is not reflected in the textbooks (Sinclair & Renouf 1988).

The argument is that in much of our language use we choose words in pairs or groups, as prefabricated 'chunks', or semi-preconstructed phrases, and that this applies far beyond recognised idioms (Sinclair 1991). It is therefore important to draw learners' attention to these phrases. To take an example from academic writing materials for EAP learners (Thurstun & Candlin 1997), the word *criteria* is introduced not just as an important item of academic vocabulary, but learners also identify adjectives which are often used with it, such as 'objective', 'proper' and 'agreed'. They also discover that the prepositions *of* and *for* are commonly used with it, and are asked to look for patterns associated with each preposition. Thurston and Candlin's workbook focuses on a small selection of vocabulary frequently used in academic writing, and it uses concordances to provide the examples of common collocations.

Concordancing software, the central analytical tool of corpus linguistics, is proving adaptable to task-based approaches with a language awareness focus. Concordances are drawn from authentic texts and provide evidence not just about individual words but also about the most common patterns, the collocations, associated with those words. There is now a growing body of experimental work in using concordances as a tool for language learning (see, for example, Thurstun & Candlin 1998; Wichmann et al. 1997). The work being developed with concordances brings together a lexical view of language and a task-based, inductive approach to language awareness. Tim Johns (1991) uses the term 'data-driven learning' for an approach which encourages students to hypothesise about the relationship between pattern and meaning, through an examination of words in context. Johns works with EAP students and is experimenting with developing concordance-based CALL (Johns 1997). The present project is exploring similar possibilities, with a particular focus on the building of a resource which can most usefully and effectively supplement existing EAP provision.

Application to a technology-based EAP context

I have indicated above that EAP students normally seek help somewhere in the planning/implementation stage of the academic writing task (if we consider drafting a paper as a form of planning). This is usually provided in one-on-one tutorial mode. In designing the language support web site, we took the need for such support as the point of entry for a student to the network, and this aspect was piloted with a small group.

Electronic one-on-one tutorials

A main need of any student undertaking academic studies in a second language is for a form of linguistic proofreading of assignments and papers they are required to submit. In the present project, five undergraduate and five postgraduate students were invited to submit their work to a tutor electronically, using an email attachment facility. The tutor devised a simple system of commenting in bold before returning the file by the same means. Those who used the system most were postgraduate students whose course requirements included regular submission of research papers. Unlike the undergraduates, these students were sufficiently organised to have the paper ready ahead of their deadline and they appreciated the time-saving nature of electronic contact, compared with having a face-to-face session with a language tutor. The undergraduate students, on the other hand, said that they preferred face-to-face sessions with a tutor, with the possibility of asking follow-up questions. The role of technology in this case was to mediate the provision of direct comment on an individual piece of work.

There is also the possibility of taking this a step further by using the technology itself as an informant. For example, Turnbull and Burston (1998) describe the use of the inbuilt proofreader in contemporary word processing software as a first check on student writing. This is an area for further research into combinations of computer-generated and teacher-generated support.

Concordance-based tasks
In the Willis model it is at the post-task stage that the focus moves to an analytical approach to language. This is the point where students may be encouraged to generalise some aspects of the language they encountered in accomplishing the task. Here too, the project examined ways in which converged computer and communications technologies could contribute to the process. A search for ways of generalising from individual problems led to a focus on lexical items, using concordances derived from the MicroConcord corpus (Scott & Johns 1993). Under development is a bank of concordance-based tasks which invite learners to explore vocabulary in academic contexts of use, presented in a key-words-in-context (KWIC) format.

Entry screen: Learning support site
    Access to the web site is through the University's Learning Support site, which will include a link to the project site, titled 'Language Link Up'.

Top screen: Language Link Up
    The top screen gives users the option to sign up for tutorial support with academic writing and/or to select the course, 'Academic Writing'. The latter links to a guide to concordance-based tasks, and a menu of 'Useful Vocabulary' which lists lexical items featured in these tasks.

Useful Vocabulary: Report (noun)
    An example of a selection within 'Useful Vocabulary' and using a set of tasks with the noun *report* is given in figure 1. This particular focus on *report* as a noun was suggested by the observation that one student consistently used the pattern, (NAME) Report (e.g. Brundtland Report) without a definite article. Other tasks were based on different sets of concordance data for *report*

featuring the use of prepositions in phrases such as 'a report on ...' (topic of report) , 'a report in ...' (place of publication; time), 'a report by ...' (author/producers/commissioners), 'a report of ...' (author/producer; topic; date).

Figure 1: Three tasks with a concordance for *report* used as a noun

REPORT (NOUN)
TASK 1 What patterns do you notice with the key word report? Make notes.

TASK 2 Where does the report name come from? Find three categories.
Official reports are usually referred to by name, as in these examples. Group them to show three different sources of names for an official report.

TASK 3 Provide examples of reports you talk about in your own field of study.

---

on Leon Krier. The Building Design report added: `One (of the witches) said `If k'. Throughout the Working Group 2 report, the tenor was that the many remaining trategy remains. Both in the Forum Report (New Ireland Forum 1983-4: xii) and in evelopment noted in the Brundtland Report, `the recent destruction of much of Af that in light of the Butler-Sloss report, there is no purpose in holding anothe contained in the Annual Borrowing Report dated 4 January 1988. <p> However, Mr lly in Chapter 4 of the Greenpeace Report shows that, even if we stop deforestat Joins in the long run. The IPCC report confines itself to projections to ificant shortcoming in the Dearing report was its failure to assess the true cos not fully assessed. The inquiry report did not even attempt to answer the ques econstruction problems. The Finlay Report discussed Pan American's route structu in this month's Economic Progress Report. <p> The measures, designed to boost t ons.<p> Ferranti said the Coopers report confirmed what its own directors and a st other recommendations, the Hill Report (Central and Scottish Health Services the riots long before the Scarman Report was published in November 1981. Any su r black members; the policy review report on economic equality; discipline proce he full implications of the Taylor Report and discover what happens over the ide plementers of the 1969 Skeffington Report, and by many idealistic councillors in rt on housing and the 1967 Plowden Report on education, as a result of which gen

Figure 2: Commentary on *report* (noun) Task 2

COMMENTARY ON TASK 2
Three sources of names for an official report:
a) Reports can take their name from the person who chaired the committee:
   the Brundtland Report*
   the Dearing Report
   *Included here on the assumption that 'Brundtland' is the name of a person.

b) Reports can take their name from the group/organisation/institution that produced or commissioned the report;
   the Working Group 2 report
   the Greenpeace report

c) Reports can take their name from the subject matter of the report:
   the Building Design report (= a report on building design)
   the Annual Borrowing report (= a report on annual borrowing)

Students are invited to enter their own observations in a text box and there is a commentary on the task available at any stage. Figure 2 provides a sample of the commentary on Task 2. Learners have the option to compare their own interpretation side by side with the commentary provided. They may do this after they have attempted the task, or in some cases they might do so before, using the commentary as a learning device. In some cases, such as Task 3 (see figure 1) open-ended responses are forwarded to a tutor.

In the context of an institution which at present provides three discrete forms of language support, such a web site could develop as a point of common focus, accessed through the University's Learning Support web site, in the following ways:

- students can sign up to be allocated a tutor for one-on-one electronic tutorials;
- tutors and language centre teachers may direct students to the academic writing task bank in follow up to specific lexical problems they may have identified;
- students access the task bank independently;
- tutors/teachers/applied linguists/MA TESOL students access the task bank, and may add to it, using the concordancing tools; and
- students ask about particular words, which may lead to the preparation of a further set of concordance tasks.

The possibility of going beyond the use of pre-selected concordance data to offer students the option of direct access to a corpus and concordancing tools is to be explored. One possible solution to the mix of disciplines usually found in a cross-campus group of EAP students would be to use electronic access to a relevant journal for the corpus. It should be possible, at least in some discipline areas, to develop a discipline-specific corpus which students would use to search for lexical information of their own choosing. Not all students would see the relevance of attaining this level of expertise in the use of concordances, but Turnbull and Burston (1998) suggest that it could be valued by some who want a greater degree of autonomy in using this learning tool.

Student response to concordance-based tasks

Delays in completing this part of the program have meant that it has not been possible to date to trial online use of concordance-based tasks by students. However, a case study conducted by the ESL Academic Skills Counsellor (Barnsbee 1999) has provided useful insights into the reactions of a group of Asian postgraduate students to working with concordances in class, using the Thurstun and Candlin (1997) workbook. Barnsbee introduced these materials to a regular EAP class in academic writing over 12 sessions of 90 minutes each. Responses of five members of the group in interview and by questionnaire included the following points:

The value of multiple examples

Students clearly saw the benefits of the opportunity to see how words behave in context through the examination of multiple examples. This is evident in comments such as, 'I like this method because we can see many examples, especially for the key words that we have to use in our reports and writing'.

Focus on a small selection of words

The above quote also conveys students' appreciation of the value of focusing on a small selection of key academic vocabulary. For example, others said, 'After we studied the word *evidence*, I checked my research proposal. Now I feel I can confidently use that word' and, 'words like *evidence*, *claim*, *research* and *criteria* we will use many many times and will make a lot of mistakes, so it's a very useful procedure how to use correctly'.

These comments are about the key words chosen by Thurstun and Candlin (1997), but they provide a useful endorsement of the similar intention of the present project to focus on frequently used words which students are seen to be using with difficulty in their academic writing.

Generalisation from multiple examples

In their comments on what they felt they could learn from studying concordances, there is a suggestion that students see the possibility of making generalisations about the use of lexical items. One student touches on a key point when he claims that he could discover 'the real meaning of a word', and another foregrounds the discovery of: 'what kind of part of speech can go with this particular word, what kind of preposition can follow this word, this word is countable or uncountable'.

An aid to memorising vocabulary

Johns (1997:112) points to anecdotal evidence that data-driven learning methods may help students to remember collocations and connotations of particular words. It is interesting to note that in the Barnsbee (1999) study, which included group discussion of students' own work using the key words, students clearly felt that the discussions they had as a class group had the strongest influence. For example, 'I will remember because we have a discussion, but if we don't have a discussion maybe I don't remember …'. This is a very useful reminder that the support which technology can provide is limited, and consideration has to be given to an appropriate mix of forms of interaction.

The support role of technology

Richards and Rogers (1986) argue that there are always assumptions about language and language learning underlying any language teaching approach, and I have tried to make these explicit for the present project. I would add that there are also assumptions about pedagogy underlying the design of materials and the identification of roles for technologies in teaching and learning a second language. Here, I turn to Vygotskian theory of teaching and learning in my conceptualisation of technology as a support tool in language awareness work.

In order to describe the roles allocated to the technology in the present project, I shall focus on three key elements arising from Vygotsky's (1987) conceptualisation of a zone of proximal development (ZPD) as a space within which a learner learns to address a particular problem with the support of someone who has greater expertise in addressing that problem.

Problem solving with assistance

In Vygotksian pedagogic theory, problem solving is the key activity, as it is in the task-based approach described above, and the assistance of more expert others is the key ingredient. In the present project, the problems are those of linguistic analysis, involving a search for patterns of collocation, and the identification of a particular usage and its associated meaning. In the Willis (1996) model, the teacher has the role of facilitator and later of informant at different points in the task cycle, as learners seek first to solve the real world problem posed by the task, and then to solve the linguistic problem of planning and delivering a report on what they did. With language awareness tasks based on concordance selections, the concordance itself can be seen as the informant, in that the concordances provide multiple examples taken from authentic texts. The doing of the task is facilitated through the selection and grouping of examples and the nature of the task set, whether this is done by a teacher preparing a lesson or the designer of the CALL program.

Flexible support
The Vygotskian concept of the zone of proximal development recognises that the need for support with the tools and techniques of problem solving varies as learners fluctuate between stages of heavy dependence, self-regulation of support resources, and autonomous control of the means of solving the problem (Tharp & Gallimore 1988). It is therefore essential that the support should have the flexibility to offer just as much help as is needed for only as long as it is needed. The concept of scaffolding (Wood, Bruner & Ross 1976) captures the character of this requirement to provide different forms of support on different occasions. Here the concept of teacher or mentor flexibility is transferred to the technology by focusing on the computer as the means of access to an informant (the concordance examples), to problems (the tasks set), and to examples of how others have solved them in the key that can be called up by users of the program.

   In this way, control is placed in the hands of the learner, in much the same way as it is in the task-based, learner-centred classroom where it is left to the learner to seek help when it is needed. For example, a learner who is unsure of what is required may choose to start by examining the solution provided before tackling another task independently. The learner decides how much of the scaffolding to use, and flexibility refers to ways of using the resource.

Problem solving as a sociocultural activity
Another important contribution of Vygotsky was the insight that mental activity originates in social activity. The sharing of problem-solving activity with a more expert problem solver is the key element in cultural as well as cognitive development, and learning to solve problems is a sociocultural activity in that the means of solving the problem are culture-specific. Hence engaging in learning can be seen as a form of apprenticeship (see, for example, Chaiklin & Lave 1993) in which learners learn to use particular tools in particular ways. From this perspective, Donato and McCormick (1994)

describe a program which set learners of French the task of building a port-
folio to document their own performance and strategies as language learners.
This approach reconceptualised language learning strategies as the product of
participation in cultural practice rather than as belonging to the domain of
individual cognitive development. Donato and McCormick interpret the outcome in terms of the results of induction into a particular social practice with
its attendant beliefs, values and behaviours.

I see parallels here in the way Johns talks of learners working with concordances as linguistic researchers (Johns 1997:101). This is a reminder that
learners in language awareness work are apprentice linguists: we are not
teaching them grammar or vocabulary, we are teaching them particular ways
of analysing language using the tools of corpus linguistics research.

Ballard (1996) reminds us that attitudes to knowledge have sociocultural
roots. She points out that international students coming into a Western university need to be made aware that they are likely to be coming into contact
with very different ways of conceptualising knowledge. She argues that there
is 'a continuum of (culturally influenced) attitudes to knowledge and
approaches to learning' (1996:153) which she summarises under the headings
reproductive, analytical and *speculative*. She suggests that in Australia the
move from school to university study requires students to move away from
the reproductive display of learned knowledge to a demonstration of the ability to analyse and critique received knowledge which is expected at undergraduate level. Postgraduate students are expected to go beyond the analytical to the speculative thinking which generates new ideas, and can lead to
creative new forms of knowledge. Ballard argues that preparatory EAP
courses need to move away from the reproductive learning approach which
they currently encourage, and to make students aware of what will be expected of them. She is not suggesting that students from non-Western societies
are incapable of other ways of thinking, but that they need to be aware that
that is what is expected of them.

In my view, the project described here could contribute to giving students
experience of different approaches to learning. A web-based CALL program
based on data-driven learning techniques clearly requires analytical rather
than reproductive thinking, and can also lead to speculative exploration of the
evidence.

Conclusion

The technical feasibility of providing access on the University network to
concordancing software and to concordance-based tasks has been established. It was also established that students would use the network to support

them in writing assignments and papers through access to linguistic proof-reading. Postgraduate students appreciated this use of technology more than did undergraduates, and were more likely to make regular use of this service.

There is accumulating anecdotal evidence that some students have a very positive response to working with concordances in a data-driven approach to the study of lexis. There is also some indication from a print-based study that rule-seeking, problem-solving language awareness tasks do lead students to make generalisations about words they study. However, there are still very few studies of student responses to this approach to language learning, and an important future research area for the present project concerns an exploration of the most effective mix of human and technological resources in the support of EAP students. There are many advocates of the value of group work on LA tasks in face-to-face contexts; is there also a viable place for web-based discussion of concordance-based tasks? Alternatively, what mix of group discussion and individual direct access to concordance-based tasks would be most acceptable to teachers and students? Another area that requires further research concerns the different forms of provision that might be appropriate for undergraduate and for postgraduate students.

As other on-campus providers of EAP support begin to work with concordances and become convinced of the value of this tool for language study by their students' response – as was the case in the Barnsbee (1999) study – I am encouraged in the view that the building of a network of the kind outlined here has the potential to provide a common focal point for various forms of collaboration. Teachers and applied linguists could collaborate over the selection of lexical items and the development of concordance-based tasks; a discipline-specific group could work with teachers to suggest useful areas of focus and to supply commentary on tasks; the work of learners in interpreting concordance data could contribute additional and alternative commentary.

The task bank can become a resource to which teachers refer students for follow-up work on lexical problems they may identify in the course of one-on-one sessions. Such a resource does provide a form of information to which teachers do not normally have ready access, and it is a flexible resource to which all users can contribute. In the ways outlined in this chapter, web-based access to concordance-based tasks makes the technology a potential catalyst for change in the design and delivery of support for teachers as well as learners in the development of language awareness.

References

Ballard, B. (1996). Through language to learning: Preparing overseas students for study in Western universities. In H. Coleman (Ed.), *Society and the language classroom*. Cambridge: Cambridge University Press.

Barnsbee, D. G. (1999). The response of Asian postgraduate students to working with concordance-based tasks. Unpublished manuscript. James Cook University,

Borg, S. (1994). Language awareness as methodology: Implications for teachers and teacher training. *Language Awareness 3*, 2, 61–71.

Carter, R. (1993). *Introducing applied linguistics*. London: Penguin.

Chaiklin, S. & Lave, J. (1993). *Understanding practice: Perspectives on activity and context*. Cambridge: Cambridge University Press.

Donato, R. & McCormick, D. (1994). A sociocultural perspective on language learning strategies: The role of mediation. *The Modern Language Journal, 78*,iv, 453–464.

Donmall, G. (1991). Old problems and new solutions: LA work in GCSE foreign language classrooms. In C. James & P. Garrett (Eds), *Language awareness in the classroom*. London: Longman.

Ellis, R. (1992). *Second language acquisition and language pedagogy*. Clevedon: Multilingual Matters.

James, C. & Garrett, P. (Eds), (1991). *Language awareness in the classroom*. London: Longman.

Johns, T. (1991). Should you be persuaded: Two examples of data-driven learning. In T. Johns & P. King (Eds), *Classroom concordancing*. Birmingham: University of Birmingham, Centre for English Language Studies.

Johns, T. (1997). Contexts: The background, development and trialling of a concordance-based CALL program. In Wichman et al. (Eds), *Teaching and language corpora*. London: Longman.

Lewis, M. (1993). *The lexical approach*. Hove: Language Teaching Publications.

Lewis, M. (1996). Implications of a lexical view of language. In J. & D. Willis (Eds), *Challenge and change in language teaching*. London: Heinemann.

Lewis, M. (1997). *Implementing the lexical approach*. Hove: Language Teaching Publications.

Newman, D., Griffin, P. & Cole, M. (1989). *The construction zone*. Cambridge: Cambridge University Press.

Richards, J.C. & Rogers, T.S. (1986). *Approaches and methods in language teaching*. Cambridge: Cambridge University Press.

Scott, M. & Johns, T. (1993). *MicroConcord*. Oxford: Oxford University Press.

Sinclair, J. (1991). *Corpus, concordance, collocation*. Oxford: Oxford University Press.

Sinclair, J. & Renouf, A. (1988). A lexical syllabus for language learning. In R. Carter & M. McCarthy (Eds), *Vocabulary and language teaching*. London: Longman.

Skehan, P. (1996). Second language acquisition research and task-based instruction. In J. & D. Willis (Eds), *Challenge and change in language teaching*. London: Heinemann.

Tharp, R. G. & Gallimore, R. (1988). *Rousing minds to life: Teaching, learning and schooling in social context*. Cambridge: Cambridge University Press.

Thurstun, J. & Candlin, C. N. (1997). *Exploring academic English*. Sydney: NCEL-TR, Maquarie University.

Thurstun, J. & Candlin, C. N. (1998). Concordancing and the teaching of the vocabulary of academic English. *English for Specific Purposes 17*, 3, 267–280.

Turnbull, J. & Burston, J. (1998). Towards independent concordance work for students: Lessons from a case study. *On-Call Journal 12*, 2, 10–21.

Vygotsky, L. S. (1987). Thinking and speech. In R. W. Rieber & A. S. Carton (Eds), *The collected works of L. S. Vygotsky: Vol. 1. Problems of general psychology*. (N. Minick, Trans.). New York: Plenum Press.

Willis, D. (1990). *The lexical syllabus*. London: Collins ELT.

Willis, J. (1996). *A framework for task-based learning*. London: Longman.

Willis, D. & Willis, J. (1988). *Collins Cobuild English Course*. London: Collins ELT.

Wood, D., Bruner, J. & Ross, G. (1976). The role of tutoring in problem-solving. *Journal of Child Psychology and Psychiatry 17*, 89–100.

Woodward, T. (1996). Paradigm shift and the language teaching profession. In J. & D. Willis (Eds), *Challenge and change in language teaching*. London: Heinemann.

Wright, T. & Bolitho, R. (1993). Language awareness: A missing link in language teacher education? *ELT Journal 47*, 4, 292–304.

19

Real Talk: Authentic Dialogue Practice

Florence Reeder, Henry Hamburger
& Michael Schoelles
George Mason University, USA

Introduction

Linguistically authentic language practice is crucial to language learning. That is, to learn a language, one must practise it, preferably with an interlocutor who makes – and expects – correct use not only of the syntax and semantics but also of the dialogue conventions of the new language. Must such an interlocutor be human, or can CALL aspire to the goal of surrogate conversational partner? This ideal of a consistent, infinitely patient interlocutor is appealing, but not yet the state of the art. Even though the aim of an authentic language practice partner is not yet realised, we can take reasonable steps toward accomplishing it. To what extent can a CALL system play a dialogue partner role? This chapter examines this question in the light of work in CALL, and particularly for the *Fluent* system, paying close attention to discourse and dialogue processing which support this.

Engaging a student in dialogues accomplishes the goal of language practice. Authentic, realistic dialogue is a complex, difficult task for ICALL (Intelligent CALL) systems. Our project, *Fluent*, is a long-term attempt to provide participation in dialogues. This is achieved by a system that supports language practice in realistic preparatory situations that assure systematic exposure to the key phenomena of the new language. The dual aim of systematic coverage with authentic communication is central to our work. In this chapter we explore its potential for supporting language learning and particularly dialogue phenomena. First, we will survey the dialogue needs for authentic language learning experiences. Then we will look at the motivations for including dialogue management into ICALL, followed by a description of dialogue management as a part of Natural Language Processing (NLP). After that, we will describe the dialogue processing needs of our system, *Fluent,* and relate these to existing support modules. Finally, we will raise some issues in this area.

The goals, methods and abilities of different ICALL systems cause a great variability in the type and style of interaction. Every ICALL system, by definition, engages in some form of dialogue with the student. Consider drill-and-practice systems: the system presents a question and the student provides a response. The scenario depicted in example 1 is a basic conversational exchange and qualifies as a dialogue, although it is not the authentic, participatory exchange one imagines in a dialogue. In the same vein, systems which provide explanations in response to student errors rely on discourse and dialogue principles to make the utterances coherent and complete, even if the explanations are static. Note that example 2 exhibits the characteristics of a coherent explanatory discourse. It starts off with a premise followed by a description which supports the premise and concludes with an example. There are indicators in the text, known as cue phrases, which tell the reader what kind of information is about to be presented (such as the word *consider* introducing an example). While these two passages qualify as discourse and serve a purpose in language teaching, they do not provide the authentic practice of language through dialogue which we are implementing.

Example 1: A drill-and-practice interaction

    T: The church _____ (past tense) located at the river.
    S: To be
    T: Incorrect. Try again using the past tense of the verb **to be**.

Example 2: Explanatory sequence

    T: 'English words can combine to form compound words, sometimes
         referred to as simply *compounds* (such as *car-phone, windmill, golf
         club*). A major indicator that a sequence of two words is a compound
         is that the relative prominence (emphasis, stress) occurs on the first
         word. Consider the words *green* and *house*. The sequence *green
         house* is a compound if *green* is emphasized (represented here as
         GREEN house)'. (Farmer & Demers 1996:11)

For a language learner the ability to participate in a meaningful dialogue signifies the last real hurdle for fluency. This participation represents both the ability to understand utterances and to generate utterances that can be understood. Typically, this takes two forms in the CALL community: written essays and dialogue participation. Written texts are judged on whether they adequately convey relevant information in a coherent manner. This ability to string together coherent thoughts with appropriate cues is part of discourse. Other elements include handling referring expressions, temporal ordering and cultural needs. Discourse phenomena are realised in written text both explicitly and also through other levels of language such as semantics, syntax and morphology.

Just as written text requires appropriate application of discourse to maintain authenticity, dialogue participation relies on it as well. Conversational principles (Grice 1975) dictate that participants provide meaningful, relevant, easily understood contributions to a conversation. In fact, it can be speculated that the nature of interaction imposes even greater system requirements for discourse than for written text. To teach these parts of language, it would be ideal for a system to be capable of processing them. Yet this is not the only motivation for designing discourse capabilities into an ICALL system. In addition to being able to teach discourse phenomena explicitly, the regular nature of dialogue and its function of relating utterances to a context can be exploited to allow for a more authentic, yet varied, interaction at the lower levels of ability. We can use conversational expectations in much the same way as we use graphical representations to constrain the interaction and to detect misunderstanding.

Fluent

The roles of dialogue principles in CALL systems vary widely, and should be understood in the context of what each system seeks to achieve and is capable of supporting. To place the *Fluent* system in such a context, we now sketch its pedagogical and computational approach. *Fluent* brings research from two sub-fields of Artificial Intelligence to CALL. These research areas are Intelligent Tutoring Systems (ITS) and Natural Language Processing (NLP). In the development of *Fluent,* a major engineering challenge is the implementation of this research in a way that is responsive to the practical needs of CALL. The practical requirements in our view are not only getting a system that is pedagogically sound into the classroom, but also one that can and will be used.

The key pedagogical observation underlying *Fluent* is that language learning requires practice. We have therefore designed a system that lets a student progress by communicating rather than by explicit study of rules and vocabulary. In *Fluent*, the student encounters a realistic situation and communicates about it with the system. This communication is either graphical, or textual with accompanying speech. Authenticity is achieved by graphically depicting familiar environments, such as a kitchen, living room or office, and performing everyday tasks in these environments. To perform the simple tasks in these microworlds, either the system or the student can pick things up and put them down, turn things on and off, open and close things, and so on. The system can move a hand around in the microworld to perform these actions and the student does them using the mouse to control the hand, which acts like a sophisticated cursor.

There are three ways in which this approach achieves authenticity, and pedagogically transcends the mere pairing of stationary pictures with concrete nouns and physically descriptive adjectives, as provided by typical commercial systems. For one thing, it brings other parts of speech into play, as shown by our work on contrasting articles (Schoelles & Hamburger 1995). Prepositions of location and direction as well as verbs expressing actions can be learned by a student because the words are coordinated with actual actions done by the student. Second, a student can learn more about words than just their core meaning. By practising the use of verbs in simple but comprehensible sentences, the student can acquire knowledge of their subcategorisation according to their various complement structures. A third and final point concerns motivation. By immersing the student interactively in an ongoing situation and conversation, *Fluent* fosters a learning style analogous to Total Physical Response, a method with proven success in motivating students to learn linguistic constructs through exposure to variations on similar situations (Asher 1977).

The pedagogical approach that *Fluent* implements is evident in other CALL systems as well. *LingWorlds* (Douglas 1995) is an intelligent object-oriented environment for second language tutoring that stresses communication and comprehension. Like *Fluent*, it generates language about graphically portrayed problem solving environments. *LingWorlds* also contains a tutoring component that implements several simple tutoring strategies.

The graphical situation-based paradigm has also been applied to the teaching of vocabulary. CAVOL (Kronenberg, Krueger & Ludewig 1994) is also like *Fluent* in that it makes use of NLP and knowledge representation techniques. One main feature of this system is that the student can access a situation through a known word or phrase to learn in context the meaning of a contextually related word or phrase. For example, if the student's target phrase (to learn) were 'pedestrian crossing', and the student knew the phrase 'traffic light', this could be used to access the traffic intersection scene.

Fluent draws from the field of Intelligent Tutoring Systems to implement this pedagogy in a systematic way. One basic idea motivating ITS is that the computer can guide the student's learning by presenting new material at an appropriate level, or by continuing to present current material until the student has obtained mastery. An ITS typically is divided into functional models which interact to achieve the desired learning effect. A domain knowledge module contains a representation of the target material. Often this knowledge representation is a set of rules, which model the knowledge of an expert in the domain. This material is conveyed to the student through an environment module such as a microworld, or simulation. A decision module infers the state of the student's progress and decides which material in the domain module to convey to the student. The inferences are often based on some model of the student's knowledge. These modules all work together to provide learning experience that is at the right level for the student in the context of an appropriate situation. In problem-solving-type tutors, 'situation' is realised as subject matter problems, in contrast to *Fluent*'s everyday plan-structured situations, which are appropriate to the task of helping the language learner focus on the language, not on new subject matter.

In *Fluent*, and in conversational CALL systems in general, the construction of a student model is problematic since the knowledge is not formulated as explicit rules. Even if the knowledge were formulated as grammatical rules it is not clear that this would be the right level at which to model the student. The reasons for this view as expressed in Hamburger (1996) are: too much minute detail; incomprehensible format; no learner-oriented relationships in the knowledge, and no notion of the difficulty of the material. As a practical compromise we have implemented a two-pronged strategy to get to the right level. The first of these is capturing teacher expertise in tutorial schemas. We consider the involvement of the teacher to be beneficial. An ITS should be thought of as a tool for the teacher to use, not as a replacement for the teacher. The second strategy is letting the student seek their own level via choice of interaction mode, and choice of action within certain modes. As an example, the Movecaster mode permits the student to perform actions which are then described by the computer.

In the traditional ITS mould, a system that has been designed to provide individualised error feedback to erroneous input is the Repairing Errors in Computer Assisted Language Learning (RECALL) project (Murphy, Kruger & Grieszl 1997). The design features a diagnostic module to analyse student input on the basis of the system's knowledge of the target language. This design also features a learner module which stores information about the learner, and a tutoring module to provide feedback and which guides the learner to suitable exercises.

Instead of an explicit expert module, *Fluent* draws from the field of Natural Language Processing in order to provide variability in the language being input to the student. The Athena Language Learning Project (Murray 1995) developed the core Natural Language Generation module (Felshin 1995) that is incorporated into *Fluent*. *Fluent* can vary the linguistic constructs being presented in form and in difficulty. The key to this variability is the generative capability of the NLP. The language generated by the NLP is based on the current situational context and the tutorial schema being executed. The tutorial schema provides the type of interaction to be performed, the action or series of actions to be performed and a linguistic specification called a *view*, for each action or series of actions. From the information provided in the tutorial schema the system creates an interlingua structure (ILS) input to the NLP, which generates a phrase or sentence from this specification. The ILS contains a predicate and its arguments, along with features and constraints on each. The action specifies the predicate and its arguments, the type of interaction specifies the sentence mood, and the features and constraints are mapped from the view. Included in the action and the view is both syntactic information and semantic information. The semantics is represented through theta roles, that is, agent, patient, goal, etc. The view also contains information about the tense and polarity to be used.

Variability in form is achieved by matching up different interaction types, actions and views in each step of the tutorial schema. For example, 'You are picking up the cup' versus 'You picked up the pot' is generated by the NLP by changing one view parameter and one action parameter. Variability in difficulty is achieved through a combination of interaction types and views. The interaction type specifies the sentence type, which varies in difficulty from declarative, then imperative, then interrogative. The number of arguments for a predicate can be varied in the view. This allows for gradual generation of longer and longer sentences.

Extensive use of NLP is a feature of other ICALL systems as well. A particularly powerful and linguistically motivated NLP system, featuring a principle-based parser for tutoring in German and Arabic, underlies the MILT tutor (Weinberg, Pennington & Suri 1995). This research team has adapted a shift-reduce parsing algorithm to make it conform to X-bar theory and incorporate case filtering constraints.

Like other forms of encoded knowledge in ITS, grammars too can be manipulated to produce representations of likely student errors, known as mal-rules. The use of mal-rules is a key feature of the Interactive Computer Identification and Correction of Language Errors (ICICLE) system (McCoy Pennington & Suri. 1996). These rules expand the grammar accepted by the system's parser. The system is a writing tool intended to foster the learning of English as a second language (L2) by learners whose first language (L1) is

American Sign Language. In ICICLE a model of the L1 is part of the learner model. It indicates places where both positive and negative transfer may take place. To acquire the requisite knowledge for the system, these researchers built an extensive error taxonomy by analysing writing samples. Having looked at *Fluent*'s place in ICALL, we will now look at the dialogue needs and supports provided by the system which bring it towards the goal of authentic interaction.

Dialogue and ICALL

An important component to support authentic interaction is a dialogue processing model. To establish the requirements, characteristics and goals of this module, we have drawn from several related fields of study: computational linguistics, CALL, non-CALL ITS and general NLP. Since the goal of our system is to provide authentic language practice, we have investigated the use of dialogue management components as characterised by these different domains. This section looks at the uses of discourse in general, and dialogue processing specifically to support a CALL environment. We will describe why dialogue management is important in ICALL; outline the field of discourse and some specific disciplines in the field; touch on dialogue management for other applications and, finally, show how it can be applied to ICALL in the *Fluent* system.

Dialogue management in ICALL

Discourse is about relating utterances to the situation and to each other. Dialogue is a subfield of discourse, which is a subfield of NLP. Discourse processing addresses diverse topics including: grammatical phenomena that relate to situations, like anaphora and definiteness; intersentential organisation via cue phrases, topic, focus and context management; cultural issues such as politeness; and knowledge of the objects, actions and plans in a given domain. The first reason for incorporating dialogue processing into an ICALL system is to teach one of these topics explicitly. For instance, the teaching of definiteness requires sufficient discourse processing to enable proper article usage. A system should be able to represent the distinction between 'the cup' referring to a specific item in the world and 'a cup' referring to a member of a class of things. Alternatively, ICALL systems, since they aim to teach usable language skills, can also concern themselves with the social and cultural aspects of language. Thai learners, as an example, learn different forms of address according to the type of relationship between participants. Another motivation for providing dialogue management is to improve the learning experience. Coherent, connected interactions with students can hold their attention. Davies (1998) describes some popular games and shows how they capture the attention and imagination of learners. To provide a sufficiently engaging language capability, these systems will need to track a conversation, contribute to that conversation in a meaningful way, and respect the grammatical realisations related to discourse. Less ambitious is the goal of coherent interaction, implying that a system should take into account when it is repeating information that has already been conveyed (Moore 1995b). Bizarre and distracting utterances need to be recognised and avoided. We will now focus more closely on some of these specific topics and how they contribute to ICALL. Along the way, we will examine some systems designed to handle some of these components, or that incorporate some elements of dialogue management.

Dialogue phenomena and ICALL

Language experiences for a student between two participants can be categorised by some basic features: spoken v. written, and interactive v. receptive. Sociolinguists (Brown & Yule 1983) add other features to characterise discourse such as politeness, formality and physical location, but these are four of the main ones. Table 1 shows the different forms and examples of each. The type of interaction typical in ITS and, to some extent, ICALL tends to be receptive as evidenced by video clip and corpus-based systems (e.g. Jaspers, Kanselaar & Kok 1994; Murray 1995; Levy 1998), yet the interactive practice of language facilitates creative learning and use of language. It is in the interactive category that we seek to implement processing modules.

Table 1: Examples of different forms

	Spoken	*Written*
Interactive	Conversation, classroom interaction	Internet Relay Chat (IRC), discussion lists
Receptive	Lectures, speeches, movies, television	Textbooks, newspapers

The interactive category can further be differentiated into those types of exercises which are rigidly structured and those which are less formal. The first type includes classroom interaction and composition practice. Examples supporting this genre are writing aids (Suri & McCoy 1993) and single sentence practice (Felshin 1995). The second type tends to be either immersive, such as study abroad, web-based IRC participation, or systems which provide dialogue exercises. To handle these high-level, active communicative exercises, discourse processing, a large field which affects all levels of NLP from syntactic to semantic to pragmatic, is necessary. As it is such a large field, we cannot describe every subfield of discourse processing in great detail, but we will look at those areas which have received attention in the ICALL community: referring expressions; conversational organisation; cultural requirements and error repair.

Referring expressions

Referring expressions can be seen in syntactic phenomena such as anaphora, ellipsis and article usage. Anaphoric reference is used in situations where an object has been named and is later referred to by a shortened reference. The most common example is pronominal usage, although other forms, such as one-anaphora, exist. Example 3 shows two different forms of anaphoric reference. This is a large subfield of discourse processing, particularly in spoken and active interaction where it tends to be prevalent. Ellipsis is another phenomenon more common to interaction than to written or receptive language use. Ellipsis occurs when an object is described and then a related feature is used instead of the object reference (example 4). This frequently happens in a question and answer interaction. In providing these types of reference, a system becomes more authentically conversational, less stilted and more varied (example 5), although few systems address the phenomena directly.

Example 3: Anaphoric references
    S: I liked the **movie.**
    S: I could recommend **it.**

Pronominal reference

    T: She baked a **batch of brownies**.
    S: I would like **one.**

One-anaphora reference

Example 4: Ellipsis example
    T: What was the date of the signing of the treaty?
    S: October 24 1998.
    T: And the participants?

Example 5: Interaction without anaphoric reference
    S: I liked the **movie.**
    S: I could recommend **the movie.**
    S: **The movie** was the best movie all year.
    S: **The movie** lasted over 2 hours.
    S: **The movie** was about two horses and a dog.

One area that has received much attention is that of definite/indefinite reference. Because of the differences between certain L1s (such as Chinese or Japanese) and L2s (such as English or French), this is an area of language learning that must be taught. Article usage has been explicitly taught by Sentance and Pain (1995), although their system focuses on written texts as opposed to dialogue interactions. Appropriate article usage is based on principles adapted from traditional linguistics including features such as the difference between mass and count nouns. Suri and McCoy (1993) utilise context tracking with semantic, pragmatic and world knowledge to determine when an incorrect referent has been used. To process these referent expressions adequately, a system must track all of the objects in the domain of the discourse. Additionally, as they have shown, it must maintain focus on the current objects of discussion. Even for their system, which analyses written texts, this is a daunting task. For a conversational system, it can be even more difficult. Fortunately, microworlds make the task more tractable by constraining the possible world of discourse.

Conversational structure

Conversation has structural properties that relate utterances to the situation and to each other. No one would expect to answer a ringing telephone with 'Goodbye'. Instead, this act would be seen as either very bizarre, or as a very specific contribution of a non-cooperative nature (such as hanging up on a romantic partner). Similarly, within utterances speakers use cues to indicate the structure: 'for instance' means that an example of a point is about to be described. The ability of a system to adequately respond with cues is essential for authentic interaction. A system should not respond to 'Thank you' with 'I don't know how to thank you'. Also, it must be able to give appropriate cues as to the information being presented: what type of information is to be presented, whether or not the information has been presented before. The mechanisms for accomplishing this include conversational structure (how we talk about things) and conversational tracking (who said what). Both are ultimately necessary for a complete, authentic conversational system. We will examine structuring tools here and tracking aids in the context of *Fluent*'s implementation of them.

The difference between discourse processing and its subfield, dialogue processing, are readily apparent when handling conversational structure. Written text concerns itself with the structure of the information to be presented: the intentional form. Theories such as Rhetorical Structure Theory (RST) from Mann and Thompson (1988) relate one sentence or utterance to the previous and preceding ones in a hierarchical nature. The relationships have given types, such as *elaboration,* and are used to accomplish specific communicative goals. For instance, if the system wants to introduce a new object into a microworld, it could do so by first naming the object, and then describing each of the distinguishing properties of that object. Moore's (1995a) work utilises this theory for explanation generation in a general tutoring environment. Like RST, Discourse Representation Theory (DRT) (Kamp 1984) attempts to describe, computationally, the relationship between successive utterances in a meaningful way. Different types of explanations and interactions are planned in the classical AI sense. While both written text and spoken interaction exhibit many of the grammatical phenomena described above, it is at the structural level of interaction that differences appear. Dialogue does require a certain structure so as to maintain coherence of conversation, allowing conversational participants to follow the thread of a conversation. Yet dialogue tends to be more varied than written text.

In some speech-based systems (e.g. Woszczyna et al. 1998; Wahlster 1993), conversational interaction is viewed as a series of related speech acts such as request information/inform, greet/acknowledge. Managing a conversation and the expectations of conversation consists of tracking context (as described in the previous section) and conforming to these speech act exchanges. A plan for conversation can be seen as a series of these exchange primitives. This formalism permits the planning of conversations, but at a more primitive and flexible manner than RST. ICALL systems, as will be seen when we discuss dialogue management, incorporate these structural properties of conversation with various techniques and to various degrees.

Cultural implications

Responding to the cultural needs of language is an area of teaching that falls into this field. Many languages differentiate the social and power relationships between the participants in the conversation. For instance, Japanese speakers utilise different grammatical forms depending on the relationship between participants. Systems explicitly designed to teach these functions typically give a scenario, and then allow the student to pick or generate the appropriate next utterance. The *Pileface* system (Lelouche 1994; Lelouche & Huot 1998) presents a description of the relevant characteristics of the participants, and the student picks the appropriate form of address. Kai and Nakamura (1995) also present situational descriptions and then use them to parse the student's utterance. Neither of these systems is conversational, yet both do provide knowledge that is necessary for authentic utterance. The system described by Levy (1998) shows cultural aspects of interaction (through video scenes), and also more social facets such as what is appropriate to ask in general conversation.

Error repair

Current error handling in many ICALL systems is not very conversational. Typically, errors are responded to with template-based explanations, or by simple right/wrong indicators. Occasionally, a system will try to convey the 'expert' knowledge of language to the student (Kempen & Dijkstra 1994). Other times, systems will point out an error and use a template-based explanation of the error (Schwind 1994). Most of these try to analyse the type or level of the error and respond appropriately (e.g. Van de Plassche 1994; Schwind 1994). Consider the possible responses to an error in a conversational language situation. If the given utterance is completely unintelligible ('cup hand place'), a system may need to respond differently than if the learner merely missed an article ('pick up cup'). In other uses, even the detection of an error depends on tying an utterance to the context. In the sequence 'Where are the pens located?' 'The stapler is blue', the response is grammatically and even semantically correct, yet is incorrect. The system should be able to respond in a way that reflects both recognition of the error and appropriate correction of it ('I know that the stapler is blue, but we were talking about pens'). Current discourse research in error repair seeks to categorise the level of error and determine an appropriate response for each level of error. Levels of errors are determined by the processing layer where failure occurs. For instance, asking to fill the stove with water, while syntactically correct, is impossible. This is a knowledge-base level error which may require a different tutoring strategy for repair than incorrect syntactic usage. In an authentic conversational environment, these levels of error repair may be more appropriate than those determined by tutoring strategy and pedagogical needs. At the same time, because this is a learning experience, the tutorial requirements may override authenticity. Example 6 shows possible reactions to the same error based on these two, sometimes conflicting, needs.

Example 6: Possible reactions to error
    S: Pick up cup.
    T: I am picking up **the** cup.

Reaction 1: Understanding incorrect utterance, responding with correct answer

    S: Pick up cup
    T: That is incorrect. In English, you must say 'the' before talking about a specific object.

Reaction 2: Template explanation for incorrect utterance

    S: Pick up cup
    T: You mean, pick up the cup.
    S: Yes, pick up the cup.

Reaction 3: Correction with verification

Dialogue management

Before looking at dialogue management, we must first acknowledge the contributions which come from the field of explanation generation. In the more traditional ITS structure used for CALL, explanation generation plays a role. (Moore 1995a; Cawsey 1992; Maybury 1992). Each follows a slightly different discourse model, but all share many characteristics. All use some form of plan primitives to represent the form of a set of utterances and then a planning system to organise them. Each tries to address some of the requirements of dialogue management systems. The organisation they each employ takes into account what was said previously, the level of the user and the domain needs. The nature of the dialogues tends to fit the more traditional model of interaction: present a problem, ask some questions, carry on a dialogue explaining relevant phenomena. This is a more receptive approach than interactive one.

For language teaching, a system that uses dialogue as a teaching mechanism is *Herr Kommissar* (DeSmedt 1995). In this system a student assumes the identity of a police inspector and attempts to solve a murder mystery by asking questions which the system answers. Yet this system permits only one type of interaction in one domain, greatly simplifying dialogue management needs. Another system, MILT (Weinberg et al. 1995), also incorporates dialogue exercises into teaching. This is accomplished this by a microworld interaction which permits only commands, and through an interrogation scenario which is much like *Herr Kommissar*. Again, the dialogue is constrained in both domain and type of interaction. CAVOL (Kronenberg et al. 1994) similarly presents a uniform interaction-type based on a set of incidents connected to a traffic accident, such as answering police questions, and testifying in court. To deal with more general dialogue phenomena, NLP systems utilise a Dialogue Management Module (DMM). For *Fluent*, we seek to apply insights from existing DMM work to ICALL. The first step in this is to examine how DMMs have been used, specifically in collaborative problem-solving applications. The kinds of functions that are allocated to DMMs show us where they can be used to enhance our system.

Two types of plans need to exist in a dialogue management situation: domain plans and discourse plans. Domain plans capture information about the actions and objects in a given area. For instance, the domain plan for baking a cake consists of the top-level actions: gather ingredients, mix ingredients, place mix in the pan, and place the pan in the oven. Discourse plans, on the other hand, capture the methods for describing the elements of the domain. Both types of plans are necessary for dialogue to generate coherent next utterances, and to be able to react adequately to the current utterance. Dialogue management in the language processing community has focused on collaborative problem-solving applications. In these applications, a shared plan for solving a problem can lend structure to the sequence of conversational moves between the student and the system. For example, to describe an object to be used, the system may first name it, and then give its relevant properties (example 7). In addition to structure, a DMM coordinates initiative, or who is controlling the interaction and focus, or what objects, actions and goals are to be discussed. In this way, both types of plans are necessary to support interaction.

Example 7: Interaction about an object
    T: This is a stove.
    T: It has four burners that can be turned on.
    T: The controls for the burners are on the front of the stove.
    T: Stoves can be used for boiling potatoes.

Two general NLP systems that have successfully utilised dialogue management modules are the *Trains* project (Allen et al. 1996), and the *Dialogue Manager* project (LuperFoy et al. 1998). The *Trains* dialogue management module was designed to overcome the limitations of the other NLP modules, especially those from speech recognisers. Due to the domain of train scheduling, the expected responses could be predicted. Also, because of the nature of the interaction, discourse structures could be predicted and this guided recognition algorithms. LuperFoy's dialogue management, much like Allen's system, was used to overcome the limitations of speech recognition for two applications: interface with a time reporting system and interface to a military simulation. Unlike Allen's system, these treat the dialogue manager as the central portion of the system, coordinating between all language modules and also with the back-end knowledge base. This work represents not only a NLP module, but also an architecture for the incorporation of dialogue management into an overall system. It tries to draw on generic world knowledge in addition to specific domain knowledge. It has, therefore, a more sophisticated NLP integration, and provides the framework for a more comprehensive error diagnosis scheme.

Dialogue management in *Fluent*
The graphical portion of *Fluent* involves two aspects of coordination (focus and initiative). In this framework, either party can use animated actions (mouse-activated for students) as well as verbal moves (example 8). *Fluent* provides dialogue management structuring via four mechanisms: tutorial schemas which supply the top-level dialogue management; plans and actions which provide collaborative context; views which manage focus; and interaction types which specify initiative. Together these components determine what to say, how to say it, and what context results from the interaction.

Looking at each of these components individually, tutorial schemas, which are built from the other three components, structure the language as conversational with pedagogical purposes, including adjusting the difficulty for the student. Two purposes served by a tutorial schema are to control graphical action and to constrain interaction by determining conversational moves. As an interaction component, a plan provides domain structure for achieving a goal and is broken down into a series of subplans which can further be reduced to a set of primitive actions. In *Fluent*, plans organise action and make it meaningful by providing goal structure. Their variability provides the flexibility necessary for authenticity. Interaction types direct the initiative in the conversation by specifying who makes the next conversational move and what form the sequence should take. Example 9 shows how interaction types can vary with conversational moves. Finally, a view specifies how to express an action including which grammatical features will be highlighted. If the pedagogical goal is article usage, the system would feature objects rather than actions.

Example 8: Series of conversational moves
    T: Turn on the faucet.
    S: (* clicks faucet handle *)
    T: You have turned on the faucet.

Example 9: Two different interaction types
    T: Pick up the pan.
    S: (* clicks pan graphic *)
    T: Turn on the faucet.
    S: (* clicks faucet handle *)

Commander mode interaction

    T: Where is the pan?
    S: The pan is on the counter.
    T: What should we do with the pan?
    S: Pick it up.

Quizmaster mode interaction

Issues in dialogue management
The issues in dialogue management can be divided into two categories: those related to language processing and those related to theoretical and pedagogical needs. In the first category, dialogue management, and discourse in general, is still a relatively new field in NLP. Because of this, it suffers from many of the problems one would expect. The first of these is the dependence on other layers of language processing: parsing, morphological analysis, and

semantic analysis. Another is that, as a growing field, there is still a wide variety of problems and a lack of a coherent framework for relating them. Researchers will focus on one aspect of dialogue management, such as anaphora resolution, without tying it back into an overall structure that other researchers can use. Unlike parsing, where there are clear computational requirements and boundaries, dialogue management still means many things to different people. Finally, a good set of corpora and other materials related to language learning does not exist. This makes a standardised evaluation of a framework or model very difficult.

For CALL, a DMM can address the tension between pedagogical and conversational aspects of interaction (Hamburger & Maney 1991:82). If a certain grammatical structure is to be practised, the DMM may want to structure the conversation to enable situations that elicit that structure. By incorporating dialogue management into an ICALL system in this way, we provide the student with the ability to practise conversational skills in a controlled, systematic way. In this way, we address the inherent tension between simulation (or controlled practising) and instruction. The components we describe give a framework for learning language in a communicatively authentic way without obviating the ability to provide more traditional instruction.

Conclusion

Authentic language practice with CALL systems is a crucial goal. We have looked at the importance of discourse and dialogue management to accomplish that aim. This processing is implicit in many systems, but we seek to incorporate it explicitly. To do so, we believe, will facilitate flexibility and authenticity for the language learner. As NLP techniques evolve, this environment will permit the continued and principled incorporation of communicative phenomena into a learning environment. It will thereby continue to improve its support of sound practice.

References

Allen, J., Miller, B., Ringger, E. & Sikorski, T., (1996). *A robust system for natural spoken dialogue.* In Proceedings of the 34th Annual Meeting of the Association for Computational Linguistics.

Asher, A. (1977). *Learning another language through actions: The complete teachers guidebook.* Los Gatos, CA: Sky Oaks Productions.

Brown, G. & Yule, G. (1983). *Discourse analysis.* Cambridge, UK: Cambridge University Press.

Cawsey, A. (1992). *Explanation and interaction.* Cambridge, Mass.: MIT Press.

Davies, G. (1998). In Proceedings of the WorldCALL 98: CALL to Creativity. University of Melbourne, Australia.

DeSmedt, W.H. (1995). Herr Kommissar: An ICALL conversation simulator for intermediate German. In V. M. Holland, J. D. Kaplan & M. R. Sams (Eds), *Intelligent language tutors: Theory shaping technology*. Mahwah, New Jersey: Lawrence Erlbaum Associates.

Douglas, S.A. (1995). LingWorlds: An intelligent object-oriented environment for second-language teaching. In V. M. Holland, J. D. Kaplan & M. R. Sams (Eds), *Intelligent language tutors: Theory shaping technology*. Mahwah, New Jersey: Lawrence Erlbaum Associates.

Farmer, A. & Demers, R. (1996). *A linguistics workbook*. Cambridge, Mass.: MIT Press.

Felshin, S. (1995). The Athena Language Learning Project NLP system: A multilingual system for conversation-based language learning. In V. M. Holland, J. D. Kaplan & M. R. Sams (Eds), *Intelligent language tutors: Theory shaping technology*. Mahwah, New Jersey: Lawrence Erlbaum Associates.

Grice, H.P. (1975). Logic and conversation. In P. Cole & J. Morgan (Eds), *Syntax and Semantics 3: Speech Acts*. New York: Academic Press.

Hamburger, H. (1996). *Yes! NLP-based FL-ITS will be important*. In Proceedings of COLING-96: The 16th International Conference on Computational Linguistics. Copenhagen.

Hamburger, H. & Maney, T. (1991). Twofold continuity in language learning. *Computer-Assisted Language Learning 4*, 2, 81–92.

Jaspers, J., Kanselaar, G. & Kok, W. (1994). Learning English with It's English. In L. Appelo & F.M.G. de Jong (Eds), *Computer-Assisted Language Learning: Proceedings of the seventh Twente workshop on language technology*. Enschede: University of Twente.

Kai, K. & Nakamura, J. (1995). An intelligent tutoring system for Japanese interpersonal expressions. In Proceedings of *AI in ED 95, World Conference on Artificial Intelligence in Education*. Association for the Advancement of Computing Education.

Kamp, H. (1984). A theory of truth and semantic representation. In J. Groenendijk, T. M. Jansen, & M. Stokhof (Eds), *Truth, interpretation and information; Selected papers from the third amsterdam colloquium* (pp. 1–41). Dordrecht: Holland/Cinnaminson: USA: Foris.

Kempen, G. & Dijkstra, A. (1994). Toward an integrated system for grammar, spelling and writing instruction. In L. Appelo & F.M.G. de Jong (Eds), *Computer-assisted language learning: Proceedings of the seventh Twente workshop on language technology*. Enschede: University of Twente.

Kronenberg, F., Krueger, A. & Ludewig, P. (1994). Contextual vocabulary learning with CAVOL. In L. Appelo & F.M.G. de Jong (Eds), *Computer-assisted language learning: Proceedings of the seventh Twente workshop on language technology*. Enschede: University of Twente.

Lelouche, R. (1994). Dealing with pragmatic and implicit information in an ICALL system: The PILEFACE example. *Journal of Artificial Intelligence in Education 5*, 501–532.

Lelouche, R. & Huot, D. (1998). How the construction of a computer system may influence language teaching practices: The communication situation variables. In Proceedings of *Natural Language Processing and Industrial Applications – Special Accent on Language Learning (NLP+IA), GRÉTAL,* Moncton, New Brunswick, Canada.

Levy, M. (1998). A multimedia design framework for the learning of culture and language discourse. In Proceedings of *WorldCALL 98: CALL to creativity.* University of Melbourne, Australia.

LuperFoy, S. et al. (1998). An architecture for dialogue management, context tracking, and pragmatic adaptation in spoken dialogue systems. In Proceedings of the *36th Annual Meeting of the Association for Computational Linguistics and 17th International Conference on Computational Linguistics, COLING-ACL '98,* Montreal, Canada: University of Montreal.

Mann, W. & Thompson, S. (1988). Rhetorical structure theory: Toward a theory of text organization. *Text 8,* 243–281.

Maybury, M. (1992). Communicative acts for explanation generation. *International Journal of Man–Machine Studies 37,* 2, 135–172.

McCoy, K.F., Pennington, C.A. & Suri, L.Z. (1996). English error correction: A syntactic user model based on principled 'mal-rule' scoring. In Proceedings of the *Fifth International Conference on User Modeling.* Kailua-Kona, Hawaii.

Moore, J. (1995a). *Participating in explanatory dialogues.* Cambridge, Mass.: MIT Press.

Moore, J. (1995b). Discourse generation for instructional applications: Making computer tutors more like humans. In Proceedings of *AI in ED 95, World Conference on Artificial Intelligence in Education.* Association for the Advancement of Computing Education.

Murphy, M., Kruger, A. & Grieszl, A. (1997). RECALL: Towards a learner centered approach to language learning. In B. du Boulay & Mizoguchi (Eds), *Artificial intelligence in education,* IOS Press.

Murray, J. (1995). Lessons learned from the Athena Language Learning Project: Using Natural Language Processing, graphics, speech processing, and interactive video for communication-based language learning. In V. M. Holland, J. D. Kaplan & M. R. Sams (Eds), *Intelligent language tutors: Theory shaping technology.* Mahwah, New Jersey: Lawrence Erlbaum Associates.

Schoelles, M. & Hamburger, H. (1995). Cognitive tools for language pedagogy. In *Computer-assisted language learning.* The Netherlands: Swets & Zeitlinger.

Schwind, C. (1994). Error analysis and explanation in knowledge-based language tutoring. In L. Appelo & F.M.G. de Jong (Eds), *Computer-assisted language learning: Proceedings of the seventh Twente workshop on language technology.* Enschede: University of Twente.

Sentance, S. & H. Pain (1995). A generative learner model in the domain of second language learning. In Proceedings of *AI in ED 95, World Conference on Artificial Intelligence in Education.* Association for the Advancement of Computing Education.

Suri, L. Z. & McCoy, K. F. (1993). Correcting discourse-level errors in a call system for second language learners. *CALL 6,* 3, 215–231

Van de Plassche, J., Bos, E. & Jongen-Junner, E. (1994). Verbarium and Substantarium: Two CALL programs for Latin. In L. Appelo & F.M.G. de Jong (Eds), *Computer-assisted language learning: Proceedings of the seventh Twente workshop on language technology*. Enschede: University of Twente.

Wahlster, W. (1993). Verbmobil: Translation of face-to-face dialogues. In O. Herzog, T. Christaller & D. Schuett (Eds), *Grundlagen and Anwendungen der Künstlichen Intelligenz*. Springer-Verlag.

Weinberg, A. & Garman, J., Martin, J. & Merlo, P. (1995). A principle-based parser for foreign language tutoring in German and Arabic. In V. M. Holland, J. D. Kaplan & M. R. Sams (Eds), *Intelligent language tutors: Theory shaping technology*. Mahwah, New Jersey: Lawrence Erlbaum Associates.

Woszczyna, M. et al. (1998). A modular approach to spoken language translation for large domains. In D. Farwell, L. Gerber & E. Hovy (Eds), *Machine translation and the information soup: Proceedings of the Third Conference of the Association for Machine Translation in the Americas*. Springer-Verlag.

20

Technological Literacy for Foreign Language Instructors and a Web-Based Tutorial

Kazumi Hatasa
Purdue University, USA

Introduction

The purpose of the project described in this chapter is to develop instructional modules which prepare pre-service teachers of foreign language for an introductory course in CALL.[1] Specifically, a World Wide Web-based tutorial on technological literacy has been implemented so that students can develop a basic understanding of, and become familiar with, computer software and hardware that is essential for daily language instruction. This tutorial was developed for the following reasons:

1   the current level of technological literacy among many foreign language instructors is not adequate;

2   short courses to introduce software packages offered by computing centres are not necessarily successful due to the lack of relevant context;

3   sufficient time cannot be spent on the development of basic technological literacy in introductory CALL courses;

4   institutions only provide limited technical support in non-alphabetic languages.

As new technology penetrates through the educational system at all levels, educators, including foreign language instructors, must not only become aware of what tools are available, but also possess sufficient knowledge of relevant technology, as well as the skills necessary to use them (Tella 1996). Most foreign language instructors probably use word-processing programs to produce handouts and tests. Also, many of them use spreadsheet programs for student records, and use email and the WWW as a part of their professional life. In this sense, these language instructors are somewhat computer literate. However, this does not mean that they are fully utilising the available tools. The continuous flow of new technology often overwhelms foreign language instructors in spite of their intention to improve themselves, and to respond to ever-increasing pressure from the administration to integrate technology into the classroom. Consequently, they reach a plateau once they feel they can do what they have to do with computers. Furthermore, some instructors who have never received formal instruction in computer applications feel so far behind in technology that they avoid using technology at all. In my personal experience, even today some instructors have admitted that they use a copying machine, a pair of scissors and adhesive tape when they need to incorporate graphics in their documents. The lack of familiarity with technology often prevents them from exploring new instructional methods and new ways of integrating technology into the curriculum.

To support these instructors as well as other users, many universities offer service courses in computer skills, and computer centres offer short courses on different software packages such as word processing and spreadsheet programs. The success of these courses, however, varies among individuals because skills are taught in a general context, and not in that of foreign language instruction. Not everybody can readily apply knowledge learned in these general courses into their own activities because of a lack of relevance to their own discipline or line of work. In fact, those who cannot make a connection are often the ones who become overwhelmed by these courses and drop out. Thus, it is essential to provide foreign language teachers and teacher-trainees with materials which reflect the needs of foreign language instructors.

In the context of teacher training in foreign languages, many institutions now offer courses in different areas of CALL in their teacher training programs, particularly for ESL and European languages (Wong 1998). These courses are typically designed to give an overview of CALL, including its history, a theoretical framework for CALL, research in CALL, courseware evaluation, multimedia, computer-mediated communication, designing and implementing CALL activities (Warschauer & Healey 1999). A large number of books, articles and resources are available (Bush & Terry 1997; Levy 1997; Dunkel 1991; Pennington 1996; Warschauer 1996). Most of these courses also incorporate, to various degrees, hands-on sessions and assignments necessary for practicing skills introduced in the courses. In reality, however, not all students who take or want to take these courses are necessarily equipped with basic skills. The difficulty lies in the fact that there is not sufficient time to teach basic technological literacy, yet it is a prerequisite for CALL courses.

Instructors of non-alphabetical languages face more fundamental problems with technology. School computing centres generally do not like to modify their computer systems to incorporate these languages because of a perceived difficulty in maintaining systems with mixed scripts. Likewise, language media centres may not be able to support the functionality in these languages as well as they can in other languages. This is often due to priority in staffing.[2] Furthermore, introductory CALL courses are also dominated by ESL and European languages. While very basic skills such as word processing and emailing can be taken for granted in alphabetical languages, the same skills present challenges to users in non-alphabetical languages (Fukada & Hatasa 1996). Thus, instructors of these languages must find a way to become more self-reliant and resourceful (Hatasa 1996, 1997).

Another factor which creates special needs for non-alphabetical languages (and other less commonly taught languages) is that students spend more time in 'the beginning level' than those in cognate foreign languages. This means that a greater amount of instruction needs to be given on fundamental language skills such as vocabulary development and basic grammar. Communicative activities need to be carried out within the confines of such restrictions, and this increases the need for classroom materials. However, since the number of learners in these languages is still relatively small in the US, textbooks are not packaged heavily with ancillaries. Thus, instructors must develop more supplementary materials by themselves. Two of the NFLRCs (National Foreign Language Resource Centers) are making efforts to improve the situation in Less Commonly Taught Languages (LCTL). One is the LCTL project at CARLA (Center for Advanced Research in Language Acquisition) at the University of Minnesota, and the other was the summer institute in LCTL at CLEAR (Center for Language Education and Research) at Michigan State University. The royalty-free clip art collection for foreign/second language instruction (Hatasa 1997b) is another example to support instructors of LCTL.

To remedy the problems described above, the project described here aims at developing a series of modularised tutorial materials on the Web, focusing on such basic areas as word-processing, spreadsheets, graphics editing, scanning graphics, scanning text, text handling and file exchange, emailing, web browsing, basic web authoring, and FTP. Each module is designed to be self-contained so that students can work through the modules in any order. The selection of the modules is based on my experience as well as on feedback from my students and workshop participants. A web-based tutorial works effectively since students can run the tutorial and software under discussion side by side on the same computer. They can read through instructions, download exercise materials, and immediately try tasks at their own pace.

Mastering skills in the tutorial will establish a minimum level of technological literacy for foreign language instructors at all levels. This minimum level of technological literacy also provides a solid base for students to study further aspects of CALL such as evaluation and development of multimedia applications, task-oriented web-based activities, and computer-mediated communication. The tutorial can be used prior to the beginning of a CALL course or it can be incorporated into the course itself. It can also be used by in-service K-12 teachers who may not have the time to attend a college course.

In order to make the objectives of the tutorial clear, a sixteen-point self-test was developed (see Appendix). The test measures the current level of technological literacy of an individual and it can be used to determine which tutorial modules should be studied. The test can also be used as an indicator of readiness for further study in CALL subject areas.[3] The self-test is divided into three categories: non network-related activities, network-related activities and other (vendor information and hardware purchase). The description for each item was intentionally phrased in such a way that some understanding of technical terms is required; this is considered to be a part of literacy.

Structure and content of the tutorial

The tutorial currently consists of ten chapters. Each chapter introduces selected topics in a context which foreign language instructors will find relevant. Students can download the material used in each chapter to their computers (Windows or Macintosh), and perform tasks described in the tutorial. Each chapter ends with additional exercises and suggestions which are designed to take students beyond the content of the tutorial. Since the tutorial is not intended to be a comprehensive how-to manual of particular software, only basic features of software are introduced. As software packages become more powerful, the possible number of ways to complete the one task increases. The tutorial aims at promoting basic understanding necessary to perform various tasks rather than teaching which button to push in a particular software package. Students can then apply their knowledge and skills with different software, or on different computers. The content of each chapter is briefly described below, illustrated with examples extracted from the tutorial.[4]

Content of the web-based tutorial

Introduction

Students learn what technological literacy is and why it is important.

Basic hardware and peripheral devices

Students become familiar with technical terminology. They learn what the current standards are in computers, modem speeds, monitor sizes, types of printers and types of scanners so that they can identify what is necessary and make recommendations for purchases.

Spreadsheet programs

Students learn how to use a spreadsheet program to keep track of student records in a FL course and to calculate grades. FL courses tend to have more scores to record than regular lecture courses (e.g. small quizzes and attendance). They may also use more complex grading criteria (e.g. dropping worst three scores). Topics include basic setup, formatting worksheets, splitting windows, printing, formula and functions, and sorting.

Example 1: A simple grading sheet

	A	B	C	D	E	F	G	H	I
		YQ	HW	COMP	ATTEND	MIDTERM	FINAL	TOTAL	GRADE
1									
2									
3	perfect student	10.0	10	10	10	100	100	100.0	A
4									
5	Kennedy	7.3	10	7.5	10	87	89	87.6	B
6	Johnson	7.0	10	5	9	90	84	82.7	B
7	Nixon	9.7	10	9.5	10	76	88	90.6	A
8	Ford	8.7	7.5	7.5	10	89	79	83.3	B
9	Carter	6.3	7.5	6	9	81	82	76.6	C
10	Reagan	7.7	7.5	8	10	86	76	80.8	B
11	Bush	7.3	7.5	8.5	10	83	70	78.4	C
12	Clinton	8.3	7.5	9	10	76	95	86.5	B

GradewithPerfect

Example 2: More complex grading criteria

5	Can you help the instructors who want to include the following conditions? If you are using other conditions, think how you can handle them.
(a)	I give 12 quizzes in total, but I discard the worst two scores for the final calculation.
(b)	I allow three absences. After that, one point will be subtracted for each unexcused absence.

In addition to student records, students will be introduced to another application of a spreadsheet using a simple item analysis of a test. The following example shows the result of eight students taking a test containing ten questions (1 indicates a correct answer and 0 indicates an incorrect answer). It clearly shows question 7 needs to be re-examined since the three best students answered incorrectly while others answered correctly.

Example 3: Item analysis

	A	B	C	D	E	F	G	H	I	J	K	L
		Q1	Q2	Q3	Q4	Q5	Q6	Q7	Q8	Q9	Q10	TOTAL
2	Student A	1	1	1	1	1	1	0	1	1	1	9
3	Student B	1	1	1	0	1	1	0	1	0	1	7
4	Student C	0	1	1	1	0	1	0	1	1	1	7
5	Student D	1	1	0	1	0	1	1	1	1	0	7
6	Student E	0	1	1	0	0	0	1	1	0	1	5
7	Student F	1	1	0	1	1	0	1	0	0	0	5
8	Student G	1	0	1	1	1	0	1	0	0	0	5
9	Student H	1	1	0	0	0	0	1	0	0	1	4
10												
11		6	7	5	5	4	4	5	5	3	5	

Word processing programs

Students are introduced to selected features of word-processing programs which are not fully utilised. These are tabs, indentations, style sheets, and

Example 4: Different paragraph formats

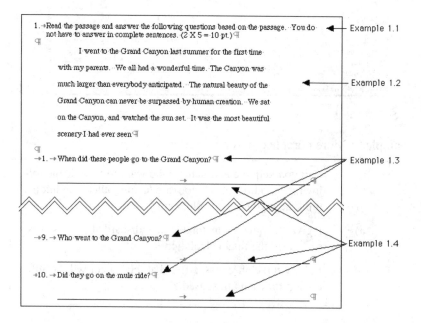

find & replace. They will learn how to format paragraphs using a sample reading test in English (e.g. question, reading passage, comprehension questions, and long underline for student answer) and register paragraph formats as styles for later use. The find & replace function is introduced in the context of converting text copied from the Web to a form able to be edited by removing unnecessary carriage returns.

Example 5: An exercise to convert text format using find & replace

Before conversion

```
I went to the Grand Canyon last summer for
the first time with my parents. We all had a
wonderful time. The Canyon was much larger
than everybody anticipated.
The natural beauty of the Grand Canyon can
never be surpassed by human creation. We sat
on the Canyon and watched the sun set. It was
the most beautiful scenery I had ever seen.
```

After conversion

I went to the Grand Canyon last summer for the first time with my parents. We all had a wonderful time. The Canyon was much larger than everybody anticipated.
The natural beauty of the Grand Canyon can never be surpassed by human creation. We sat on the Canyon and watched the sun set. It was the most beautiful scenery I had ever seen.

Text file and file exchange

Students learn what happens when spreadsheet data is saved as a text file and what they can do with it (the concept of delimiter is introduced). A solid understanding of ASCII file or text file helps students when they face the problem of exchanging text and documents with somebody else. This chapter also introduces students to exchanging files across different software packages and across different computer platforms.

Example 6: An exercise for file exchange between spreadsheet and word processing software

4.   An MS-Word file is given to you by your friend who does not know much about formatting. When you open the file, you find it looking like the one shown in Figure 5.7. Your friend wants to add another column for average scores of the two tests. You recognize the computation is better to do using a spread sheet program (e.g. MS-Excel). You would like to open the file in MS-Excel, but the present form is not good for MS-Excel.

(1)   Manipulate the text using the replace function so that you can open the file in MS-Excel.

(2)   Compute the average of two numbers for each person, put the result in the third column in MS-Excel, and sort according to the average score (highest to lowest).

(3)   Finally, create a MS-Word file so that your friend can see the file looking like the one shown in Figure 5.8.

Figure 5.7: An open file

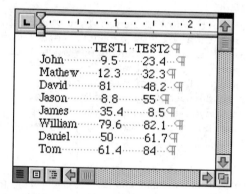

Figure 5.8: An MS Word file

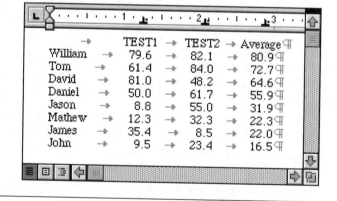

Basic graphics manipulation

Students learn the basics of graphics by incorporating graphical images into handouts, tests and props for communicative activities. Sample graphic files (a picture of a room and a map of a town) are provided and students are instructed to modify them in order to make information gap activities. The basic knowledge and skills of graphical images include the distinction between paint and draw types of graphics and their characteristics, editing tools, the relationship between image types and file sizes, different file formats. Clip art collections for FL instruction are also introduced for students to use (Hatasa 1997b).

Example 7: An exercise to edit a paint image to make a find-difference
activity

Example 8: A draw graphic to create an information gap activity

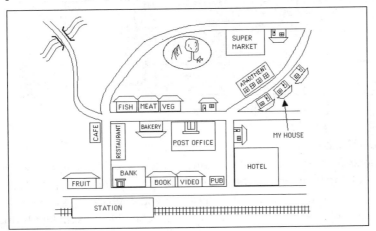

Graphical scanning and text scanning

Basic concepts of graphical scanning are introduced, including image types and the relationship between originals and scan resolution. Students are instructed to modify scanned graphics by using the skills learned in the relevant chapter and incorporate them into their work.

Text scanning (or OCR) is also introduced. While text scanning in alphabetic languages is relatively straightforward once students have a basic understanding of scanning in general, attention will be paid to scanning text in non-alphabetical languages such as Chinese and Japanese, in which an OCR software must identify a letter out of thousands of possible letters. The example shows a window displaying the result of a newspaper scan in Japanese.

Example 9: Sample of Japanese OCR

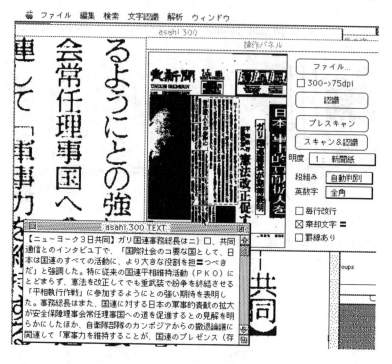

Email and listservs

Students learn the basics of emailing in their target languages and the use of listservs for their professional enhancement. Attention is paid to ensure students in non-alphabetical languages can accomplish the same goal. This chapter includes other topics such as file attachment to exchange formatted files and connection methods to mail hosts (e.g. modem, Ethernet, ISDN and PPP). Instructional applications of email and other computer-mediated communication, such as MOO and IRC, are beyond the scope of this chapter.

Web browsing and authoring simple web pages

We assume students are already browsing the Web. In this chapter, they learn to:

1   view the Web in their target languages;
2   listen to audio and view video images;
3   use search engines in their target languages;
4   copy and paste text/graphics into their documents; and
5   organize bookmarks.

For authoring web pages, students will be instructed to use an WYSIWYG HTML editor so that learning of the HTML language will be minimised. They learn about relevant graphic formats such as GIF and JPEG. Students will create a course syllabus for language courses, a resource page for their language courses, and their own home page (including curriculum vitae). In conjunction with chapter 10, they learn how to upload HTML files to update web pages.

Example 10: A web page of clip art collection for FL instruction
<www.sla.purdue.edu/fll/JapanProj/>

Anonymous and person-to-person FTP

In addition to downloading files using a Web browser, students learn to use FTP programs such as WindowFTP and Fetch. While downloading and uploading files are integrated in Web browsers, the students need to understand what is happening during the process. Students also learn person-to-person FTP in order to exchange files such as teaching materials with a particular person, as file attachment to an email message is limited in size, and generally works only on the same computer platform. Knowledge of file compression and file conversion methods are introduced as well.

Uses of the tutorial

The principal purpose of the tutorial is to supplement introductory courses in CALL so that students with little experience in technology are not over-whelmed. The tutorial would help an instructor conduct a course by ensuring a minimum level of computer skills. It can also be used for remedial work for students with weaknesses in particular areas. The chapters on spreadsheet programs, word-processing, and text-manipulation have been tried with students taking a course on technological literacy for foreign language instruction at Purdue University. Although no formal evaluation has been conducted yet, the students responded to the materials positively, and I was able to spend less time in classroom talking about actual operation of software and coordinating students' activities.

The tutorial can also be used independently. There are a large number of in-service instructors of foreign languages who are interested in improving their skills in the technology area. As was mentioned earlier, taking summer courses or participating in workshops is certainly a good option. They can go through the tutorial in advance so that they will be ready for these courses. Furthermore, the tutorial provides a training environment for those who cannot take these courses for reasons such as family commitment during summer.

In closing

Like many well-maintained web sites, the content of the tutorial and the self-test must be periodically examined and updated to keep up with the changes in technology and in-coming students' computer literacy. Some modules may become obsolete and be abandoned while others may require modification. At the same time, new modules may have to be created. The Web is an ideal medium of instruction for the tutorial since updating the materials is relatively easy.

It is hoped that this web-based tutorial will contribute to the improvement of technological literacy among foreign language instructors, and will provide the necessary link between the instructors and further study in CALL.

Notes

[1] This project is supported by the Center for Technology-Enhanced Language Learning at the Department of Foreign Languages and Literatures, Purdue University.

[2] There is no doubt about the willingness of language media centres to support non-alphabetical languages.

[3] Available at <http://tell.fll.purdue.edu/literacy/selftest.html>.

[4] The tutorial is available at <http://tell.fll.purdue.edu/literacy/index.html>.

References

Bush, M. D. & Terry, R. M. (1997). *Technology enhanced language learning.* Lincolnwood, Chicago: National Textbook Company.

Dunkel, P. (Ed.) (1991). *Computer assisted language learning and testing: Research issues and practice.* London: Ellis Horwood.

Fukada, A. & Hatasa, K. (1996). Making electronic communication possible in Japanese on the Internet. In M. Warschauer (Ed.), *Telecollaboration in foreign languages* (pp. 219–231). Honolulu: University of Hawaii Second Language Teaching and Curriculum Center.

Hatasa, K. (1996). Nihongo kyoshi no tameno computer literacy (Computer literacy for Japanese language instructors). *Gekkan Nihongo* (Monthly Japanese), December 1995 – June 1996.

Hatasa, K. (1997a). Computer literacy for Japanese language professionals – What do we need to know about applications of the computer? In Hubbard, Sakamoto & Davis (Eds), *Progress in Japanese linguistics and pedagogy: A collection in honor of Professor Akira Miura* (pp. 263–274). Tokyo: ALC Press.

Hatasa, K. (1997b). *Royalty-free clip art collection for foreign/second language instruction.* URL <http://www.sla.purdue.edu/fll/JapanProj/>

Levy, M. (1997). *Computer-assisted language learning: Context and conceptualization.* Oxford: Clarendon Press.

Pennington, M. C. (Ed.) (1996). *The power of CALL.* La Jolla: Athelstan.

Tella, S. (1996). Foreign languages and modern technology: Harmony or hell? In M. Warschauer (Ed.), *Telecollaboration in foreign languages* (pp. 3–17). Honolulu: University of Hawaii Second Language Teaching and Curriculum Center.

Warschauer, M. (1996). Computer-assisted language learning: An introduction. In S. Fotos (Ed.), *Multimedia language teaching* (pp. 3–20). Tokyo: Logos International.

Warschauer, M, & Healey, D. (1998). Computers and language learning: An overview. *Language Teaching 31,* 57–71.

Wong, C. J. (1998). *CALL links.* URL <http://tiger.coe.missouri.edu/~cjw/call/links.htm>

Appendix

Elements of Technological literacy for Foreign Language Instructors
A self-test

This is a 16-point check list to test how technologically literate you are as a foreign/-second language instructor. Read the brief description of each item carefully. Check if you can perform the task without extensive help from others. You should be familiar with the terminology used in the text.

Non–network-related activities

1 *Making the personal computer ready for your target language*
   Check if you can make a computer ready to process your target language. You may need to install a special language support system for your target language. (important for non-alphabetic languages).
2 *Using a spreadsheet*
   Check if you can use a spreadsheet program to record student records, handle different grading criteria, use formula for calculation of scores, and sort the records according to different criteria.
3 *Word processing*
   Check if you can correctly use the following features: inserting pictures, using different types of tabs, using tables, and using style sheets.
4 *Electronic reference tools* (on-line dictionaries and CD-ROMs)
   Check if you can use dictionaries and other reference tools available in electronic format.
5 *Text files and file/data exchange*
   Check if you can read files created by other software or by other computers, and create files in such a way that other people using different software or a different computer can read them. Terminology: formatted file, ASCII file and text file.
6 *Graphics scanning and printing*
   Check if you can use a scanner to scan line-drawings and photographs, print them (in colour, if necessary), and make OHP (black-&-white and colour) if necessary. Terminology: resolution, dpi, bit-depth (or colour depth), file formats for graphics.
7 *Graphics editing*
   Check if you know the differences between 'paint' and 'draw' in an electronic context, and if you can use a basic paint/draw program to create and edit graphics for picture flash cards, props for communicative activities (e.g. information gap), and quiz/tests. Terminology: file formats for graphics such as BMP, EPS, and PICT.
8 *Character scanning* (Optical Character Recognition)
   Check if you can use a scanner and the necessary software for character recognition in your target language (e.g. newspaper and magazine articles), and incorporate the scanned text into documents (Important for non-alphabetic languages).

Network-related activities

9 *Network connection*

Check if you can connect your computer to a network through a school's computer, or an Internet service provider using necessary devices such as a modem. Terminology: bps and PPP.

10 *Email*

Check if you can write and receive email in your target language, participate in the listservs (mailing lists) of your professional interest, bring messages into your word-processing program, and exchange formatted and unformatted files with other people, using attachments. Terminology: MIME.

11 *Web browsing and information gathering*

Check if you can search and browse web sites of your interest, read information in your target language, incorporate authentic text in your instructional materials, locate various resources (dictionaries, photos, clip art, etc.), and copy them in your documents. Terminology: http and URL.

12 *Web basic authoring*

Check if you can create and maintain simple web pages for the dissemination of information such as course outlines, schedules, personal profile/CV, etc. (Knowledge of the HTML language is not necessary if you use an HTML editor. You must be able to upload files to the web site and update them as necessary.) Terminology: HTML, GIF.

13 *Anonymous FTP*

Check if you can use anonymous FTP to download various files in public domain such as utility programs, language corpus, etc. You need to know methods of expanding files. Terminology: ZIP, LZH, Stuff It, Bin-Hex, and self-extracting/expanding archives.

14 *Person-to-person FTP*

Check if you can use FTP to exchange formatted files with particular individuals instead of sending floppy disks/ZIP disks. You need to know how to compress files as well as how to expand them. Terminology: ZIP, LZH, Stuff It, Bin-Hex, and self-extracting self-expanding archives.

Other

15 *Vendor information*

Check if you know where (or how to find where) to purchase software for your target languages if not available in the main channel such as major mail order companies (more important for less-commonly taught languages).

16 *Purchase of computer and peripheral device*

Check if you can make a purchase decision for a computer and necessary peripheral devices such as a modem, a scanner, and a printer. Merely being able to state your needs is not sufficient. You must be able to carry out conversation with technical support on particular issues regarding hardware selection. Terminology: bps, dpi, resolution, laser printer, ink-jet printer, RAM, hard disk, CD-ROM drive, and etc.

Index